Genes, Genesis, and Evolution

Genes

Genesis
and Evolution

By JOHN W. KLOTZ
Professor of Natural Science
Concordia Senior College
Fort Wayne, Indiana

Second, Revised Edition
Second Printing 1972

CONCORDIA PUBLISHING HOUSE · SAINT LOUIS

Copyright 1955, 1970 by
CONCORDIA PUBLISHING HOUSE
Saint Louis, Missouri
Library of Congress Catalog Card No. 55-6434
ISBN 0-570-03212-1

MANUFACTURED IN THE UNITED STATES OF AMERICA

6 7 8 9 10 11 12 13 14 WP 90 89 88 87 86 85 84 83

To my wife

Introduction

Scientists pride themselves on being fair, objective, open-minded, and unprejudiced. Yet science also has its sacred cows, and today one of these is the theory of evolution. Any attack or criticism of the theory as such is regarded as a part of the cult of antiscientism. Scientists may point out weaknesses and defects and may attack parts of it, but the theory itself must remain unchallenged. It must always remain the great unifying principle of biology.

It is the author's thesis that evolution in the generally accepted sense of the term has not taken place. He does not believe that life as we know it is the result of a gradual process of development, that man, for instance, is the descendant of simple, unicellular forms. He believes that, in general, organisms have remained relatively constant and have reproduced after their kind.

This is not to deny the fact of change. There have been changes in the landscape and changes in the flora and fauna. Both plants and animals have become extinct. There has been the development of varieties within the species, yes, even the development of forms which can be classified as new species. Mutations have occurred in the past and still occur at a fixed, measurable rate. But all of this change, insofar as the organic world is concerned, has taken place within limits fixed by the Creator when He fashioned the different "kinds" in the beginning. In summary, it is the thesis of this book that what has occurred is not the development of higher organisms from lower organisms but rather a finite amount of change within a fixed and closed system.

The manuscript was read in whole or in part by H. H. Gross, W. F. Kruse, R. A. Lange, Byron C. Nelson, and Paul A. Zimmerman. I am indebted to all these men for their valuable suggestions. I also wish to express my appreciation to the Committee on Scholarly Research for its encouragement and for making this book possible. Recognition is also due those who have given permission for quotations and for the use of illustrations. Individual acknowledgment is made in the "Notes" and after each of the figures. I should also like to express my appreciation to the art department and to the staff of Concordia Publishing House for their interest and assistance.

Fort Wayne, Ind.

JOHN W. KLOTZ

Contents

1. Science and Scripture

"What is truth?" This well-known question of Pilate addressed to the Savior has intrigued men for many centuries. Is there such a thing as truth? Can man ever be certain that he has the truth? The great minds have all grappled with the problem. Socrates dealt with it; the Epicureans discussed it. Kant, Hume, Hegel — all of these men made their contribution to this, the essential problem of epistemology, that branch of philosophy or metaphysics which deals with knowledge. And the question also has a bearing on our problem, the problem of the origin of the organic world.

There are those who ask why we are so willing to accept the statements of the Bible in preference to scientific theories and hypotheses. They are quick to point out that the Bible does not claim to be a textbook of science, and they ask why we are willing to listen to its pronouncement on a scientific problem, such as the problem of the origin of the earth and the organic world. It is, of course, true that the Bible is not and does not claim to be a textbook of science or, for that matter, of history or anthropology or economics or sociology. The Bible has only one purpose, and that is to make us wise unto salvation through faith in Christ Jesus. It is essentially a book designed to prepare man for the life that is to come.

Scripture and Absolute Truth

And yet the Bible is true in its every word. Jesus, who declared that He is the Way, the Truth, and the Life, said of the Bible, "Thy Word is truth." The Bible asserts that all its statements are true and correct, and this declaration applies also to historical, anthropological, sociological, and scientific statements.

Purported Errors in Scripture

Nor need we apologize for this teaching of the Scriptures. Time after time the Bible has been vindicated and its critics put to shame. For instance, in Acts 13:7 the governor of Cyprus is called "the deputy." This implies that the island at that time was a senatorial province governed by a proconsul, or deputy. For many years critics charged Luke with error in this section of his book. They said that Cyprus at that time was an imperial province governed by a general, known either as a *legatus* or a *propraetor*. However, recent archaeological discoveries have shown that while it was originally an imperial province, it was made a senatorial province in 22 B. C. Thus at the time Paul and Barnabas visited the island it was indeed a senatorial province governed by a proconsul.[1]

Similarly Solomon was charged with a biological error when, in Prov. 6:8, he referred to the ant as providing her meat in the summer and gathering her food in the harvest. Critics were quick to point out that, so far as was known, ants do not store up food. They implied that Solomon had been guilty of faulty observation. They said that he had probably kicked open an anthill and had mistaken the pupal cases which he saw there for grain. Men such as Gould, Latreille, Huber, Gene, Kirby, Spence, and Blanchard, who were recognized authorities on the life and habits of ants, expressed skepticism as to the existence of harvesting ants. But we now know that there are harvesting ants. Wheeler, who today is a recognized authority on ants, believes that the ancient peoples, too, were undoubtedly familiar with the grain-storing and seed-storing habits of such species of ants as *Messor barbarus* and *Messor structor* and probably with those of a third species, *Messor arenarius*. The first two occur in Palestine and other Mediterranean countries. *M. arenarius* is found in the deserts of North Africa. He says: "To them refer many allusions in the writings of Solomon and the Mishna, and of classical writers. . . . The entomologists of the early portion of the last century, however, failing to find any harvesters among the ants of temperate Europe, began to doubt or even to deny their existence. . . . All doubt was removed by Moggridge's excellent work . . . in 1871 and 1872 on *Messor barbarus* and *M. structor,* the very species that had been observed by the ancients. . . . He opened the nests of these ants, and studied their granaries. . . ." [2]

The Bible's claim of absolute truthfulness applies also to the account that it gives us of the origin of the world. It tells us that the world in which we live, the plants and animals which are found on it, and man himself were all created by God. They did not come into existence by chance. They did not develop gradually. But they were created in a wide variety of forms, many of them very complex, and all of them "very good," Gen. 1:31.

Only Relative Truth Possible in Science

Only the Bible claims infallibility for itself. The scientist, for one, does not claim to have absolute truth. He says that what he presents is at best relative truth. Mavor, for instance, points out that no law or principle of science can ever be regarded as absolutely proved. All laws and principles, he says, are subject to modification with the accumulation of more data and the increase of knowledge. [3]

Warren Weaver, president of the American Association for the Advancement of Science, defines science as "that amazingly successful, interesting, intriguing, elusive, and rewarding human process by means of which, within one particular framework of reference, men approach truth. This process moves in the direction of increasing precision and validity, but it does not reach perfection. It deals with certain very important aspects of experience — chiefly those that lend themselves to classification through quantitative regularities — but it excludes many other important aspects of experience." [4]

Dryden says that science advances by purposely taking a limited and incomplete view of complex events. It is, he says, a partial view of life and in many respects a narrow view. [5]

This relativity of scientific truth is inherent in the tools and methods with which the scientist must work. Essentially there are two steps in scientific operations. The scientist first makes observations with his sense organs and then interprets these with his mind.

How reliable are these two?

a. The Reliability of Sense Impressions

While it is possible for his sense organs to give him an incorrect picture, in general we must assume that observations which he reports and which can be confirmed by other disinterested observers are correct. It is possible for our senses to deceive us. We are all familiar with optical illusions and mirages — instances in which our eyes deceive us. We also know that at times we have difficulty in distinguishing momentarily between heat and cold. If we plunge our hands into hot water, it may momentarily feel cold. If we handle solid carbon dioxide, it may seem to burn us.

Similar erroneous impressions arise when we are in a train or plane which is taking a sharp turn so that the vertical axis of our body no longer coincides with terrestrial gravity: in such moments buildings, trees, and the like seem to be in an oblique position. If we touch the upper row of our incisors with the lower surface of our tongue, we get an equally wrong impression. Yet the instances in which our sense organs deceive us are comparatively few. God has given us these sense organs. They are intended to keep us in touch with our environment. They are our sources of information about what is going on both outside and within our bodies. It is unreasonable to assume that they are in error unless it can be proved that they are.

b. The Reliability of Logic

These observations are then interpreted by the scientist. This second step is not always so dependable. It is this interpretation by the scientist which leads to his hypotheses and theories. These may very well be — and often are — wrong, and we may well disagree with them. For that reason we distinguish between facts and observations, and the conclusions drawn from these. The former cannot ordinarily be questioned, but the latter may very well be questioned. For in interpreting observations, in reaching conclusions, the scientist has at his disposal human reason and logic. Accordingly, he must work either deductively or inductively.

1. *Weaknesses of Deduction*

In employing deductive reasoning he begins with a generalization and applies this generalization to a specific instance. Its most common form is the syllogism. It begins with a general statement, known as the major premise, followed by a more restricted statement, known as the minor premise, and from these two a conclusion is drawn.

Deduction leads to the truth only if the major and minor premises on which it is based are correct. If they are faulty, the conclusions drawn from them may also be faulty (though, of course, the conclusion may be correct even if the premises are faulty).

2. *Weaknesses of Induction*

Modern science depends largely on the inductive method. To be sure, modern science is not exclusively inductive. It is self-evident that also deductive processes must enter into scientific reasoning. But the chief reliance is placed upon induction and inductive processes. In this method of reasoning we make a number of particular observations and from them draw a general conclusion. Thus, we observe that an oak tree has leaves, a maple tree has leaves, an elm tree has leaves, a locust tree has leaves, and an apple tree has leaves. From these and similar observations we reach the conclusion that all trees have leaves. In this way, new information is added to the sum total of human knowledge.

But induction also has its weaknesses. The chief of these is that we can be certain that our conclusions or generalizations are correct only after we have examined every possible instance of the occurrence of the phenomenon. It is just possible that the cases we have not examined are the exceptions which show our conclusion or generalization to be incorrect and which, therefore, nullify the principle we have come to accept. Even one fact that is an exception to a generalization forces us to seek another explanation.

As a matter of fact, it is impossible to examine every occurrence of any phenomenon that is at all widespread. And for that reason we can never be absolutely sure of the validity and correctness of our conclusions. We must be satisfied to work with relative rather than absolute truth. We must also expect that at times it will be necessary to reexamine and revise laws and principles which have come to be universally accepted.

3. *The Importance of Experimentation and Direct Observation*

Science progresses most rapidly when it is able to use direct observation and controlled experimentation. The latter method, the genius of modern science, enables the scientist to establish with reasonable certainty cause-and-effect relationships. Indeed, modern science arose through the wedding of Greek abstract reasoning to the experimentation developed by the metallurgists and alchemists of the Middle Ages. Through controlled laboratory experimentation, the scientist is able to supply the facts which he uses in reasoning processes and in establishing cause-and-effect relationships.

Yet with all these techniques the scientist can have at best only relative truth. To be sure, we can get along in science by working with relative truth. Indeed, it is true that modern science has contributed a great deal to our twentieth century civilization, and it has done this by making relative truth work. But we must recognize that the truths of science are at all times relative. And we must also realize that science does not claim for itself absolute truth.

For that reason the scientist has always been extremely cautious and modest in his statements and claims and always ready to admit his ignorance when he is not certain. It is that attitude which Galileo recommended to his readers when he urged them "to pronounce that wise, ingenious, and modest sentence 'I do not know.' " [6]

Most scientists recognize that science is an ongoing and constantly changing thing. Scientists generally do not concern themselves with absolute truth. Some question the validity of the concept, and all recognize that if there is such a thing as absolute truth, it cannot be attained by the scientific method. Conceptual schemes in science are constantly changing things; the picture of reality that we have on any given time level is essentially a two-dimensional as opposed to a three-dimensional picture of reality. As a result some scientists estimate that the duration of a revisionary cycle in a median science is fifteen years, and one of them states that in that period of time the body of knowledge becomes as obsolete as the notion of body humors, the ether, or the impenetrable atom.[7] Whitehead is quoted as saying, "When I was a young man . . . I was taught science and mathematics by brilliant men. . . . Since the turn of the century I have lived to see every one of the basic assumptions of both set aside." [8]

Interpreting Scripture

It goes without saying that we must be sure we understand what Scripture says. It is possible to argue that a statement is Biblical and therefore must be true when the Bible says no such thing. There have been those who have argued that the earth must be flat, because the Bible speaks of the four corners of the earth. They refer to a passage such as Is. 11:12. Now, as a matter of fact, this is a poetical expression for the four points of the compass. The words used mean literally "the four wings of the earth." And the reference to God in Is. 40:22 as sitting upon the circle of the earth may just as well be regarded as an indication of a spherical earth.

So we must also be sure in discussing evolution that we are properly representing the statements of the Scriptures. There are those who insist that there have been no new species and can be no new species, because God's Word forbids the development of one species from another. As we shall see, this position is not tenable, for the Bible nowhere uses the term "species." There are also those who insist that the world can be only 6,000 years old, because Scripture says this. Again, as we shall see, the Bible nowhere tells us the exact age of the earth.

In studying the Bible we must recognize that the language of the Bible is everyday, popular language, a sort of newspaper language. It is not the technical language we find in a scientific treatise. It is nonscientific, yet not unscientific. Just as we use popular expressions such as sunrise and sunset in our daily speech without thereby committing ourselves to the Ptolemaic theory, the Bible in describing scientific phenomena uses everyday, phenomenal language rather than the technical scientific language of a particular age.

Defining Terms

Sincere defenders of the Scripture have sometimes harmed their cause by making the Bible say something that it does not say; for example, equating "species" and "kind" and insisting that the world is only 6,000 years old. Terms must also be defined. In discussing evolution it is especially necessary to do this. There are those who accuse the critics of evolution of denying the observable "fact" of change. There is no question but that change takes place. The landscape changes. Living things change. New species arise. But evolution means more than change. As generally understood, it is the concept that nonliving materials became alive through natural processes by chance alone, that all things now alive are descended from a single or a very few initially living organisms, and that man himself is the product of a process of chance development over millions of years from nonhuman ancestors.

Some have found it helpful to distinguish between microevolution and macroevolution or between the general theory of evolution and the special theory of evolution. By "microevolution" is meant the changes which we are able to observe in living things, including the origin of new species. "Macroevolution" refers to the generally held concept of evolutionists today that life originated from nonliving matter and that all living things are descendants of a single or a few organisms which initially acquired the properties of life. The special theory of evolution is generally synonymous with microevolution, and the general theory of evolution is usually equated with macroevolution. No knowledgeable person questions microevolution or the special theory of evolution; the controversy comes when we deal with macroevolution and the general theory of evolution.

The Widespread Acceptance of the Theory of Evolution

The hold that evolution has on the scientific world has often been underestimated. Repeatedly we meet people who have questioned the importance of discussing this topic, because, they insist, evolution is on the way out. Actually the very opposite is true. Some form of evolution is accepted

by almost all biologists today. It would be difficult to point
to a biologist of national or international repute who does
not accept evolution in one form or another. The theory is
still very much alive and will continue to be alive for the
forseeable future.

It is not difficult to understand why the erroneous idea
that evolution is on the discard has become current. For
one thing, we have tended to overemphasize the statements
of biologists who have disagreed with one form of the theory
of evolution, and inadvertently we have given the impression that they were disagreeing with evolution itself. It is
true, of course, that scientists are by no means agreed on the
details of evolution. Probably there are about as many
theories of evolution as there are biologists. It is this disagreement among the scientists that has been called to our
attention so repeatedly and has led us to the idea that scientists were repudiating evolution. Because a man has questioned some phase of Darwinism or has perhaps repudiated
it entirely, we have gotten the idea that he was repudiating
evolution entirely and championing the Genesis account.
But these men whom we quote are still evolutionists,
although they may disagree with one another.

Let it be stated at the outset that, to the best of the
author's knowledge, all of the scientific authorities referred
to in the chapters that follow are evolutionists. The criticisms of evolution that they make are made because they
are sincere seekers after the truth, and these criticisms refer
to details of different evolutionary theories. The fact that
they make these criticisms does not mean that they have
discarded or repudiated the theory of evolution.

The Problem of Problems

It is also a mistake to feel that we can answer all questions and solve all problems. Our source of information, the
Bible, does not give us all the information we should like
to have. The account in Genesis is a very sketchy and in-

complete one. It portrays God's activities in Creation only in broadest outline. After all, the final purpose of Scripture is the salvation of men's souls. God did want us to know something about Creation, but He did not feel it necessary that we should know every detail of that grand process. For that reason the Bible does not give us all the information we should like to have. Scripture does not claim to be a textbook of science, nor does it pretend to give us a scientifically detailed account of Creation. We need not feel apologetic or on the defensive when we cannot answer all questions or solve all problems. The Bible does tell us that the world came into being through the almighty power of God, and it gives us a few details of the creative process. But it does not claim to answer all our questions or solve all our problems.

Reasons for the Conflict

It may be well for us at this point to explore the reasons for the conflict between Genesis and the theories of the scientists. Scripture is God's revelation of the truth. It presents to us what God tells us of Himself, of the universe, and of its origin. And that must be true and correct, since only He has the wisdom and omniscience to know the absolute truth. Science, on the other hand, is man's groping for the truth. True science is the glimpse that God permits us to gain of the way in which the world operates. Science involves the fallible intellect and wisdom of man, so that that glimpse may at times be obscured and muddied by man's imperfect mental powers. Nevertheless, science is man's groping for the truth. And so we ask: Why is it that science has not come to know the truth of the creation of the universe as revealed in the Book of Genesis? Why this disagreement?

Let us emphasize at the beginning that scientists as a group and evolutionists too are, by and large, men of intellectual honesty. They do not promulgate their theories with the avowed intention of undermining the faith of

Christians. Though many of them do not hold the faith we hold, they are not anxious to make suggestions which are contrary to the account which God gives us in the Bible, merely to disturb and antagonize Christians. There may be, and undoubtedly are, some who delight in pointing out the conflict between evolution and Genesis and who delight in scoffing at and ridiculing the faith of those who continue to champion the account of Genesis. But these are small men, petty men, men of few intellectual gifts, and they are in the minority. Most evolutionists are not at all concerned with theological problems. They are not interested in the supposed conflict. They do not feel obliged to defend their theories against the account that Moses gives us.

Most scientists and most evolutionists are earnest seekers after the truth. They are trying to discover how the world actually came into being. True, the methods that they employ — apart from natural man's animus against the revealed truth — make it difficult, if not impossible, for them ever to arrive at an acceptance of what God has told us has actually happened. But by and large the motives of these men are not to be criticized or faulted. They are not deliberately attacking our faith. They are not conscious tools of Satan, though they may, of course, be his unwitting agents. Because they are earnest seekers after what they regard as truth, we find them at times criticizing details of the very theory which they have espoused. They point out the weaknesses, the faults, and the problems of the various theories of evolution.

The reason for the conflict lies not only in the carnal mind of man but also in the nature of science — the area with which it deals and its limitations. Science deals only with the natural, with things that can be apprehended by the sense organs. It deliberately limits itself to this area of reality but does not thereby deny the reality of that which cannot be apprehended by the sense organs; it simply does not deal with such aspects of reality. One scientist has described the scientist as a fisherman repeatedly dragging a net with two-inch mesh through a lake. He brings to shore his catch, sorts and classifies it, and on the basis of his observations makes certain conclusions. Many conclusions are justified on the basis of such a procedure, but one conclusion that dare not be made is that there are no fish in the lake smaller than two inches; they may well be there but will have eluded the fisherman's net. So the scientists dare not deny the realities of the supernatural; it simply cannot be apprehended by the net which he is using. Science deals with those things which can be measured. Its tools are the rule and the balance. It attempts to describe things in quantitative or mathematical terms. To come within the area of science a phenomenon must be capable of measurement,[9] and it must be possible for another man to repeat that measurement and arrive at the same result as did the first worker. Because the phenomena of the social sciences cannot be described in the same exact quantitative terms as can the phenomena of the natural sciences, many would exclude the social sciences from the realm of true science. For this same reason biology is the least exact of the natural sciences. Living things change and do not lend themselves to the exact measurement that nonliving things do.

The scientist is also looking for a measurable cause-and-effect relationship. He seeks some explanation for the universe and for the world about him that has this relationship as its basis.

Now, you cannot observe God directly. You cannot observe Him with your sense organs or apply to Him the tools of measurement. He is a Spirit, and you cannot describe Him in mathematical terms. He also does not fit into the scientific scheme, because He is Himself the First Cause. He created heaven and earth. He established the scientific laws which govern this universe. God in this sense is outside the realm with which science deals.

This, of course, does not mean that science denies the

existence of God. It simply cannot bring Him within the scope of those things with which it deals. Most scientists will admit that there is a reality which cannot be measured. Unlike a minority of their colleagues, they do not deny the reality of that to which they cannot apply the tools of their art; nor do they deny God's existence because they cannot feel and handle and touch and measure Him.

Indeed, of late, more and more have come to recognize not only the reality but also the importance of the spiritual. Dryden says that scientists have come to realize that atrophy of the moral and spiritual life is inconsistent with well-rounded development. Man's life, he continues, is a trinity of activity — physical, mental, and spiritual. Man must cultivate all three, he says, if he is not to be imperfectly developed.

Dryden quotes with approval several men in this connection, among whom are Eddington and Harbison. Eddington, the great physicist, said that you can no more analyze the great imponderables by the scientific method than you can extract the square root of a sonnet. Harbison of Princeton believes that we have paid a heavy price for electric lighting, nylon, standardized radio entertainment, subways, and airplanes and that price has been the loss of spiritual values.[10]

Most scientists today recognize that science cannot be completely objective and that it has basic assumptions which are not capable of experimental examination and demonstration. One of the contributions that philosophers are making to science today is that of assisting the scientist in examining his assumptions. Science, to a degree, is indeed a matter of faith. Ehrlich and Holm say: "A biologist may scoff at the religious, saying that they accept on faith a system of beliefs that cannot be put to a rational test. The scientist all too often overlooks the articles of his own faith, a faith that almost always includes a belief in a real world in which a sort of statistical order exists. He believes that internal con-

sistency of a theoretical construct is 'good,' that quantifica-
tion is 'good,' that curiosity is 'good,' and that certain kinds
of logic are pertinent to his real world. He may even resort
to appeal to authority. Virtually all scientists dogmatically
accept as fact that there has been a past and that there will
be a future although neither concept is readily amenable
to operational analysis." [11]

The Christian Approach to Research

Now, it is quite proper that scientists seek cause-and-
effect relationships. As a matter of fact, we Christians do
this very thing when we engage in scientific research. We
seek the cause-and-effect relationships which govern the
universe. We seek the laws which rule this world of ours.
In medical research we seek to explain disease in terms of
cause and effect. We do not simply throw up our hands and
announce that these are scourges of God, but we try to find
the laws and principles that govern their occurrence. To be
sure, we recognize that these so-called "scourges" come with
God's permission and sometimes by His will. Nevertheless
we are concerned with discovering the laws and principles
through which He works, the laws and principles, for
instance, which govern the occurrence of cancer, polio,
rheumatic fever, and similar disorders.

We do, however, go beyond the mechanistic scientist in
recognizing that behind these laws, these principles, these
cause-and-effect relationships, there stands God, who has
established them and who works through them. We believe
that He is the First Cause. We cannot agree with the
mechanists that these are the result of blind chance.

Then, too, we give God credit for sustaining the world.
God has not withdrawn from the world which He created,
leaving it to function automatically. No, He still uses His
divine power to keep this universe ticking. And we believe
that without His sustaining hand the world would quickly
collapse into chaos.

We go beyond the mechanist in still another respect. We recognize that God, who has set up the laws of cause and effect and ordinarily works through them, is not bound by them. We believe that He can also suspend their operation and interfere directly in the affairs of this universe. We, of course, are bound by these laws of nature. But God can and does suspend these at will, and when this happens, a miracle has occurred. It is this confidence that leads us to pray. We pray God so to govern the ordinary course of events that good will come to His church, or to His Christians, and, if necessary, to interfere directly in a miraculous way to effect that good.

Finally, we take God's Word as the absolute and final truth, which need not be subjected to further study and verification. We therefore do not put its record to the test of experiment. We do not consider it on the same level with human hypotheses, but we regard it as being in a class by itself.

Scientific Hypotheses, Theories, and Laws

A word about the nature of the various types of scientific conceptual schemes is also in order. Hypotheses and theories are intended to explain, to relate collections of facts to one another. These are developed through insight after observations and experiments have been made. Their correctness is then checked by other experiments.

A scientific law is entirely different. Laws are not explanatory but rather represent records of observations. They usually describe mathematical relationships. For instance, the law of gravity does not really tell us why objects fall to the center of the earth or what these forces really are which cause these bodies to attract one another. Newton himself, after discussing the various phenomena associated with gravity, said: "The *cause* of gravity is what I do not pretend to know." [12] The law of gravity merely reports that in all observations that have been made, objects fall to the center of the earth and that objects attract one another with the force that is directly proportional to the product of their masses and inversely proportional to the square of the distance between them. Accordingly, a large body attracts another body with greater force than a small body. Moreover, the closer the two bodies are to one another, the greater the force with which they attract one another. Such a scientific law makes it possible for us to predict that this same observation will be made again and again in the future.

The law of gravitation does not explain this phenomenon; what is needed is a theory, and this we do not have at present. There was a time when scientists thought that it would be possible to develop theories to explain phenomena such as gravitation, magnetism, and the like. Today the quest for theories to explain these phenomena has been all but abandoned. Many scientists believe that we should seek to explain only those things characterized by regularities; they believe that we cannot hope to explain initial properties such as gravitation. The Christian believes that the First Cause for gravitation and other such phenomena is God, who established these phenomena and is responsible for their continued operation. Scientific laws merely record the ways in which God operates.

The Breadth of the Problem

One serious difficulty that the scientist has in dealing with the problem of the origin of the earth, of the plants and animals, and of man is the very breadth of the problem. By its very nature no one man can have a broad overview of the whole problem. He can see only one facet. He can know only a small part of it. In the time of the Greeks it was possible for Aristotle to be an authority in all the fields of science. But that day has long passed. The consequence has been an increasing specialization, in the course of which someone has said facetiously that a man gets to know more and more about less and less, until finally he knows everything there is to know about nothing.

Today it is a very rare individual indeed who can explore a given subject without overlooking some pertinent information. This is especially true of any field at all removed from his own. As a result important data are often overlooked for many years. Mendel's laws, to which we shall refer later, are a classic example. They were overlooked for thirty-five years. DDT was synthesized forty years before it was used and methods of collecting and coordinating information and making that information available to scientists.[13]

The limitations and disadvantages of this very necessary specialization are nowhere better seen than in the problem of evolution. It is simply impossible for one man to be familiar with all the scientific disciplines that affect evolution. This has been rather widely recognized and almost universally acknowledged. Julian Huxley writes:

> Evolution is an alarmingly large and varied subject. The students of a particular aspect of evolution are prone to think that their conclusions are generally applicable, whereas in most cases they are not. The paleontologists unearth long evolutionary series and claim that evolution is always gradual and always along a straight course which may be either adaptive or non-adaptive . . . the comparative physiologist and a certain type of naturalist will inevitably be struck by the adaptive characters of animals and plants: organisms are seen by them as bundles of adaptations, the problem of evolution becomes synonymous with the problem of the origin of adaptation, and natural selection is erected into an all-powerful and all-pervading agency. . . . The systematist, on the other hand, and often the ecologically minded naturalist, struck by the apparent uselessness of the characters on which they determine species and genera, are apt to overlook other characters which are adaptive but happen to be of no use in systematics and to neglect the broad and obviously adaptive characters seen in larger taxonomic groups and in paleontological trends.[14]

Bruce Stewart in discussing the teaching of evolution quotes Conant's discussion of the scientific method. "Take up a textbook of these subjects and see how very simple it all seems as far as method is concerned and how very complicated the body of facts and principles soon becomes. Indeed, before you have got far in a freshman course you will find the harassed professor under pressure to be up to date in bringing in subjects which cannot be adequately analyzed by the class. Having insufficient knowledge of other disciplines . . . the students have to take on faith statements about scientific laws and the structure of matter which are almost as dogmatic as though they were handed down by a high priest." [15]

The differences in plant and animal processes are also marked and complicate the problem of evolution. Thompson believes that plants are fundamentally different from animals, and White suggests that evolutionary processes in the two forms differ so much in certain features that plant and animal evolution are best discussed separately.[16]

Also to be considered is the fact that evolution does not lend itself to direct observation and experimentation. It is generally agreed that much of the useful theoretical structure in biology, including the various ideas about the origin of life and the general theory of evolution, is not amenable to direct observational analysis. Dobzhansky calls attention to this when he says: "Anti-evolutionists have said again and again that evolution is not 'proven.' We cannot reproduce in the laboratory the changes which transformed the three-toed horse into the one-toed one or those which led *Australopithecus* to *Homo*. It is an inference (and at that one questioned by some competent authorities) that the bones of our ancestors were once upon a time not very different from those of *Australopithecus*. Darwin did not claim to have observed evolution except that under domestication. He claimed that evolution can be inferred from what he did observe." [17]

Rostand says: "The three cardinal problems of biology —
the problem of how a living creature grows, the problem of
how species evolve, the problem of how life originated
— have scarcely been touched by scientists. . . . We have
hardly any idea of the way in which the organic meta-
morphoses that must have gone to produce the human
species from some original virus may have been accomplished in the course of the ages." [18]

Ehrlich and Holm feel that this leads to a great deal of
dogmatism. They say: "The most obvious aspect of evolutionary theory that may be at least partially explained as
reaction to the Bishop Wilberforce approach has been the
development of a rather stringent orthodoxy. This orthodoxy is easily detected in the compulsion of biologists to
affirm *belief* in evolution (rather than to accept it as a
highly satisfactory theory) and to list *proofs* that evolution
has occured. . . . The discipline is close enough to the danger
area to call for some critical re-examination of basic
tenets." [19]

They also say: "The strong urge to believe in present
evolutionary theory, which is so evident among workers in
the field, seems to stem partly from a very common human
error, the idea that one of a number of current explanations
must be correct." They go on to say that demonstrating
special creation to be scientifically meaningless (and it is
obviously scientifically meaningless, since science excludes
consideration of the supernatural) does not "prove" that the
theory of evolution is correct. Current faith in the theory,
they say, is reminiscent of many other ideas which at one
time were thought to be self-evidently true and supported
by all available data — the flat earth, the geocentric universe,
the sum of the angles of a triangle equaling 180°. Perpet-
uation of today's theory as dogma, they believe, will not en-
courage progress toward more satisfactory explanations of
the observed phenomena.[20]

Evolutionists readily admit that their theory is an incomplete one, but they often argue that the facts they have gathered force them to accept it. Yet we must recognize that it usually depends upon your point of view, and there have been many instances in the history of science where facts which were thought to support one theoretical approach were found to give no support to it at all. Hanson writes: "Facts are always facts about, or with respect to, or set out in terms of some theoretical framework. Should the framework deliquesce the objects, processes, and facts will dissolve conceptually. Where now are the 'facts' of alchemy, of the phlogiston theory? Or must we grant that no observations ever really supported such frameworks of ideas? Where can one now locate a sample of caloric, or a magnetic effluvium? How easy and doctrinaire to remark these as chimerae, as illusions of fact. They are actually once descriptive references whose supporting rationale has disappeared. Their articulators were in their way dedicated empiricists groping, struggling, to delineate *the facts* concerning intricacies of a nearly incomprehensible world. But effluvia, caloric, phlogiston, influences, virtues, humors, essences, harmonies, attractions, and powers — these are no longer sustained by laws as once they appeared to be and as *our* now recorded facts, processes, and objects seem so surely to be. But the negative-energy electron of 1928, the luminiferous ether, and the planet Vulcan of the nineteenth century are not so long departed from the scientific stage. May not the solid acquisitions of our own laboratory performances yet grow pale before the chilling winds of new doctrine — doctrine opposed to our presently accepted theories?" [21]

Some scientists have recognized that evolution is a problem which science itself cannot solve. They recognize that it has metaphysical implications and is a problem for such disciplines as religion and philosophy. Albert Vandel says that we must recognize very frankly that the problem of evolution does not fit into a strictly scientific form. He believes that to envision evolution solely in its objective aspects means to mutilate it, to renounce the understanding of its essence, and to misjudge its true significance. Evolution, he says, has metaphysical projections which we cannot ignore.[22]

The Contributions of Science

Now, all of this is said, not to minimize the importance of modern science, but rather to point out its limitations. There is no doubt that through science the Lord has blessed the human race. Consider the very matter of life expectancy. In 1750 the average man could expect to live about thirty years. By 1850 his life expectancy had increased to thirty-eight years, and today it has increased to more than seventy years. This tremendous increase in life expectancy has been due largely to scientific research and investigation. The findings of the scientists have been God's gifts enabling more and more men to live out their allotted span of three score and ten.

Science has also provided us with a means of making life more comfortable. It has shifted the burden of work more and more from the shoulders of men to the machines which it has provided. In place of manpower we now have the power of electricity, of coal, of gas, and of oil. Within the past years we have seen the beginning of the harnessing of the atom, which promises new leisure and new luxury.

The scientist has also made life more enjoyable. Today we have rapid comfortable transportation by auto, train, and air. We have the radio and television and motion pictures for our entertainment. These, too, can rightly be regarded as gifts of God.

Finally, we should point out that these gifts of God through science have also been important in the spread of the Gospel. Radio has enabled us to reach hitherto inaccessible places. Television promises to be a new medium for the mass spread of the Gospel. The auto and airplane have made the work of missionaries more effective. Certainly, also for these gifts we ought to thank God.

NOTES

1. Hastings, James. *Dictionary of the Bible* (New York: Scribner's, 1908), III, 731.
   Hogarth, D. G. *Devia Cypria* (London: H. Frowde, 1889), p. 114.
   Robertson, A. T. *Epochs in the Life of St. Paul* (New York: Scribner's, 1935), pp. 107 f.

2. Wheeler, William Morton. *Ants: Their Structure, Development and Behavior* (New York: Columbia University Press, 1913), pp. 269 f.

3. Mavor, James W. *General Biology* (New York: Macmillan, 1948), p. 5.

4. Weaver, Warren W. *Science,* CXIX (Feb. 26, 1954), 3A.

5. Dryden, Hugh L. "The Scientist in Contemporary Life," *Science,* CXX (1954), 1053.

6. Galileo, *Dialogue on the Great World Systems,* trans. T. Salusbury (Chicago: U. of Chicago Press, 1953), p. 407.

7. Schwab, Joseph J. "Enquiry, the Science Teacher, and the Educator," *The Science Teacher,* XXVII (October 1960), 7.

8. Weaver, Warren W. "Science and People," *Science,* CXXII (1955), 1257.

9. Moody, Paul Amos. *Introduction to Evolution* (New York: Harpers, 1953), p. 202.

10. Dryden, pp. 1052 f.

11. Ehrlich, Paul R., and Holm, Richard W. *The Process of Evolution* (New York: McGraw-Hill, 1963), pp. 312 f.

12. Newton, I. *Opera* (Horsley's edition), iv., 437. Quoted by Dingle, p. 514.

13. Beard, Raimon L., and Heumann, Karl F. "The Chemical Biological Coordination Center: An Experiment in Documentation," *Science,* CXVI (1952), 553 f.

14. Huxley, Julian. *Evolution, the Modern Synthesis* (New York: Harpers, 1943), p. 30.

15. Stewart, Bruce. "On Teaching Evolution," *The American Biology Teacher,* XXIV (April 1962), 272.

16. Thompson, Betty Flanders. "Letters," *Science*, CL (1965), 289. White, M. J. D. *Animal Cytology and Evolution* (Cambridge: Cambridge University Press, 1948), p. 1.

17. Dobzhansky, Theodosius. *Mankind Evolving* (New Haven: Yale University Press, 1962), p. 321.

18. Rostand, Jean. *Can Man Be Modified?* (New York: Basic, 1959), p. 23.

19. Ehrlich and Holm, p. 309.

20. Ibid., p. 310.

21. Hanson, Norwood Russell. "Galileo's Discoveries in Dynamics," *Science*, CXLVII (1965), 472 f.

22. Vandel, Albert. *L'Homme et L'Evolution* (Paris: Gallimard, 1949), p. 8.

2. History of Evolutionary Theories

The theory of evolution, the idea of the development of complex organisms from simple organisms, is nothing new. There were evolutionists among the early Greeks. Thales, Anaximander, Anaximenes, Epicurus, and Lucretius — all suggested that living things as they knew them might have developed from simple forms.

Two men among the ancients developed rather extended theories on this subject. Empedocles (493–435 B. C.), the first of these, believed that plants and animals were not produced simultaneously. Plants, he thought, originated first, and animal life came into existence only much later. He also suggested a sort of "survival of the fittest" theory. Aristotle (384–322 B. C.), the greatest of all the ancient scientists, believed in a complete gradation in nature. He believed that there had been a gradual transition from the imperfect to the perfect. He also believed that man stood at the highest point of one long continuous ascent.

Early Modern Theories of Evolution

But just as modern science began with the Renaissance, so the modern theories of evolution began with that movement. Interestingly enough, the early contributions to the theory of evolution were made by philosophers rather than by biologists. Bacon (1561–1626) called attention to the variations in animals and the bearing of this variation upon the origin of new species. Descartes (1596–1650) was one of the early mechanists. Leibnitz (1656–1716) believed that all the different classes of animals were connected by transitional forms. Kant (1724–1804) believed that the higher organisms had developed from simpler forms, but doubted whether any human investigation would ever come to an understanding of the laws governing this development.

The first of the biologists to make a contribution to the theory of evolution was the great French naturalist, Buffon (1707–1788). His ideas are expressed in his *Natural History of Animals*. He spoke of the direct modifying influence of the environment. He also suggested the concept of a struggle for existence.

After Buffon came Erasmus Darwin (1731–1802), the grandfather of Charles Darwin. He, too, accepted the idea of evolution through environmentally controlled forces. This action of the environment, however, was not a direct one. Rather the modifications came from within the organism by reactions of the organism to its environment.

Lamarckianism: Inheritance of Acquired Characteristics

The first man to suggest a fairly complete theory of evolution was Jean Baptiste Pierre Antoine de Monet, better known as the Chevalier de Lamarck (1744–1829). In the year 1800 he became professor of invertebrate zoology at the Museum of Natural History in Paris. In his opening lecture he outlined his views on evolution. Later, in 1809, he published his theories in greater detail in *Philosophie Zoologique*.

He developed his theory in the form of four postulates:

1. Life by its own efforts tends continually to increase the volume of everything which it possesses and to increase the size of its parts up to a limit which life itself determines.

2. The formation of a new organ is the result of a new need which has arisen and continues to be felt by the organism.

3. The extent of development of organs and their power of action is proportional to their use.

4. All changes occurring during the lifetime of an organism are transmitted to its offspring by the process of reproduction.

Perhaps a concrete example of Lamarck's theory will better explain it. Lamarck would explain the long neck of the giraffe in this way: For many generations there was a drought on the plains of Africa, and the giraffes there were obliged to stretch their necks to reach the few leaves that were found on the trees. The first generation stretched their necks perhaps a fraction of an inch and passed this longer neck on to their offspring. The second generation started out with necks somewhat longer than their parents' and proceeded to stretch their necks farther. Again they succeeded in stretching their necks, so that they were a fraction of an inch longer than they had been originally, and passed these longer necks on to their descendants. Through this process continuing for hundreds of generations, the giraffe acquired its long neck.

Lamarck believed that this action of the environment was not a direct one but that the environment acted on internal structures through the nervous system. Since plants lack a nervous system, he believed that they were directly influenced by their surrounding conditions. Thus he agreed with Erasmus Darwin rather than with Buffon, though Erasmus Darwin believed that plants as well as animals reacted through internal stimulation.

An Analysis of Lamarck's Postulates

With the first of Lamarck's postulates, we would probably agree. It is merely a description of the growth process of the organism, and so long as we understand that God is behind the process of growth, we can very easily accept this principle. Lamarck was himself a vitalist and recognized that behind the phenomenon of growth there was a vital force.

The second postulate, however, is unacceptable to us

and to scientists today. No evolutionist believes that the development of an organ is the result of a need which the organism felt for that particular organ. This would mean that a worm by wanting eyes could develop them, or even that we could develop eyes in the back of our heads merely by wishing for them intensely enough. At the same time it is interesting that we often find evidences of this sort of Lamarckian thinking in the writings of evolutionists today. Even though they have repudiated the idea, they at times speak of the development of an organ coming about in response to the organism's feeling a need for that particular organ.

The third postulate expresses a truth that is very easy to observe. A blacksmith develops a large biceps by using his arm constantly to pound on his anvil. It is a generally accepted rule that a muscle that is used a great deal will grow larger and that a muscle that is not used will grow small and flabby. This increase or decrease in size does not involve the number of cells, but only their size.

The fourth postulate is the most important of Lamarck's postulates, and, like the second, it is no longer accepted in scientific circles today. This principle is usually called the inheritance of acquired characteristics. It was disproved by Weismann, a champion of Darwinism, who cut off the tails of twenty-two generations of mice and found that the tails of their descendants were no shorter than those of a similar group whose tails had not been cut off. This latter group, in a scientific experiment, would be known as the control group. Such a control group must be as similar to the test group as possible. Wherever possible in a scientific experiment, a control group is used so that factors other than the one being tested can be eliminated as the responsible agents for the changes noted in the test group.

No one has ever been able to demonstrate conclusively the inheritance of a single acquired characteristic, and for that reason the theory has been discarded. It is true, of

Figure 1. A Blind Cave Fish, *Typhlichthys.* Fish like this one are found in caves in various parts of the world. Their origin is often explained on the basis of the rejected use-disuse theory of Lamarck. Some evolutionists believe they developed through loss mutations. (Courtesy Chicago Natural History Museum)

course, that this is a negative approach and that it is always possible for some new evidence to appear. But at the present time, as Stebbins points out, there is no valid experimental evidence in either plants or animals to indicate that acquired characteristics are inherited, and there are some experiments to show that they are not.[1]

It is interesting to note that there are many examples also of this type of Lamarckian thinking still to be found in scientific literature today. Again and again we find a character explained on the basis of its having been acquired by an ancestral form during its lifetime and passed on to all the descendants. The blind fish to be found in caves in various parts of the world, for instance, are often stated to have originated in keeping with the use and disuse theory of Lamarck. It is believed that seeing fish wandered into the subterranean streams and in the course of living there for centuries lost their vision because it was not used or needed. Packard, one of the outstanding students of this habitat, believes that their development cannot be explained on the basis of natural selection alone but that Lamarckianism in a modern form is necessary to explain their development.[2]

Other neo-Lamarckians include Eimer, whom we shall mention in connection with the theory of orthogenesis; Naegeli, who is also associated with the theory of orthogenesis; Haeckel, who is famous for his recapitulation theory; Spencer; Cope; Hyatt; Dall; and Gadow. Some of these, it should be noted, worked before Weismann published his objections to Lamarck's ideas. Pathologists, who deal with disease and the changes which disease brings, and paleontologists, who concern themselves with fossils, have been particularly impressed with Lamarck's theory.

Lamarckianism Today

There are also a number of reputable scientists who have even more recently expressed themselves in favor of at least a moderate amount of Lamarckianism. Hopwood, a paleontologist, says that to the geneticists — men who study inheritance — the idea that external conditions can so influence an organism that in course of time their effect becomes heritable is almost absurd; but to him it is axiomatic.[3] G. G. Simpson says of Lamarckianism that until the utopian day when the processes of evolution are really well understood, we cannot afford to close our minds conclusively to any factors that might conceivably prove to be at the root of the many mysteries still remaining.[4] In his last work Professor Cuénot confesses that he is not satisfied with the modern evolutionary ideas. He still thinks that a modified kind of doctrine of inheritance of acquired characteristics of the type proposed by Baldwin and Schmalhausen will be needed.[5]

Lindsey says that now that the realm of genetics has been fairly well explored, the inadequacy of the present explanations for evolution is becoming apparent.[6] He believes that Lamarckianism must be reconsidered and reevaluated. He lists eight experiments which he believes furnish evidence from plants, from cold-blooded and from warm-blooded animals, that changes resulting from the reaction of individuals to unusual environmental conditions may be transmitted to their offspring in the absence of the condition that brought the change about.

Lindsey complains that because of the genetic bias of present-day writers on the subject of evolution few men today even discuss Lamarckianism seriously. Indeed, he says, the experiments he refers to have been ignored in the bibliographies of the two outstanding books on organic evolution which have appeared in the past decade.[7]

It should be pointed out that today the change from Type II pneumococci to Type III pneumococci, one of the eight experiments listed by Lindsey as an example of Lamarckianism, is well understood as an example of DNA transduction and is no longer regarded as evidence for Lamarckianism.

Other recent proponents of Lamarckianism have referred to the work of the French botanist Bonnier as evidence for their theories. He carried on large-scale transplant experiments with native plants. In these, he asserted, environmental factors brought about differences as great as those seen in different species. Most biologists, however, are skeptical of his results. We shall have occasion to refer to these experiments later. The results of Clements, Martin, and Long, to which we shall also refer, must also be considered in evaluating Lamarckianism.

Stebbins refers to other experiments which seem to support the idea of the inheritance of acquired characteristics. He speaks of a series carried out at Aberystwyth, Wales, on the response of flax to fertilizer and says that in these experiments there was some increase in the vigor of the plants which they acquired following heavy fertilization and which was transmitted to their offspring.[8]

As an example of the cautions that must be observed in evaluating evidences that seem to support Lamarckianism, the experiments of McDougall should be considered. He trained white rats to escape from a tank of water by following a certain route. The trained rats were mated, and their offspring, in turn, were taught the problem and became the parents of a third generation. This was repeated for forty-four generations. McDougall reported that there was a marked and progressive decrease in the number of errors made in learning the problem as generation followed generation.[9]

This experiment was repeated by Agar, Drummond, and Tiegs, who carried out the experiment for thirty-six generations. They divided their rats into two groups, an experiment and a control group. McDougall used no control, a fact criticized by Agar, Drummond, and Tiegs. The experimental group was trained: the control group was not. They found that during the first fifteen or sixteen generations the number of errors in both the experimental and control groups decreased progressively for some obscure reason. From the sixteenth to the twenty-eighth and thirtieth generations the number of errors remained low in both groups. After the thirtieth generation the number of errors increased slowly generation by generation in both lines. At the end of the experiment the rats in both groups were making more errors than their ancestors of the sixteenth to thirtieth generations.[10]

Darwinism: Struggle for Existence and the Survival of the Fittest

The second important theory of evolution was the theory of Charles Darwin (1809–1882), first published in 1859 in *The Origin of Species by Means of Natural Selection or the Preservation of Favored Races in the Struggle for Life.* Darwin himself was a reputable scientist. Sometimes he is represented as a charlatan and a fraud, a man whose sole claim to fame rests on his championing an anti-Scriptural theory. But Darwin was a careful worker, a keen observer.

We would disagree, of course, with his conclusions on evolution, but we cannot deny the contribution he has made to science. His research on the role of the earthworm in ploughing and fertilizing soil entitles him to a place as one of the leading scientists of his day and, for that matter, of all times.

Darwin was born the same day as the Great Emancipator, Lincoln, February 12, 1809. He first studied medicine and then theology. His greatest interest, however, was natural science, and in 1831 he began a five-year exploratory voyage on the small British brig *H. M. S. Beagle.* This voyage extended around the world, and Darwin worked incessantly, reading and making exploratory trips into the interior of different islands and countries he visited. After his return, Darwin spent ten years in studying his notes and reworking them. From these he developed his ideas of the origin of species and finally published his book in 1859.

Darwin lived in ill health most of his life. Huxley believes this was an escape mechanism fostered by the devotion of his wife, who became an ideal nurse just as Darwin became the ideal patient. His reluctance to commit himself publicly and in print to belief in evolution sprang ultimately, Huxley believes, from some unacknowledged inner conflict partly rooted in his relations with his father and partly due to his deeply religious wife, who was opposed to his unorthodox ideas. His father, Robert, deplored Charles' intense devotion to nature and natural history and was apparently hostile to the whole idea of evolution. Darwin's chronic ill health did not begin until after his marriage, and in 1844 he wrote Hooker that to assert that species are immutable is "like confessing a murder." [11]

Darwin first wrote out his ideas on the origin of species in rough form in 1842, and a more complete draft was drawn up in 1844, but he continued to assemble facts until 1856. Then, urged by Lyell, he started to write up his material in a work which he expected to fill four volumes. This undertaking was nowhere near completion when he received a manuscript from Alfred Russel Wallace (1822–1913), who had come to many of the same conclusions as Darwin. Darwin was asked to comment on the manuscript and to send it on to Lyell for his opinion. Darwin was completely unnerved by the receipt of Wallace's manuscript and considered abandoning his work altogether. However, he was persuaded to present a joint paper with Wallace to the Linnean Society of London in 1858, and both papers were published in a single number of the *Journal of the Linnean Society*.

The theories were very much alike. However, Wallace favored environmental selection eliminating organisms that cannot survive under severe conditions, whereas Darwin postulated a competitive selection which was essentially intraspecific. Darwin's theory was much more carefully developed. Then, too, Darwin presented a great deal more data in support of his theory so that he, rather than Wallace, generally receives credit for the theory. Later Wallace became an ardent champion of Darwin's theory.

Darwin's theory, like that of Lamarck, may be arranged in a series of postulates and conclusions.

1. First postulate: *variation*. Individuals of the same species differ.

2. Second postulate: *overproduction*. In most cases far more individuals are born than can possibly survive to maturity.

First conclusion: *struggle for existence*. The individuals that are to survive must compete with other members of the same species.

3. Third postulate: *survival of the fittest*. In this struggle for existence those individuals will survive which are best fitted for their environment.

4. Fourth postulate: *inheritance of favorable characteristics*. Fit individuals pass their fitness on to their descendants.

Final conclusion: *New species arise by the continued survival and reproduction of the individuals best fitted or adapted to the particular environment.*

An Analysis of Darwin's Postulates

Examining the theory, we find that there are some things to which we must agree and others with which we cannot agree. Certainly we will agree to the first postulate. It is undeniable that there is variation among the individuals of a given species. We see that in the human race itself. It would be a dull world if God had made the human race a race of identical individuals. A similar variation is found within the various species of plants and animals.

We shall also have to agree to the second postulate that there are far more offspring produced in most species than can possibly survive to maturity. An example of this over-production often cited is that of the female codfish, which, in a single breeding season, produces an average of six million eggs, almost all of which are fertilized. And yet the codfish population does not increase, but remains just about stationary. As a matter of fact, there is some evidence that the number of codfish is on the decline. This means that, disregarding the population cycles to which we shall refer later, the average pair of codfish is survived by only a single pair of codfish in each generation.

There is, of course, a reason for this high reproductive rate. First of all, it is a guarantee of the survival of the species. The lower organisms have not been provided by God with the means of protecting their young both before and after birth that the higher forms have. This means that they must produce a large number of offspring in order to insure that some will survive. Then, too, those that do not survive often provide food for the higher organisms and in that way fit into the scheme of God's creation.

We cannot agree that there is the struggle for existence that Darwin postulated. Certainly there is not the conscious struggle and competition that Darwin seems to have had in mind. Nor is it a necessary consequence of the variation among organisms and their high reproductive rate that there should be a struggle for existence. Even evolutionists themselves do not emphasize it in the same way that Darwin did, and many of them question the concept entirely.

For example, it is clear to scientists today that there is little competition between members of the same and closely allied species. Instead of fighting for the food supply, they co-operate in securing it. Montagu points out that the tendency today is to emphasize co-operation instead of struggle. Favored races, he says, are preserved not by conflict, but by co-operation.[12]

Darwin was convinced that as a consequence of this struggle there would be mass starvation, particularly in the animal world. He was greatly influenced by the gloomy theories of Malthus (1766–1834), who believed that human populations increase geometrically, whereas food supply increases only arithmetically. Darwin was convinced that this was true also of animals. Today scientists believe that starvation is rarely a cause of death in wild populations. The often-cited examples of wild animals starving in our national parks and national forests are instances of an upset of the balance of nature by man's interference.

Elton, for example, points out that animal numbers seldom grow to the limit of food supply and, except in some parts of the sea, not often to the limits of available space. Mass starvation of herbivorous animals—those which depend on plants for their food—he says, is a comparatively rare event in nature. He believes, though, that it may occur more often in predatory animals.[13]

So far as fitness as a favorable characteristic is concerned, McAtee points out that it is a distinct qualification that must be individually acquired and is not inherited or transmitted. He believes that for this reason it loses most of its importance for the theory of natural selection.[14]

There are also many instances in which the fittest individual does not survive. Often the survival of one individual and the death of another is a matter of chance. This criticism of Darwin's theory was pointed out very early. It may be that one individual is not exposed to the same environmental stresses as another member of the same species. In this way he may survive, even though he may not be as fit as his less fortunate neighbor. This is especially true where animals are the victims of predators. Here it is often a matter of chance which individual supplies the predator with his dinner. Defenders of Darwin have pointed out that not all deaths are due to elimination by chance, and they base their theory on that proportion of the cases in which natural selection rather than chance is the factor involved. It should, however, be pointed out that this does reduce the number of cases to which natural selection applies and that it increases the chance of the elimination of the fit individual.

So far as the fourth postulate is concerned, biologists today would say that the correctness of this statement depends upon whether the character is a somatic or germinal character. A somatic character is one which is determined by the environment rather than by the genes and chromosomes, the tiny structures within the cell which determine heredity. Such a character would be the powerful biceps developed by a blacksmith. Somatic characters are not inherited. Germinal characters are those characters which are determined by the genes and chromosomes, and these characters are inherited. Darwin did not distinguish between these two kinds of traits. In fact, he probably did not know that there was such a distinction. In his theory he was concerned with the fact that favorable characters were inherited, and he did not concern himself with the mechanism of this inheritance. He himself believed that the use and disuse mechanism proposed by

Lamarck was one way, though not the only way, that favorable characters could be developed and inherited.

There was much in common between Lamarck and Darwin. The important difference was that Darwin did not stress the way in which favorable characters are inherited, and Lamarck did not stress natural selection as the guiding factor in evolution. Darwin would explain the long neck of the giraffe somewhat as follows: There was a long period of drought on the African plains. Only those animals could survive which had long necks. Some of the giraffes had in some way or other acquired necks that were longer than those of the other members of the species. These survived and passed on those longer necks to their descendants, while the others starved to death. Those offspring inherited the long necks of their parents, so that the average length of neck was greater in this generation than in the previous generation. In this generation, as in the previous generation, there were some with shorter-than-average necks, some with average-length necks, and some with necks that were longer than average. Again this selective process went on, and those with necks shorter than average as well as those with average-length necks died of starvation, while those with longer-than-average necks survived and reproduced. In this third generation the average neck length was again longer than the average in the second generation. Once more there were some giraffes with necks of shorter-than-average length, others with average-length necks, and still others with necks longer than average length. Only the latter survived to reproduce; the shorter-than-average-neck individuals and the average-length-neck individuals died of starvation.

The Survival Value of Species Differences

There are many weaknesses in Darwin's theory, and we shall point out some of them later. For the present we would like to emphasize the fact that his theory requires that the differences between species of the same genus (the category in the scheme of classification immediately above a species) should have survival value, for it is this survival value which has been responsible for their separation into distinct species. This means that the differences between a species which lives in the highland and one which lives in the lowland should be of such a nature that they adapt the two species to their respective habitats. It means that the differences between the blacktail deer, the whitetail deer, and the mule deer, all three of which belong to the same genus, should be of such a nature that they adapt these species to their particular habitats. But we do not find this in nature. The differences between such species are such that there is scarcely an instance in which even by a stretch of the imagination we can see a survival value in them. Often they are differences in coat pattern or differences in the number of bristles or fin rays, or the like, totally unrelated to the environment.

A great many scientists recognize this difficulty. Lancelot Hogben, for instance, says that the alleged selective value of differences between closely allied species, like the blue and the brown hare, sometimes demands an effort of the imagination, if not an act of faith.[15] And Charles Elton says that closely allied species do not seem to differ in ecologically adaptive characters, that is, in characters which adapt them to their habitats. He points out that this fact creates a difficulty for Darwinism for which no one has as yet found a satisfactory explanation.[16]

It is true that we can see an adaptation to the environment in the classes and in the phyla, larger categories in the scheme of classification. The fish are especially adapted to life in the water, and the birds are especially adapted to life in the air. Sometimes we can see what appear to be adaptive differences between members of different orders of the same class, as pelicans and humming-birds. But very rarely can we detect such evidences of adaptation in the differences between species. Now, if Darwin were correct, then we should see these evidences of adaptation in the differences between species. According to his theory, adaptive differences are the reason for the development of new species.

Fitness and Survival

It is also true that adaptation to the environment does not necessarily increase the number of a species in a given area. It will, of course, for a time increase the proportion of the variety especially adapted. But instead of increasing the number permanently, it may actually decrease the number. Elton points out that a very favorable adaptation may set up oscillations that become too high and too low, leaving the population near the margin of extinction. For instance, an insect may develop a mutation which enables it better to blend in with its background and thus escape detection by the birds which prey on it. Its numbers increase greatly, creating a food problem. At this point the population becomes particularly vulnerable to the attack of disease or of parasites, both of which are favored by the crowding and by the inadequate food supply. Disease and parasites may take such a tremendous toll that the insect is brought to the margin of extinction. Elton believes that extreme adaptation to the environment may actually bring about the extinction of the species. He is of the opinion that moderate efficiency in adaptation is to be preferred.[17]

It should also be pointed out that Darwin thought largely in terms of individual fitness and of the survival of individual organisms. He was looking for factors that would ward off death from the individual and prolong his life. Today evolutionists look for factors which will increase the number of progeny or benefit the species as a whole rather than lengthen the life of the individual. Indeed, a favorable factor may actually bring about the death of the individual. Dobzhansky suggests that a disease such as cancer may actually be a favorable characteristic so far as

evolution is concerned. It kills ordinarily after the reproductive age is past and thus eliminates useless, nonproduc-
tive members of the species.[18]

Thus fitness today is measured in terms of the individual's contribution to the gene pool of future generations.
One biologist says: "The genetic usage of 'fitness' is an extreme attenuation of the ordinary usage: it is, in effect, a
system of pricing the endowments of organisms in the cur-
rency of offspring, i. e., in terms of net reproductive per-
formance. It is a genetic valuation of goods, not a statement
about their nature or quality." [19]

De Vries and the Mutation Theory

Darwin did not suggest a mechanism whereby these
variations between species would come about. He did not
tell us how the individual acquired these characteristics
which he regarded as having greater survival value. It remained for Hugo de Vries, a Dutch botanist, to suggest a
mechanism for these changes and thus for evolution. In 1905
he published his *Species and Varieties, Their Origin by
Mutation.*

The form that De Vries worked with was *Oenothera
lamarckiana,* the evening primrose. This is a weed which
is very common in the United States and which was found
by De Vries growing in an abandoned potato field. Specimens were transplanted by De Vries to his garden, and there
in the course of his experiments he noticed a number of
abrupt changes which he called "mutations." Some of these
plants were so different that De Vries called them new
species, and on the basis of his experiments he suggested
that new species might arise by mutation.

However, the new "species" of De Vries were not species,
but rather varieties — varieties, to be sure, which were quite
different, but nevertheless only varieties. Moreover, most,
if not all, of De Vries' "mutations" were not mutations as
we know them today, but were due to the breeding out of

recessive characters present in the stock but not showing themselves (similar to the birth of an albino child to two normal parents both of whom are "carriers" of the trait) and to chromosomal rearrangements within the cells similar to those which we shall refer to in chapter 8.

Today we do see mutations in various plants and animals. These are sudden, abrupt changes in the organism which are due to changes in the genes. They are inherited, and hence are passed down from generation to generation.

Orthogenesis and the Origin of Nonuseful Characteristics

Darwin's theory requires that the differences between species have survival value. It follows from this requirement that the course of evolution will be ever upward, that there will be constant improvement within the species and among the different species. Accordingly, only those characteristics which are useful and helpful should develop in the organism in the course of evolution. Characteristics which are of no adaptive significance or are actually harmful to the organism should be quickly eliminated from the species.

Now, as a matter of fact, in the course of evolutionary history as outlined by the evolutionists themselves, there have been a great many nonuseful characteristics — characteristics which are either useless or else actually harmful to the organism. For instance, there are the dorsal spines of the Permian reptiles, *Edaphosaurus* and *Dimetrodon,* which apparently elongated to such a degree that they proved to be harmful to these animals and brought about their extinction. Similarly extinction seems to have come to the saber-toothed "tiger," *Smilodon,* as a result of the gradual lengthening of the canine or eye teeth. Another animal that appears to have become extinct because of harmful developments in the course of its history is the Irish deer, *Cervus megaceros.* The antlers of this animal became so overdeveloped and so heavy that they apparently brought about its extinction.[20]

H. H. Swinnerton calls attention to the pelecypod *Gryphaea* — a shelled animal belonging to the same group as the clam — as another example of this harmful type of development. In some of the individuals the umbo — the prominence on the shell near the hinge — of the left valve actually pressed against the outer surface of the right valve so that this could be opened only slightly, if at all. Such a situation could lead only to the death of the individual and the extinction of the race.[21]

To meet this objection a number of suggestions have been made, particularly by paleontologists. These are usually grouped together under the term "orthogenesis," a term originally proposed by Haacke in 1893. Two of the leading proponents of orthogenesis were the paleontologist

Figure 2. Irish Deer Restoration. The antlers of this animal are supposed to have become so heavy that the animal became extinct. (Courtesy Chicago Natural History Museum)

Theodor Eimer and the botanist Karl von Naegeli. They and their co-workers suggested that the guiding factor in evolution might not be natural selection at all, but some undefined force within the organism which would cause it to evolve along certain lines. Thus, when an undesirable character developed, its development was due to this force within the organism that was causing it to evolve in this direction. This would very easily explain the development of nonuseful and even harmful characters.

Most scientists today have rejected orthogenesis. For them it is too philosophical. An undefined force within the organism does not lend itself to measurement. Most of them concur in the opinion of Simpson that this appeal to the unknown, inherent in all theories such as orthogenesis, is metaphysical and not scientific.[22]

Supporters of Darwinism explain the appearance of structures such as the overdeveloped antlers of the Irish deer as due to one of three factors. First, they believe the structure may actually have selective value at a certain stage in the life cycle, for instance, in the case of the young elk, or in certain environments. They also suggest that sexual selection leads to reproductive success and is therefore favored unless counteracted by components of natural selection. Most of the "excessive" structures referred to in the literature are secondary sexual characters, they point out. They also believe that what we see evolve is only the visible phenotype and that the genes producing it may have been selected for other cryptic functions which contributed positively to the survival of the bearer. The widespread occurrence of the Irish deer and its relative abundance, they believe, indicate that in its particular environment and at the time it lived it very definitely had superior survival value and was not handicapped by its giant antlers.

Yet most scientists insist that there is no evidence for orthogenesis. Jepsen, an outstanding paleontologist himself, says that after a considerable search he has not found

among vertebrate fossils a single proved example of orthogenesis in either the descriptive or the theory sense. Each
case that has been called orthogenesis, he says, seems to be
at least as well described or explained by other figures
or theories.[23]

However, the problem of nonuseful and harmful characteristics still remains, and there are many scientists today
who favor some degree of orthogenesis. Such a man as
Huxley believes that a little orthogenesis is necessary to
account for certain apparently harmful trends which
preceded extinction in such forms as the Ammonites,
another group of shelled animals no longer alive. He believes that it is difficult to account for these without appeal-
ing to some degree of internally directed evolution.[24] Shull
sums up the feeling by saying somewhat facetiously that
what the world most needs is not a good five-cent cigar but
a workable and correct theory of orthogenesis.[25]

Emergent Evolution

A final theory that has been suggested for a number of
years by some is the theory of emergent evolution. Basic to
all the suggestions of emergence in evolution is the idea that
the whole is more than the sum of its parts. An example of
such emergence that is commonly cited is the result of combining hydrogen and oxygen to form water. Both are color-
less, odorless, and tasteless gases, and from these a new
compound, water, with qualities quite different from either
of the two parent substances is formed. Still another
example is the combination of finely ground charcoal and
sulphur to form a compound, carbon bisulfide, with properties entirely different from the two parent substances. The
term "emergence" is usually attributed to George Henry
Lewes. Later the theory was worked out by C. Lloyd
Morgan.

Emergent evolution has been championed particularly
by philosophers and psychologists. For the average biologist

it is too philosophical. Gregory, however, points out that there is something to the idea and that it cannot be completely discarded. He says that it is true at least in one sense.[26] In general, however, the theory has met with very little acceptance among biologists.

NOTES

1. Stebbins, G. Ledyard. *Variation and Evolution in Plants* (New York: Columbia University Press, 1950), p. 75.

2. Packard, A. S. "The Cave Fauna of North America." *Memoirs of the National Academy of Sciences,* IV (pt. 1), 116–143.

3. Hopwood, A. Tindell. "The Living Mollusc, II. How It Works," *Proceedings of the Malacological Society of London,* XXVI (1945), 111.

4. Simpson, George Gaylord. "Rates of Evolution in Animals," *Genetics, Paleontology, and Evolution,* ed. Glenn L. Jepsen, Ernst Mayr, and George Gaylord Simpson (Princeton: Princeton University Press, 1949), p. 222.

5. Cuénot, Lucien, with the collaboration of Andrée Tétry. *L'Evolution Biologique: Les Faits, Les Incertitudes* (Paris: Masson et Cie, 1951). Reviewed in *Science,* CXIV, 310.

6. Lindsey, Arthur Ward. *Principles of Organic Evolution* (Saint Louis: Mosby, 1952), p. 342.

7. Ibid., pp. 284–287.

8. Stebbins, G. Ledyard. *Processes of Organic Evolution* (Englewood Cliffs: Prentice-Hall, 1966), p. 21.

9. McDougall, William. "Fourth Report on a Lamarckian Experiment," *British Journal of Psychology,* XXVIII (1938), 321 to 345, 365–395.

10. Agar, W. E., Drummond, F. H., and Tiegs, O. W. "Third Report on a Test of McDougall's Lamarckian Experiment on the Training of Rats," *Journal of Experimental Biology,* XXV (1948), 106.

11. Huxley, Sir Julian. *Essays of a Humanist* (New York: Harper and Row, 1964), p. 31.

12. Montagu, M. F. Ashley. "A Consideration of the Concept of Race," *Cold Spring Harbor Symposia on Quantitative Biology,* XV (1951), 326.

13. Elton, Charles. "Animal Numbers and Adaptation," *Evolution,* ed. G. R. De Beer (Oxford: Clarendon Press, 1938), p. 130.

14. McAtee, W. L. "The Role of Fitness in Evolution," *Ohio Journal of Science,* XXXVI (1936), 240.

15. Hogben, Lancelot. "Problems of the Origins of Species," *The New Systematics,* ed. Julian Huxley (Oxford: Oxford University Press, 1940), p. 272.

16. Elton, p. 134.

17. Ibid., pp. 136 f.

18. Dobzhansky, Theodosius. "Human Diversity and Adaptation," *Cold Spring Harbor Symposia on Quantitative Biology,* XV (1951), 394.

19. Williams, George C. *Adaptation and Natural Selection* (Princeton: Princeton University Press, 1966), p. 158.

20. Simpson, George Gaylord. *Tempo and Mode in Evolution* (New York: Columbia University Press, 1944), p. 171.

21. Swinnerton, H. H. *Outlines of Paleontology* (London: Arnold, 1923), pp. 222 f.

22. Simpson, *Tempo,* p. 76.

23. Jepsen, Glenn L. "Selection, 'Orthogenesis,' and the Fossil Record," *Proceedings of the American Philosophical Society,* XCIII (1949), 495.

24. Huxley, Julian. "Toward the New Systematics," *The New Systematics,* ed. Julian Huxley (Oxford: Oxford University Press, 1940), p. 12.

25. Shull, A. Franklin. "Weismann and Haeckel: One Hundred Years," *Science,* LXXXI (1935), 449.

26. Gregory, William King. *Evolution Emerging* (New York: Macmillan, 1951), I, 553.

3. The Species Problem

In any discussion of evolution the term "species" is probably encountered and used most frequently. Darwin's famous book bore the title *The Origin of "Species."* It is probably best, then, that we should begin by defining this term.

The Term Defined

But this is not easy, for we meet a strange situation. Biologists are not at all anxious to define the term. They feel that present ideas and definitions of the term are not at all adequate. And they themselves do not feel competent to bridge the gap. Dobzhansky sums up this feeling by saying that of late the futility of attempts to find a universally valid criterion for distinguishing species has come to be rather generally, if reluctantly, recognized.[1] This diffidence, he says in the first edition of his book, has prompted an affable systematist to propose the following definition of a species: "A species is what a competent systematist considers to be a species."[2]

Darwin's definition, which Mayr suggests is still valid in a slightly modified form, is similar. He said: "In determining whether a form should be ranked as a species or a variety, the opinion of naturalists having sound judgment and wide experience seems the only guide to follow."[3]

At the same time it should be stated that the concept of "species" is as real a concept as can be found in any of the taxonomic categories of biology. It is a term which is of considerable value in arranging and classifying plants and animals. Most biologists are agreed that this category has greater objectivity than the categories of a higher level.[4]

And we shall have to agree with them. However, defining the term is a different thing, and it is no exaggeration to say that there are probably as many definitions of the term "species" as there are competent systematists.[5]

Let us look at a few more of these definitions. One biologist suggests the following: "A species is a group of individuals which, in the sum total of their attributes, resemble each other to a degree usually accepted as specific, the exact degree being ultimately determined by the more or less arbitrary judgment of taxonomists."[6]

Again, we are told that "a species is a community, or a number of related communities, whose distinctive morphological characters (those concerned with the form and structure of the organism) are, in the opinion of a competent systematist, sufficiently definite to entitle it or them to a specific name."[7]

Both these definitions, as well as Darwin's referred to above, obviously are extremely subjective. They define the concept in terms of an opinion expressed by a recognized authority — a practice at which everyone shudders. They can scarcely be regarded as satisfactory, but they do point out the difficulty of the problem and the tendency of some biologists to take refuge in the supposed authority of experts.

Huxley gives us a more exact definition. He believes that species are natural units which meet four criteria: First, they have a definite geographical range. Second, they are self-perpetuating groups. Third, they are distinguishable in form and external appearance from other related groups, or in the rare cases where they are externally similar they may be distinguished by apparent chemical differences in the structure of their protoplasm. Finally, they normally do not interbreed with related groups, in most cases showing partial or total infertility on crossing with them.[8]

Another definition to be found in the literature on the

subject reads: "In sexually reproducing organisms, a species is a system consisting of one or more genetically, morphologically, and physiologically different kinds of organisms which possess an essential continuity maintained by the similarity of genes between its members. Species are separated from each other by gaps of genetic discontinuity in morphological and physiological characteristics, which are maintained by the absence or rarity of gene interchange between members of different species."[9] Though it is reported by Stebbins, it is not his own, for he recognizes that several species definitions are possible within this framework.

Sturtevant lays down these three criteria for a species:[10]

1. Species must be separable on the basis of ordinary preserved material.

2. Cross fertility between distinct species is generally absent or so slight as to make unlikely any transfer of genes from one to another in nature.

3. Subspecies usually replace one another geographically. Species may do so, but are more likely to show extensively overlapping distribution areas.

Generally Accepted Criteria

In studying these definitions several criteria seem to run through all of them. A form that meets these criteria is usually spoken of as a "good" species, that is, a group of organisms which most taxonomists agree deserves to be known as a species. First of all, there is considerable emphasis on the idea that to belong to the same species two organisms must be capable of interbreeding. For that reason reproductive isolation is repeatedly mentioned as a criterion for distinguishing species.

A second criterion is that the offspring itself must be fully fertile. That is almost self-evident, for if this is not the case, the progeny will gradually become extinct. There are a number of instances in which species will cross and produce offspring, but the offspring is sterile. The mule, the offspring of mating a horse and an ass, is an example of this phenomenon. Sometimes it is possible to cross rather widely separated forms and still produce offspring, though these are sterile. It is believed that the widest such cross is between two rushes, *Cyperus dentatus* and *Rhynchospora capitellata,* which belong to separate subfamilies of the Cyperaceae.[11] The hybrid is completely sterile.

Third, the group must have a definite geographical range which can be marked off and delimited, though there is some disagreement as to whether this criterion is a valid one.

Finally, the members of one species are usually separated by differences of structure and appearance (morphological differences) from members of another species.

But even these criteria are difficult to apply objectively. Moreover, there are many forms, such as asexually reproducing forms, to which these criteria cannot be applied.

Kinsey takes a rather extreme position and attacks the whole species concept. He says that a species is a "nebulous something which everybody calls a species but which nobody can define, describe, or recognize in a fashion which is quite acceptable to the next student in the field." He further adds: "We are ready to question the reality of any grouping of local populations into species or any other category." [12] Ehrlich and Holm take much the same point of view. They say that many concepts in population biology have low information content and little or no operational meaning. In this category they place the concept of "species." [13]

Reasons for the Problem

There are good reasons for the existence of this species problem. We want to discuss some of them in detail.

1. Arbitrariness Inevitable in Classification

With any definition that attempts to be so broad as to encompass the whole of the plant and animal kingdoms, there is bound to be some arbitrariness. This is apparent throughout the world of living things, but is especially pronounced in the classification of fossil organisms. Here the problem is multiplied by the fact that it is impossible to do breeding tests. Then, too, in studying fossils we are dealing only with bones and other hard parts. These give little real indication of the external morphology. It is generally agreed, moreover, that bones are very likely to be modified by external and internal environmental forces which do not bring about permanent heritable change. Dietary deficiencies or endocrine defects are likely to bring about tremendous skeletal changes which are not passed down to descendants. It is inevitable, then, that in classifying fossils we should find a great deal of arbitrariness. In the Paleoniscoids (a group of fossil fish), for instance, differences of body scale ornament are used to separate the species, while differences of head scale ornament are used to separate the subspecies.[14] Even in classifying living fish we see this arbitrariness. The degree of fusion of lower pharyngeal bones to form a single plate is used in the perch to separate the genera, but in the order Synentognathi it is used as a characteristic of the order.[15]

2. The Difficulty of Carrying Out Breeding Tests

Even today it is difficult to do breeding tests. We noted above that it is generally agreed that ability to interbreed is one criterion of a species. In many cases it has not been possible to observe the interbreeding or lack of interbreeding of different animals in nature. To overcome this difficulty animals have been observed in captivity. But the lack of interbreeding in captivity is no indication that the animals do not interbreed in nature. We know that many wild species simply will not breed in captivity, and this may account for the lack of interbreeding between the forms we are studying. Robson and Richards point out that at the present time we do not know whether interbreeding is possible in the majority of species.[16] Baker says the same thing of the vast bulk of the world's flora and believes that therefore we have no alternative but to apply morphological and geographical criteria of species delimitation.[17]

3. Forms Normally Separate Which Interbreed When Brought into Contact

There are organisms which are normally separate but which will interbreed to produce fully fertile offspring when they come into contact with one another. Their ranges are normally separated; hence they meet the third criterion to which we referred above. But when they do meet, they interbreed, and hence, according to the first and second criteria, they seem to belong to the same species. For instance, the two oaks *Quercus robur* and *Q. sessiliflora* are kept separate not only by the fact that the first grows on a lime soil and the second does not, but also by preferring heavy and light soils respectively. However, where these two types of soils meet abruptly, a narrow belt of hybrids is found. In intermediate soils the entire wood may consist of a mixed population of the two pure forms together with a number of the hybrids.[18]

Similarly, there are two species of the bladder campion, *Silene maritima* and *S. vulgaris*. *S. maritima* is confined to the coastal regions of England, whereas *S. vulgaris* is an inland form. Only in the north does *S. maritima* penetrate inland, but *S. vulgaris* does not extend so far north. Ordinarily, therefore, the two do not cross. However, under experimental conditions the two species can be crossed to yield fully fertile hybrids.[19]

Platanus occidentalis, the American buttonwood, or sycamore, is found in the eastern part of the United States. *P. orientalis* occurs in the eastern Mediterranean region. These have been considered separate species. The artificial hybrid between them, *P. acerifolia,* is vigorous, highly fertile, and shows a perfectly normal meiosis. The habitats of the two parent forms are quite different, and each appears to be especially adapted to its habitat.

Still another example is that of the catalpas. *Catalpa ovata* is found in China and *C. bignonioides* is found in the eastern United States. The artificial hybrid between the two is fully fertile. In this case the habitats are similar, and the two parents could presumably exist side by side.[20]

There are some forms which do not cross in nature, but do cross in captivity. The true nightingale (*Luscinia megarhyncha*) and the northern nightingale, or sprosser (*L. luscinia*), will cross if they are kept together in captivity, but out in nature they remain distinct in the region between the Vistula and Oder, where their ranges overlap. The same thing is true of the yellow-bellied and red-bellied species of the fire-bellied toad *Bombina* (*Bombinator*), which will breed in captivity but remain distinct out in nature. Similarly, the land snails *Clausilia dubia* and *C. bidentata* breed in captivity but remain distinct out in nature.[21] Most biologists do not regard these and similar instances as violating the criterion of intersterility, since these forms are intersterile in nature. By interbreeding they mean that in nature the organisms normally and successfully interbreed.

4. The Wide Variety of Living Things

Another problem is that created by the wide variety of living things which we are attempting to classify. It is simply a fact that plants and animals are different, and for that reason the attempt to impose the same categories on the different groups is bound to create serious difficulties. Deevey pleads for recognition of the fact that the species is actually only a category of convenience. He points out that bird species are not the same kinds of entities that insects or plant species are and that some organisms such as sponges and lichens may not even be divisible into species in the ordinary sense of the word.[22]

Ehrlich and Holm state that many taxonomists "feel" that biological species exist at least in diploid out-crossing organisms, and they take the point of view that the principle difficulty is in finding or delimiting them, though they state that virtually every well-studied case turns out to be borderline or "a problem." They go on to state that the attempt to force all organisms including apomictic and allopolyploid plants into a species category is indefensible.[23]

5. Differences in the Amount of Intraspecific Variation

There are wide degrees of differences of external form and appearance within the species of different kinds of animals. In some only slight morphological differences are found between distinct species. Among the skippers (butterflies) the species *Hesperia pahaska* and *H. viridis* are so similar that only the expert can distinguish them and then not with absolute certainty. The form of a single spot on their wings is the only superficial difference, and in an occasional individual this spot is not characteristic.[24]

In cuckoo gentes there is no difference except in the type of egg they lay. Each gens lays an egg that matches the egg of its host. Ehrlich and Holm say that it seems unlikely that gentes are genetically isolated from each other. There is no sign of differentiation among them, they point out, except the egg habitus; yet such differentiation would be expected if each gens was an isolated evolutionary unit.[25]

In other forms there may be wide morphological differences without any barriers to free interbreeding. Huxley says: "Experience has taught that in some cases large differences in appearance are possible within an interbreeding group. The color phases of some birds and mammals are examples, but the most striking cases are those of polymorphic mimicry in butterflies. The older entomologists were shocked at the idea that such diverse types might belong to the same species." [26] This poses the problem as to how much morphological difference is needed before organisms are to be classified as separate species.

Huxley also calls attention to the fact that in the deer mice marked intersterility appears with a small degree of morphological difference. However, in pheasants intersterility begins with what have been considered generic differences, and in some ducks even generic crosses may be quite fertile. In other animals, too, intergeneric crosses seem to occur normally in nature. There is also some evidence that the different types of Canidae — members of the family to which the dog, fox, and wolf belong — may be interfertile in spite of wide taxonomic divergence. [27]

Another complication of this sort occurs in the fungi where problems of classification are complicated by the occurrence of saltations. These are instances in which a portion of a fungus colony takes on an entirely different appearance from that of the rest of the colony. The morphological range is so great that a single saltation gives what might well be considered a new species. This situation is still further complicated by what Hansen calls the "dual phenomenon." According to this, three types of colonies may be distinguished. In one, the mycelia (strands of fungus protoplasm, the body of the fungus) produce few or no conidia (reproductive cells). In the second a great many conidia are produced and little aerial mycelium. A third type is intermediate between the other two types. [28]

A very unusual situation is that referred to by Hubbs and Hubbs. They report that one of the cyprinodont fishes, *Mollienisia formosa*, is characterized by always being associated with one or the other of two closely related species, *M. sphenops* and *M. latipinna*. *M. formosa* seems to consist solely of females. The eggs of this species are fertilized by the sperms of the other species. Thus it is believed that *M. formosa* is a sort of reproductive parasite on the others.

Mating normally occurs between *M. formosa* and them, though there is no resultant true hybridization.[29] It has been suggested that *M. formosa* is a natural hybrid formed where the other two species meet and that it maintains itself in this peculiar fashion. But is it a separate species? Or indeed are the three separate species? Are they not rather varieties of a single species?

6. The Tendency to Overemphasize Differences

There is a natural and understandable tendency among taxonomists to emphasize the differences between forms and to minimize the similarities. It is natural that an individual should seek to be the discoverer of a new species or genus, because in this case his name will go down in the history of taxonomy. This is a particular temptation in classifying fossils. Here it is complicated by the uncertainties resulting from the incompleteness of the available fossils, by doubts concerning the identity and relative age of species (whether two or more given "types" are time successive or contemporaneous), and by questions relative to the possible existence in the past of ecological barriers that would have separated the groups geographically.[30]

7. Differences Brought About by the Environment

Environmental effects often create differences which in the absence of breeding tests appear to be great enough to warrant classifying the organisms as different species. This also makes possible a great deal of morphological variation within a freely interbreeding species. For instance, the common plantain, *Plantago major,* shows a great deal of plasticity in transplant experiments. Phenotypes have been produced within two years from seedlings and from pieces of a single clump or clone which have been classed as varieties and subspecies in a recent monograph of the genus.[31]

There are also the experiments of the French botanist Bonnier, to which we referred earlier. He conducted transplant experiments on a large scale with native French plants.

Figure 3. The Effects of an Environmental Factor, Temperature. These fruit flies are all homozygous for "vestigial" wings. The first fly was raised at room temperature, about 72° F. The second fly was raised at 80° F. and the third fly at 88° F. (From A. M. Winchester's *Genetics,* Houghton Mifflin Co.)

Some of these apparently showed tremendous environmentally induced changes. His usual method was to choose plants of perennial herbaceous species, divide a given individual plant into approximate halves, and plant half in a lowland garden near Paris, and the other half at a high altitude in the French Alps or Pyrenees. A few plants from the plains died at the high altitudes, but 58 were able to maintain themselves. Bonnier reports that these underwent striking changes which often made them resemble native high mountain species. They showed a relatively large development of subterranean parts as compared with aerial parts, a shortening of the leaves and of the internodes of the stems, an increased hairiness, and a relatively larger development of bark and protective tissues. The leaves were thicker in proportion to their surface. They had a more highly developed palisade tissue and were of a deeper green, with a large number of chloroplasts — the tiny structures in which the green coloring matter is found — per cell. The flowers were larger and more highly colored. In at least 17 species Bonnier reports that the changes were so great that they had apparently been transformed into distinct alpine species. Thus *Lotus corniculatus* L., the bird's-foot trefoil, began to be identical with *L. alpinus* Schleich. *Helianthemum vulgare* Gaertn, one of the rockroses, became very much like *H. grandiflorum* DC. *Leontodon proteiformis* Vill, one of the hawkbits, became almost identical with *L. alpinum* Vill.

These results have been criticized on the basis of no proper precautions against replacement by neighboring seedlings having been taken. It has been suggested that Bonnier did not have the same plants that he had transplanted, but native alpine plants that had replaced them. Yet Turrill says that while these results must be received cautiously, they cannot be completely ignored.[32] It would be interesting to know whether the plants would have reverted to "plains" types upon retransplanting. It would also have been interesting to gather seeds from the alpine plants and plant them in Bonnier's garden near Paris. If they did not revert to type, or if their seeds did not produce the same plants as their supposed parents, there would be strong suspicion that they had indeed been replaced by alpine seedlings.

Other amazing results are reported by Clements, who claims to have converted timothy, *Phleum pratense* L., into *P. alpinum* L. by means of the water transect and to have changed fireweed, *Epilobium angustifolium* L., into *E. latifolium*.[33]

Clements, Martin, and Long even go so far as to speak of the conversion of one genus into another. They say that while such conversions are much more difficult, they are far from impossible.[34] Certainly in appraising these results caution is in order, but they do suggest that the environment itself may effect considerable changes in organisms.

8. Self-Fertilizing and Asexual Forms

It is impossible to apply these definitions of species to forms which are self-fertilized or which do not reproduce sexually. There are a great many forms, particularly in the plant kingdom, of which this is true, and any division of these into species is purely arbitrary. Indeed, it is generally agreed that the species concept as we understand it cannot be applied to these and that different criteria will have to be worked out for these. It is for that reason that the classification of the genera *Rubus* (the brambles), *Rosa* (the roses), *Salix* (the willows), and *Crataegus* (the hawthorns), is very difficult, and few taxonomists have been able to agree on how they should be divided into species.[35]

The species problem is particularly acute in those forms where sexual reproduction does not occur. The general term applied to these organisms is *apomicts*, and the process is known as *apomixis*. Apomixis and self-fertilization both permit the building up of large populations of genetically similar individuals, but they are mutually exclusive genetic systems. In apomixis there is no fertilization at all. In self-fertilization, which occurs in the garden pea and bean, the organism is fertilized by pollen grains which it itself has produced. Apomixis has not been found in self-fertilized plants.

Apomixis is also used to refer to forms which reproduce vegetatively by bulbs, bulbils, corms, runners, layering, etc. It appears that the phenomenon of apomixis is related in some way to hybridization and polyploidy. Stebbins believes that the existence of such agamic complexes as *Crepis* (the hawk's beard), to which we shall refer shortly, indicates such a relationship. However, there is no evidence that hybridization by itself can induce apomixis. Nor is there any direct correlation with polyploidy. It is believed that hybridization promotes apomixis by bringing together the genes necessary for apomixis and by bringing about a tolerance for a wide range of ecological conditions. It is believed that apomixis is genetically controlled. It seems to be recessive to sexuality, but it is brought about by a number of genes and not by a single gene.[36]

Stebbins goes so far as to say that, in attempting to set up species categories similar to those found in sexual groups in forms such as these, we are looking for entities which are not there.[37] It is self-evident that failure to interbreed can scarcely be regarded as a criterion for establishing species in these forms.

The microorganisms present a special problem. Wilson is quoted as saying that in their case the task of defining species seems to be almost insuperable; yet he believes that to abandon the concept of species would be most unfortunate. He suggests that the only practical method of classification in naming microorganisms is to establish a series of nodal points along the continuous chain of variance and to record the organisms at these nodes and for some distance on either side of them as constituting species.[38]

Another situation in which we have real classification

problems is in the case of agamic complexes. This term is applied to forms in which hybridization, polyploidy, and apomixis seem to be involved. The classical example of an agamic complex is the American species of the hawk's beard, *Crepis*.

Huxley points to still other forms in which this same difficulty of classification is to be found. He mentions hybrid swarms presumably formed by introgressive hybridization, to which we shall refer later, such as are found in the New Zealand plants, in the plants of the Balkans, and in North American moths.[39]

Over a short period of time agamic complexes and similar forms are believed to be capable of a rapid burst of evolution in terms of the production and establishment of new genotypes. Frequently they develop into apomicts. However, once the agamic complex consists chiefly of apomicts, its evolutionary history is decidedly limited. There is no evidence that apomicts have ever been able to evolve a new genus or even a subgenus. In this sense all agamic complexes are closed systems and more or less evolutionary blind alleys.[40]

Results of the Species Problem

1. Recognition That No Universally Valid Definition Can Be Expected

Several results have come from a recognition of the difficulty of defining "species" and classifying organisms accordingly. First of all, it has been recognized that no universally valid definition of the term can be given or can be expected in the near future, if at all. For the foreseeable future there is going to be considerable disagreement as to the way in which individual species should be classified. This is true not only of pigeonholing organisms into the proper species category, but also of the whole taxonomic system. Mayr says that it must be realized that no system of nomenclature and no hierarchy of systematic categories is able to represent adequately nature as it actually is.[41]

2. The Tendency to Reduce the Number of "Good" Species

A second effect has been a reduction in the number of generally recognized species. At the present time the total number of generally recognized metazoan animal species is approximately as follows: Insects, 500,000–750,000; Sponges, 4,500; Coelenterates, 9,000; Echinoderms, 4,200; Annelids, 7,600; Other worms, 9,000; Molluscoids, 3,300; Mollusks, 80,000–104,000; Crustacea, 15,500; Myriapods, 8,100; Arachnids, 28,000; Vertebrates, 40,000–70,000.[42]

For many years there has been considerable controversy among taxonomists, who in general have fallen into two groups, the "splitters" and the "lumpers." The "splitters" were inclined to separate a single species and to make of it several species. The "lumpers," on the other hand, were inclined to group together several species into a single species.

Recent work in the field of taxonomy has favored the "lumpers." Huxley, for example, thinks that the number of species should be reduced and the number of subspecies increased.[43] Turrill, a botanist, says that the results of combining genetical with taxonomic methods are sometimes surprising and indicate that at least many species must be accepted only as categories of scientific convenience, with a very considerable amount of internal or intraspecific variation (variation within the species) and sometimes a large amount of character overlapping with other species.[44] He concludes that it is not improbable that genetical studies may reduce considerably the number of accepted species in the plant kingdom.[45]

Stebbins, another botanist, points out that in plants we recognize today a great many polytypic species and subspecies, which at one time were regarded as separate species. This has been true of the genera *Quercus* (the oaks), *Poten-*

tilla (the cinquefoils), and *Aquilegia* (the columbines). This reduces the number of species. Actually this is another evidence of the great variety possible within the species.[46]

In 1916 Rydberg recognized 122 species of the *Artemisia*. Seven years later the genus was monographed by Hall and Clements who accepted only 29 species. Ross refers to five native species of field crickets of the genus *Acheta* which have widely overlapping ranges but distinctive mating songs and will not interbreed. Only average differences in size or proportion have been found among them. He also refers to a freshwater copepod in which a few noninterbreeding species can be differentiated reliably only by breeding tests.[47]

In 1910, 19,000 species of birds were recorded. Since that time 8,000 additional forms have been described, making a total of 27,000. However, these 27,000 forms are classified as 8,500 species. It is now recognized that many forms which were classified as separate species are actually varieties of polytypic species.[48]

Mayr, too, sides definitely with the "lumpers." He believes that in many cases careless work has unnecessarily multiplied the number of species. He says that it is both distressing and embarrassing to a careful and conscientious taxonomist to have to admit that a great many new species have been created by less conscientious taxonomists on the basis of phenotypic differences — differences of appearance which have no hereditary basis — within the species.

It should be pointed out that in the insects, contrary to the general trend, the present tendency is to increase the total number of species. This is due to the fact that a number of "cryptic species" — similar in external morphology but incapable of fertile interbreeding — have been discovered by genetic tests. One example of this is to be found in the fruit flies, *Drosophila melanogaster* and *D. simulans*, to which we shall refer later.

The various species of the malarial mosquito, *Anopheles*

maculipennis, are another example of this. Mayr calls these "sibling species." He, however, believes that the application of modern taxonomic principles will reduce also the number of insect species. He believes that the total will be reduced from one million to one third of that number or less.[49]

3. The Coining of New Terms

A third effect has been an attempt to coin new terms which will be more meaningful than the general term "species." These terms are usually suggested to fit a particular situation which cannot well be brought under the definition of species. Thus Rensch uses the term *Rassenkreis* to speak of a species which is made up of a number of subspecies. Huxley uses the term "polytypic species" to cover the same group of organisms. Mayr uses the term "superspecies" to describe such forms. All three terms, then, are applied to groups which show a great deal of morphological variability but the members of which are capable of free interbreeding to produce fully fertile offspring.

Another term used by Rensch is *Art,* which corresponds to Huxley's "monotypic species." In these forms there are no subspecies within the species. Huxley also uses the term "polymorphic species." He applies this to a species within which there are sharply contrasting types.[50]

Another series of terms is used by Clausen, Keck, and Hiesey. The first of these is the term "ecospecies." This term is applied to a series of populations or ecotypes which are so related that they are able to exchange genes freely without the loss of fertility or vigor in the offspring. This term is synonymous with what we generally call a "species." The term "cenospecies" is applied to all the ecospecies which are so related that they may exchange genes among themselves to a limited extent through hybridization. Their hybrids are at least partially fertile. This is a wider term than "ecospecies," though it may sometimes be the same as "ecospecies." Often, though, it consists of a section or subgenus of the group in question. Still another term in this series is "comparium." This includes all the cenospecies between which hybridization is possible, either directly or through intermediaries.[51]

Another term frequently used is the term "cline." This refers to several groups of organisms which gradually replace one another geographically.[52] Instead of a sharp division into subspecies, the characters change gradually and continuously over large areas. The groups adjoining one another will interbreed, but in some cases the groups at either end of the cline may not interbreed. Thus subspecies A will interbreed with subspecies B and C; subspecies B will interbreed with subspecies A, C, and D; subspecies C will interbreed with subspecies A, B, D, and E; subspecies D will interbreed with subspecies B, C, E, and F. But subspecies A may not interbreed with subspecies F.

It is also possible for such a cline or series of intergrading populations to turn itself around in a circle leading to populations which occupy the same territory without interbreeding. The range of the herring gull *Larus argentatus* extends around the Arctic Ocean, and the two ends of the range, represented by different subspecies, meet in northwestern Europe. These two forms do not hybridize but live together like two distinct species even though they are connected genetically through a range of intermediate interbreeding populations.[53] Such is the situation also in the deer mice *Peromyscus maniculatus bairdii* Hoy and Kennicott and *P: m. gracilis* Le Conte.[54] Huxley believes that this is an unusual situation. He believes that different parts of a cline do not ordinarily differentiate into separate species, but continue to evolve as a part of the whole interbreeding complex to which they belong.[55]

Still another term that is used is "karyotype," a term devised by Delaunay. This concerns itself chiefly with chromosomal structure. A karyotype was at first defined as a group of species resembling each other in the number, size, and form of their chromosomes. More recently the term has been used to refer to the phenotypic appearance of the somatic chromosomes — what they look like under the microscope — in contrast to their gene contents.[56] Interestingly enough the karyotypes of most animals are far more asymmetrical than those of most plants. Increase in asymmetry of the karyotype is thought to be an evolutionary trend. However, there is no explanation for it.[57]

Still another term is "deme." By this is meant a group of organisms of one species living together in a community. A species consists of a large number of demes. Carter believes that the deme is the fundamental and important unit in evolution. Sometimes demes are the equivalent of subspecies.[58]

Some of these terms have gained some acceptance, but none is as universally used as the term "species." One difficulty is that different authors sometimes use them in different senses. Another difficulty is the fact that sometimes two terms are used for the same situation, as *Rassenkreis* and "polytypic species." The terms are also somewhat limited in their application, since some of them apply to special situations which are by no means universal throughout the biological world. The fact that they have been suggested and used does, however, point out the unsatisfactoriness of the present "species" concept and the almost universal desire to improve the situation.

Defining the Lower and Higher Categories

Even greater difficulty is experienced when we attempt to define categories below the species category. Among the terms found are variety, race, and subspecies. Very often these are looked upon as species *in statu nascendi,* or incipient species, and their origin and development is regarded as a model for the origin and the development of species. However, the fact that we can point to the development of varieties and show the various ways in which they have originated does not mean that we have solved the problem of the origin of species. Goldschmidt insists that subspecies are actually neither incipient species nor models for the origin of species. He says that they are more or less diversified blind alleys within the species.[59] There is, moreover, no clear definition of what constitutes a subspecies and what constitutes a variety. In fact, Huxley believes that the term "variety" should be dropped entirely, because he believes it is too confusing.[60]

A similar difficulty is experienced in defining the higher categories. Separating genera, families, orders, and classes is often an arbitrary process. Nor can the bounds of these categories be defined. For instance, Muir has suggested that a genus is the stage at which obviously adaptive structural characters are developed.[61] Other systematists object that this definition makes for genera which are too large. Mayr pleads for an honest admission that any definition of a genus must be subjective.[62]

It is rather interesting that no new phyla have appeared in the geological record during the last several hundred million years. Even more striking is that no phylum clearly worthy of that rank is known ever to have become extinct.[63]

Species and Evolution

We have seen the difficulty in defining the term "species." Even greater difficulty is experienced in explaining how the species come to be separate. Most biologists believe that this is the fundamental problem of evolution, and many will admit that it is far from solved.

Timofeeff-Ressovsky states flatly that we still know very little about species *in statu nascendi* in nature.[64]

Actually, as we shall see, the problem of evolution involves far more than the origin of species. The problem of evolution is the monophyletic origin of all the species which exist on our time level and an explanation of how the differences which separate the larger groups have arisen. Evolutionists extrapolate from microevolution to megaevolution; yet extrapolation is always hazardous.

Clements, Martin, and Long believe that the important unit in evolution is not the species but the phylad, which is related to the phylum rather than to the species. The familiar species units are only knots in a thread. The phylad is a continuum in which the many parts are subordinate to the whole. This unit, they believe, is the dynamic unit in evolution.[65]

Huxley says that the major processes in evolution consist essentially in a greater extension of life's activities into new areas and into new substances; in a greater intensity of exploration and in a progressive increase of life's control over, and independence of, the environment. Superimposed upon these processes, he says, and having little or no bearing on them are the processes of species formation, which are the consequence of accidents in the environment or in the genetic machinery of life. Much of the minor systematic diversity to be observed in nature is irrelevant, he believes, to the main course of evolution, a mere frill of variety superimposed upon its broad pattern. He believes that though it is inevitable that life should be divided into species and that the broad processes of evolution should operate with species as units of organization, far fewer are necessary for the process of evolution than the number which actually exist. Species formation is one aspect of evolution, he says, but a large fraction of it is, in a sense, an accident, a biological luxury, without any bearing upon the major and continuing trends of the evolutionary process.[66]

Species and the "Kinds" of Genesis

Now what is the relationship of this species problem to the account that we find in Genesis 1 and 2? Can new

species arise? Or does the Bible mean to tell us that no
new species have ever arisen or can ever arise? Disregarding the criteria of geographical range and of morphological
difference because these are difficult to measure and establish, let us agree that species are ordinarily forms which are
capable of interbreeding and whose progeny are also fully
fertile.

What is the relationship between this term and the
"kind" of Genesis?

We shall have to agree that the Bible does not use the
term "species." The Hebrew word used is *min*, which is
probably best translated "kind." The word does not mean
species in the same sense that we use the term today. Moses
would scarcely have used a term which was unknown to his
contemporaries and which men would not have understood
for over 3,000 years after the Book of Genesis was written.
The Bible was written for men of all times, and that certainly included the contemporaries of the writer. It is also
unlikely that Moses would have used a term which has
so many varying meanings as does the term "species" today.

Accepting the definition of species given above, we shall
certainly have to admit that there have been new species.
We cannot go along with Linnaeus who said: *"Species tot
sunt, quot formae ab initio creatae sunt"* (there are as many
species as there were forms created in the beginning). True,
most of the demonstrable instances have arisen in very artificial situations and under laboratory conditions, so that
it is unlikely that they could have arisen in that way out
in nature. Nevertheless they are new species in the generally
accepted sense of the term. And it is not correct to say that
no new species have arisen since Creation. Nor is it correct
to assume that evolution has been proved when we have
demonstrated the origin of new species.

It should be pointed out in all fairness that it is unreasonable to expect to be able to demonstrate the origin
of a number of new species in the field. The very nature

of the problem requires that we be satisfied with laboratory demonstrations of the development of new species. After all, if we are to say that a form is a new species, we shall have to be able to show which plants or animals were its parents, and that is almost impossible under field conditions.

New Species That Have Arisen Out in Nature

Let us look first at an example of a new species which is believed to have originated out in nature. The form is rice grass or cord grass, *Spartina townsendii* H. and J. Groves, which was first collected in 1870 at the edge of Southampton Water in England. Since that time it has spread over much of the south coast of England and to France. It seems to have arisen as a hybrid between *S. stricta* Roth, which is a European species, and *S. alterniflora* Loisel, an American species. The latter was apparently introduced from America with some shipment of merchandise. *Spartina townsendii* is fertile and breeds practically true.[67]

In the study of supposedly new species, one of the important things to be observed is the chromosome number. Chromosomes are threadlike structures that are found in the nucleus of a dividing cell. Each species has a fixed chromosome number. Man, for instance, has forty-six chromosomes or twenty-three pairs of chromosomes. Human eggs and sperms each contain twenty-three chromosomes.

The chromosomes carry the hereditary characteristics. It is generally believed that two forms can interbreed only if their chromosomes are compatible. Incompatibility may be due to incompatibility of genes, or it may be an incompatibility of whole chromosomes. It is generally believed, that hybrids are sterile because chromosomal pairing is impossible, and they suffer from a chromosomal incompatibility. They have received a single set of chromosomes from each parent. These do not match and therefore cannot pair up in the process which produces eggs and sperms.

It is also possible for gene incompatibility to cause sterility. Such is believed to be the case in the fruit flies *Drosophila melanogaster* and *D. simulans*.[68]

Spartina alterniflora has a chromosome number of seventy (thirty-five pairs). *S. stricta* has a chromosome number of fifty-six (twenty-eight pairs), and *S. townsendii* has a chromosome number of 126 (sixty-three pairs). Apparently by some accident the new form received a full or paired set of chromosomes from each parent instead of a half set. This made it possible for the chromosomes of the hybrid to pair.

Another species believed to have developed in a similar way out in nature is one of the primroses, *Primula kewensis*. This resulted from a spontaneous cross at Kew, just outside London, England, between *P. verticillata*, and *P. floribunda*. Both of the parent forms have a chromosome number of eighteen. The hybrid proved to be completely sterile. However, it was cultivated vegetatively for a number of years until a shoot appeared which proved to be fertile. The fertile form had thirty-six chromosomes — apparently a pair of each set of chromosomes from each parent.[69] It should be noted that this form would have died out completely had it not been cultivated vegetatively. It could not have maintained itself without human interference and care.

Another species which is supposed to have developed by hybridization in nature is the cultivated ornamental sunflower, *Helianthus multiflorus*. This form is sterile and is propagated by the division of the rhizomes. It is believed to be a triploid resulting from a cross between *Helianthus annuus* and *H. decapetalus*. An artificial hybrid between the two presumed putative parents has been obtained with some difficulty.[70]

Ownbey reports the origin of a new allotetraploid species. He first observed sterile hybrids between three species of *Tragopogon*. Some years later, doubling of the genomes occurred resulting in two completely fertile allo-tetraploids and a third that was partially sterile.[71]

Laboratory Experiments in the Formation of New Species

1. Interspecific and Intergeneric Hybrids

Let us look at some of the new species developed in the laboratory. The first of these, developed by polyploidy (the presence of more than the normal or diploid number of chromosomes), was the synthesis of one of the tobaccos, *Nicotiana digluta,* from *N. tabacum* and *N. glutinosa.* This was reported by Clausen and Goodspeed in 1925.[72] *N. digluta* has 72 chromosomes; *N. tabacum* has 48 chromosomes; and *N. glutinosa* has 24 chromosomes. It is believed that *N. digluta* doubled its chromosome number after fertilization.

In 1928 Karpechenko crossed a radish and a cabbage. Both of these forms had the same number of chromosomes, eighteen. The hybrids also had eighteen chromosomes, nine from the radish and nine from the cabbage. Nearly all of these hybrids were sterile, but under favorable conditions some produced a few seeds. Some of these germinated and produced plants like the hybrid parents; others were intermediate between it and the radish parent. Those which resembled the hybrid were found to have thirty-six chromosomes, the sum of the chromosome numbers of the two parent species. They were thus tetraploid hybrids with two pairs of each chromosome (instead of one pair as in a diploid) and proved not only to unite certain characters from both parents but also to be fully fertile and to breed true to the hybrid and tetraploid characters. The hybrid is known as *Raphanobrassica,* since it is a combination of the radish, *Raphanus sativus,* and the cabbage, *Brassica oleracea.*

A careful study of these experiments showed that when the reproductive cells of the radish-cabbage hybrid were formed, the eighteen chromosomes were usually distributed

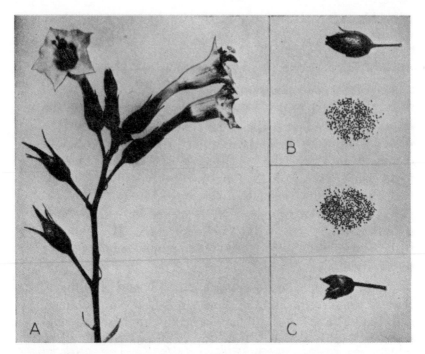

Figure 4. Nicotiana Hybrids. This is the tobacco plant from which the first "synthetic" species was produced. *A* shows the plant with its flowers; *B* and *C* show the seed pod and seeds of two of the species. (Courtesy *Journal of Heredity*)

at random so that each cell received from six to twelve chromosomes. Such gametes (eggs or sperms) were not functional, and this accounts for the fact that very few seeds were produced. Occasionally, however, cell division was abnormal, so that a few gametes were produced which contained all eighteen chromosomes, nine from the radish and nine from the cabbage. Undoubtedly the true breeding tetraploid was the result of the union of two such gametes, so that its thirty-six chromosomes consisted of eighteen from the radish and eighteen from the cabbage. In cell division the nine pairs of radish chromosomes and the nine pairs of cabbage chromosomes lined up together. In this way a new set of characters was perpetuated in a fertile intergeneric hybrid breeding true to its own type and infertile with both parents.[73]

Another experiment which produced a new species was one performed by Muentzing. In this he synthesized a new species from the two species from which he thought it had developed. The forms that he worked with were nettles. All of them were members of the same genus, *Galeopsis*. As the female parent in his experiment he used *G. pubescens* and as the male parent he used *G. speciosa*. Both have eight pairs of chromosomes. The hybrid was highly sterile. Its anthers contained only from 8.9% to 22.3% of visibly good pollen, and few good ovules were produced. From these hybrids a single plant was produced which proved to be triploid (having three times the unpaired number of chromosomes), with twenty-four chromosomes. This triploid was backcrossed to *G. pubescens*. A single seed resulted from the backcross. It gave rise to a plant which proved to be tetraploid with thirty-two chromosomes. This tetraploid was fertile and became the progenitor of a strain which has been named *artificial tetrahit*. This *artificial tetrahit* is like the real *G. tetrahit* in that it possesses the same number of chromosomes, and also in other ways. Cell division is, with few exceptions, normal. A cross between the artificial and the natural *tetrahit* gives normally developed offspring which are externally similar to either plant. The fertility is complete in some individuals, while in others partial sterility has been observed. It should be noted that partial sterility has been observed in some lines of the natural *G. tetrahit*.

It is postulated that this is the way in which the species *Galeopsis tetrahit* originated. It is believed that in some way the two parent species interbred, and the result was the species which we now know as *Galeopsis tetrahit*.[74]

2. Tetraploids

Far more common than such interspecific and intergeneric crosses which result in new species is the production of tetraploid plants (plants which have twice the normal or paired number of chromosomes, or four times the unpaired number) from diploid plants (those which have the normal or paired number of chromosomes) of the same species. A number of these have been developed which are sterile with the original parent plants and are therefore new species. We shall have occasion to refer to this phenomenon again in our discussion of the mechanisms of evolution.

Among these is a tetraploid tomato which has been developed by Lindstrom. The tetraploid tomato is cross-sterile with the diploid species. It was produced asexually by decapitating young heterozygous *pimpinellifolium* plants and allowing a callus to form on the cut stem. Nuclear or chromosomal doubling occurred. From these calluses a number of adventitious sprouts arose. Only three of the 100 tested sprouts proved to be tetraploid. From one of these larger sprouts three generations were bred. These proved to be completely cross-sterile with the parent species.[75]

An Evaluation of These New Species

If we accept the generally accepted definition of a species, then these are new species, for they are sterile with their parents and are themselves capable of fertile reproduction indefinitely. But let us remember that the concept "species" is an artificial one and not a natural one. And even though these are new species, they are still no proof or even evidence for evolution. They do not contradict Genesis, for each is reproducing after its kind. Their characters are the same characters which their parents had, except that in some cases, as the tomato, they have been accentuated. No new character which did not exist before is brought into the world by them. There is no evidence of the start of a process which would lead to the development of an entirely different form.

Moreover, the means by which these plants were produced were extremely artificial. True, as we have said, we shall have to be satisfied with these laboratory demonstrations of new species. And yet it is difficult to believe that any of these phenomena would have occurred exactly in this way out in nature. Under ordinary circumstances a cabbage is rarely if ever fertilized by radish pollen or vice versa. Lindstrom's tomato was not only a freak, but it was a pathological freak as well, for chromosomal doubling is in itself abnormal.

The fact that so few of the new species were produced at first is also striking. Muentzing tells us that under the most favorable conditions only 22.3% of the pollen was good and that there were but few good ovules. Then, too, only a single seed resulted from the second cross. Karpechenko tells us that under favorable conditions some of the F_1 plants produced a few seeds, and he admits that these were the result of an abnormal cell division. Lindstrom reports that of the 100 sprouts tested, only three proved to be tetraploid. His work was confined entirely to one of these tetraploid sprouts.

All of these instances are only of academic interest. As we shall see in our discussion of the mechanisms of evolution, they make no real contribution to the problem of evolution. They do, however, show us that "species" and "kind" in Genesis are not to be regarded as exact synonyms. There can be no evolution from "kind" to "kind," but there can very rarely be the development of one species from another. In most cases "kind" and "species" may be regarded as synonyms, but they are not exact equivalents.

NOTES

1. Dobzhansky, Theodosius. *Genetics and the Origin of Species* (New York: Columbia University Press, 1951), p. 262.

2. Ibid. (1937 ed.), p. 310.

3. Mayr, Ernst. *Systematics and the Origin of Species* (New York: Columbia University Press, 1942), p. 115.

4. Huxley, Julian Sorell. "Towards the New Systematics," *The New Systematics*, ed. Julian Huxley (Oxford: Oxford University Press, 1940), pp. 3 ff.

5. Mayr, p. 115.

6. Gilmour, J. S. L. "Taxonomy and Philosophy," *The New Systematics*, ed. Julian Huxley (Oxford: Oxford University Press, 1940), pp. 468 ff.

7. Regan, C. Tate. "Organic Evolution," *Report of the British Association*, 1925, XCIII (1926), 75.

8. Huxley, p. 17.

9. Stebbins, G. Ledyard, Jr. *Variation and Evolution in Plants* (New York: Columbia University Press, 1950), pp. 189 f.

10. Sturtevant, A. H. "The Classification of the Genus Drosophila, with Descriptions of Nine New Species," *University of Texas Publication* No. 4213 (1942), pp. 32 f.

11. Huxley, Julian Sorell. *Evolution, the Modern Synthesis* (New York: Harpers, 1943), p. 388.

12. Kinsey, Alfred C. "Isolating Mechanisms in Gall Wasps," *Biological Symposia*, VI (1942), 253–259.

13. Ehrlich, Paul R., and Holm, Richard W. "Patterns and Populations," *Science*, CXXXVII (1962), 653.

14. Huxley, *Evolution*, p. 158.

15. Norman, J. R. "Zoological Classification," *School Science Review*, XVIII (1936), 244.

16. Robson, G. C., and Richards, O. W. *The Variation of Animals in Nature* (New York: Longmans, Green, 1936), p. 131.

17. Baker, H. G. "Reproductive Methods as Factors in Speciation in Flowering Plants," *Cold Spring Harbor Symposia on Quantitative Biology*, XXIV (1959), 177.

18. Salisbury, E. J. "Ecological Aspects of Meteorology," *Quarterly Journal of the Royal Meteorological Society*, LXV (1939), 337.

19. Huxley, *Evolution*, pp. 268 f.

20. Stebbins, pp. 199 f.

21. Huxley, *Evolution*, p. 246.

22. Deevey, Edward S., Jr. "General and Historical Ecology," *Bio-Science*, XIV, 7 (July 1964), 35.

23. Ehrlich, Paul, and Holm, Richard W. "Population Biology," *Science*, CXXXIX (1963), 239.

24. Lindsey, Arthur Ward. *Principles of Organic Evolution* (Saint Louis: Mosby, 1952), pp. 35, 327.

25. Ehrlich, Paul R., and Holm, Richard W. *The Process of Evolution* (New York: McGraw-Hill, 1963), p. 245.

26. Huxley, *Evolution*, p. 159.

27. Ibid., p. 294.
   Carter, G. S. *Animal Evolution* (London: Sidgwick and Jackson, 1951), p. 130.

28. Ramsbottom, J. "Taxonomic Problems in the Fungi," *The New Systematics*, ed. Julian Huxley (Oxford: Oxford University Press, 1940), pp. 413–417.

29. Hubbs, C. L., and Hubbs, L. C. "Apparent Parthenogenesis in Nature in the Form of Fish of Hybrid Origin," *Science*, LXXVI (1932), 628.

30. Simons, Elwyn L. "Some Fallacies in the Study of Hominid Phylogeny," *Science*, CXLI (1963), 881.

31. Turrill, W. B. "Experimental and Synthetic Plant Taxonomy," *The New Systematics*, ed. Julian Huxley (Oxford: Oxford University Press, 1940), p. 57.

32. Ibid., pp. 55 f.

33. Ibid., p. 56.

34. Clements, Frederic E., Martin, Emmett V., and Long, Frances L. *Adaptation and Origin in the Plant World* (Waltham, Mass.: Chronica Botanica, 1950), p. 241.

35. Huxley, *Evolution*, p. 351.

36. Stebbins, pp. 383–396.

37. Ibid., p. 409.

38. Wilson, G. S. Quoted in V. D. B. Skerman, "Species Concept in Bacteria," *The Evolution of Living Organisms*, ed. G. W. Leeper (Victoria: Melbourne University Press, 1962), p. 213.

39. Huxley, "Towards," pp. 20 f.

40. Stebbins, pp. 415–417.

41. Mayr, *Systematics*, p. 103.

42. Hesse, R. "Bericht über das 'Tierreich,'" *Sitzungsberichte Preuss. Akad. Wiss.* 1929:xl.

43. Huxley, "Towards," p. 36.

44. Turrill, p. 63.

45. Ibid., p. 66.

46. Stebbins, pp. 54–66.

47. Heiser, Charles B., Jr. "Methods in Systematic Research," *BioScience*, XVI, 1 (January 1966), 32.

48. Mayr, *Systematics*, p. 127.

49. Ibid., p. 141.

50. White, M. J. D. *Animal Cytology and Evolution* (Cambridge: Cambridge University Press, 1948), pp. 8 f.

51. Clausen, Jens; Keck, David D.; and Hiesey, William M. "Experimental Studies on the Nature of Species, II. Plant Evolution

through Amphiploidy and Autoploidy with Examples from the Madiinae," *Carnegie Institute of Washington Publication* No. 564 (1945), vi.

52. Huxley, "Towards," pp. 33 ff.

53. Ross, Herbert H. *A Synthesis of Evolutionary Theory* (Englewood Cliffs: Prentice-Hall, 1962), p. 138.

54. Wright, Sewall. "The Statistical Consequences of Mendelian Heredity in Relation to Speciation," *The New Systematics,* ed. Julian Huxley (Oxford: Oxford University Press, 1940), p. 162.

55. Huxley, *Evolution*, p. 210.

56. Stebbins, p. 444.

57. Ibid., pp. 462 f.

58. Carter, pp. 119–127.

59. Goldschmidt, Richard D. *The Material Basis of Evolution* (New Haven: Yale University Press, 1940), p. 183.

60. Huxley, "Towards," p. 37.

61. Muir, F. "The Role of Function in Taxonomy and Its Relationship to the Genitalia in Insects," *Transactions of the 4th International Congress of Entomology,* II (1928), 600.
    Muir, F. "Some Remarks on Function as a Base for Classification and Its Relationship to Form," *Proceedings of the Hawaiian Entomological Society,* VII (1928), 135.

62. Mayr, *Systematics*, p. 283.

63. Simpson, George Gaylord. *The Geography of Evolution* (Philadelphia: Chilton, 1965), pp. 5 f.

64. Timofeeff-Ressovsky. "Mutations and Geographical Variation," *The New Systematics,* ed. Julian Huxley (Oxford: Oxford University Press, 1940), p. 127.

65. Clements et al., p. 259.

66. Huxley, *Evolution*, p. 389.

67. Crane, M. B. "The Origin and Behavior of Cultivated Plants," *The New Systematics,* ed. Julian Huxley, (Oxford: Oxford University Press, 1940), pp. 540 f.
    Srb, Adrian M., and Owen, Ray D. *General Genetics* (San Francisco: Freeman, 1952), p. 228.

68. Muller, H. J. "Bearings of the 'Drosophila' Work on Systematics," *The New Systematics,* ed. Julian Huxley (Oxford: Oxford University Press, 1940), p. 206.

69. Huxley, *Evolution* p. 340.

70. Heiser, Charles B., Jr. "Origin of Helianthus multiflorus," *Science,* CXXX (1959), 1418.

71. Scagel, Robert F., Bandoni, Robert J., Rouse, Glenn E., Schofield,

W. B., Stein, Janet R., and Taylor, T. M. C. *An Evolutionary Survey of the Plant Kingdom* (Belmont, Calif.: Wadsworth Publishing Co., 1966), p. 5.

72. Clausen, R. E., and Goodspeed, T. H. "Interspecific Hybridization in Nicotiana, II. A Tetraploid *Glutinosa-Tabacum* Hybrid, an Experimental Verification of Winge's Hypothesis," *Genetics,* X (1925), 278–284.

73. Karpechenko, G. D. "Polyploid Hybrids of *Raphanus sativus* L.×*Brassica oleracea* L.," *Zeitschrift für Induktive Abstammungs- und Vererbungslehre,* XLVIII (1928), 1–85.

74. Muentzing, Arne. "Ueber Chromosomenvermehrung in *Galeopsis*-Kreuzungen und ihre phylogenetische Bedeutung," *Hereditas,* XIV (1930), 153–172.

75. Lindstrom, E. W. "A Fertile Tetraploid Tomato Cross Sterile with Diploid Species," *Journal of Heredity,* XXIII (1932), 115–121.

4. Days of Creation and Age of the Earth

In order to reconcile what are believed to be evidences for an old earth and for evolution with Genesis 1, much attention has been given to the length of the creation days. Many regard these as long periods of time. They point to the fact that the Hebrews did not have the exact quantitative sense that we Occidentals have and that they were more inclined to the use of poetical expressions. They ask whether it is not possible that these were long periods of time, eons, in which evolution may have taken place. Thus, the process of evolution may have been God's way of effecting Creation. Others look for long periods of time in the creation days, because they are convinced that the world is older than the 6,000 years postulated by Bishop Ussher.

Basic to any discussion of evolution and of the length of the creation days is agreement on the way in which the Genesis account is to be interpreted. There are those who believe that it is historical; others believe that it is of a different literary genre and that it must be regarded as an allegorical or poetical account. The latter usually apply this principle to the first eleven chapters of Genesis, believing that the first two chapters state nothing more than that God is behind the process of creation, that the third chapter states only that man is evil, that the story of the Flood tells us that God punishes wickedness, and that the story of the tower of Babel is intended to teach us that God will punish pride and rebellion. History, they believe, begins

82

with Genesis 12, and even this history is not written in the same way in which we of the Western world write history.

It is true, as we have pointed out, that the language of Genesis is not the technical scientific language of the 20th century; it is popular, everyday commonsense, phenomenal language. It is also true that the Hebrews did not have the exact historical sense that we have. It is further true that there are different literary genres in Scripture, and we must take these into account in interpreting it. The Bible does have poetical and prophetic books as well as historical books. Poetry is characterized by imagery and figurative language; prophecy by pictures. Yet even poetry and prophecy have a message; they are intended to convey God's truth to us.

The suggestion that the first chapters of Genesis are allegory or parable is not new. Medievalists sought to find an allegorical meaning as well as a literal meaning in interpreting Scripture. Luther was a literalist in interpreting the historical books of the Bible; this is apparent from his approach to the doctrine of the Lord's Supper at the Marburg Colloquy, and he reacted violently against the allegorical interpretation of Genesis that was current in his day. He says: "Nor does it serve any useful purpose to make Moses at the outset so mystical and allegorical. His purpose is to teach us, not about allegorical creatures and an allegorical world but about real creatures and a visible world apprehended by the senses. Therefore . . . he employs the terms 'day' and 'evening' without allegory, just as we customarily do." [1] Later, in his interpretation of chapter 2, he says: "These, then, are all historical facts. This is something to which I carefully call attention, lest the unwary reader be led astray by the authority of the fathers, who give up the idea that this is history and look for allegories." [2] Still later he says: "According to our ability, we have treated all these facts in their historical meaning, which is their real and true one. . . . Almost all of these [Latin, Greek, and Hebrew in-

terpreters of the Scripture] not only do not concern themselves with the story but bury and confuse it with their
nonsensical allegories." [3]

There are those who believe that Genesis must be interpreted as a historical book but still believe that the "days"
of Genesis must be regarded as long periods of time. They
point to the fact that the Bible itself uses the term *yom* for
a period greater than twenty-four hours. Thus, already in
Gen. 2:4 the statement: "In the *day* that the Lord God
made the earth and the heavens," refers to the entire period
of creation. There are other passages, too, which use such
expressions as "the day of the Lord," where the term "day"
clearly refers to a period of time.

It is also urged that passages such as Ps. 90:4 and 2 Peter
3:8 define the term "day" and show that it is meant to be
a long period of time. It is further argued that the sun was
not created until the fourth day and that therefore the
preceding days could not have been ordinary solar days.
There are those, too, who believe that the seventh day upon
which God is said to have rested extends through all succeeding time. Therefore, they argue, the preceding days
must have been long periods of time.

Evidences that the Days of Creation Were Not
Long Periods of Time

Yet the Scriptures speak very clearly on the length of
the creation days. It is a general principle of Biblical interpretation that a word is to be taken in its everyday meaning
unless there is compelling evidence that it must be taken in
a different sense. So in Gen. 2:4 it is very clear from the
text itself that the word "day" here means a period of time
longer than twenty-four hours. And that is also true of the
other passages of Scripture where the word "day" clearly
refers to a long period of time. But there is nothing in the
text or context of Genesis 1 which indicates that these were
long periods of time. Sound principles of Biblical inter-

pretation require that we accept this "day" as being an ordinary day.

Passages such as Ps. 90:4 and 2 Peter 3:8 are not meant to interpret Genesis 1 and 2. Their purpose is to show God's eternity. They have no connection at all with the creation story.

Insofar as the view is concerned that these could not be ordinary days because the sun had not been created, we should like to point to the fact that we still measure time in terms of days even though the sun does not appear or is not visible. For instance, north of the Arctic Circle and south of the Antarctic Circle the sun does not appear for periods of time up to six months at the poles themselves. We would not think of measuring time in terms of the appearance or lack of appearance of the sun in these areas. No one would contend that at the North or the South Pole a day is the equivalent of six months elsewhere.

Finally, it should be stated that there is no evidence in Scripture that the seventh day on which God rested is to be conceived of as extending through all succeeding time. True, the work of creation is finished, and God is resting from that work. But there is no reason to believe that this resting of God on the seventh day is meant to imply that the seventh day extends through all eternity.

Evidences that the Days of Creation Were Ordinary Days

There is also clear evidence from the text that these were ordinary days. The repetition of evening and morning would almost indicate that God anticipated some of the controversies of our day and that He wanted to make it clear that the creation days were ordinary days. It is hard to escape the conviction that these were ordinary days when we read the almost monotonous repetition of evening and morning. Then, too, the sun was created to rule the day.

Are we to believe that in those early days of the earth the sun continued to shine for thousands of years without setting?

There are difficulties in assuming that these were long periods of time. In the account in Genesis the plants were created on the third day and the sun only on the fourth day. Today the plants are dependent on the sun for their energy. And because animals are dependent on the plants, we can say that the animals are also dependent on the sun for their energy. It would be possible for the plants to exist for one day without the sun, but it would be inconceivable that they should have existed for a long period of time without the sun. True, it may be argued that for the era represented by the third day the plants had some other source on which they depended for their energy — the general "light," for instance, created on the first day. But it can also be argued that it is unlikely that God would have made the plants dependent on some other source for energy for a long period of time and then transferred their dependence to the sun.

This is also the interpretation which other portions of Scripture indicate. In Ex. 20:11 we are told that the Sabbath day was to be observed in the Old Testament because "in six days the Lord made heaven and earth, the sea, and all that in them is, and rested the seventh day." This statement clearly implies that the days of creation were ordinary days and that God rested on the seventh *day* rather than on the seventh era, for the Jews were required to rest for a day and not for an era.

Then, too, in the Old Testament where the term *yom* is associated with a definite number, it is always used to designate an ordinary day. The repetition of the first day, the second day, the third day, indicates that these were ordinary days.

The repetition of evening and morning creates still

another problem. Does this mean that for half the period represented, let us say, by the fourth day, the sun did not shine and that for half the period it did? The text speaks of evening and morning, implying a period of darkness and a period of light. It is hard to believe that the plants could survive an extended period of darkness lasting for hundreds or even thousands of years.

Finally, we should point out that little is gained in reconciling Genesis with evolution by assuming that these were long periods of time. It is hardly conceivable that anyone would question the interpretation of these as ordinary days were it not for the fact that people are attempting to reconcile Genesis and evolution. And yet, ironically enough, seven thousand or seven million years will not satisfy the evolutionist. He requires an even greater length of time than can be had by saying that the days of creation were thousand- or million-year periods rather than days.

The Theory of a Gap Between Gen. 1:1 and Gen. 1:2

Another problem in connection with the Genesis account is the possibility of hiatus between Gen. 1:1 and Gen. 1:2. It has been suggested that possibly the world was created originally for the angels and that is why their creation is not mentioned in Genesis 1. According to this suggestion, it is the creation of the world intended for the angels that is reported in Genesis 1:1. Some time after this angel world had been created, the evil angels, led by Satan, fell into sin. As a punishment for this sin, the world was destroyed and the evil angels cast into hell. It is this condition of the earth which is reported in Gen. 1:2: "and the earth was without form and void."

Proponents of this theory believe that it would account for the passage of a considerable amount of time and in that way would make it possible to reconcile the Bible with the findings of some geologists who believe that the world is about four and one-half billion years old. They also believe that this theory would account for many fossils. These, they believe, are remnants of animals which were created for the angel world but were destroyed when the angel world was destroyed.

However, this theory does not fit in with Scripture. Gen. 1:2 does not say that the world was *disorganized,* as it would have been as a result of the destruction of such an angel world. Rather the Hebrew indicates an *unorganized* condition. In other words, the matter had been created, but it was not organized in the way in which it is organized today.

The etymology of the two Hebrew words for "without form and void" has been lost, but according to Keil and Delitzsch the meaning here is "waste and empty" or "barren." They do not imply a "laying waste" or a "desolating." Thus these words describe the coming earth and tell us that at first it was a desolate, formless, lifeless mass.[4]

Furthermore, at the end of the creation account we are told: "And God saw everything that He had made, and, behold, it was very good" (Gen. 1:31). This could hardly be said if part of the world had already been destroyed and the angels had already fallen into sin. The angels as well as the rest of creation were still in a state of perfection at the end of the sixth day. Keil and Delitzsch say that the application of the term "good" to everything that God had made and the emphatic "very" at the close of the whole creation denies absolutely the existence of anything evil in God's creation.[5]

The Ussher Chronology

Another of the problems that must be discussed in the light of its Scriptural background is that of the age of the earth. Many of our English Bibles have the date 4004 B. C. in the margin of Genesis 1. This is the figure arrived at by Bishop Ussher, an Anglican bishop who worked out the chronology of Scripture and published his results in 1654. In 1701 these dates began to be printed in the margins of many Bibles, and they have been printed in most editions of the King James Version of the Bible ever since.

The figures were arrived at by a study particularly of Genesis 5 and 11. There we are told that an individual lived a certain number of years, begat so-and-so, lived a certain number of years after begetting so-and-so and then died. Ussher assumed that these were father-and-son relationships and on that basis constructed his chronology. If this premise is granted, then the figures arrived at are approximately correct.

Scriptural Evidence that These Were Not Always Father-Son Relationships

However, there is some evidence that these may not be simple father-and-son relationships. We know that abridgment of genealogies is very common in Scripture and may almost be said to be the rule. Time after time we find the term *son* used where clearly the term means *descendant*, not *son*. For instance, in the very first verse of Matthew's Gospel, Christ is called "the Son of David, the Son of Abraham." In the same chapter in verse 8 three names are omitted between Joram and Ozias (Uzziah).

Comparing the genealogy of Ezra 7:3 f. with 1 Chron. 6:6-10, we find six names omitted between Meraioth and Azariah.

EZRA 7:3 f.	1 CHRON. 6:6-10
Zerahiah	Zerahiah
Meraioth	Meraioth
	Amariah
	Ahitub
	Zadok
	Ahimaaz
	Azariah
	Johanan
Azariah	Azariah
Amariah	Amariah

There are many other instances that could be cited, but

from these it will be apparent that abridgment of genealogical records is quite common in Scripture.

The most convincing evidence comes from another genealogy in the Bible itself. Luke, in the third chapter of his Gospel, traces the genealogy of Christ back to Adam. And in that genealogy he mentions a name which is not recorded in the account of Moses in Genesis.

LUKE 3	GENESIS 11
Sem	Shem
Arphaxad	Arphaxad
Cainan	
Sala	Salah
Heber	Eber
Phalec	Peleg

Now, certainly Luke was inspired by the Holy Spirit in recording his genealogy of Christ. It cannot be by mistake that an extra name crept in. It must be that Cainan actually has a place in the genealogy. Undoubtedly Luke used a genealogical table which was somewhat different from the one in Genesis. Clearly this indicates that there is at least one name omitted by Moses in the Genesis account. And if there is one omission, is it not possible that there are more?

It should be noted in passing that Cainan is included in the genealogical table of Genesis 11 in the Septuagint. Here he is said to have had a life span of 565 years. It is possible that the translators of the Septuagint had access to the same genealogical tables that Luke studied and copied and they felt it necessary to correct the Hebrew text. Some scholars feel that originally Cainan was included in the Hebrew text and that his omission from the Bible we have at present is due to a corruption which has crept into the Hebrew text which we now have. Others feel that his mention in the Septuagint is due to a corruption in that text.

Those who accept the historical interpretation of Genesis

but believe that more time is involved than Ussher assumed point to the fact that if we construct a chronology using the genealogies of Genesis 11 and the following chapters and assume these to be father-son relations, we find that Shem lived as a contemporary of all his descendants through Abraham and Isaac. It is hard to believe that he was a contemporary of the two patriarchs and died only shortly before the birth of Jacob. Even a cursory reading of the Old Testament gives the impression that a great deal of time elapsed between the life of Shem and that of the patriarchs.

The Purpose of the Genealogical Records

It may be helpful to consider the purpose of the genealogical tables in Genesis. Certainly the purpose was not to give us an exact chronological account of those times, for if that were the case, there would be no omissions. The Holy Spirit would not have permitted Moses to omit any names if that had been His purpose. It seems rather that God wanted to give us the names of the most important men who lived between Adam and Abraham and wanted to give us a brief account of what occurred in that period. It is also evident that the Lord wanted to show us how the earth was populated in keeping with His command (Gen. 1:28 and Gen. 9:1). By the time of the Flood the human race had spread over much of the face of the earth, and it is the purpose of Genesis 5 to show how this spread was accomplished. In Genesis 11 the emphasis is on the spread of the descendants of Shem after the Flood. But why should God have included the ages of these patriarchs? Chiefly to show how the human race could have increased in numbers so rapidly. Because these men attained such great ages, they were able to beget large numbers of sons and daughters. In this way, the world was populated rather quickly. Then, too, God apparently did want to show us that the earth is not billions of years old.

Scripture and the Age of the Earth

What shall we say, then, about the age of the earth? We shall have to say that Scripture gives us no exact dates before the time of Abraham. It is impossible to give an exact date for Creation, and we cannot say on the basis of Scripture how old the earth is. God simply did not feel that it was necessary for us to know its exact age. Apparently the age of the earth has no bearing on our salvation. This is not to be regarded as a plea for the acceptance of the figures of some geologists and evolutionists: it is merely a statement that on the basis of Scripture we cannot establish definitely how old the earth is.

Scientific Hypotheses on the Age of the Earth

What age is assigned to the earth and to the universe by scientists today — the geologists, physicists, and astronomers? Most scientists believe that the earth is somewhere between 4½ and 6 billion years old and that the age of the universe is not much greater than that of the earth itself. Estimates of the age of the universe, however, run as high as 10 billion years.

Hoyle's steady-state theory of the origin of the universe, which postulates that matter is being continuously created throughout space, has been largely abandoned today. The age of the universe is estimated by assuming that the universe is expanding. Astronomers believe that the stars, of which our sun is one, are moving out from a common point. Estimates of the age of the universe are gotten by projecting the paths of the stars backward to their apparent point of origin. The universe is believed to have originated suddenly at that time.[6]

Older Methods of Estimating the Age of the Earth

How are estimates as to the age of the earth made? A number of methods have been employed, and at one time each of these was thought to be very accurate. For a while, for instance, it was thought that rates of erosion and depósition or sedimentation would give us a fairly accurate figure as to the age of the earth. Careful measurements were made in the various delta areas, such as the Nile Delta in Egypt and the Mississippi Delta here in the United States. It was thought that projections based on these figures would give us a fairly exact figure for the age of the earth.

Another method of determining the age of the earth employed at one time was that of measuring the amount of salt (sodium chloride) in the seas. It was believed that all of the salt to be found in the oceans came originally from land areas. The rain, as it percolated through the soil, was supposed to have leached out, or dissolved out, the salt and to have carried it into the sea. It was assumed that by measuring the rate at which salt is being brought down to the sea today it would be possible to determine the age of the oceans on the basis of the amount of salt which they contain. Figures based on the amount of sodium in the sea and the present rate of erosion place the age of the earth at 50 million years.[7]

Today it is recognized that erosion-deposition rates are not constant, and this method of dating the earth has been discarded. It is also believed that sodium may form a closed cycle, an equal amount moving into and out of the sea. As salt is carried down into the ocean by the rivers, it is possible that an equal amount is being removed from the oceans by crystallization into rock. If the cycle is completely closed, as is suggested, then the calculations of the age of the oceans from estimates of their sodium content and of loss of sodium to them by the weathering of crystalline rock are, of course, invalid.[8]

It is recognized, too, that many of the inorganic elements form similar closed cycles. Cycles have been suggested for strontium, sodium, carbon, nitrogen, oxygen, calcium, potassium, and magnesium. Odum says that it is possible that the whole sedimentary cycle is in a state of equilibrium.[9] For that reason any dating that is based upon the quantity of inorganic salts in various areas is probably invalid.

More Recent Methods for Estimating the Age of the Earth

Today it is generally recognized that these older methods do not give an even reasonably accurate indication of the age of the earth. They seem to agree that the earth is very old — much older than Ussher assumed it was. However, for accuracy, scientists today depend on other newer methods. Recently, for example, it has been suggested that rocks be dated on the basis of their helium content. This method has been successfully applied to iron meteorites, which have been assigned an age close to that estimated for the earth's crust. This, of course, agrees with the idea that the other heavenly bodies are of about the same age as the earth. However, it is generally believed that this method is unreliable in determining the age of rocks, because helium, being a gas, is likely to escape. As a result, different figures are gotten from the constituent minerals found in a single rock. Moreover, where comparisons are possible, the helium ages are lower than those derived from the uranium time clock. This, too, is believed to be due to the fact that some of the helium escapes. At the same time, though, there are cases where there is too much helium present in the rock, and the helium ages are higher than the uranium time clock ages. This situation creates a real problem. It is believed to be due to the fact that during crystallization the mineral in which this excess helium is found absorbed considerable amounts of short-lived radioactive elements or that there has been a selective occlusion or absorption of helium from that left in the magma, the molten rock mass.[10] This method of age determination by helium content is a part of the radioactive methods to which we shall refer later.

Still another radioactive method is a measurement of the decay of rubidium to strontium. The half-life of rubidium is believed to be about 5×10^{10} years. Rubidium-bearing minerals are less common than lead-bearing minerals, and there are some problems in determining its precise half-life.[11]

Recently some dating of rocks has been done on the basis of ratios of K^{40} (Potassium—40) to A^{40} (Argon—40). K^{40} is a naturally occurring radioactive isotope which decays to Ca^{40} (Calcium—40) and A^{40}. In general the age determinations have agreed with those made by the uranium time clock, and where it has been possible to date a rock by the uranium time clock as well as by this method, the results have agreed within what are regarded as acceptable margins of variation.[12] This method, like the rubidium-strontium method, is believed to be very promising.

The Uranium Time Clock

The most widely employed method of dating the rocks today is the so-called uranium time clock. This is based on a measure of the relative amounts of certain radioactive substances to be found in various rocks. Uranium, the heaviest naturally occurring element, breaks down spontaneously into a series of elements, finally becoming lead. The rate at which this breakdown occurs is constant: it can neither be speeded up nor slowed down by forces or agencies which we know today. It has been found that 7,600,000,000 grams of uranium yield about 1 gram of lead a year. Hence the age of the rock can be determined by the formula:

$$\text{Age of rock} = \frac{\text{weight of lead}}{\text{weight of uranium}} \times 7.6 \times 10^9 \text{ years}$$

Actually there are four possible methods of determining the age of a rock according to this process. U^{238} * decays

---

* U is the chemical symbol for uranium, Pb the chemical symbol for lead, Th the chemical symbol for thorium, and Ac the chemical symbol for actinium. The superscripts indicate atomic weight. The superscripts are important in distinguishing the different kinds (isotopes) of uranium and lead.

to Pb^{206}, U^{235} decays to Pb^{207}, and Th^{232} decays to Pb^{208}. It is also possible to determine the age of a rock by determining the ratio of Pb^{207} to Pb^{206}. U^{238} is believed to have a half-life of 4.51×10^9 years, U^{235} is believed to have a half-life of 7.13×10^8 years, and Th^{232} is believed to have a half-life of 1.39×10^{10} years.[13] Because U^{238} and U^{235} decay at different rates, it is possible to determine the age of a rock by determining the relative quantities of Pb^{207} and Pb^{206}. Pb^{206} is sometimes known as RaG, Pb^{207} as AcD, Pb^{208} as ThD, and U^{235} as AcU. Both U^{238} and U^{235} have an atomic number of 92; Th has an atomic number of 90; and all lead has an atomic number of 82. In addition to these three kinds of radiogenic lead there is a fourth isotope of lead, Pb^{204}, which is nonradiogenic and which is found in small quantities in some rocks.

There are a number of substances formed in the course of the disintegration of uranium and thorium to lead. Each of these substances disintegrates into the next one in line in a certain period of time. This disintegration is usually measured in terms of half-life, the period it takes half of a given amount of a radioactive substance to disintegrate. The substances in the U^{238}/Pb^{206} series, their atomic weights, and their half-life periods are shown in Table 1.

NAME	ATOMIC WEIGHT	HALF-LIFE
Uranium I	238	4.5×10^9 years
Uranium X_1	234	24.1 days
Uranium X_2	234	1.14 minutes
Uranium Z	234	6.7 hours
Uranium II	234	2.7×10^5 years
Ionium	230	83,000 years
Radium	226	1600 years
Radon (Emanation)	222	3.825 days
Radium A	218	3.05 minutes
Radium B	214	26.8 minutes
Radium C	214	19.7 minutes
Radium C'	214	1.5×10^{-4} second
Radium C''	210	1.32 minutes
Radium D (Radiolead)	210	22.3 years
Radium E	210	5.0 days

Radium F (Polonium)	210	140 days
Radium G (Uranium lead)	206	∞

Table I: The Uranium Series of Radioactive Disintegrations
Adapted from *General Inorganic Chemistry*, M. Cannon Sneed and J. Lewis Maynard (New York: Van Nostrand, 1942), p. 876

It is assumed that at the time of their formation the rocks contained only uranium or thorium. The rate at which these decay, as we noted above, can be neither speeded up nor slowed down. Most chemical reactions can be speeded up by heat and slowed down by cold. However, this is not true of radioactive reactions, which involve the nucleus rather than the planetary electrons. For that reason it is believed that by a careful study of the amounts of these radioactive substances present the exact age of a given rock can be determined.

Premises on Which the Dating Is Based

Both the "ore method" and the "meteorite method" depend on the uranium time clock. The "ore method" assumes (1) that the rocks contained only uranium, thorium, and nonradiogenic lead (lead which is not the product of radioactive decay) at the time the earth's crust was formed; (2) that changes in the ratio of uranium and lead or thorium and lead have not occurred since the time the earth's crust was formed except for radioactive decay; (3) that each lead ore has been derived from a single area and has not been mixed with lead from another source; (4) that we can determine the amounts of uranium, thorium, and non-radiogenic lead originally present; (5) and that the rate of decay, which is constant today and can be neither speeded up nor slowed down, has been constant since the time of the origin of the rocks.

None of these assumptions is necessarily true. Assuming that the story of Genesis is correct, we find no reason why God should not have placed some of the decay products, such as radium, into the rocks when they were created. The rocks might very well have contained substances of the

uranium series other than uranium, thorium, and nonradiogenic lead.

In studying the half-life of the various radioactive
elements, it should be noted that only Uranium I and
Uranium II have a very long half-life. The other elements
in the series disintegrate relatively rapidly. It is because
of the long half-life of these two members of the series that
the age determinations by the uranium time clock are so
high. If these were not present from the beginning, if, for
example, God placed ionium or radium or one of the members of the series in the rocks at Creation, the actual ages
would be much lower than those arrived at because of the
assumption that only uranium was present in the rocks at
the beginning.

Geologists and physicists have themselves recognized
that the second, third, and fourth premises are not necessarily correct. The discrepancies in the age determinations
to which we shall refer are interpreted by evolutionists
themselves as evidence that alteration has taken place in
the rocks. Hahn and Walling say that unaltered thorium
minerals are practically unknown.[14] Patterson, Tilton, and
Inghram report studies which indicate that nearly all of
the uranium in the earth is concentrated near its surface
and most of the lead is not. Assuming that the earth is
4.5 billion years old, they note that there is less radiogenic
lead in the crust of the earth than would be expected. This
deficiency they account for by assuming that uranium has
been transferred in proportion to its concentration in the
interior and that the transfer of lead has been negligible.
They also present evidence which indicates there has been
quite a bit of differentiation and mixing of rocks on the
earth's crust. They believe that this mixing may have
exerted a first-order effect on the composition of leads found
in the earth's crust. The evidence for extensive mixing is
so clear, they say, that it would be contrary to the facts to

postulate the continued existence of unchanged lead to uranium ratios for billions of years.

Patterson, Tilton, and Inghram also call attention to the problem of the "anomalous" leads which are usually excluded from age calculations. These are leads which are believed to have been excessively contaminated by radiogenic lead or are leads which have resulted from a marked increase in the ratio of U^{235} to Pb^{204}. If these were included, age determinations would not be possible, or they would be very unusual. They point out that the exclusion of these "anomalous" leads has not as yet been justified on acceptable theoretical grounds. They also state that while "anomalous" leads can be recognized in extreme cases, there is no means of detecting slightly anomalous leads. The inclusion of these latter, they say, may lead to serious error.[15]

Hurley points out that we have no assurance that we have an accurate estimate of the amounts of the parent isotopes present or that some of the parent or daughter atoms have not escaped from the rock.[16]

Uniformity and Uniformitarianism

In connection with the fifth premise it is necessary to give consideration to the principle of uniformity and to uniformitarianism. In all scientific work we are bound by the principle of uniformity, the assumption that scientific principles have remained the same throughout time and space and that natural processes have not changed in time and space. Without this assumption — and we must recognize that from a philosophical point of view it is just that — science would be impossible, for the natural world, instead of being ordered, would be capricious. Uniformity fits also with our Christian concept of God as a God of order who ordinarily operates through the natural processes which He set up at Creation.

There are some who question this principle so far as the distant past is concerned. Caullery, a well-known French biologist, in discussing problems in connection with life and its origin, mentions as an interesting possibility that the natural laws of today may not have applied rigorously throughout the vast stretches of past geological time.[17]

The principle of uniformitarianism deals primarily with rates of scientific processes. One of the bitterest geological controversies was that between the uniformitarianists and the catastrophists. The former believe that the present was the key to the past and that the explanation for geological phenomena must be sought in the way in which geological processes were going on at present. The catastrophists postulated a series of catastrophes to explain geological phenomena. Geologists came gradually to accept uniformitarianism, but in recent years the principle of uniformitarianism has met with some criticism. Following the 1963 meeting of the American Geological Society, a popular magazine quoted Norman Newall, a paleontologist from the American Museum of Natural History, as saying: "Geology suffers from a great lack of data and in such a situation any attractive theory that comes along is taken as gospel. That is the case with uniformitarianism. Geology students are taught that 'the present is the key to the past,' and they too often take it to mean that nothing ever happened that isn't happening now. But since the end of World War II, when a new generation moved in, we have gathered more data, and we have begun to realize that there were many catastrophic events in the past, some of which happen just once." [18] Newall is further quoted as saying that he is in favor of junking both terms, catastrophism and uniformitarianism, because they are just too confusing.

Beck says: "When all is said and done there seems to be evidence that even the 'laws of nature' are changing. Modern physics suggests the possibility that changes are taking place in the speed of light and the rates of chemical reactions. In other words, the universe is changing, and it becomes hazardous to attempt calculations concerning the very remote past and the future." [19]

In discussing the quasars Hurlburt says that some scientists suspect that many currently held fundamental concepts of physics, such as the speed of light or the nature of time, differ now from what they were at this very early date in the history of the universe. Possibly, he says, the fundamental laws of physics are not everlasting and immutable but rather have evolved from earlier different forms.[20]

We have been able to observe many developments which took place more rapidly than was once thought possible. The volcano Paricutin in Mexico erupted in 1943, continued erupting until 1952, and built up a cone over fifteen hundred feet in height.

Hough in commenting on the rate of shore erosion says: "The question will be raised . . . of how much time is required for the development of shore features of this magnitude. Observations bearing on this question were made in an area near Woods Hole, Massachusetts, after the hurricane of 1938. The amount of shore erosion which occurred during the hurricane in a period of a few hours exceeded that which had occurred during the previous fifty years. The geological doctrine of uniformitarianism, stressing the slow orderly working of familiar processes, has perhaps blinded us to the importance of the unusual and catastrophic event." [21]

There is little evidence of any change in the rate of radioactive decay. However, two Westinghouse researchers reported small changes in radioactive decay rates of Sn^{119} and Fe^{57}; the actual increase in the lifetime was 1.5 per cent for Sn^{119} and 2.2 per cent for Fe^{57}.[22]

There is also some evidence for shifts and even reversals of the geomagnetic field.[23] One wonders what would happen during the period of the reversal of the magnetic field when cosmic and solar rays are not stopped by matter in orbit and the earth's magnetic field. This matter — ice crystals, charged and uncharged particles of dust, and molecules — may be brought along with the "solar wind," particularly

hydrogen ions. These are so "hard" (high in energy) that
one scientist believes they can split atoms into pieces without the benefit of fission decay energy. They would produce neutrons that are absorbed by the rock minerals to
build up atomic weight and radioactive nuclei, and they
would penetrate deep into the earth.

Accuracy of the Dating

In considering the question of dating we must distinguish
between precision and accuracy. The age as determined in
the laboratory may be precise without being accurate. By
this we mean that the proper technique has been followed
and that if the assumptions are correct, the age as determined
is correct. In discussing the age of *Zinjanthropus,* for example, Straus and Hunt say that isotopic age determinations,
including those made by the potassium-argon method, may
be analytically precise, yet may not be accurate because of
errors wholly unrelated to the sampling, concentrating, and
analytical procedures. Consistency in a series of isotopic
dates, they say, is evidence only of precision and not of accuracy. Dates that are not consistent may still be precise,
of course, but they cannot be accurate.[24]

We have already commented on the assumptions underlying the uranium dating; these must also be considered.

There are also discrepancies when more than one "clock"
is used. Hurley says that no single "clock" is entirely
trustworthy. Unfortunately, it is not very often that more
than one clock is at hand to date the rocks, and for that
reason most determinations cannot be regarded as entirely
trustworthy. Moreover, when more than one clock is con-
sulted, they rarely agree. Hurley points out that very
close agreement of the three clocks is the exception rather
than the rule.[25] Zeuner says that the clocks rarely agree.[26]
Patterson, Tilton, and Inghram say that the requirements
of the assumptions in the ore-lead method are so extreme
it is unlikely that this method should give a correct age.[27]

These facts certainly throw doubt on the accuracy of the procedure.

As an example of such disagreement there are the results of age determinations of rocks from the Sunshine Mine near Kellogg, Idaho. An uncorrected age determination $(\frac{Pb}{U+Th})$ gives 1050 ± 50 M. Y. (million years). This uncorrected determination does not take into consideration alterations in the rock; loss of radon, which is a gas; etc. The ratio of Pb^{206}/U^{238} gives an age of 710 ± 10 M. Y. On the same basis Pb^{207}/U^{235} gives 750 ± 10 M. Y. The graphic solution proposed by Nier (the man who has done the largest number of these determinations) for Pb^{207}/Pb^{206} gives 850 ± 50 M. Y.

To explain these differences it is assumed that radon loss is the major source of divergence in the age ratio, and certain adjustments are made accordingly. On that basis it is assumed that the rocks are 750 ± 50 M. Y. old.[28] Certainly it is striking that by employing these various methods we get four different figures for the same rock: 1050 ± 50 M. Y.; 710 ± 10 M. Y.; 750 ± 10 M. Y.; and 850 ± 50 M. Y., and that by making adjustments we get a fifth figure, 750 ± 50 M. Y.

Another determination which shows this same difficulty is one reported for the Martin Lake specimen from near Beaverlodge, north of Lake Athabasca, Canada. Here the uncorrected age $(\frac{Pb}{U+Th})$ is 870 M. Y. The Pb^{207}/Pb^{206} determination gives us 900 ± 10 M. Y. The Pb^{206}/U^{238} gives us 860 ± 5 M. Y.

In that same article Kerr and Kulp refer to the determination made of the age of the Caribou specimen from near Nederland, Colo. The age determination on the basis of Pb^{206}/U^{238} is 23 ± 10 M. Y., but the authors point out that the large amount of common lead present in the rock invalidates this uncorrected age.[29] Here again there is a recognition of the difficulties associated with the method.

A. O. Nier gives the following results as typical of various determinations (ages in millions of years):[30]

	RaG/UI	ThD/Th	AcD/RaG
Parry Sound Uraninite	1003	945	1030±15
Connecticut Samarskite	253	266	280±60
Woods Mine Pitchblende	57		
Parry Sound Thucholite	265	245	430±40
Huron Claim Monazite	3180	1830	2570±70
Las Vegas Monazite	1730	770	1340±200

In recent years considerable progress has been made in solving the problem of discordant ages. Yet discordant mineral ages continue to be reported. In a study of the geochronology of the midcontinental region of the United States, Goldich, Muehlberger, Lidiak, and Hedge report that mica ages by both Rb-Sr and K-A methods are commonly lower than the corresponding Rb-Sr ages for whole rock or feldspar samples, and they believe this reflects a loss of the daughter products during metamorphism. They suggest that Rb-Sr ages particulary of biotite may be low as a result of incipient weathering.[31] Arriens, Brooks, Bofinger, and Compston report examples of discordant Rb-Sr mineral ages in the granitic rocks from Australia. Biotite, they believe, retains the age of crystallization measured from the total rock samples, but K-feldspar gives a younger age and plagioclase an older age if the calculations are made using the total-rock initial Sr87/Sr86. They believe this can only be explained by an internal isotopic redistribution of rubidium and strontium.[32]

As an instance where it has been possible to correlate the uranium time clock with fossil evidence we have the dating done on an oil shale known as kolm, found in Sweden. According to the fossil evidence — it contains trilobites, extinct crustacea belonging to the same class as the modern crayfish, and other fossils — this kolm is believed to date from the late Cambrian period, roughly 500,000,000 years ago. The Pb^{206}/U^{238} determination gives a figure of 380 M. Y. The Pb^{207}/Pb^{206} determination gives 770 M. Y. To reconcile the two and the fossil evidence of the rock's age, it has been suggested that some of the radon escaped so that the actual amount of Pb^{206} formed is smaller than it should be. Therefore the Pb^{207}/Pb^{206} figure is too large and the Pb^{206}/U^{238} figure is too small. On this basis it is assumed that the probable real age is 440 M. Y., much closer to the geological age than either of the two determinations.[33]

In accounting for discrepancies in the various figures, Blum suggests the possibility that the remelting of rock may have altered the relationship of the uranium or thorium and lead. In this way the rocks may actually be older than they appear, or they may be younger.[34] If this is true, any figure from the uranium time clock is of questionable reliability. Mattauch judges that of the many lead age determinations of various types only five to eight are even apparently free from objectionable features.[35] Goodman and Evans express the same opinion.[36]

Dymond points out that the usual assumption of K-A dating (a closed system and no argon present at time zero) must be amplified if the age obtained from volcanic materials is to correspond to the time of deposition. He points to the following requirements: (1) the volcanic material must arrive at the deposition site soon after its formation during the volcanic episode; (2) continental detritus, submarine erosional products, or authigenic marine minerals must not be present in the analyzed materials. He believes these problems can be solved by careful selection of samples.[37]

In discussing the isotopic composition of lead and strontium from Ascension and Gough Island, Gast, Tilton, and Hedge suggest that unexpected variations in ratios could have arisen either by a mixture of surfacal or crustal lead and strontium in the primary magma or from chemical and ensuing isotopic heterogeneities in the source of the magma-forming mechanisms which tended to preserve these heterogeneities. They conclude: "If the uranium-lead ratio in different parts of the mantle has been differentiated at various times in the last three to four billion years as we have inferred, the existence of terrestrial lead evolved in a chemically closed system formed at the same time as the planet is open to question. Also if the isotopic variations observed at these two islands are due to chemical processes occurring in the mantle, the initial isotope ratios of lead and strontium in extrusive igneous rocks may not be used in continental regions as unambiguous indicators of contamination with older crustal rocks." [38]

Determining the Amount of Nonradiogenic Lead

Another problem is the fact that it is difficult to determine the actual amount of nonradiogenic lead present. We have indicated that Pb^{204} is generally assumed to be nonradiogenic. It is believed, though, that also some of the Pb^{206}, Pb^{207}, and Pb^{208} is nonradiogenic. The atomic weight determinations for common or nonradiogenic lead vary less than 0.02%, but their isotopic composition may vary somewhat more. Nier reports [39] the following extremes in variation in a number of samples:

ISOTOPIC RATIOS OF "COMMON" LEADS REFERRED TO Pb^{204}
$Pb^{204} = 1.00$

	206	207	208
Sample 13 from Greenland	14.54	14.60	34.45
Sample 14 b from Joplin, Mo.	22.48	16.15	41.3

This means that the per cent of "common" lead made up of the different isotopes varied as follows:

	204	206	207	208
Sample 13	1.54	22.51	22.6	53.35
Sample 14 b	1.23	27.77	19.95	51.15

The Joplin lead, Sample 14 b, is one of the "anomalous" leads to which Patterson, Tilton, and Inghram refer.

Dating by the uranium time clock depends on the amount of radiogenic lead present. If Pb^{204} is absent, it is generally assumed that the lead present is radiogenic. If Pb^{204} is present, however, there must be some common or nonradiogenic lead present, and the problem faced is that of determining how much is radiogenic and how much is nonradiogenic.[40] But how is one to determine exactly how much of the Pb^{206}, Pb^{207}, and Pb^{208} is radiogenic if there is variation in the amount that is radiogenic and the amount that is common lead?

Second-Order Effects in the Ore-Lead Method and an Evaluation

Patterson, Tilton, and Inghram point out that the calculations of the ore-lead method depend on second-order effects and that therefore small errors in the underlying assumptions may introduce large errors into the results. They conclude that while this method uses terrestrial materials, and in that respect has the advantage over the meteorite method, it still gives rise to serious uncertainty in the determination of the age of the earth's crust.[41]

The Meteorite Method and Its Problems

The meteorite method of calculating the age of the earth depends on a comparison of the isotopic composition of lead found at present in the earth's crust with the isotopic composition of lead found in iron meteorites in which there is an insignificant concentration of uranium. It is assumed that when the earth was formed, it contained lead with an isotopic composition the same as that found in iron meteorites and that the ratio of lead to uranium has been changed only by radioactive decay in the surface of the earth since the surface was formed. It is on this basis that the age of the earth is estimated at 4.5 billion years.

It is evident that some of the same criticisms raised against the ore method apply to this method, too. Moreover, there is no evidence that compels us to assume that when the earth was formed, it contained lead with the same isotopic composition as that in iron meteorites. The lead found in iron meteorites may have been exposed to an environment containing higher concentrations of uranium for a period of time before the meteorites were formed. We have no way of knowing whether the lead existing on earth was exposed to a similar environment.[42]

Rancitelli, Fisher, Funkhouser, and Schaeffer described the application of the potassium-argon method of dating to iron meteorites and report that many of them date out to be about 6.3 billion years. They conclude that the potassium-argon dating technique as applied to iron meteorites gives unreliable results.[43]

In coming to a final evaluation of their method, Patterson, Tilton, and Inghram say that while it uses primordial lead of accurately known isotopic composition and gives an accurately determined age, it makes use of extraterrestrial materials whose relationship to the earth is uncertain. In concluding their discussion of both the ore-lead and the meteorite method they say that it should be recognized that an approximate age value is sufficient and should be viewed with considerable skepticism until the basic assumptions that are involved in the method of calculation are verified.[44]

The Fluoride Dating of Organic Remains

For dating of organic remains two other methods may be employed. These methods have little if any bearing on the problem of the age of the earth except that presumably they set a minimum age. However, they are of interest, and we shall mention them in passing. The first of these is by measuring the quantity of fluorides to be found in bones. The hydroxyapatite originally present in bones is gradually changed to fluorapatite by their being percolated by fluorine-charged water. Since fluorapatite is extremely weather resistant, a measure of the fluoride contents of the bones, it is assumed, will give a fairly reliable indication of their age.

However, of late there have been some who have questioned the accuracy of this method. Stewart, for example, believes that it is of limited reliability and warns against the subjective pitfalls that surround chemical dating.[45] For one thing, it is known that water varies in its fluoride content from time to time and place to place. It is also possible for humans to have access during their lifetimes to water from deep wells to which animals do not have access. Such water from deep wells is likely to contain relatively large quantities of fluorine compounds.

Radiocarbon Dating

Another method is the so-called C^{14} method of dating organic materials. This method is also known as the radiocarbon method or the atomic calendar. It depends upon a measure of the amount of radioactive carbon to be found in organic remains. Cosmic rays which enter our atmosphere from outer space change nitrogen to C^{14} — radioactive carbon with an atomic weight of 14. Ordinary carbon has an atomic weight of 12. Some of this C^{14} unites with oxygen to form a radioactive CO_2, and this is used by plants in the process of food manufacture known as photosynthesis. In this way C^{14} is incorporated into plant and animal tissues. The incorporation of C^{14} into tissues ceases with the death of the organism, and the C^{14} gradually decays. The half-life of C^{14} is 5,730 years; this is believed to be more accurate than the previously suggested half-life of 5,568 years. The age of organic material is determined by the amount of C^{14} still present in the tissues. This method of dating organic remains is supposed to be accurate up to about 25,000 years. After that time there is so little radioactivity left that accurate dating by this method is impossible. However, some workers using recently developed methods believe C^{14} dating is accurate to 44,000 or even 70,000 years. Because of this limitation on accurate dating and because it deals with living materials and not with the age of the rocks, it is of little value in attempting to determine the age of the earth.[46]

Where it has been possible to correlate these dates with known historical dates, radiocarbon dating appears to be fairly reliable. A number of tests have been made, and these have agreed rather closely with known historical dates.

It is interesting to note that this method has moved up the close of the Ice Age. Formerly it was thought that the last phase of the last Ice Age occurred about 20,000 years ago, but it is now believed to have occurred only 11,500 years ago. Libby and Arnold dated a number of wood and peat samples from the Two Creeks Forest Bed in Manitowoc County, Wis. Apparently a spruce forest here was submerged, pushed over, and buried under glacial drift by the last advancing ice sheet in this region. Five samples were examined. The age determinations were quite close to one another, and the average age was 11,404±350 years.[47] Studies reported by Iversen of deposits from Denmark, Germany, and the British Isles have confirmed this dating of the last Ice Age.[48]

This earlier dating of the close of the Ice Age is also confirmed by other studies made by Libby. He reports that wood from beach deposits apparently of the Glenwood stage of glacial Lake Chicago appears to be about 10,972±350 years old. Lake Chicago is believed to have been formed by the last glacier as it retreated northward. The Glenwood stage is the earliest stage of the lake. It has been variously dated from 25,000 to 50,000 years ago.[49]

Still another confirmation of this later dating of the close of the Ice Age is supplied by Rubin and Suess. They dated a sample of wood collected from peat in a deep cut along the Ohio turnpike near Streetsboro, Ohio. It appears to have come from a swamp overwhelmed by a late Cary ice advance. The sample dated 8,600±300 years. Because this sample showed an unexpectedly young age, a second sample was dated. This sample dated 8,450±250 years.[50]

The Cary substage was formerly thought to have occurred 35,000 years ago and to have lasted for 10,000 years.[51]

Yet there are difficulties associated with this method of dating that should be noted. It is possible for materials to have their radioactivity diminished by the entry of "dead" carbon, which will increase the apparent age. It is also possible for the radiocarbon content of materials to be enriched by physical and chemical processes. This would decrease their apparent age.[52]

Until recently the radiocarbon dating of archaeological bone samples was based primarily on the dating of associated charcoal and in some cases on the natural calcium carbonate contents of bones. However, dates by correlation with charcoal may not always be correct, and even greater doubts exist on the accuracy of dates based on calcium carbonate which may have been replaced by ground water carbonate of varying ages. It is now possible to date bones directly from their content of organic carbon or collagen, and there is no known mechanism by which collagen may be altered to yield a false age. However, the collagen content of bone decreases with age to such a low concentration that isolation of sufficient collagen for radioactive dating becomes difficult with the oldest bones, and unfortunately collagen does not decrease uniformly with age for finds around the world.[53]

In discussing anomalous ages from sediment cores from the Arctic and subarctic, Ericson, Ewing, and Wollin say that they can think of no effect which could make the ages spuriously low but believe that certain conditions in the Arctic Ocean would tend to make the ages spuriously high by some unknown amount. Among these they list contamination of the samples by detritus from old carbonate rocks and the incorporation of old carbon during secretion of the foraminiferal tests and redeposition of old tests by ice rafting.[54]

Still other sources of error are erratic changes in cosmic

ray background, slight changes in counter efficiency, counting of spurious pulses from carbon dust or other sources, and nonlaboratory errors.

Rainey and Ralph report oscillations in the C^{14} inventory between A. D. 1400 and 1700 and also describe deviations about 1600 B. C. They believe studies ought to be conducted to determine the magnitude and the duration of these B. C. deviations and raised the question as to whether these deviations may be due to variations in the cosmic ray intensity of the earth's magnetic field, which is also suggested as a possible factor in connection with other types of radioactive dating.[55]

Studying Carbon[14] variations in connection with tree ring samples, other workers have suggested as the probable cause of short-time fluctuations the variation in sunspot activity.[56]

A recent conference discussing the variation in atmospheric radiocarbon level reported evidence of variation at several different time levels. The concluding paper of this conference, however, suggested that atmospheric uniformity over the past 25,000 years is approximately true despite the smaller scale variations which have frequently been reported.[57]

Other Methods of Dating

Other methods of dating include a study of varves, tree rings, cores of deep sea sediments, and thermoluminescence studies. Varves are regular layers which are laid down annually in some lakes. This technique has been best developed in Scandinavia, and it has also been applied to some deposits in the United States. Dendrochronology is based on the counting of annual tree rings whose varying thicknesses reflect seasonal weather conditions and which, in sequence, form a pattern that is distinctive for a given region. Once a master pattern is established in any area, the ring pattern of a particular specimen can be matched against it, thus providing a fairly exact indication of the year in which the specimen was cut and presumably used. Tree ring dating has been used most successfully in the southwestern part of the United States.

Most of these methods can be applied to only relatively recent times and many of them have a great many problems. For example, Damon calls attention to the problem of Pleistocene time scales. Erickson and his co-workers estimate the base of the Günz glaciation at 1.5 million years, and Emiliani estimated it at about 300,000 years. These chronologies differ by a factor of five; the wide divergence is of particular interest because they are based on the same radiometric dates for deep sea cores which were studied by both groups of workers. Damon says that the factor of five is a result of different methods of extrapolating ages to basal Günz, and he believes it would seem preferable to declare a moratorium on the construction of Pleistocene time scales until firmer data is available on which to base such chronology. He also says that Erickson and his co-workers who assigned an age of 1.5 million years to the base of the Günz have greater faith in the doctrine of uniformitarianism than he has.[58]

An Evaluation of the Scientific Evidences

What shall we say then so far as scientific evidence as to the age of the earth is concerned? There are many observations and evidences which have been interpreted by some to indicate that the age of the earth is greater than the 6,000 years postulated by Bishop Ussher. Since Ussher's calculations cannot be proved accurate, we must be careful not to insist that the earth is only 6,000 years old. Scripture gives the impression that we are dealing with a young earth, an earth whose age must be measured in thousands of years rather than in millions or billions, but the Bible does not permit us to arrive at any accurate figure. We cannot help but be impressed by the overwhelming evidence for an old earth. Most of the observations we are able to make give us the impression that the earth is an old one rather than the young earth that the Bible seems to indicate. We must recognize, of course, that things are not always what they appear to be and that initial studies of a subject often give us an impression which later proves to be incorrect. Yet the overwhelming evidence for an old earth is impressive.

At the same time we must recognize that radiometric methods are not as accurate and as reliable as they appear at first glance to be. All too often, these determinations are pointed to as a final proof that the earth is of great age. But at the present time it can hardly be maintained that the uranium time clock possesses the reliability and accuracy we should like to find in science. The problem of discordant datings cannot be ignored. At the same time we must recognize that none of the uranium dates point to a young earth even though the dates may vary by a factor of three or even more.

It might also be pointed out that processes once thought to take long periods of time — millions and millions of years — are now known to occur in much shorter periods of time. It is generally assumed, for instance, that oil is formed only after the original complex organic matter is covered by several thousands of feet of overburden and after a lapse of several millions of years. Yet Smith has found hydrocarbons (oil is a mixture of hydrocarbons) in sediments dated as "Recent." A composite sample of hydrocarbons taken from the Gulf of Mexico and dated by the C^{14} method gave an age of $12,300\pm1,200$ years,[59] — a far cry from the millions of years previously thought necessary for their formation.

Mulik and Erdman report that the mild heat treatment of water-wet marine muds resulted in the genesis of three aromatic hydrocarbons characteristic of crude oils but which are seldom found in significant quantities in recent sediments.[60]

It might also be pointed out that the age of the earth is not connected directly with the problem of evolution. In a sense they are separate and distinct. It would be possible to have a very old earth and still have no evolution at all. There is, however, this connection. An earth that is relatively young is unfavorable to the evolutionist. An old earth suits his purposes much better. It would be very difficult to have evolution occur in six or seven thousand years, or even in six or seven 10,000-year periods.[61]

Mayr believes that the evolution of a species requires a minimum of several hundred thousand years and averages probably a million years or more. For its completion, he says, speciation requires a time interval equivalent roughly to 30,000 human generations.[62] And Huxley says that in a form such as the horse the time needed to effect a change of specific magnitude is in the order of 100,000 generations and of a generic magnitude, of a million generations.[63] Moreau believes that it takes a minimum of 5,000 years for the development of distinct races, at least in the birds.[64] Evolution, therefore, is more plausible if we assume that the world has stood for three billion or more years. For that reason evolutionists are favorably inclined toward any evidence which makes the earth very old.

NOTES

1. *Luther's Works,* ed. Jaroslav Pelikan, I (St. Louis: Concordia, 1958), 5.
2. Ibid., p. 93.
3. Ibid., p. 231.
4. Keil, C. F., and Delitzsch, F. *Biblical Commentary on the Old Testament,* trans. James Martin (Grand Rapids: Eerdmans, 1949), I, 48.
5. Ibid., p. 67.
6. Holmes, Arthur. "A Revised Estimate of the Age of the Earth," *Nature, CLIX* (1947), 127 f.
   Blum, Harold F. *Time's Arrow and Evolution* (Princeton: Princeton University Press, 1951), p. 10.
7. Blum, p. 53.

8. Odum, Howard T. "The Stability of the World Strontium Cycle," *Science*, CXIV (1951), 411.

    Hasler, Arthur D. "Limnologists and Oceanographers Discuss Lakes, Rivers, and Aquatic Life," *Science*, CXXXVIII (1962), 698.

9. Odum, p. 411.

10. Hurley, Patrick M., and Goodman, Clark. "Helium Retention in Common Rock Minerals," *Bulletin of the Geological Society of America*, LII (1941), 546.

    Chlopin, V. G., and Abidov, S. A. "Radioactivity and Helium Content of Beryllium, Boron, and Lithium Minerals of the U. S. S. R.," *Comptes Rendus (Doklady) de l'Académie des Science de l'U. R. S. S.*, XXXII (1941), 637–640.

11. Aldrich, L. T., and Wetherill, G. W. "Geochronology by Radioactive Decay," *Annual Review of Nuclear Science*, VIII (1958), 266.

12. Shillibeer, H. A., and Watson, K. "Some Potassium-Argon Ages for Ontario," *Science*, CXXI (1955), 33 f.

13. Aldrich and Wetherill, pp. 259–261.

14. Hahn, Otto, and Walling, Ernst. "Über die Möglichkeit geologischer Alterbestimmungen rubidiumhaltiger Mineralien und Gesteine," *Zeitschrift für Anorganische und Allgemeine Chemie*, CCXXXVI (1938), 78.

15. Patterson, C., Tilton, G., and Inghram, M. "Age of the Earth," *Science*, CXXI (1955), 71–74.

16. Hurley, Patrick Mason. "Radioactivity and Time," *Scientific American*, CLXXXI (1949), 48.

17. Caullery, Maurice. *Les Etapes de la Biologie* (Paris: University of France, 1941), p. 125.

18. "God, Man, and Geology," *Newsweek*, LXII (Dec. 23, 1963), 48.

19. Beck, William S. *Modern Science and the Nature of Life* (New York: Harcourt, Brace, 1957), p. 170.

20. Hurlburt, Everett H. "Signals from Space," *The Science Teacher*, XXXI, 7, (November 1964), 11.

21. Hough, Jack L. *Geology of the Great Lakes* (Urbana: University of Illinois, 1958), pp. 32 f.

22. Ruby, S. L., and Ferber, R. R. "Imprisonment of Gamma Radiation with Resulting Lifetime Increase," Westinghouse Research Laboratories, Scientific Paper 64-802-115-P1 (Sept. 1, 1964), 1.

23. Kobayashi, Kazuo, and Schwarz, E. J. "Magnetic Properties of the Contact Zone between Upper Triassic Red Beds and Basalt in Connecticut," *Journal of Geophysical Research*, LXXI (1966), 5357–5364.

24. Straus, William L., Jr., and Hunt, Charles B. "Age of Zinjan-thropus," *Science,* CXXXVI (1962), 293.

25. Hurley, p. 48.

26. Zeuner, Frederick E. *Dating the Past* (London: Methuen, 1952), p. 328.

27. Patterson, Tilton, and Inghram, p. 74.

28. Kerr, Paul F., and Kulp, J. Laurence. "Pre-Cambrian Uraninite, Sunshine Mine, Idaho," *Science,* CXV (1952), 86 f.

29. Kerr and Kulp, loc. cit.

30. Nier, Alfred O., et al. "The Isotopic Constitution of Radiogenic Leads and the Measurement of Geological Time III," *Physical Review,* LX (1941), 112–116.

31. Goldich, Samuel S., Muehlberger, William R., Lidiak, Edward G., and Hedge, Carl E. "Geochronology of the Midcontinent Region, United States," *Journal of Geophysical Research,* LXXI (1966), 5375–5388.

32. Arriens, P. A., Brooks, C., Bofinger, V. M., and Compston, W. "The Discordance of Mineral Ages in Granitic Rocks Resulting from the Redistribution of Rubidium and Strontium," *Journal of Geophysical Research,* LXXI (1966), 4981–4994.

33. Knopf, p. 5.

34. Blum, p. 10.

35. Mattauch, J. "Stabile Isotope, Ihre Messung und Ihre Verwendung," *Zeitschrift für Angewandte Chemie,* A 59 (1947), p. 40.

36. Goodman, Clark, and Evans, Robley D. "Age Measurements by Radioactivity," *Bulletin of the Geological Society of America,* LII (1941), 534 f.

37. Dymond, Jack R. "Potassium-Argon Geochronology of Deep-Sea Sediments," *Science,* CLII (1966), 1239.

38. Gast, Paul W., Tilton, G. R., and Hedge, Carl. "Isotopic Composition of Lead and Strontium from Ascension and Gough Islands," *Science,* CXLV (1964), 1181.

39. Nier, A. O. "Exhibit 2," *Report of the Committee on the Measurement of Geological Time,* ed. Alfred Lane (Washington, D. C.: National Research Council, 1941), pp. 56–60.

40. Friedlander, G., and Kennedy, J. *Introduction to Radiochemistry* (New York: Wiley, 1949), p. 18.

41. Patterson, Tilton, and Inghram, p. 74.

42. Ibid., pp. 69 f.

43. Rancitelli, L., Fisher, D. E., Funkhouser, J., and Schaeffer, O. A. "Potassium-Argon Dating of Iron Meteorites," *Science,* CLV (1967), 999 f.

44. Patterson, Tilton, and Inghram, pp. 74 f.

45. Stewart, T. D. "The Problem of the Earliest Claimed Representatives of *Homo Sapiens*," *Cold Spring Harbor Symposia on Quantative Biology*, XV (1950), 100.
    Idem. "The Fluoride Content of Associated Human and Extinct Animal Bones from the Conkling Cavern, N. Mex.," *Science*, CXVI (1952), 457 f.

46. Arnold, J. R., and Libby, W. F. "Radiocarbon Dates," *Science*, CXIII (1951), 116 f.

47. Arnold and Libby, loc. cit.

48. Iversen, Johs. "Radiocarbon Dating of the Alleröd Period," *Science*, CXVIII (1953), 9–11.

49. Libby, Willard F. "Chicago Radiocarbon Dates IV," *Science*, CXIX (1954), 137 f.

50. Rubin, Meyer, and Suess, Hans E. "U. S. Geological Survey Radiocarbon Dates II," *Science*, CXXI (1955), 481 f.

51. Dunbar, Carl O. *Historical Geology* (New York: Wiley, 1949), p. 451.

52. Bartlett, H. H. "Radiocarbon Datability of Peat, Marl, Caliche, and Archaeological Materials," *Science*, CXIV (1951), 55 f.

53. Berger, Rainer, Horney, Amos G., and Libby, W. F. "Radiocarbon Dating of Bone and Shell from Their Organic Components," *Science*, CXLIV (1964), 999.

54. Ericson, David B., Ewing, Maurice, and Wollin, Goesta. "Sediment Cores from the Arctic and Subarctic Seas," *Science*, CXLIV (1964), 1191 f.

55. Rainey, Froelich, and Ralph, Elizabeth K. "Archeology and its New Technology," *Science*, CLIII (1966), 1482.

56. Stuiver, Minze. "Carbon-14 Content of 18th and 19th Century Wood: Variations Correlated with Sunspot Activity," *Science*, CXLIX (1965), 533.

57. Olson, Edwin A. "Carbon-14 and Tritium Dating," *Science*, CL (1965), 1490.

58. Damon, Paul E. "Pleistocene Time Scales," *Science*, CXLVIII (1965), 1037 f.

59. Smith, Paul V. Jr. "The Occurrence of Hydrocarbons in Recent Sediments from the Gulf of Mexico," *Science*, CXVI (1952), 437–439.

60. Mulik, James D., and Erdman, J. Gordon. "Genesis of Hydrocarbons and Low Molecular Weight in Organic-Rich Aquatic Systems," *Science*, CXLI (1963), 806.

61. Simpson, George Gaylord. "Rates of Evolution in Animals," *Genetics, Paleontology, and Evolution*, ed. Glenn L. Jepsen, Ernst Mayr, and George Gaylord Simpson (Princeton: Princeton University Press, 1949), p. 216.

62. Mayr, Ernst. "Speciation and Selection," *Proceedings of the American Philosophical Society*, XCIII (1949), 514.
63. Huxley, Julian. *Evolution, the Modern Synthesis* (New York: Harpers, 1943), p. 61.
64. Moreau, R. E. "On the Age of Some Races of Birds," *Ibis*, VI (1930), 239.

5. Evidences for Evolution

In this section we want to examine critically the various observations and facts which have been regarded by evolutionists as evidence that evolution has occurred. It should be pointed out once more that, as we indicated in chapter one, a distinction must be made between facts and observations and the hypotheses and conclusions drawn from them. The facts and observations themselves cannot ordinarily be questioned. It is unreasonable to assume that the observations which we make with our sense organs are frequently in error. Though sometimes our senses deceive us, we must assume that what they tell us is true and correct unless it can be shown to be erroneous. This is especially true when these observations can be repeated by other competent observers.

For this reason we must assume them to be factual. We cannot disagree with them or place them into the category of mirages and other deceptive phenomena. We must assume that they are true. But we can disagree with the conclusions that are drawn from these facts and with the hypotheses which they are believed to support. In this section we hope to show that many of the facts and observations generally regarded as evidence for evolution do not necessarily give support to the theory.

I. The Evidence for Evolution from Classification

A. Nature of the Evidence

These facts and observations have been drawn from various areas of biology. The first of these evidences which we want to consider is the evidence of classification.

Biologists have set up a number of pigeonholes into which they place all living things. The species concept, which we discussed in detail in chapter three, is one of these pigeonholes.

The living world is divided first of all into two or three kingdoms, the plant kingdom, the animal kingdom, and by some taxonomists, one-celled organisms. These are then divided into phyla or divisions. Most taxonomists divide the plant kingdom into about sixteen divisions and the animal kingdom into some twenty phyla. The phyla or divisions are further divided into classes, the classes into orders, the orders into families, the families into genera, and the genera into species.

All the members of a given phylum have certain characteristics in common. Thus, all members of a phylum Chordata have a notochord — a solid line of cells which gives support and protection to the nerve chord — in some stage of their development, and a dorsal, tubular nerve chord. Similarly, all members of the same family have certain characteristics in common, and all members of the same genus have certain characteristics in common. Members of the same family have more things in common than members of the same phylum, and members of the same genus have more in common than members of the same family.

It should be noted that there is no exact agreement among systematists as to exactly where these lines of classification should be drawn. At this point we are not concerned with this particular problem of the systematists. Nor has it any direct bearing on the evidence for evolution from classification. There is no doubt that a system of classification is possible and that a given organism resembles some organisms more than it resembles others. The evolutionists argue that the fact that such a system of classification is possible and that such resemblances can be demonstrated shows that evolution has occurred. They believe that the degree of resemblance is a measure of the remoteness or the closeness of a common ancestor. They believe that all the members of the same phylum have had a common ancestor in remote antiquity. They believe that members of the same order have had a common ancestor in the not too distant past. And they believe that members of the same genus have had a common ancestor in relatively recent times. In other words, they believe that similarity is proof or at least evidence of descent from a common ancestor.

B. An Evaluation of the Evidence

1. Disagreement as to the Nature and Extent of the Categories

We have referred before to the fact that there is no agreement with regard to the nature and extent of the various categories. We should also note that it is not always possible to place an organism into a given category. After the characteristics for the given categories have been established, it is found that some organisms have the characteristics of several categories. For instance, there is a little microscopic organism, *Euglena,* which has both plant and animal characteristics. It has chlorophyll and manufactures its own food. This is clearly a plant characteristic. On the other hand, it is capable of locomotion. It has a long whip-like hair, a flagellum, and by means of this it moves through the water. This is a distinct animal characteristic.

The same thing is true of bacteria. Many of them have cilia or other means of locomotion. They lack chlorophyll and cannot manufacture their own food. And yet in other characteristics they resemble very closely the blue-green algae and appear to be plants.

For this reason many taxonomists have set up a third kingdom in their system of classification, the Protista. In this they have placed relatively simple one-celled organisms which do not show sharply differentiated plant and animal characteristics. Usually these in the Protista are said to include the Protozoa, flagellates, bacteria, slime molds, and certain other primitive organisms.

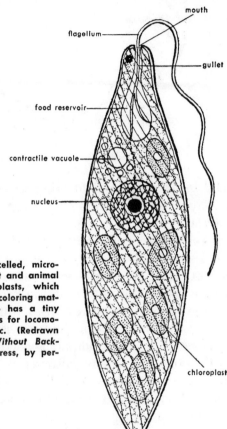

Figure 5. Euglena. This one-celled, microscopic organism has both plant and animal characteristics. It has chloroplasts, which contain chlorophyll, the green coloring matter found in plants, and also has a tiny whiplike flagellum which it uses for locomotion — an animal characteristic. (Redrawn from Buchsbaum's *Animals Without Backbones*, University of Chicago Press, by permission)

2. Phylogenetic Trees

But let us look at the argument itself. It is believed that the scheme of classification is itself an evidence of descent from a common ancestor. Very often the scheme of classification is presented as a phylogenetic tree, similar to the one presented in Table 2.

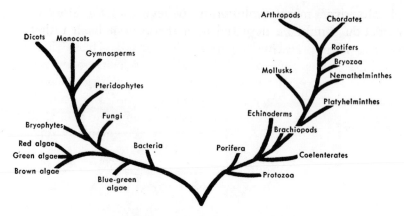

Table 2: The Phylogenetic Tree

The forms associated together in species, genera, classes, or phyla are supposed to have descended from a single common ancestor.

Yet it is generally recognized that all such phylogenetic trees are highly speculative. Allan describes them as being invented and based on what we have read into classification rather than deduced from a true knowledge of descent.[1]

And there is good reason for this statement. In classifying organisms, taxonomists have usually examined characteristics of external morphology — the external appearance of the organism. Today, however, it is generally agreed that classification must be based not only on the evidence of external morphology, but also upon the genetic makeup of the individual — the genes and chromosomes which determine what he has inherited and what he will pass on to his offspring. Indeed, today it is generally recognized that this classification is even more important than a classification based on external morphology. Therefore there is much dissatisfaction with the present system of classification among taxonomists themselves. Repeatedly the plea for a new system of classification has been made, and much work has been done in reclassifying organisms on the basis of their genetic makeup as well as their external morphology.

Moreover, many evolutionists believe that the story of evolution should be depicted as a shrub or a bush rather than as a tree, and indeed most phylogenetic "trees" look shrublike when they are drawn today. Because they are artificial and speculative, there are some evolutionists who believe they serve very little purpose. Kraus says there is a growing number of scholars who are coming to feel that the two-dimensional representation of phylogenetic relationships is not an adequate way of conveying the story of evolution but it is quite apt to be misleading in that it neglects the very nature of evolution.[2]

3. Breeding Test Problems

A classification system based on genetics as proposed presents real problems in so far as evolution is concerned. In the first place, it is not possible to examine the genetic makeup of organisms no longer alive. The only evidence that can be used in classifying them is the evidence from external morphology, and this makes their classification less certain. Then, too, it is difficult to do breeding tests even with those organisms which are alive. Some cannot be bred under controlled conditions of observation. For instance, some animals do not breed in captivity. Finally, the very task of making all of these detailed observations as to whether organisms are capable of interbreeding is an overwhelming one.

4. Similarity and Relationship

We should also like to comment on the basic assumption in this argument, and this is that similarity is evidence of descent from a common ancestor. It is true, of course, that organisms that are closely related are usually quite similar. Brothers and sisters are marked by family resemblances. And yet it is also true that similarity is in itself not a proof of family relationship. Two individuals may resemble each other so closely as to be mistaken for each other and yet be totally unrelated.

Ross says that one may observe many robins nesting and note that they always lay blue eggs. Upon seeing a robin starting a nest, he says, one can say with a high degree of probability that it will lay blue eggs. But, he goes on to say, if one finds a nest having blue eggs, it is not logically safe to say that these eggs were laid by a robin.[3] It is just this latter sort of reasoning that is employed when it is argued that similarity is evidence of descent from a common ancestor.

Fossils also present a problem, for what the evolutionists regard as the consecutive stages of development within a single line may be less similar than analogous stages in different lines.[4] Though Dobzhansky believes that this difficulty is more abstract than real, it does nevertheless create a problem. For that reason it is extremely hazardous to argue that since two organisms resemble each other, they must be descended from a common ancestor.

5. *Parallel Mutations*

There is also the well-known phenomenon of parallel mutations. This is the occurrence by mutation of similar characteristics in different species. For instance, the fruit flies *Drosophila melanogaster* and *D. simulans,* two separate species, have both experienced mutations of eye color to prune, ruby, and garnet; of body color to yellow; of bristle shapes to forked and bobbed; of wings to crossveinless, vesiculated, and rudimentary. It might be assumed by those who regard similarity as a proof of descent from a common ancestor that two flies, both of which have ruby eyes, have descended from a common ancestor who had ruby eyes, but this is not necessarily the case. The same type of mutation has occurred in both species, and the two ruby-eyed flies may not be related at all.

This phenomenon of parallel mutation is not confined to *Drosophila.* It is a widespread phenomenon, and has been clearly established in a number of forms.

Evolutionists argue that parallel mutation is in itself an evidence for evolution. They argue that parallel mutations are possible only because the organisms are closely related and have the same sort of germ plasm. Hadorn lists a number of instances where parallel mutations are due to mutations of homologous loci.[5] This would seem to support this sort of argument. However, there are other instances in which parallel mutations or parallel variations are known not to be due to the same ancestral germ plasm. Dobzhansky says: "Here is a caveat — phenotypically similar or mimetic mutants are produced also at different fully complementary and not even linked genes within a species. . . . A few of the mimetic genes may conceivably have arisen through reduplication of the same ancestral genes. But for the majority such a supposition is quite gratuitous. Our powers of observation are limited and what to our eyes are phenotypically similar changes may actually be due to different genes." [6] Rensch says that similar or identical organs may arise from quite different anatomical substrata. He uses as his example the vasa malpighii which originate from the ectoderm in insects and from the endoderm in spiders, and the stridulating ridges and spines of insects which may develop on various parts of the legs, wings, thorax, or abdomen.[7]

In cases in which parallel mutation has not been clearly established there are similarities described as being due to parallel variation. These may or may not be due to parallel mutations. In any case they are similarities which are not derived from a common ancestor but which appear in different species. They are so common in plants that Stebbins says that morphological similarity is much less indicative of phylogenetic relationships — those of evolutionary descent — in plants than it is in animals.[8]

A good example of such a parallel variation is albinism, which appears as a mutation in a great many animal forms and also in many plants. In some cases it is probably a parallel mutation, but in many cases different genes are involved. These are frequently known as mimic genes.

6. Differing Degrees of Relationship at Different Stages of Development

There are also instances in which larval forms are similar while adult forms are different. Such is the case with the butterflies *Acraea alciope* Hew. and *A. humilis* E. M. Sharpe; with *Acraea terpsichore* L. and *A. alicia* E. M. Sharpe; and with the amphibians *Megalophrys montana* Kuhl and *M. parva* Boulenger. It is possible to emphasize larval similarities while ignoring adult differences.

7. Special Creation and Observed Similarities

We should also like to question the reasoning of those who insist that if plants and animals had been separately created, it would not be possible to classify them; that, instead of falling into distinct groups with a number of characteristics in common, they would be scattered. Our God is a God of order. It is but natural that organisms which are supposed to occupy the same place in the scheme of life should have similar characteristics. There is no reason at all why God should have to follow a separate pattern in the creation of each organism.

II. The Evidence for Evolution from Homology

A. Nature of the Evidence

A second type of evidence for evolution is drawn from homology, a detailed comparison of structure after structure in different organisms. When this is done, we find not only that the skeletons are similar but also that in many instances there is a bone-for-bone correspondence. Practically all mammals, for instance, have seven cervical vertebrae. Organisms as diverse as man, the giraffe, and the whale have these seven. However, there are not only similarities but also differences which are regarded as significant. Hence biologists distinguish between homologous and analogous structures. Homologous structures are those which correspond to one another but do not necessarily have the same function. Analogous structures are those which have the same function but do not necessarily correspond to one another. For instance, the wing of a bird and the wing of a bat perform the same function. They are analogous. However, structurally they are quite different, and for that reason are not regarded as being homologous. On the other hand, the wing of a bat is similar in structure to the forefoot of a dog or the arm and hand of man. They are therefore homologous, but since they do not serve the same function, they are not analogous.

Studies such as these are regarded as supplying evidence for evolution. The fact that the wing of a bat resembles the arm of a man more than it resembles the wing of a bird, is pointed to as evidence for the fact that the bat is more closely related to man than to the bird. Essentially this argument is once more based on the premise that similarity is evidence or proof for descent from a common ancestor.

B. The Evidence Evaluated

1. Parallel Mutations

We should like to refer again to the phenomena of parallel mutation. They show us clearly that similar structures need not indicate descent from a common ancestor. This is the chief reason why the argument from homology is not stressed today. Many evolutionists themselves are of the opinion that the evidence from homology is of little importance in establishing the facts of evolution.

2. Homologies Produced by Different Genes

The fact that it is possible to develop eyes in eyeless *Drosophila* stocks by inbreeding also has a bearing on this argument. Fruit flies that are homozygous for "eyeless" may develop eyes if they are inbred. These eyes are homologous with the eyes of the wild type, but they are not produced by identical genes, because it can be shown that the factor for "eyeless" is still present in the stock.[9]

Dobzhansky says that the presence of homologous organs is not necessarily evidence of persistence of identical, similar, or even homologous genes. The genetic system which brings about the development of the eye in a fish, he says, is probably quite different from that in a bird or man.[10]

3. *Homologies and Early Development*

It is also worth pointing out that correspondence between homologous structures cannot be pressed back to similarity of the position of the cells in the embryo or of the parts of the egg out of which the structures are ultimately composed.[11] However, if the facts of homology are to prove evolution true, there should be such similarity. Homologous structures should always arise from the same position of the cells in the embryo or from the same parts of the egg. But this does not always occur. Embryologists believe that different organizers perform the same task in different forms. This possibility, too, casts a grave doubt on the correctness of the conclusions drawn from homology.

4. *Similarities Not Regarded as Evidences of Relationship*

But there are still other facts that bear on this problem. There are times when organisms which are very similar are not classified as being closely related. The platypus, one of the strange mammals of Australia, is not regarded as a link between birds and mammals. It has a bill, but that resembles the bill of a duck only superficially. It has webbed feet and tarsal spurs, but these, too, are believed to be only superficial resemblances.[12] But if this is true, isn't it possible that many of the other resemblances referred to in the argument from homology are superficial too?

5. *Variations in Degree of Resemblance at Different Stages of the Life Cycle*

Sometimes, too, there are variations in the degree of resemblance between seedling and adult. The seedlings of the *Eucalyptus* (an evergreen of the myrtle family native to Australia and the surrounding regions which has been brought over to the United States) have leaves more similar to supposedly related forms than to the leaves of the adult plants. This is also true of the bush poppy (*Dendromecon rigidum*) and the chamise bush (*Adenostoma fasciculatum*). These variations are explained on the basis of growth habits. The seedling leaves, which are broad and flat, appear in wet seasons, when a maximum amount of food production is desirable. Later, in the dry season, the adult plant must be protected against undue loss of water, and this necessitates a different type of leaf, one which is protected against water loss.[13] All these observations throw doubt on any argument drawn from similarities.

6. Similar Glands Producing Different Substances

Identical glands may produce substances which are quite different chemically. In the beetles of the family Carabidae the defensive glands, which are generally regarded as homologous throughout the group, have been shown in various species to produce compounds as different as formic acid, m-cresol, p-benzoquinones, salicylaldehyde, and tiglic and methacrylic acid. In the millipedes the orders Julida, Spirobolida, and Spirostreptida secrete p-benzoquinones, the Polydesmida produce cyanogenic secretions, and the single species of the Chordeumida that has been studied produces a phenol. Eisner and Meinwald believe that despite some difference in structure the glands in these various orders are probably homologous.[14]

III. The Evidence for Evolution from Vestigial Organs

A. Nature of the Evidence

A third evidence for evolution which we want to consider is the occurrence of what are known as vestigial organs in various forms. These are organs for which no function has been demonstrated. It is postulated that these organs were once functional, but that in the course of evolutionary history they lost their usefulness and gradually deteriorated. In the human body, for instance, we have the appendix and the caecum in the digestive tract; the coccyx at the end of the vertebral column; the tonsils; ear muscles; and the like. There are supposedly vestigial organs also in other forms. The wings of the ostrich and the kiwi are supposed to be vestigial. The hind legs of whales are missing except for small bones. There are literally hundreds of structures in different organisms which are supposed to be vestigial.

B. The Evidence Evaluated

1. A Lamarckian Argument

In a sense the argument that these have deteriorated through disuse is a Lamarckian argument. There is no genetic evidence for a method whereby useless organs will necessarily deteriorate. So far as we know structures are retained even though they are not used. Evolutionists who do not accept Lamarck's theories believe they disappear through "loss mutations," but there is no real evidence that this is actually the case.

2. The Possibility that the Function of an Organ Has Not Yet Been Discovered

Besides, the fact that a function has not been demonstrated for an organ is no real evidence that it has no function. It is quite possible that these structures have a function that has not yet been discovered. For many years the endocrine glands — glands of internal secretion, such as the thyroid, the pituitary, and the adrenals, which pour their products into the blood stream — were regarded as vestigial organs. They could be seen and described anatomically, but no function was known for them. Today, of course, we know that these structures are very important for life.

3. *The Possibility that the Function of an Organ May Be Taken Over by Another Organ When It Is Removed*

It is even possible that an organ such as the appendix, which can be removed without any discernible effect, may have a function which is taken over by other structures after it has been removed. The "margin of safety" phenomenon, which consists in man's having more tissue of a specialized type than he really needs, is an example of this. Man can live with only one kidney or one lung, but God has provided him with two as a sort of margin of safety.

Organs may also take over functions which they do not

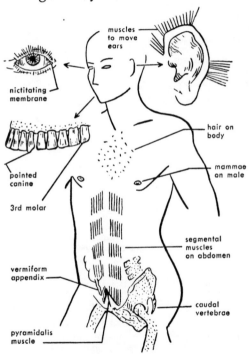

Figure 6. **Vestigial Structures in Man.** The structures indicated in this diagram are some of the supposedly vestigial organs in man. They are believed to have served man at one time in his evolutionary history but to have no function today. (Redrawn from Storer's *General Zoology*, McGraw-Hill, by permission)

ordinarily have. The spleen produces red corpuscles before birth, but in the adult it ordinarily does not. In cases of severe hemorrhage, however, it may resume this function until the emergency is over.

4. The Appendix

The structure which probably is referred to most frequently as a vestigial organ is the appendix. In most primates other than man it is larger than it is in man, and in mammals which eat a coarse diet containing a considerable amount of cellulose the appendix and the caecum, to which it

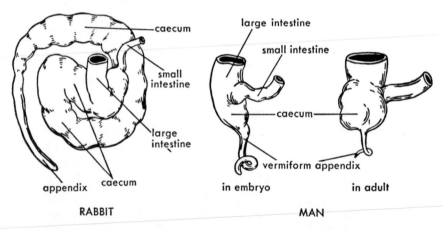

Figure 7. The Caecum and Vermiform Appendix in the Rabbit, in the Human Embryo, and in the Human Adult. These are two of the most frequently mentioned vestigial organs in man. The rabbit, being a herbivore, has a large appendix and caecum in which partially digested food is stored while being acted upon by bacteria. It is suggested that at one time a remote ancestor of man ate a great deal of plant tissue and required an appendix and caecum. These have been retained even though man's diet has changed and he no longer needs them. (Rabbit redrawn from Bensley's *Practical Anatomy of the Rabbit*, E. Horne Craigie, ed., University of Toronto Press, by permission. Human redrawn from Walter's *Biology of the Vertebrates*, Macmillan, by permission)

is attached, form a large sac in which mixtures of food and enzymes can react for long periods of time. The fact that in embryonic life it is relatively large and conspicuous has persuaded a great many people that it must be a vestigial organ. And yet Sir Arthur Keith, a well-known anthropologist and paleontologist, believed that it is not a vestigial organ but an organ, the function of which is not known.[15] There are some physicians today who believe that the appendix has a function in embryonic life and early infancy though none has been demonstrated. For that reason they are reluctant to perform an appendectomy on an infant. Moreover, the appendix is larger and better developed in the anthropoid apes than it is in man. This fact might seem to indicate that man is further along in his evolution. And yet while it is present in some lemurs, the simplest primates, it is absent in tarsiers, in New World and in Old World monkeys.[16] Does this mean that the Old World and New World monkeys have evolved even further in this direction than man?

5. *The Thymus*

Only recently have we learned how important the thymus is. For a long time it was not possible to assign any function to it. Now we know that it plays a key role in directing the establishment of a functioning immunologic apparatus. If the thymus is removed in early life before the immune system is fully developed, there is a disturbance of immune functions. Yet once the immunologic mechanisms are well established, the effects of thymectomy are negligible. However, if in an adult we destroy the cellular basis for immunologic reactions, a thymectomy is again associated with serious defects in immune functions. Thus the thymus is necessary not only for establishing normal immunological potential during development but also for restoring such potential after it has been destroyed or damaged and possibly for maintaining it as it becomes depleted with time.[17]

6. *Vestigial Organs That Prove Too Much*

Actually there are some vestigial organs which prove too much. The presence of vestigial mammary glands in the male might suggest that at one time males suckled the young. The large rounded head of the human fetus might indicate that our ancestors once had large rounded brain cases. Likewise, the absence of an opposable great toe should exclude from our ancestors animals with an opposable great toe, such as the great apes, since the presence in the fetus of an external tail, the lanugo (fetal hair), and the cartilaginous nodule which fuses with the navicular bone (supposed to be an evidence of an *os centrale*) are regarded as evidences that man descended from simple primates.[18]

IV. The Evidence for Evolution from Comparative Physiology and Biochemistry

A. Nature of the Evidence

Another argument for evolution is that which is drawn from the fields of comparative physiology and biochemistry. Physiological processes and the chemical make-up of various cells and tissues in different organisms are compared. Similarities are regarded as evidence of kinship and of descent from a common ancestor.

It is often pointed out that protoplasm itself seems to be basically one substance. Throughout the living world chromosomes seem to consist of basic proteins in combination with nucleic acid. The nucleic acids themselves are said to be rather uniform. Very similar or even identical enzymes and hormones are found in large groups of animals. Trypsin, which digests proteins, is found in a great many animals from protozoa to mammals. Amylase, which digests starches, is found in many animals from sponges to man. Thyroxin is found in all vertebrates.

Much of the work in this area has been done with blood. It is a readily available tissue and one which lends itself in a peculiar way to a very careful analysis.

B. The Evidence Evaluated

1. Similarity and Descent

Obviously, the chief premise of this argument is once more that similarity is evidence of descent from a common ancestor. It is assumed that the reason for similarities in physiological processes and in the chemical structure of tissues is that the organisms have descended from a common ancestor.

Dobzhansky cautions against this sort of reasoning. He says that to an evolutionist the fact that certain enzymes are widely distributed in most of earth's organisms is very impressive but that to conclude that these chemical constituents are produced everywhere by the same genes is going far beyond what is justified by the evidence. In the first place, he says, what we really know is merely that some enzymes extracted from different organisms facilitate the same chemical reactions. These enzymes, he says, are not necessarily identical in their protein structure. Second, the functional similarity of enzymes is not necessarily conferred upon them by identical genes in different organisms.[19]

Mabry, Alston, and Turner point out that the ability of two different organisms to synthesize the same secondary compounds can be interpreted in at least two different ways: it may reflect a common ancestor, or alternatively it may be a case of parallel evolution. This latter explanation is used when organisms that are not believed to be closely related produce identical or very similar compounds.[20] For instance, ants and phasmids produce similar compounds. Cavill and Robertson conclude that this simply suggests that the ability to synthesize terpenoids may be widespread among the Insecta.[21] Mollusks may excrete their wastes as urea, uric acid, ammonia, adenine, guanine, or creatinine. Insulin composition in sperm whales is identical with that in pigs and quite different from that of sei whales: this is believed to be an example of the confusion that may be brought about by convergent evolution.[22] Tarichatoxin, a powerful neurotoxin that has recently been isolated in crystalline form from eggs of various species of western American newts as well as in newt eggs and embryos, is very different chemically from other known salamander toxins, but it appears to be identical to a toxin known as tetrodotoxin, which occurs in the Japanese fugu or puffer fish.[23]

While recent studies of evolutionary relationships are believed to have confirmed generally held evolutionary ideas, they have nevertheless also turned up some problems. Fitch and Margoliash carried out a series of studies using mutation distances as estimated from cytochrome *c* sequences. Many of the relationships which they found agreed with generally accepted evolutionary relationships, but they report three notable exceptions. They found that the penguin seems closely related to the chicken whereas they would expect the "birds of flight" to be more closely related to each other than to the penguin. The kangaroo was found to be closely associated with nonprimate mammals whereas most zoologists maintain that the placental mammals, excluding the primates, are more closely related to each other than to the marsupials. Third, they discovered that the turtle appears more closely associated in their studies with birds than with its fellow reptile, the rattlesnake.[24]

2. The Blood

Let us look carefully at the argument that is drawn from a study of the blood of different organisms. It is this evidence that is mentioned most frequently by evolutionists. Blood is a complex tissue containing a number of chemical substances. These studies are particularly concerned with the antigen-antibody relationships and with the resulting agglutination or lack of agglutination of the blood. (Antigens are substances produced by another organism which harm the individual and cause his body to produce protective substances, or antibodies. The toxins of bacteria are antigens which cause the body to produce various types of antibodies.)

a. *Protein Tests.* — It is a well-known fact that transfusion of blood from one human being to another is not always a safe procedure. If the individual receives blood of the wrong type, he may very easily die as a result of the transfusion. Accordingly, before a blood transfusion is given today, blood is typed, and, in addition, the blood of the donor is cross-matched with that of the prospective recipient by mixing a drop of blood from each to see whether clumping will occur. For the blood of some people contains substances which will cause such clumping and actually destroy the blood of other individuals. Among humans there are four well-known blood types: O, A, B, and AB. The red corpuscles of the individual contain complex chemical substances known as antigens. The plasma, or liquid part of the blood, contains other complex chemical substances called antibodies. The antibodies of the plasma will cause corpuscles containing certain antigens to clump together and will also cause them to disintegrate.

In addition to the O, A, B, and AB blood types, a number of other blood types have been discovered among human beings. Perhaps the best known of these are the Rh blood groups. In these, two groups are distinguished, Rh^+ and Rh^-. These blood groups, like the O, A, B, and AB blood groups, are inherited. In cases where the mother's blood group does not match that of her child (if the mother is Rh^- and the child is Rh^+), the child sometimes may be stillborn or die shortly after birth. Other blood groups are the MN blood groups, the P blood groups, the Kell blood groups, the Lewis blood groups, and the Duffy blood groups. It appears that these blood groups are somewhat similar to the O, A, B, AB, and the Rh blood groups. However, only the Kell blood groups, in addition to the O, A, B, and AB blood groups and the Rh blood groups, appear to be involved in human disease.

Evolutionists are particularly interested in studying similarities between the agglutination reactions of humans and the agglutination reactions of other organisms. Two general types of serological tests are made — tests for proteins and tests for haptenes, or polysaccharides. In the former the foreign proteins and the neutralizing antibodies in the immune serum are the cause of precipitation. In the latter the haptenes and their corresponding antibodies cause the precipitation.

Protein tests may be carried out by testing the blood of other animals with an antihuman serum. Such a serum is produced by injecting human blood into a rabbit or some other experimental animal. The human blood acts as a sort of poison to the rabbit, and his body reacts to protect itself by producing antihuman antibodies. These antibodies clump and destroy human blood. The blood of the rabbit who has received an injection of human blood is then processed and used as an antihuman serum.

The antihuman serum so produced is mixed with the blood of other animals, and the degree of clumping and precipitation is noted. With dogs and cats and many other mammals there is no agglutination or precipitation. However, when this antihuman serum is mixed with the blood of primates (apes, monkeys, and the like), agglutination and precipitation frequently occur. It is the precipitation reactions that have been most widely studied. The greatest precipitate is noted when antihuman serum is mixed with the blood of chimpanzees. Taking the human reaction to antihuman serum as 100, the precipitate between antihuman serum and chimpanzee blood is 130. The precipitate, however, is less compact. With gorilla blood the precipitate is 64. With orangutan and mandrill blood it is 42. With Guinea baboon and spider monkey blood it is 20. Old World monkeys generally show slighter reactions than the reactions shown by the blood of the great apes. New World monkey blood shows only the faintest reactions, and there is no reaction at all with the blood of lemurs and tarsiers.[25]

This result is taken as evidence of a relationship between

man and the other primates. He is believed to be only dis-
tantly related to the lemurs and tarsiers. He is more closely
related to the Old World monkeys than he is to the New
World monkeys, and he is most closely related to the great
apes. This would also appear to confirm the opinion of the
Yerkes who believe that of the great apes the chimpanzee
is the most similar to man.[26]

However, there are other blood relationships which do
not match this particular evidence from antihuman serum.
The chimpanzee has blood group A and O but no blood
group B or AB. The orangutan, gibbon, and baboon have
A and B but no O. The gorilla has a B-like group but neither
A nor O.[27] The macaques, however, seem to have all of the
blood groups. And this is also true of the other Old World
monkeys and of the New World monkeys, though these
blood groups may not be identical with the corresponding
human factors.[28]

It is striking that the macaques, the other Old World
monkeys, and the New World monkeys seem to have all of
the blood groups, whereas the great apes, which are supposed to be more closely related to man, lack at least one
of the blood groups. Could it not be argued that man is
more closely related to these than to the great apes? It is
also striking that in some cases the O-blood group should
be the one that is missing, since it is believed that the
O-blood group was the original blood group among humans,
that A was acquired later, and that B was acquired still later
in the course of evolutionary history.

Hooton admits that these investigations create a problem
and says that the interpretation of these recent findings concerning blood groups is not altogether clear. He believes
that it is possible that these originated as more or less parallel
mutations in the different stocks. However, even this explanation presents difficulties, since it does not explain the
absence of blood group O, apparently the original blood
group, in some of the higher apes.

b. *Problems in Blood Relationships.* — There are also problems associated with the origin of these blood groups. Why is it that these antibodies are inherited, while the antibodies which protect us against disease germs are not?

There are problems, too, in connection with the distribution of the various blood groups in different human stocks which may or may not have a bearing on evolution. It is generally believed that the Rh$^+$ blood group is the original blood group and that Rh$^-$ developed later. However, among the Basques more than 50% of the people tested are Rh$^-$. This proportion compares with an Rh$^-$ frequency of about 15% among white Americans and a very low occurrence of Rh$^-$ among people living in the Orient and on the islands of the Pacific.

3. Disease Relationships

The whole argument from comparative physiology and biochemistry is based upon similarities. However, many similarities are ignored because they prove the wrong things. Some diseases are limited almost entirely to man. Polio is well-nigh exclusively a human disease. It cannot be transmitted from one animal to another. Monkeys can acquire it only by inoculation. The trypanosome of sleeping sickness attacks man, antelopes, other African mammals, and domestic cattle. Is this evidence that man is closely related to these animals? Rabies attacks man, the dog, and a few other animals. Is this evidence of a relationship? Tetanus is spontaneous in man, horses, cattle, and sheep. Malta fever affects only man and goats spontaneously, while the plague occurs spontaneously chiefly in man and rats.[29] Are these evidences of a relationship?

4. Hemoglobin

Another similarity that strikes us as strange is that the vertebrate forms (protoheme combined with globin in a ratio of four to one) of hemoglobin, the coloring matter of the red corpuscles which enables them to transport oxygen, are found in paramecia, fish, amphibia, reptiles, birds, and mammals. The invertebrate forms are found in roundworms (nematodes); segmented worms (annelids); crayfish, insects, and the like (arthropods); clams and oysters (mollusks); starfish (echinoderms); and hagfish and lamprey eels (cyclostomes). Hemoglobin is also found in the root nodules of leguminous plants.[30] Why should the paramecium, a one-celled protozoan, have the vertebrate form of hemoglobin? Should it not have the invertebrate form? Why should the cyclostomes — simple vertebrates — have the invertebrate form? Would it not be reasonable to expect them to have the vertebrate form? Why should a plant have hemoglobin in its root nodules?

Also impressive is the wide variety of methods that have been developed for carrying oxygen. In addition to hemoglobin there are other iron-containing compounds, there are copper-containing compounds, there is a vanadium-containing compound, and it has even been suggested that there is a manganese-containing compound. There are also some achroglobins that have no metallic components which are capable of binding oxygen. Rensch says that when we consider these findings it is apparent that there are various ways of satisfying the same organic need. He points out that quite a number of different ways can be found in a single group such as the Mollusca, where we meet hemocyanin, hemoglobin, pinnaglobin, and achroglobin.[31]

It is rather interesting that the hemoglobin of the New World monkeys appears to resemble human hemoglobin rather closely; yet the New World monkeys are not believed to be closely related to man. The hemoglobin of tarsiers is similar to, if not identical with, elephant hemoglobin.[32]

The type of hemoglobin varies with the stage of development of the organism. The human fetus, which secures oxygen through the placenta, has a different type of hemoglobin than the adult who secures oxygen through his lungs. Huehns, Dance, Beaven, Hecht, and Motulsky comment on

a study by Muirhead and Perutz which shows how beautifully the structure of hemoglobin is adapted to its function
and says that it is therefore not surprising that hemoglobins
of the same species which function under different physiological conditions have different structures. Tadpole hemoglobin differs from that found in a frog, and the hemoglobin
found in chicken embryos differs from that of the adult
hen.[33]

5. Physiological and Biochemical Complexities

There are also many physiological and biochemical complexities which are difficult to explain on the basis of evolution and mere chance development. The complicated chemical relationships of the body are themselves an example.
This complexity is well illustrated by the chemistry of the
digestive system. The mouth is only slightly acid, and the
enzymes of the mouth can digest food only in a medium
close to neutrality. The stomach, however, is very acid, and
its enzymes work effectively only in an acid medium. Of all
the acids investigated, hydrochloric acid is the most effective
in promoting peptic action,[34] and this is the very acid that
occurs in the stomach. The small intestine is alkaline, and
its digestive enzymes work only in an alkaline medium. Let
us assume that originally the entire digestive tract was acid.
Then, we ask, how did the intestinal enzymes develop, and
how did the intestine become alkaline? If we assume that
the enzymes developed first, then it is unlikely that they
would have been retained by the human organism, for they
would not have worked in an acid medium. If, on the other
hand, we assume that the first change was a change in the
intestine itself to an alkaline condition, then this would not
have been retained, for it would have interfered with the
continuation of protein digestion, which begins in the
stomach and could continue in an acid intestine, but not in
an alkaline intestine.

The amino acids used in protein synthesis are all alpha
amino acids (those in which the NH_2 and the $COOH$ groups

are attached to the same carbon). With possible rare exceptions, they are all "l" forms (rotating a beam of polarized light to the left) as opposed to "d" forms (those that rotate a beam of polarized light to the right). This is the case in spite of the fact that if an optically active substance is synthesized in the laboratory, a mixture of "d" and "l" forms is obtained.[35]

All of these complexities can only lead us to ask whether they could have arisen by chance. Could any system of evolution have produced them? Isn't it more logical and more reasonable to seek their origin in a creation by an infinitely wise God? Certainly we are inclined to agree with Dr. George Gallup, who said: "I could prove God statistically. Take the human body alone — the chance that all the functions of the individual would just happen is a statistical monstrosity." [36]

V. The Evidence for Evolution from Embryology
A. Nature of the Evidence

Another field that is said to furnish evidence for the theory of evolution is the field of embryology. Here we have the famous recapitulation theory, or biogenetic law, of Haeckel — "Ontogeny recapitulates phylogeny." Haeckel meant to say that in the course of embryonic development (ontogeny) the organism repeats the evolutionary history of the phylum (phylogeny). In the case of man he begins as a single fertilized cell — the protozoan stage. Then he develops through a sort of jellyfish stage and a worm stage. Finally he becomes a chordate. This process, we are to believe, is merely a repetition of his evolutionary history, an abridgment of the stages he passed through in the course of his development.

This development can also be traced out in the various systems. His kidneys pass through a worm stage, then through a frog stage, and finally become human. His heart develops first as a pulsating tube — the worm stage. Then it becomes a two-chambered structure — the fish stage.

It continues and becomes three-chambered — the frog stage. It then develops into a four-chambered stage, but there is a connection between the right and left sides of the heart — the reptile stage. Only at birth does the heart finally become fully human.

The development which is probably referred to most frequently by embryologists is the development of the so-called "gill slits," or branchial grooves, and "gill arches." These are found in the throat and resemble superficially the gill slits and gill arches of a fish. They are supposed to be evidences that at one time man passed through a fish stage.

The argument from embryology also emphasizes the fact

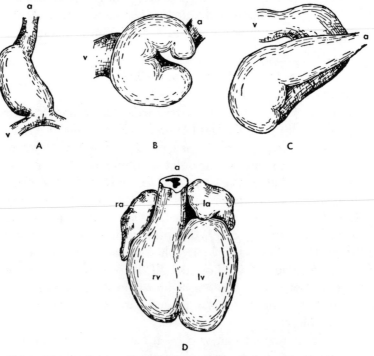

Figure 8. Stages in the Development of the Human Heart. The auricle is indicated by a, the ventricle by v. Evolutionists believe that this development repeats the stages in the evolutionary development of the heart from the time it was a simple pulsating tube until it became a four-chambered human heart. (Redrawn from Lindsey's *Principles of Organic Evolution*, Mosby, by permission)

that in early embryonic stages mammals are all very much alike. Indeed, in early embryonic life, until about the eighth week of development, it is difficult to tell a human embryo from the embryo of any other mammal. That is regarded by the evolutionists as evidence that they are descended from a common ancestor.

B. The Evidence Evaluated

1. An Increase in Complexity to Meet the Needs of the Developing Organism

At first glance this reasoning seems rather telling. It would almost seem as if these organisms are passing

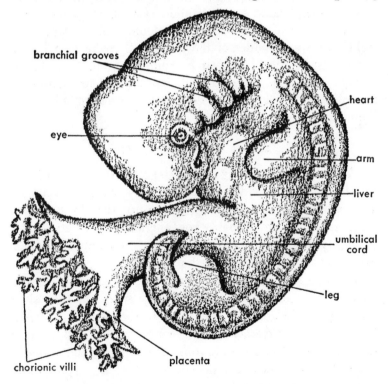

Figure 9. Human Embryo at Four Weeks. Note the branchial grooves, which are supposed to be remnants of a fish stage. (Redrawn from Gilbert's *Biography of the Unborn,* Williams and Wilkins Co., by permission)

through these various primitive stages. And yet much of the development referred to is just what we should expect in the course of normal development. It is but natural that organs and systems should develop from simple to complex. The human being starts out as a single fertilized cell, not because he was once a protozoan, but because that is the simplest form possible. In the case of the heart, too, it is but natural that there should be a development from simple to complex. In the early stages only a pulsating tube is needed. Why should a complex four-chambered heart spring into being at once? The development of the heart meets the needs of a developing organism. As the need develops for a more complicated transportation system, the heart itself becomes more complicated. The connection between the right and the left sides of the heart is there so that before birth most of the blood can be shunted around the lungs. Oxygen is supplied before birth, not by the lungs, but by the placenta, and there is no point in sending all of the blood to the lungs.

2. *The Test of Function*

Another striking thing is that the structures do not function in the way in which the organs they resemble function. The worm kidney (pronephros) and the frog kidney (mesonephros) are probably not functional in excretion. It is generally agreed that the pronephros does not function in excretion. It has been suggested that the mesonephros may function as a temporary excretory organ. In man (and in some other mammals) it is relatively small; in the rabbit and pig it is large. The small size in man makes it doubtful that it functions as an excretory organ in early human development. In later embryonic development the pronephros and mesonephros are incorporated into the reproductive system. Only the last kidney (the metanephros), which is distinctively human, is used in excretion. It functions already before birth.[37]

This is also true of the so-called gill slits. If they are to recapitulate a fish stage, they should be functional in respiration, but they are not. As a matter of fact, except for the more cephalic which occasionally break through, they are never completely open in man, but are closed by a membrane. They develop as an inpocketing from the neck and an outpocketing from the pharynx. In later embryonic life they are incorporated into various other organs. The first becomes the Eustachian tube, which connects the throat and the middle ear, and the tympanic cavity of the middle ear. The second is greatly reduced and incorporated into the palatine tonsils. The third, fourth, and fifth become incorporated into the thymus, parathyroids, and postbranchial bodies.[38] In no way are they ever associated with the respiratory system or with respiratory processes.

The gill arches, too, are incorporated into other organs. The anterior branches persist on both sides to form the internal and external carotids, the arteries going to the head. The third gill arches form portions of the internal carotids. The right side of the fourth gill arch forms part of the right subclavian artery which feeds the arm. The left side of the fourth gill arch forms the aortic arch. The sixth arch forms the ductus arteriosus which is cut off at birth.[39]

Experience should teach us to be very cautious in naming or assigning functions to structures which resemble superficially other structures whose function is known. In the *Euglena*, to which we referred earlier, there are structures the names of which would indicate they were part of the digestive system. There is a mouth, a gullet, and a food reservoir. All these names would seem to imply that these structures are associated with the ingestion and digestion of food. And, superficially, they look as if they would serve that purpose. The mouth appears to be an opening which might very well serve for taking in food. The gullet appears to connect the mouth and the food reservoir. And the food reservoir resembles a structure which might well be used for storing food. Yet these structures, so far as we know, are not associated with food getting and digestive processes in the *Euglena.* The animal manufactures its own food, and there is no evidence that under any circumstances it takes in food through its mouth.[40] In short, we have structures which superficially seem to have a certain function. However, when we examine them carefully we find that they do not have the function which their names imply and that their resemblance to these structures is only superficial.

Today the recapitulation theory is not as important in knowledgeable circles as popularizations of evolution would indicate. Ehrlich and Holm refer to it as a "crude interpretation of embryological sequences," and they say it will not stand up on close examinations. Its shortcomings have been almost universally pointed out by modern authors, they say, but the idea still has a prominent place in biological mythology. The resemblances of early vertebrate embryos is readily explained, they believe, without resort to mysterious forces compelling each individual to climb its phylogenetic tree.[41]

3. *Explanations for Embryonic Relationships*

Actually it is coming to be more and more recognized by evolutionists themselves that in many cases embryonic development can be explained on the basis of increasing complexity and developing needs just as reasonably as on the basis of recapitulation. De Beer says that the failure to recognize this principle of parallelism of increasing degrees of complexity was a grave error in the theory of recapitulation.[42]

For instance, many invertebrates excrete nitrogen in the form of ammonia. Fish and amphibia excrete it as urea, and adult birds excrete nitrogenous wastes as uric acid. The embryo bird first excretes ammonia, then later urea, and finally, as an adult, it excretes uric acid. At first glance this appears to be a fine instance of recapitulation. Yet Needham points out that it is no evidence at all for recapitulation.

He believes that it represents the order and sequence in which biochemical reactions of increasing degrees of complexity can be performed. In addition, he points out that the production of urea by the chick embryo by means of the arginine-arginase system is not identical with that which occurs in fish and amphibia. In these organisms urea is produced by the ornithine cycle.[43]

A similar example is cited by Simpson, who criticizes Wald for considering the fact that tadpoles resemble fishes in a number of biochemical characteristics whereas adult frogs have a biochemistry like that of land vertebrates as an example of "the most striking instances of recapitulation we know." Simpson says that in his opinion there is no reason to invoke recapitulation and definite reason not to. Tadpoles, he says, are adapted to live in the water, and adult frogs to live on land. Wastes are secreted as ammonia in water, urea out of it. He calls attention to the evidence cited by Wald that when amphibians go from land to water as some do, the changes tend to go in the opposite direction; they antirecapitulate.[44]

Stebbins believes that seedling similarity in plants, which at first seems to exemplify recapitulation, is the result of an entirely different phenomenon. He believes that the genetic factors which alter the growing tip of the plant (the apical meristem) so that it produces appendages of a more specialized type often begin their action relatively late in development.[45] Thus a number of plants follow the same general plan for a relatively long time, and it is only relatively late in their development that specialization appears. Genetic factors, and not recapitulation, account for seedling similarities.

4. The Contributions of Experimental Embryology

Much additional evidence in this area has come from the field of experimental embryology. It now appears that developing organisms "make themselves." They utilize successive internal and environmental causes (many of which are now recognized as chemical and physical) to effect certain changes by means of "organizers" which induce a differentiation of particular qualities out of the reacting tissues. It is the inherited and undeveloped germ plasm which gives each organism the capacity to respond to certain stimuli in the manner recognized as development from the egg, insuring that if development occurs at all, it conforms to the type of the species.[46] The development proceeds, under the guidance of these organizers, in a way which meets the needs of an increasingly complex organism, and this, rather than recapitulation, is responsible for what can be observed during embryonic life.

The case of the notochord, which is crowded out by the vertebrae almost as soon as it is formed in the embryo, is discussed by Merrell. He asks why the notochord is retained and answers that while it may seem to be a clear-cut case of recapitulation, it can hardly be such. The cells that form the notochord are intimately bound up with the organizing and inducing of the essential axial structures of the embryo — the spinal cord and the brain, the heart, kidneys, muscle, and so on. Thus these cells must be present in order to bring about such organization and induction.[47] These structures, which are considered evidence of recapitulation, may be present because they are needed in embryonic or larval life.

5. The Scarcity and Unreliability of the Evidence

Carter concludes that the evidence for an elongation of the life history (hypermorphosis), which is basic to Haeckel's theory, is slight and hard to find. He believes that recapitulation is not at all basic in animal evolution. Nor does he believe that it is the cause of the resemblances that we find between the young stages of animals.[48]

De Beer says that larval convergence (similar larvae and dissimilar adults), larval divergence (dissimilar larvae and similar adults), and incongruence (classification based on larval relationships does not agree with that based on adults) are more common in subspecies and mutants than in species.[49] In short, the more closely the organism is presumably related, the more deceptive the story from embryonic life. Certainly this is disconcerting when we are looking for evidence of relationships in embryonic development. De Beer believes that this is due to the fact that in the course of evolution species have diverged to such an extent that only similarities appear and dissimilarities are lost.

C. Paedomorphosis, Neoteny, Fetalization

In view of all this, De Beer concludes that embryology cannot with any degree of certainty reconstruct ancestral types. He believes, though, that embryology may give some indication of affinity.[50] The descendant, he says, may be derived from a larval form of the ancestor, and in such a case the resemblance between the young form of the descendant and the young form of the ancestor may convey little or no information concerning the adult form of that ancestor. His own theory, which was also suggested by W. Garstang,[51] is known as paedomorphosis. He believes that in many cases the embryonic or undeveloped ancestor resembles the adult descendant. For instance, the adult modern man is believed to resemble the young Neanderthal man or the newborn ape. Vertebrates, he believes, have developed from larval echinoderms. Insects have developed from larval myriapodlike forms.[52] Recapitulation, he says, is now discredited and generally abandoned.[53] Other names for his theory or variations and modifications of it are neoteny, paedogenesis, caenogenesis, and fetalization.

As can be seen, this idea, which has gained rather wide acceptance, is almost the opposite of recapitulation. In fact, De Beer calls it the very opposite of recapitulation.[54] De Beer and Garstang believe that in many cases higher forms have evolved by having their embryonic development arrested.

Instead of continuing embryonic development to its final completion, for some reason or other the embryonic development stopped at a certain point, and this stoppage resulted in the development of a higher form. Certain embryonic features which are ordinarily passed through before the adult stage are sometimes retained in the adult by the lagging of later growth stages either in vigor or in timing. Females of some moths and beetles are larviform; certain salamanders do not metamorphose into adults but reproduce as larvae. Many of man's peculiarities are regarded as fetalizations. The most noteworthy examples of these are the unique relations between the head and the spine, the position of the face and orbit relative to the brain case, the inability to rotate the great toe, certain peculiarities of hair distribution, and the late appearance of skin color.[55] Schultz believes that fetalization in the face region occurs not only in man, but also in some of the monkeys and apes.[56]

There is believed to be some evidence for a sort of paedomorphosis also in plants. Stebbins says that De Beer's conclusion that the recapitulation theory is more misleading than helpful and should be rejected is partly true also of plants. He does not believe, however, that the situation is quite as marked in plants.[57]

Most of the same objections which apply to recapitulation apply also to paedomorphosis. The development which we find is only that which we would expect in the course of the development from simple to complex. Moreover, with the suggestion of a number of types of possible embryonic and evolutionary development, it is but natural that we should occasionally find some superficial resemblance to one of the types suggested.

VI. The Evidences for Evolution from Color Patterns, Etc.

Other phenomena which are believed to be evidences for evolution are those associated with the color patterns of animals. It is believed that the patterns which the organisms have today have evolved in the course of time from relatively simple patterns and from neutral colors. All of these phenomena were emphasized by Darwin. Subsequently for a time they were de-emphasized. But today the pendulum seems to have swung again in the direction of some emphasis on these phenomena.

A. Protective Resemblance

The first of these is the phenomenon which has been called protective resemblance. According to this concept, organisms are protected against predators by blending in with their background. Two types of protective resemblance have been distinguished. According to one type the animal resembles its general background; according to the other, the organism resembles some particular object in its background.

There are a great many examples of this phenomenon which come to mind at once. Fish, for instance, are dark colored above, so that they blend in with the dark bottom when observed from above. However, they are light colored on their under parts, so that they blend in with the sky when observed from below. Bright green parrots are relatively inconspicuous in the bright tropical vegetation of South America. Lizards are dark gray or tawny-colored like the soil, sand, rocks, or bark of trees near which they live. Some animals, such as the chameleon, have the power to change their color, and this, too, is said to render them less conspicuous.

There are also many examples of the second type of protective coloration. The grayish caterpillars of certain geometrids, when disturbed, hold themselves rigidly at an angle to the twig on which they rest, thus looking like branches of the twig. Certain spiders look like the buds of plants on which they rest. The wings of some katydids, long-horned grasshoppers, and mantids are green and have a net-veined structure like leaves. The famous Kallima butterfly of India has wings which, when folded, are colored and marked like a dead leaf. The tobacco sphinx moth has a pattern which resembles to a striking degree the markings on an old weathered board or the furrows and ridges of tree bark.

Many evolutionists believe that this is evidence of evolution. They believe that originally the animals lacked this protective resemblance to their environment or to the objects in the environment. In the course of evolutionary history, however, they acquired this protective resemblance as a means of survival. Those which lacked it were quickly destroyed by predators, and only those which had such protection were able to survive.

1. The Protective Value of Protective Patterns

There is no doubt that there is some degree of resemblance to the background in animals. But its extent has been greatly exaggerated by evolutionists. And, as Robson and Richards point out,[58] there is no evidence that it has developed as a result of selection and evolution.

McAtee goes so far as to conclude from his experiments that the whole idea of protection is largely a myth. He studied the stomach contents of a large number of North American birds and found that protection did not exist for some of the prey species thought to be protected. In brief, these protected species were eaten just as often as those that were not supposed to be protected.[59] After reviewing the various ways in which animals change color the Milnes come to much the same conclusion. They believe that protective coloration in land animals is generally overrated.[60] Changes in the chameleon, for instance, appear to have no relationship to his background.

2. The Visual Powers of Predators

Another difficulty in discussing protection is the problem of determining the visual powers of the predator. We know that some insects are able to see parts of the spectrum that we humans cannot see. Ants, for instance, can apparently see ultraviolet light which we do not see, and they cannot see some of the red zones which we can see. Likewise bees cannot see red, but can perceive ultraviolet light. It has also been learned that they confuse yellow with orange or green, and they confuse blue with violet.[61]

It can be demonstrated that the color pattern of some of these protected organisms is different under ultraviolet light from the pattern under visible light. It may be that many animals which appear to have a sort of protective resem-

Figure 10. Protective Resemblance. The walking stick at the left illustrates the type of protective resemblance according to which the organism resembles some particular object in the background. This insect resembles a twig. At the right, the underwing moth, *Catocala*. The bright color of the hind wings, shown when the wings are spread in *A*, is hidden by the fore wings when the insect is at rest on the bark of a tree, as in *B*. In this latter condition the insect blends in with its background, appearing as a discolored patch or clump of moss on the bark of the tree. (From Folsom and Wardle's *Entomology*, P. Blakiston and Co., by permission)

blance do not have that protective resemblance when viewed
by their predators.

3. *The Problem of Relative Size*

Still another factor is the size of the object relative to
the observer's field of vision. An object which may occupy
only a small part of our field of vision and hence may escape
detection by us may occupy a very large part of the field
of vision of the predator and may easily be seen by him.

4. *Length of Time Spent Against a Protected Background*

Another point to be considered is the relative length of
time that the organism spends against the protected background. An animal is not able to spend all of his time against
the sheltering background. He must move about from time
to time, and when he does, he loses the supposed advantages
of protection. Actually, animals spend only a portion of the
time against a protected background.

5. *The "Capricious Incidence" of Protective Resemblance*

Still another thing to be considered is what Robson and
Richards call the "capricious incidence" of protective resemblance. They point out that it is well developed in some
forms, such as the phasmids (a group of insects belonging
to the same order as the grasshopper), and yet is nearly
entirely absent in forms such as the land mollusks.[62]

Robson and Richards conclude that there is often insufficient quantitative evidence as to the association of animals
with appropriate backgrounds, that in some examples,
e. g., nocturnal animals, it is possible that the habits of the
animals do not require protective coloration, and that there
is no evidence that selection has actually produced the
observed color correspondences.[63]

B. Aggressive Resemblance and Alluring Resemblance

Another difficulty that presents itself is the fact that some
predators appear to be protectively colored. This hardly
fits with the general theory of protective resemblance, since
they do not need protection. Protection is needed by the

animal which is eaten, not by the organism that does the eating.

To meet this objection two other theories have been proposed: the theory of aggressive resemblance and the theory of alluring resemblance. According to the first, a predator resembles his environment in order that he may sneak up on his prey and catch him unawares. He blends into the background to such a degree that he becomes invisible to the animal that is to serve as his dinner. The white color of the polar bear and of the arctic fox is explained on this basis.

This theory is open to the same objections which have been advanced against the theory of protective resemblance. In addition, the factor of movement must be considered. Animals that appear to be protected by a sort of camouflage achieve that protection by remaining absolutely still. They quickly become visible as soon as they move. However, in order to capture his prey, a predator must move, and it is hardly likely that he would remain invisible to his prey under such circumstances.

The other type of similarity to the background to be found in a predator, alluring resemblance, is found in organisms that are passive in the pursuit of their prey. Instead of coming on its prey unseen, it entices the prey to come to it. For instance, there is a spider in Java which is supposed to entice butterflies as its prey by its resemblance to the excrement of birds. There is a lizard in Algeria which has red spots on its tongue. These resemble a desert flower to such an extent that it is believed insects approach it, only to be devoured.

Again, this theory, too, is open to the objections that have been advanced against the idea of protective resemblance.

C. Warning Coloration

Another difficulty of the idea of protective resemblance is the fact that there are some organisms which actually stand out from their environment. They are not only neutral, failing to blend with the environment, but they are actually brilliantly colored in such a way as to stand out from the environment. This has given rise to the theory of warning coloration. Animals supposed to be warningly colored are those which are dangerous or unpalatable in some way. These are conspicuously colored in order to advertise this fact. A predator may try one of these animals once but soon learns to avoid a strikingly colored animal.

Probably the best example of an animal supposed to be warningly colored is the skunk. Instead of having the dull brownish-gray agouti pattern of most wild animals, his fur is a solid black with a conspicuous white stripe. Other examples of animals supposed to be warningly colored are the yellow jacket, the Gila monster, and the blister beetle.

1. Distastefulness a Subjective Judgment

But there are difficulties also with this theory. For one thing, it is difficult to say that an animal which is distasteful or unpalatable to man is also distasteful or unpalatable to a predator. Such a decision is highly subjective, and it is hard to believe that all animals have the same tastes as man. The studies of McAtee on the stomach contents of birds emphasize this fact. The chinch bug is said to be warningly colored and is supposed to have an objectionable taste. But McAtee found that this bug was eaten by 29 species of birds, three of which — the meadow lark, bobwhite, and brown thrasher — ate more than 100 bugs in a single meal.[64] Either the bug is not distasteful to the birds, or the birds do not learn.

2. Reighard's Studies of Reef Fish

The experiments of Dr. Reighard are also interesting. He worked with a number of brilliantly colored reef fishes in the Gulf of Mexico. It was generally believed that these were warningly colored and were distasteful to potential predators. The most common predatory fish in this area is the gray snapper. It was first determined that the predator could distinguish colors by coloring artificially a number of *Atherinas,* small fish on which the gray snapper ordinarily feeds. Those that were red were made disagreeable by sewing into their mouths pieces of jellyfish tentacle. At first these were eaten, but finally the fish learned to reject them. When the experiment was begun again after a three-week lapse the gray snapper still rejected the red-colored fish.

After this, some of the highly colored reef fish were tossed to the gray snapper. These were eagerly eaten, not only once but repeatedly. Dr. Reighard concluded that these reef fish were protected in their normal habitat, not by the fact that they were warningly colored, but by the fact that

Figure 11. Reef Fish. These brightly colored fish were at one time thought to be examples of warning coloration. It was assumed that they were distasteful to potential predators and hence not eaten. Reighard's experiments showed that, as far as the forms he studied were concerned, this was not the case. (Courtesy Chicago Natural History Museum)

the gray snapper usually takes its prey with a swift rush, and in the neighborhood of the sharp reefs did not dare risk injuring itself.[65]

3. Evidence for a Degree of Warning Coloration

The work of Frank Morton Jones, on the other hand, does indicate a degree of protection for some brightly colored insects. "Bird tables" provided with water and food were set up on the edge of a woodland. During each experiment an average of 50 freshly killed insects were arranged on a tray. Bird visits were recorded, and at intervals the insects remaining were tabulated. He found that the majority of insects are more or less palatable or are eaten at least occasionally, that large insects are favored over similar forms of smaller size, and that a number of species with very conspicuous black and yellow markings or brilliant metallic colors are very unacceptable. He also found that none of the insects which were in the group of most frequently eaten insects had a conspicuous pattern, at least when the insect was at rest. At the same time, a number of other types of color pattern conspicuous to the human eye do not seem to be associated with a lower-than-average acceptability. Finally, he found that the most strikingly marked and unacceptable species were those which feed on the milkweeds (Asclepiadaceae) and the dogbanes (Apocynaceae), plants with acrid or poisonous juices.[66]

4. Warning Coloration Evaluated

These experiments certainly indicate that birds are able to distinguish between very conspicuous and dull-colored insects and between very nauseous and harmless or tasty insects. Nor are these facts out of keeping with the creation account. It is very possible that God endowed some of His creatures with this sort of protection, just as it is possible that He provided some organisms with an inconspicuous pattern.

It is doubtful, however, that these data indicate an ability in birds to discriminate between minor variations of these properties of color and taste. And it is that ability which birds would have to have if this conspicuous pattern developed by evolution. It is difficult to believe that brilliant color developed in one step. It is generally assumed that it was a gradual process in which one insect or a few insects were slightly more brightly colored than other members of the same species and that this coloring served as a sort of warning marker. But there is no evidence at all that birds or predators can discriminate between such minor variations.

Then, too, there is no evidence at all that this conspicuous pattern has developed by selection or evolution. It is just as reasonable to assume that God gave to these animals at Creation the protection which they have in their brilliant colors.

Robson and Richards summarize their discussion of warning coloration by saying that the great extent to which certain groups usually supposed to be distasteful are preyed on cannot but make one hesitate to regard them as specially protected. They conclude by saying that even though a selective attack constituting a very small part of the total predation might lead to important evolutionary changes, the degree of selective attack recorded, unless deceptively low, is minimal compared with the enormous changes that such attacks are supposed to have brought about.[67]

D. Mimicry

Another explanation for bright color patterns in animals is the theory of mimicry. According to this theory, an edible species imitates or mimics an inedible one. Actually two forms of mimicry are proposed: Batesian mimicry, according to which an edible species mimics or imitates an inedible one; and Muellerian mimicry, according to which two or more inedible species have evolved the same pattern. Muellerian mimicry assumes that some members of the inedible species will be eaten until the predator learns to avoid animals with that particular pattern. When two or more inedible species evolve the same pattern, they economize on the number eaten experimentally. Thus they spread this "experimental" loss among them.

Most of the examples of mimicry are from the insects and spiders. In these groups the greatest number of examples are to be found among the moths and butterflies, the bees and the wasps, and the various kinds of flies. Most of these are from tropical species. Probably the most commonly cited example of mimicry is that of the viceroy butterfly (*Basilarchia archippus*), which is said to mimic the monarch butterfly (*Anosia plexippus*). The viceroy is the mimic and the monarch the model. The monarch is distasteful to humans — it feeds on the milkweed which has an acrid juice — and presumably it is distasteful also to its predators. The viceroy, by resembling the monarch, profits from the disagreeable taste which the monarch presumably has, and is protected by it.

1. Distastefulness in the Models

There are a number of objections to the theory of mimicry. In the first place, there is seldom any real proof that the model is distasteful. The experiments that have been made have by no means been conclusive. True, there is some evidence that some insects are distasteful to birds, and it is a fact that insects feeding on plants with acrid or poisonous juices are apparently distasteful. But it has by no means been established that the majority of those insects and spiders regarded as models are distasteful.

2. The Real Enemies of Butterflies and Moths

Another difficulty is concerned with the supposed enemies of insects, particularly of butterflies and moths. It is generally assumed that since these are aerial insects, their chief enemies are birds. Poulton has supplied a number of instances in which attacks by birds upon butterflies and moths presumably occur. But some of them are observations

Figure 12. Mimicry. The monarch butterfly *(Anosia plexippus)* is believed to have a disagreeable taste and is presumably avoided by predators for that reason. The viceroy butterfly *(Basilarchia archippus)* is believed to have developed a mimicking wing pattern similar enough to the wing pattern of the monarch to fool potential predators. Thus it profits from the bad taste of the monarch. The monarch is above, the viceroy below. (Redrawn from Hegner's *College Zoology,* Macmillan, by permission)

made on birds in captivity, and it is generally agreed that captivity reactions are not reliable guides to normal behavior. McAtee in examining the stomach contents of 80,000 birds found only 87 adult butterflies, and 69 of these were found in a single species of bird, the pigeon hawk.[68] This finding would certainly throw doubt on the contention that birds are important predators of moths and butterflies.

Heikertinger, who has investigated this problem, believes that birds rarely eat butterflies.[69]

3. *The Visual Pattern Seen by Predators*

Even assuming that birds are the chief predators there is no evidence that they see the same parts of the spectrum that we see. Indeed, there is evidence that some birds — chickens, doves, and kestrels — do not see colors as we do.[70] If birds do not see the same visual areas that we do, then the pattern that they see is probably a different one, too.

4. *Museum Specimens and Mimicry*

Still another difficulty is that decision as to the mimicry pattern is usually made on the basis of museum specimens. Most cases of mimicry have been discovered not out in nature but by an entomologist working with his collections in a museum. Sometimes, however, museum specimens, because of the way in which they are dried and mounted, are more alike than living specimens. If this is the case, the predator might be deceived by the museum specimens, but would hardly be deceived by the living specimens.

5. *Other Problems of the Mimicry Theory*

Merrell questions whether the resemblance of the viceroy to the monarch is actually an example of Batesian mimicry or for that matter even of Muellerian mimicry. He points out that recent evidence has shown that the viceroy, though more palatable to birds than the monarch, is eaten somewhat less often than other butterflies. He says that while the whole subject of mimicry is of extreme interest, much work remains to be done to clarify many of the questions in the field.[71] Sheppard accepts mimicry but says, "Unfortunately no direct experiments to test the effectiveness of mimicry in the wild have ever been undertaken." [72]

Robson and Richards summarize their discussion of mimicry by concluding that the data which we have are not sufficiently quantitative to be very conclusive. They point out that there are few, if any, pairs of model and mimic in which all of the desirable evidence is available for that particular pair. They believe that it is dangerous to use the mimicry theory as one of the main lines of support for natural selection and evolution.[73]

E. Sexual Selection

Another explanation for brilliant colors among animals, one which was stressed especially by Darwin, is sexual selection. Evolutionists have assumed that characters such as the bright color of the male are due to the fact that in the course of time females have always chosen the most brightly colored males as their mates. It is generally assumed that both sexes were originally dull-colored. Gradually, however, individual males developed some color, and this aided those particular individuals in gaining the females. These colored males became the fathers of the next generation and passed on the bright colors to their descendants. This process continued for many generations, and in the course of time many of the males acquired the bright color that characterizes them in some species. In addition to the brilliant color of the male, other characteristics that are believed to have developed as a result of sexual selection are the mane of the lion, the crests of certain male birds, the feathery tails of some crustaceans, and weapons used in fighting, such as spurs, antlers, horns, and teeth.

1. Female Choice

There are a number of objections to this theory. First of all, it appears that only in very few cases does the female actually exercise choice with regard to the male with whom she mates. Among most animals it is the male who makes the choice if any choice is made. Yet there are few instances in which the female is brightly colored. The only instances in which female choice may occur are in such birds as the ruff, the blackcock, and probably the various species of birds of paradise.[74]

2. *The Aesthetic Sense of Animals*

Then, too, this theory presupposes that the female has an aesthetic sense. There is no evidence at all that any animal has the sense of beauty that man possesses. Certainly there is no reason for the development of these brilliant colors if they cannot be appreciated by the female.

3. *Display Characters*

Many evolutionists, recognizing the problem, have suggested that many of these characters regarded as having developed by sexual selection are intended as display characters, to call attention to the male, and are not intended to appeal to the aesthetic sense of the female. It should be pointed out, though, that in some cases sexual display cannot be favorable to the male who has developed this particular behavior pattern. In the case of some of the newts, courtship takes place after the little packets of sperms, the spermatophores, have been deposited on the bottom of the pond. This courtship behavior cannot favor one newt over another, for how can the female know which newt has produced which spermatophore? This same situation occurs in some of the migratory birds. In warblers the courtship display occurs after the birds have already paired off for the season.[75]

Huxley believes that this sort of behavior favors the species as a whole, that it stimulates the female so that more eggs are produced and fertilized. But this cannot account for the development of display characteristics. For if this were the case, the male who developed the behavior patterns characterizing this courtship display would not have been favored. He would not have been the father of more progeny than the male who did not develop this behavior pattern. The latter, too, would have left progeny and within the species there would have been some males showing this pattern and others not. Yet so far as is known, all males in a given species show this pattern and not just a certain group of males.

4. Harmful Secondary Sex Characteristics

It might also be pointed out that some characteristics that are supposed to have developed by sexual selection are actually harmful to the organism. That is the case with the train of enormously overgrown tail-covert feathers found in the peacock, which are so long and cumbersome that they are actually a handicap in flight. The beautifully adorned wings of the male argus pheasant are of little value in flight, for the male bird is able to fly only for short distances.[76]

5. Sexual Selection Evaluated

Robson and Richards conclude that most secondary sexual characters should be classified as apparently of no value so far as the survival of the form is concerned. They also point to the sporadic distribution among species of such structures. In some groups they are very common, in other groups rare.[77] Huxley himself says that it has now become clear that the hypothesis of female choice and selection between rival males irrespective of general biological advantage is inapplicable to the great majority of display characters.[78] While he believes that they have developed by selection, he believes that other factors are also involved. He points out that intrasexual selection between males of the same species would be of little importance in monogamous species and would be of advantage only in polygamous species.[79] Yet he says that Darwin's theory, though wrong in many details, was essentially right, since no other explanation for the bulk of characters concerned with display in the male is possible.[80]

NOTES

1. Allan, H. H. "Natural Hybridization in Relation to Taxonomy," *The New Systematics*, ed. Julian Huxley (Oxford: Oxford University Press, 1940), p. 516.
2. Kraus, Bertram S. *The Basis of Human Evolution* (New York: Harper and Row, 1964), p. 30.
3. Ross, Herbert H. "The Logical Bases of Biological Investigation," *BioScience*, XVI, 1 (January 1966), 15.

4. Dobzhansky, Theodosius. *Genetics and the Origin of Species* (New York: Columbia University Press, 1941), p. 364.

5. Hadorn, Ernst. *Developmental Genetics and Lethal Factors* (London: Methuen, 1961), p. 41.

6. Dobzhansky, Theodosius. "Evolution of Genes and Genes in Evolution," *Cold Spring Harbor Symposia on Quantitative Biology*, XXIV (1959), 22.

7. Rensch, Bernhard. *Evolution Above the Species Level* (London: Methuen, 1959), p. 279.

8. Stebbins, G. Ledyard, Jr. *Variation and Evolution in Plants* (New York: Columbia University Press, 1950), p. 506.

9. De Beer, G. R. "Embryology and Evolution," *Evolution*, ed. G. R. De Beer (Oxford: Clarendon Press, 1938), p. 66.

10. Dobzhansky, "Evolution," p. 23.

11. De Beer, "Embryology and Evolution," p. 70.

12. Gregory, William King. *Evolution Emerging* (New York: Macmillan, 1951), I, 361.

13. Stebbins, pp. 489 f.

14. Eisner, Thomas, and Meinwald, Jerrold. "Defensive Secretions of Arthropods," *Science*, CLIII (1966), 1344.

15. Keith, Sir Arthur. *The Human Body* (London: Williams and Norgate, 1912), pp. 236 f.
    Keith, Sir A. "The Nature of Man's Structural Imperfections," *Nature* (London), CXVI (1925), 867–869.

16. Hooton, Earnest Albert. *Up from the Ape* (New York: Macmillan, 1946), p. 224.

17. Miller, J. F. A. P. "The Thymus and the Development of Immunologic Responsiveness," *Science*, CXLIV (1964), 1519.

18. Hooton, pp. 222–224.

19. Dobzhansky, "Evolution," 23.

20. Mabry, Tom J., Alston, R. E., and Turner, B. L. "The Biochemical Basis of Taxonomy," *The Science Teacher*, XXXII, 9 (December 1965), 20.

21. Cavill, G. W. K., and Robertson, Phyllis L. "Ant Venoms, Attractants and Repellents," *Science*, CXLIX (1965), 1342.

22. Simpson, George Gaylord. "Organisms and Molecules in Evolution," *Science*, CXLVI (1964), 1537.

23. Mosher, H. S., Fuhrman, F. A., Buchwald, H. D., and Fischer, H. G. "Tarichatoxin-Tetrodotoxin: A Potent Neurotoxin," *Science*, CXLIV (1964), 1100.

24. Fitch, Walter M., and Margoliash, Emanuel. "Construction of Phylogenetic Trees," *Science*, CLV (1967), 283.

25. Hooton, pp. 44 f.
26. Yerkes, Robert M., and Yerkes, Ada W. *The Great Apes* (New Haven: Yale University Press, 1929), p. 550.
27. Wiener, Alexander S., and Moor-Jankowski, J. "Blood Groups in Anthropoid Apes and Baboons," *Science,* CXLII (1963), 68.
28. Hooton, p. 46.
29. Zinsser, Hans, Enders, John F., and Fothergill, Le Roy D. *Immunity: Principles and Application in Medicine and Public Health* (New York: Macmillan, 1939), pp. 113–115.
30. Blum, Harold F. *Time's Arrow and Evolution* (Princeton: Princeton University Press, 1951), pp. 182–188.
31. Rensch, p. 65.
32. Buettner-Janusch, John, and Hill, Robert L. "Molecules and Monkeys," *Science,* CXLVII (1965), 838–842.
33. Huehns, E. R., Dance, N., Beaven, G. H., Hecht, F., and Motulsky, A. G. "Human Embryonic Hemoglobins," *Cold Spring Harbor Symposia on Quantitative Biology,* XXIX (1964), 327.
34. Carlson, Anton J., and Johnson, Victor. *The Machinery of the Body* (Chicago: University of Chicago Press, 1948), p. 279.
35. Blum, p. 131.
36. *Reader's Digest,* LVII (July 1950), 137.
37. Patten, Bradley M. *Human Embryology* (Philadelphia: Blakiston, 1946), pp. 549–560.
38. Ibid., pp. 460 f.
39. Hooton, pp. 218 f.
40. Buchsbaum, Ralph. *Animals Without Backbones* (Chicago: University of Chicago Press, 1948), pp. 39 f.
41. Ehrlich, Paul R., and Holm, Richard W. *The Process of Evolution* (New York: McGraw-Hill, 1963), p. 66.
42. De Beer, "Embryology and Evolution," p. 60.
43. Needham, Joseph. "The Biochemical Aspect of the Recapitulation Theory," *Biological Reviews,* V (1930), 150 f.
    Needham, J. *Advances in Modern Biology* (Moscow: 1935), IV, 239. Quoted in De Beer, "Embryology and Evolution," p. 60.
44. Simpson, George Gaylord. "Organisms and Molecules in Evolution," *Science,* CXLVI (1964), 1537.
45. Stebbins, p. 492.
46. De Beer, "Embryology and Evolution," pp. 62 f.
47. Merrell, David J. *Evolution and Genetics* (New York: Holt, Rinehart and Winston, 1962), p. 90.
48. Carter, G. S. *Animal Evolution* (London: Sidgwick & Jackson, 1951), pp. 323, 326.

49. De Beer, "Embryology and Taxonomy," *The New Systematics,* ed. Julian Huxley (Oxford: Oxford University Press, 1940), p. 374.

50. De Beer, "Embryology and Evolution," p. 61.

51. Garstang, Walter. "The Theory of Recapitulation: A Critical Restatement of the Biogenetic Law," *Journal of the Linnaean Society of London (Zoology),* XXXV (1922), 81–101.

52. De Beer, "Embryology and Evolution," pp. 58 f.

53. De Beer, "Embryology and Taxonomy," pp. 375 f.

54. De Beer, "Embryology and Evolution," p. 59.

55. Schultz, Adolph H. "The Specializations of Man and His Place Among the Catarrhine Primates," *Cold Spring Harbor Symposia on Quantitative Biology,* XV (1950), 50.

56. Ibid., p. 47.

57. Stebbins, p. 488.

58. Robson, G. C., and Richards, O. W. *The Variations of Animals in Nature* (New York: Longmans, Green, 1936), p. 313.

59. McAtee, W. L. "Effectiveness in Nature of the So-Called Protective Adaptations in the Animal Kingdom, Chiefly as Illustrated by the Food Habits of Nearctic Birds," *Smithsonian Miscellaneous Collections,* LXXXV, 7 (1932), 144.

60. Milne, Lorus J., and Milne, Margery J. "How Animals Change Color," *Scientific American,* CLXXXVI, 3 (1952), 64.

61. Von Frisch, Karl. *Bees: Their Vision, Chemical Senses, and Language* (Ithaca: Cornell University Press, 1950), pp. 8 f.
Michener, Charles D., and Michener, Mary H. *American Social Insects* (New York: Van Nostrand, 1951), pp. 9 f.

62. Robson and Richards, p. 234.

63. Ibid., p. 313.

64. McAtee, p. 44.

65. Reighard, Jacob. "An Experimental Field Study of Warning Coloration in Coral-Reef Fishes," *Department of Marine Biology of Carnegie Institute of Washington, Papers from the Tortugas Laboratory,* II, 9 (1908), 261–321.

66. Jones, Frank Morton. "Insect Coloration and the Relative Acceptability of Insects to Birds," *Transactions of the Royal Entomological Society of London,* LXXX (1932), 345–371.

67. Robson and Richards, p. 251.

68. McAtee, p. 60.

69. Robson and Richards, p. 252.

70. Hess, C. *Vergleichende Physiologie des Gesichtssinnes* (Jena: Gustav Fischer, 1912), pp. 9–15.

71. Merrell, p. 12.

72. Sheppard, P. M. "The Evolution of Mimicry: A Problem in Ecology and Genetics," *Cold Spring Harbor Symposia on Quantitative Biology,* XXIV (1959), 132.

73. Robson and Richards, pp. 264 f.

74. Huxley, Julian. *Man in the Modern World* (London: Chatto and Windus, 1950), pp. 89–91.

75. Ibid., pp. 89, 92.

76. Huxley, *Man in the Modern World,* p. 184.

77. Robson and Richards, p. 296.

78. Huxley, J. S. "The Present Standing of the Theory of Sexual Selection," *Evolution,* ed. G. R. De Beer (Oxford: Clarendon Press, 1938), pp. 20 f.

79. Ibid., p. 24.

80. Huxley, *Man in the Modern World,* pp. 86 f.

6. Fossils and Geographical Distribution

There are two areas which present problems for us in reconciling the account of Creation in Genesis with the facts and evidences that we find. These are the fossils and the geographical distribution of plants and animals. The fact that there are a great many forms found as fossils which do not exist today would seem to indicate that some change has taken place. Then, too, the fact that we find certain species of plants and animals limited to small areas of the earth's surface is difficult to explain on the basis of the Bible account. It is these two evidences that we want to examine carefully in this section.

How Fossils Are Formed

Let us look first at the fossils. These are the hard parts of plants and animals which have been preserved by petrification. Sometimes bones and teeth are preserved by having their pores filled with mineral matter, and in this case the hard material of the bone or tooth remains intact and unaltered. In other cases the original substance of the hard part is dissolved away and replaced, often particle by particle, by mineral matter, such as silica or carbonate of lime. Wood is commonly preserved in this way, and the process may be so delicate that the cells and other microscopic structures of the wood are preserved even after all the organic matter has disappeared. In addition to fossils themselves, we find evidences of plants and animals no longer alive in the form of casts, footprints, insects preserved in amber, whole animals preserved in ice, and the like.

We must admit, of course, that fossils are quite common and, further, that many of them, or even most of them, are different from the plants and animals that we know today. It is also true that we find the fossils grouped together so that certain kinds of fossils are characteristic of certain rock layers.

The evolutionist believes that the fact that many fossils are quite different from the forms we know today is evidence that evolution has taken place. He believes, too, that in many cases it is possible to arrange the fossils in a sequence so as to show how evolution has taken place.

The Fossil History of the Horse

The most famous of these fossil series is that of the horse. It is traced from an animal about the size of a fox terrier, known as *Hyracotherium* or *Eohippus*, through several forms which are said to represent steps in its evolutionary development to our present horse. In general the trend in horse evolution is supposed to have been toward an increase in size, a lengthening of the limbs, a reduction and loss of toes, and a change in dentition so that the modern horse is fitted as a grazer. *Eohippus* had an arched back and had four toes on its front feet, with three toes and remnants of two others on its hind feet. Its teeth had low crowns and rough surfaces. Fossils of this form are found in Wyoming and New Mexico. It is supposed to have lived in the Eocene period. Later in this same period *Orohippus*, a slightly larger horse, is supposed to have evolved. Its fossils, too, come from Wyoming and New Mexico. This form, in turn, gave rise to a still more advanced Eocene form, known as *Epihippus*. In the Oligocene period *Mesohippus* is supposed to have developed. It was between 18 and 24 inches tall and had three toes on each foot. The middle toes on all four feet were the largest. Later *Miohippus*, a little larger but quite similar, is supposed to have evolved. In the early part of the Miocene period, or Lower Miocene, *Parahippus*, a transitional form between *Miohippus* and *Merychippus,* which followed it in the Middle Miocene period, developed. *Merychippus* had long-crowned, fully cemented molars. It had three toes, but the lateral toes never reached the ground, so that it was functionally one-toed. It was followed by *Protohippus* in the late or Upper Miocene, and *Pliohippus* in the Pliocene period. The latter is the first one-toed horse and was about 40 inches tall. *Protohippus* is also supposed to have given rise to *Hipparion* in the Miocene, and this form persisted as a sort of side branch into the Pliocene.

Pliohippus is supposed to have given rise to *Plesippus,* which shows no trace at all of the lateral toes, and this form in turn gave rise to the modern horse, *Equus,* which is supposed to have appeared in the Upper Pliocene period. Until the Miocene, horses are supposed to have been browsers. In the Miocene some of the horses gave up browsing and took to grazing. These grazers became ancestors of the modern horse. Most horse fossils are known from American rocks: only a few are found in European formations.

Horse evolution today is no longer regarded as a straight line development, but rather as a much-branched type of development in which a great many forms become extinct without giving rise to the modern forms.

Evaluating the Fossil Evidence

There are some possible explanations for the various findings and phenomena which may help us reconcile their existence with the Biblical account. We want to discuss these. In addition, there are many problems which fossils pose for the evolutionist, and we want to describe these. Then, too, we want to point out that the fossil record, even today, a hundred years after Darwin, is at best a very incomplete and sketchy one.

1. Problems of Fossil Classification

First of all, there is a real problem in classifying organisms which we know only as fossils. The paleontologist has

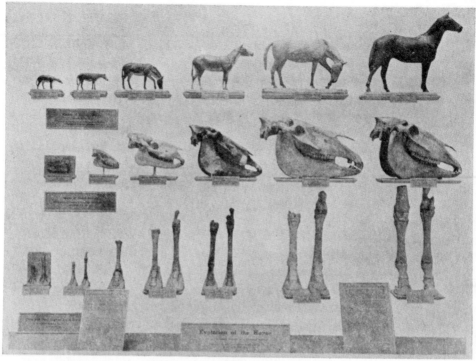

Figure 13. The Evolution of the Horse. Top: restorations of the different stages from *Eohippus* to *Equus*. Middle: skulls, showing tooth structure and arrangement. Bottom: foot structure, showing gradual loss of toes. All are to scale. (Courtesy Chicago Natural History Museum)

only the remnants of the skeleton to work with, and often these are only fragments. As Davis points out, the paleontologist must infer the major part of each functional system, the functioning of those systems, and the conditions under which they functioned. Certainly, as he says, these limitations are extremely difficult, often insurmountable. The problem is great enough in working with those forms which are similar to forms which are still alive today, but it is even greater in the case of those forms which have no existing counterparts or of lines that have died out completely.[1]

Boyd calls attention to five grave defects in using bones as a basis for classification of human and prehuman remains. Some of his criticisms apply also to fossils of animals and plants. He points out that skeletal characteristics alter rapidly in response to the environment. The form of the skull, for instance, depends partly on the muscles that are attached to it. Differences in skeletal structure may not indicate a difference of specific magnitude at all. Two forms with different skeletons may well belong to the same species; the differences may be due to environmental effects which are not passed on to descendants. Then, too, the characters of the skeleton are dependent upon the action of a number of genes, any or all of which can bring about extensive changes within the species. The exclusive use of skeletal material, he believes, makes the anthropologist the slave of his material. Boyd says that he becomes interested in *Homo osseus*, not *Homo sapiens*. Finally, Boyd says anthropometry — the science of human measurement — and craniometry — the science of measuring the skull — were never very logical, nor were they developed as exact sciences.[2]

There are still other examples of this problem. In 1936 Jenks described a skeleton which he believed to belong to the Pleistocene age. He said that it was quite different from the physical type of modern American Indians.[3] The following year Dr. Aleš Hrdlička published a paper in which he concluded that the skeleton represented a modern Sioux burial.[4]

Stensiö has proposed a new classification of fossil fish in which the geological younger members of the group are postulated in his system as being the structural antecedents of the oldest known forms.[5]

The Pyrotheres were ungulates of a kind. *Pyrotherium* itself was the size of an elephant and was remarkably similar to one. In fact, it would probably be classified with the proboscideans, were paleontologists able to explain its appearance early in the Tertiary in Patagonia. All its structures suggest relationship to the true elephants, but because there is no trace of proboscideans in North America before the second half of the Tertiary — it is believed they were developing in Africa — the origin of the Pyrotheres has been a mystery, and it has been suggested that they were actually marsupials related to the kangaroos or an unusual notoungulate.[6]

2. The Fossil Record an Incomplete and Nonrandom Sample

The chance of a given organism being fossilized is very slight; it is estimated to be not greater than one in a million. Indeed, Simpson estimates that the available fossils represent only a fraction of one per cent of the species which have existed during the evolution of life. Immediate burial is a first prerequisite for fossilization, and this should be such as to exclude the air so as to prevent oxidation of the organism. Usually this burial is effected by water-borne sediment. Thus, the record is not only very incomplete but, as Stebbins points out, a strongly biased sample. In most places where organisms die, their remains are quickly destroyed by other organisms such as the bacteria and fungi of decay. Since fossils are preserved chiefly under water, in water, or in water-soaked ground, nearly all the deposits of terrestrial animals and plants are in or near ancient river or lake beds. Organisms which live in such habitats are more likely to be preserved than those who live in uplands or on mountainsides. This also means that periods of the earth's history when shallow seas, lakes, and large rivers were widespread are more strongly represented in the fossil record than are those periods when mountain ranges were high and there was a much larger proportion of dry land. Another problem is that almost no organisms are preserved in their entirety. Soft parts are very rarely preserved as fossils; the larger or harder an animal or a structure is, the greater its chance of being preserved. Insects which are both small and fragile are preserved in only a few deposits. Plants are most often represented by leaves, wood, and particularly pollen, parts which botanists find difficult to use in classification.

Still another problem is that many past periods are represented by fossil beds which are found in only a small number of places on earth.[7]

Stebbins says that the bias inherent in the fossil record is exactly of the wrong kind for evolutionists who wish to learn how the major groups of organisms originated. In modern floras and faunas the greatest diversity of races and species exist in mountainous habitats, where climate, soil, and other factors can vary greatly in a small area. In such regions also new habitats are opened up much more often than in the flat lowlands, and as a result stages in the origin of modern species can be found most easily in upland regions or on islands which are hilly or mountainous. But these are the places in which the chances that fossils will be preserved are the lowest. Stebbins believes, however, that in spite of these imperfections the paleontologists have been able to supply us with a great deal of information regarding the course of evolution.[8]

Merrell says much the same thing. He says that whole groups of species may be virtually absent from the fossil record because they do not meet the requirements for fossilization, and for that reason the fossil record is by no means a random sample of all previously existing species but only a specially selected group.[9] Scagel et al. call attention to the same problem and agree with Stebbins' point of view that much of the evolution of terrestrial organisms occurred in the upland regions where the fossil evidence has been lost as a result of the forces of erosion and disintegration.[10]

Black reports the unexpected discovery in Central Wyoming of several groups of archaic mammals in late Eocene rock which were previously thought to have become extinct in earliest Eocene times, and he raises the question of how representative of middle Eocene life the mammal faunas which we now know are. He believes this is due to the limited sampling available and feels that the upland communities in which we might expect to find these mammals are unlikely to be represented in the fossil record which we have.[11]

Ehrlich and Holm also believe that fossils must be viewed as a very biased sample of the remains of past life. In addition to some of the problems pointed out by Stebbins, they call attention to the fact that factors favorable to the preservation of plant remains often are not suitable for animal preservation. Acid conditions, which might preserve leaves, will dissolve shells and bones. They agree with Stebbins that the fossil record is nevertheless sufficiently ample and diverse that paleontologists have been able to recognize many patterns and have been able to describe the processes thought to be responsible for their development.[12]

Deevey points out that only about 30 percent of the modern benthic species and individuals — organisms living at the bottom of the sea — have fossilizable parts.[13]

Davis says that the paleontologist has threads of a cross-section disconnected and fragmented because of deficiencies in the record and, further, his study is limited by being restricted to a single system, the skeletal system. All these deficiencies, which are inherent in the record, present a real problem to the evolutionist.[14]

There are some instances, of course, in which whole organisms may be well preserved. Wind-borne materials such as loess or volcanic ash sometimes yield fossils of land-living animals, and mire in bogs and quicksands has also provided fossils of land animals.

Perhaps the most remarkable instance of organisms mired in bogs and quicksands is the death trap found in the Rancho La Brea on the western border of Los Angeles. Here oils have distilled under the influence of sun and wind to form a viscous asphalt in which even large mammals, such as mastodons and saber-toothed cats, have been trapped. It appears that the trapping of one mammal acted as a bait to attract various carnivores that were in turn trapped.

3. The Difficulty of Reconstructing Forms from Their Fossil Remains

Another related problem is the problem of reconstructing forms from their fossil remains. Cuvier thought that, given an ungulatelike tooth, he could infallibly predict that it would be associated with a particular sort of hoofed foot, even though the feet had not yet been found. It was not long until people came to believe that Cuvier could restore a whole animal from one fragment of bone.

It is true, of course, that a great deal can be learned from a single bone, let us say, of a human being. It is often possible to predict the age, sex, height, and other physical characteristics quite accurately. However, it is not possible to predict the exact physical appearance. It should be remembered, too, that this sort of thing is done with living human beings on the basis of thousands and thousands of measurements that have been made. Accurate restorations of extinct forms from one or a few fossil bones are simply not possible. Simpson classifies this supposed ability as "folklore." He goes on to say that this marvelous ability is ascribed to paleontologists, to their great distress. He criticizes many of the restorations that have been made and says that a prudent paleontologist is sometimes appalled at the extent of restoration indulged in by anthropologists. Some of them, he says, seem quite willing to reconstruct a face from a partial cranium, a whole skull from a piece of lower jaw, and so on.[15]

There have been many instances in which the restoration did not match the animal when it was finally found. Such was the case with the many restorations of the mammoth which were found in various museums before the whole animal was found encased in ice in Siberia. And there have been other suggestions, too, which have been shown to be wrong. W. D. Matthew suggested that the Sauropods, one of the extinct lizardlike reptiles, could not walk on land.[16] He believed that they were so heavy that they would have collapsed without water to support their weight. It was his opinion and that of a number of other paleontologists that these animals lived in the water at the edge of the ocean or in marshes or lakes, where part of their weight was supported by the buoyancy of water. However, a set of fossil footprints was recently excavated by Barnum Brown which indicates very clearly that the Sauropods did walk on land.[17]

Among the Mediterranean dry-land snails of the family Helicidae there are some types, belonging to well-differentiated genera distinguished by their different genitalia, which possess shells of nearly identical shape and structure. Rensch discusses other problems of snail classification and calls attention to the problem that this creates for paleontologists who must classify on the basis of empty or fossil specimens without knowing the anatomical details of the snails.[18]

4. Variations Within Living Species; Their Bearing on Fossil Classification

Even assuming that the forms are quite different, it is not possible to state with certainty that all fossils which are different actually belong to different species. It is quite possible, and indeed probable, that many of them are varieties of the same species. This, too, would reduce the number of species found as fossils and not extant today. If we today were to find the fossilized bones of all the varieties of dogs from, let us say, the tiny Chihuahua to the Great Dane, it is unlikely that we would conclude that they were all members of the same species. We would probably conclude that we had at least several different species. But we are living in the age when these animals exist, and we are able to recognize that they are all members of the same species.

This is true also of the various forms which go through several stages in their life cycle. The larva of a butterfly is quite different from the adult. Many of the coelenterates (jellyfishes of various sorts) show a polyp and a medusa stage. In the polyp stage they frequently resemble plants; in the medusa stage they frequently look like the common jellyfish.

Similarly, there are various species in which polymorphic forms occur. In ants, for instance, there are not only two kinds of females as in bees — the workers and the fertile queen — but also several kinds of workers. There is sexual dimorphism — bright-colored males and dull-colored females — in the birds. In some forms there are seasonal variations. In the varying hare, the ermine, and the ptarmigan the animals are white in winter and more or less brownish in summer. Many birds are brightly colored during the breeding season and more or less dull-colored at other times of the year. There are also seasonal generations in the insects and short-lived invertebrates. Individuals hatching in the cool spring are quite different from those hatching in the summer. Dry-season individuals are quite different from wet-season individuals. Mayr points out that seasonal generations have caused confusion and much complication of nomenclature in butterflies.[19] If this is true in the case of forms that are alive today and can be carefully examined, imagine what the result would be in studying fossil remains. Mayr also calls attention to habitat forms which he calls ecophenotypes. These are instances in which different, though genetically identical forms of the same species, are found in different habitats. Habitat forms occur in corals, freshwater snails, and mussels.[20] Indeed, it would be very easy to regard all these different forms of the same species as separate species if we knew them only as extinct forms.

5. Hybrids and Fossil Histories

It is possible, too, that not all the organisms arranged in a series, such as the horse series, actually belong there. It may very well be that some of the fossils are remnants of interspecific and intergeneric hybrids. These are sterile and could make no contribution to the course of evolution. For instance, it is possible to mate a female horse and a male ass.

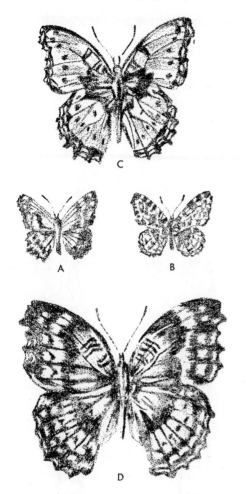

Figure 14. Seasonal Forms of Butterflies. A and B, *Araschnia levana,* summer-form *prorsa* and normal-form. C and D, *Precis octavia natalensis,* dry-season form, and wet-season form *sesamus.* (Redrawn from Lindsey's *Principles of Organic Evolution,* Mosby, after Doflein, by permission)

The offspring is a mule, which is ordinarily sterile and cannot reproduce. If we did not know these three forms today — the horse, the mule, and the ass — and found them as fossils, it is conceivable that they might be arranged in a series to show how the ass evolved into the mule and the mule evolved into the horse. There is no way of doing genetic tests on fossils and no way of identifying sterile organisms. We should have no way of knowing that the mule is a sterile hybrid and not an evolutionary link between the two forms. It is quite possible that a number of the fossils we have found are not good species but are rather sterile interspecific or even intergeneric hybrids.

6. The Possibility of Atypical Fossils

It is also possible that some of the fossils are fossils of organisms which for some reason or other have developed a peculiar or abnormal skeletal structure. We have referred above to the fact that environmental conditions often bring about considerable change in the skeletal structure. Such effects may be brought about by either the external or internal environment — forces without the body or chemical

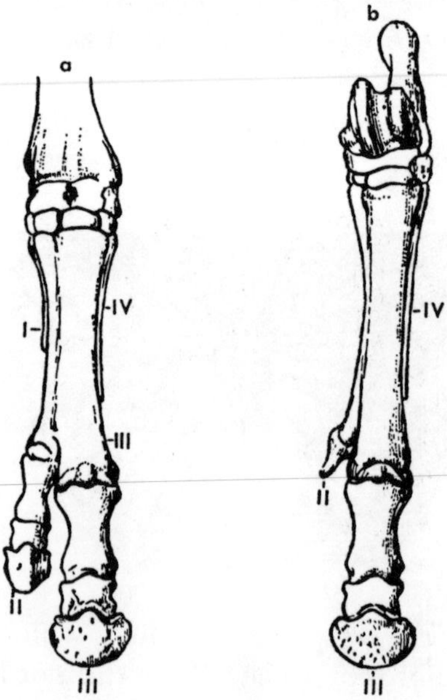

Figure 15. A Modern Multitoed Horse. a is the forefoot, b the hindfoot. Roman numerals indicate the phalanges, or toes. Note the hoof at the end of Toe II. (Redrawn from the American Journal of Science, Vol. 23, by permission)

changes within it. An animal with a peculiar skeletal structure might conceivably be fossilized. This fossilized skeleton would be very different from the fossils of others of the same species.

Occasionally a horse is born with one of the splint bones bearing phalanges or toes. The terminal one may even bear a greatly reduced hoof.[21] This condition is similar to that found in some of the fossils of supposedly prehistoric horses. In modern horses the third digit forms the hoof, and the second and fourth digits have disappeared except for their metacarpals, which are present as the rudimentary splint bones referred to above. It would be very easy to conclude that the fossilized remains of such a horse represented a form ancestral to the modern horse, when in fact this is not the case at all. The four-toed guinea pig stock reported by Huxley, which will be discussed in chapter 8, is another example.

In recent years a wrestler by the name of Maurice Tillet, known professionally as "the Angel," achieved considerable notoriety. Not only did he win a number of bouts and gain recognition in that way, but his physical appearance attracted considerable attention. Apparently he suffered from acromegaly, an endocrine disorder. As a result

Figure 16. Maurice Tillet, "The Angel." In spite of his appearance, M. Tillet, who died in September 1954, was a highly educated and cultured individual. (Courtesy Minnesota Mining and Manufacturing Company)

his head and his face became very large, his hands and his feet thickened, and his torso, too, became broadened. Certainly if his bones were fossilized, it is not hard to believe that they might be regarded as those of a pre-human form. And yet M. Tillet was a twentieth-century human being, and a cultured, well-educated member of our society at that. Similarly, it is possible that pituitary giants, who suffer from a related endocrine disturbance, might well be regarded as examples of a prehistoric race of giants.

It should be pointed out that we must be careful not to press the argument that all fossils are exceptional forms — sterile hybrids or victims of skeletal disorders. In all probability, of course, most of the fossils represent organisms typical of the age and geographical area in which they are found. But it must be granted that at least some of them may be abnormal forms.

7. Supposedly Extinct Forms That Are Still Alive

Then, too, it is possible that some of the forms regarded as extinct are still alive in some parts of the globe. We commonly believe that most of the globe has been explored. However, there are still several land areas on which no white man has ever set foot. And there is one very large area of the globe which has still not been explored at all. That is the sea depths. We know that very bizarre, unusual forms are found there. Some we have seen, but many have never been seen by man. Possibly some of the forms we regard as being extinct are still very much alive in these unexplored areas.

For instance, for many years it was believed that the dawn redwood, *Metasequoia glyptostroboides*, had been extinct for almost 20 million years. However, in 1944 its existence was reported by a Chinese forester, Tsang Wang. He found it growing in the province of Szechwan in central China. Later an entire grove of these trees was found growing in the Shuihsa valley. Far from being·extinct, the tree is still very much alive.

Another living fossil is the ginkgo, or maidenhair tree, which has been planted extensively here in the United States. It is believed to have been preserved by the Chinese, who planted it in their cemeteries. Unlike the *Metasequoia*, it is unknown except where it has been planted and preserved by man.

Another fossil that has been found to be alive is the coelacanth (a fish), *Latimeria chalumnae.* A living specimen was taken off the coast of Africa in 1937. Until that time it was believed to have been extinct for from 50 to 120 million years. A second specimen was taken in December 1952 off Great Comoro in the Indian Ocean, near

Figure 17. A Coelacanth. This specimen was taken in 1952 between Mozambique and Madagascar by a fisherman named Ahmed Hussein. The species was supposed to be extinct for between 50 million and 120 million years. It was about five feet long. (Courtesy *Life* Magazine. © Time, Inc.)

Figure 18. Fossil Coelacanth, *Undina penicillata,* from Bavaria. (Courtesy American Museum of Natural History)

Madagascar, and a third specimen in August 1953. To date over thirty specimens have been captured, all but the first in the vicinity of the islands of Anjouan and Great Comoro in the Comoro Archipelago between Madagascar and Mozambique.

The Somasteroidea, echinoderms, are known from fossils in the lower Paleozoic rocks and until recently were thought to have become extinct in early Ordovician times, about 400 million years ago. A living Somasteroid is now known to have survived in tropical eastern Pacific waters bordering on southern Mexico.[22]

McKenzie reports the discovery of a new ostracod "living fossil" in samples of recent marine sediment collected from several Pacific islands. Members of this genus are very similar to the superfamily Healdiacea, which was a characteristic of the Devonian and Pennsylvanian periods.[23] Still another recently discovered living fossil is the *Neopilina galatheae* which was discovered off the west coast of Mexico during explorations conducted in connection with the International Geophysical Year. It was thought to be extinct since Paleozoic times, possibly as much as 500 million years ago.

The discovery of these living fossils does not suggest that we shall find alive most of the forms which we today regard as extinct, but it does suggest that some forms believed to be very ancient may have survived down to the present day. It shows how hazardous it is to argue the nonexistence of an organism from its failure to appear in the fossil record. These were all believed to have become extinct because they left no fossils, and it may well be that other organisms have existed much earlier or later than they appear in the fossil record.

Criticisms of the Horse Series

As was pointed out earlier, the best-known fossil history is that of the horse. Yet it is generally admitted that only one in several million horses has survived the hazards of fossilization, solution in rock, removal by erosion, and failure to be discovered.[24] For that reason this record can hardly be regarded as even partially complete. The study of horse evolution, says Simpson, has barely begun, and he adds that although the series as arranged would indicate straight line evolution, the fossils themselves indicate a great deal of branching and also several periods of evolution in spurts.[25]

Nor is the change from the browsing habit to the grazing habit, believed to have occurred in the Miocene period, easily accomplished. A browsing horse could not suddenly take to grazing. As Carter points out, such a change demands widespread reorganization of the body. A browser, he says, would almost certainly die if kept from reaching its normal food. He believes that this presents a real problem and suggests preadaptation as a solution.[26]

The Geological Time Scale

We might at this point call attention briefly to the fossil history of the earth as it has been worked out by geologists and paleontologists. The so-called geological time scale is presented in a brief form in Table 3. In discussing this

Era	Time*	Periods	Epochs	Geological Features	Forms of Life
Cenozoic	1	Quaternary	Recent		Dominance of man.
			Pleistocene	Periodic glaciation.	Extinction of large mammals.
		Tertiary	Pliocene	Large continental areas. Mountain building, including Alps and Himalayas. Climate warm at beginning of period, gradually cooling.	First men.
			Miocene		Culmination of mammals and land flora.
			Oligocene		Extinction of ancient mammals; rise of anthropoids.
	60		Eocene		Spread of modern mammals and origin of modern groups. Rise of grasses.
			Paleocene		Origin of modern mammals. Lemurs and tarsioids.
Mesozoic			Cretaceous	Great swamps, followed by formation of Rockies and Andes and cooler climate.	Rise of ancient mammals and birds. Extinction of dinosaurs, pterodactyls, and toothed birds. Spread of modern insects and flowering plants.
			Jurassic	Great areas of lowlands near the seas.	Spread of primitive mammals, rise of toothed birds, spread of pterodactyls.
	200		Triassic	Great desert areas.	Rise of dinosaurs, pterodactyls, and primitive mammals. Spread of cycads and conifers.
Paleozoic			Permian	Mountain building.	Spread of amphibians and primitive insects. Extinction of trilobites and paleozoic corals.
			Pennsylvanian	Mountain building. Warm climate. Humid.	Spread of reptiles. Extensive forests of tree ferns, horse tails, and club mosses.
			Mississippian	Lowlands. Great inland seas.	Spread of ancient sharks. Culmination of crinoids.
			Devonian	Inland seas and gradual emergence of land. Dry climate in eastern North America and western Europe.	Rise of fish and amphibians. First spread of forests.
			Silurian	Great inland seas. Warm, mild climate.	Rise of primitive fish. Sea scorpions. First land plants.
			Ordovician	Great submergence of land. Mild climate extending to arctic.	First primitive fish. Culmination of trilobites. Spread of mollusks.
	540		Cambrian	Lowlands and inland seas. Probably mild climate.	Dominance of trilobites. Rise of mollusks and brachiopods. Sudden appearance of most phyla.
	3,350 or 4,500		Proterozoic Era	An early and a late glacial period.	First fossils. Sponges, protozoa (radiolaria), and algae.
			Archeozoic Era	History obscure.	Living things, but no fossils.

* Approximate time that has elapsed in millions of years.

Table 3: The Geological Time Scale

For evaluation see pp. 196—202

time scale, we shall follow the terminology and suggestions of the evolutionists.

The earliest rocks that can be seen are said to be the Archeozoic. They are known chiefly in North America, Europe, China, and Australia. Fossils are unknown in these formations. The occurrence of graphite in them, however, is taken as proof that at least simple plants existed.

What are believed to be the oldest known fossils are peculiar layered structures found in the limestone at Bulawayo, Southern Rhodesia. These fossils consist of finely layered rings of limestone remarkably like deposits being produced now by lime-secreting blue-green algae. They have been dated as at least 2.6 billion and possibly in excess of 2.7 billion years old.[27] These have not been isolated from the rock, but a series of fossils found in flint deposits in Ontario have been isolated from the rock. These are well preserved structurally and are believed to be about 1.6 billion years old. Of approximately the same age are a series of fossils from Precambrian rock in central Australia. These are believed to be green and blue-green algae and occur in chert.[28] A Dartmouth College geological team headed by Prof. Andrew H. McNair of the Geology Department recently reported the discovery of brachiopods in Precambrian sedimentary rocks in the Shaler Mountains of the Canadian Arctic. The brachiopods are believed to be about 720 million years old.[29] Burdick reports finding spores of plants at least closely related to pines in Precambrian rock at the Grand Canyon.[30]

The Cambrian Outburst

In what is known as the Cambrian period there is literally a sudden outburst of living things of great variety. Very few of the groups which we know today were not in existence at the time of the Cambrian period. One of the problems of this Cambrian outburst is the sudden appearance of all of these forms. All of the animal phyla are represented

Figure 19. Paleozoic Landscape. A restoration of the earth as it is supposed to have appeared in the Paleozoic era. Note the giant tree ferns. (Courtesy Chicago Natural History Museum)

already in the Cambrian period except two minor soft-bodied phyla (which may have been present without leaving fossil evidence) and the chordates. Even the chordates may have been present, since an object which looks like a fish scale has been discovered in Cambrian rock.[31] It is hardly conceivable that all these forms should have originated in this period. And yet there is no evidence for the existence of many of them prior to the Cambrian period.

In the Middle Paleozoic era — the Silurian and Devonian periods — it is believed that there was a gradual emergence of the land from the vast seas which spread over the North American continent during the Early Paleozoic era. Land plants appear during this period. The Devonian period is known especially for its fossil fish, chiefly sharks and lung-fish. The lungfish of this period show rapid evolutionary change, but since the Paleozoic period they have shown practically no change.[32] Lungfish are still extant today. Primitive amphibians also appeared at this time.

In what geologists have called the Late Paleozoic era — Mississippian, Pennsylvanian, and Permian periods — the

south and central portions of North America were submerged. Later they emerged to such a degree that the
coast line extended even beyond its previous limits. This
was the period of the great tree ferns, and the coal beds are
believed to have been formed at this time. Large insects —
some with a wingspread of over two feet — were also found,
but this was particularly the age of amphibians — frogs,
toads, salamanders, etc.

The Mesozoic Era

In the Early Mesozoic — Triassic and Jurassic periods —
we find a great many insects. Most of the modern orders
except the moths and butterflies are represented. Bony fish
appear at this time. The Mesozoic, however, is especially
the age of reptiles. The dinosaurs were terrestrial reptiles
which walked with their bodies clear of the ground. Some
walked on all fours; others walked on their two hind feet
balanced by a long tail. The pterosaurs were winged lizards.
The enaliosaurs, including the ichthyosaurs and plesiosaurs,
were aquatic animals apparently living largely on fish. Birds
and mammals also appear in this period.

The Late Mesozoic era is synonymous with the Cretaceous period. Here the flowering plants appear rather suddenly. The species were different from those we know
today, but many of the genera were the same. Fish were
rather abundant, snakes appear for the first time, and more
than thirty species of toothed birds are known. Toward the
end of this period a great many of the animals which
flourished during the period became extinct.

The Cenozoic Era

The Early Cenozoic era is known as the Tertiary period.
It is divided by geologists into five epochs, the Paleocene,
Eocene, Oligocene, Miocene, and Pliocene. The climate
seems to have been very mild at the beginning of this period.
Toward the middle of the period it appears that there were

vast areas covered with grassy prairies. This is the period during which mammals became very abundant. Of these early mammals only the insectivores — represented today by the moles and shrews — seem to have persisted to the present day. By the Oligocene, however, many of the modern orders of the mammals had appeared.

The Quaternary period, or Late Cenozoic era, is known as the age of man. It includes the Pleistocene epoch and the Recent epoch. Four ice ages are recognized by evolutionists, separated by three interglacial stages. Many people believe that we are living in a fourth interglacial stage today. During the ice ages a great ice cap is believed to have covered much of North America, including all of Canada, the Great Lakes, New York State, and through Ohio, Michigan, Indiana, Illinois, Wisconsin, and Minnesota to the banks of the Ohio and Missouri Rivers. During the interglacial periods the climate is supposed to have been even milder than it is today.

It is believed that from the first appearance of life until what is known as the Pleistocene period the number of species of plants and animals progressively increased. However, since the last Ice Age the absolute number of species apparently has decreased, and that same thing is true also for the number of organisms. In the Late Pleistocene period we find a drastic and unexplained destruction of the mammals. It has been suggested that the glaciers had something to do with the disappearance of these mammals or that possibly even men had something to do with their decrease.[33] But it is generally agreed that seldom in geological history has there been a comparable extinction of great groups.

An Evaluation of the Geological Time Scale

No one will deny that the whole scheme of arrangement in the geological time scale is highly speculative, has many gaps, and presents a great many problems for the evolutionist. Nor is this unexpected. After all, he is working with a very imperfect record. For one thing, only the hard parts of the animal — teeth, bones, etc. — can be preserved. Then, too, the chance of an organism's being fossilized is very slight. And even if it is fossilized, the chance of that fossil being discovered is very slight. Moreover, even if the fossil does come to light, it is quite possible that it will be damaged by wind and water erosion before it can be carefully studied by paleontologists.

1. Dating the Rocks

Let us look at some of the problems in connection with the geological time scale. First of all, there is the problem of dating the rocks. Some dating has been done by means of the uranium time clock, which we have discussed in chapter four. But since it is not often possible to find a rock which contains radioactive materials and also contains fossils, much of the dating of the rock depends upon the discovery of index fossils in the rocks. Certain forms are believed to have been very abundant in different periods and to have been characteristic of those different periods. Thus the fossils are used to date the rocks. But how are the fossils dated? All too often the only basis for dating them is the rock in which they are found. This sort of reasoning is evidently a gigantic argument in a circle. For example, F. H. Knowlton, in discussing the sandstones and shales covering the greater part of Alaska north of the 69th parallel, insists that these sandstones and shales could not be earlier than the Upper Cretaceous period, because he found in them a very few dicot leaves, and he believes that the dicots did not originate until the Middle or Late Cretaceous period.[34] In other words, these rocks were dated not on the basis of the rocks themselves, but on the basis of the fossils which they contained.

Stebbins points out that we must remember that the dating of the fossil beds is always approximate and that it becomes less precise the older the beds are. In dating the older beds which contain the forms most critical for determining how major groups of organisms arose, errors of one or two billion years are to be expected. Consequently, he says, the fossil records of these events will never be sufficiently complete or so precisely understood that we can interpret them in terms of the evolutionary processes which we are following in modern biota except in a general indirect fashion.[35]

2. The Range of Fossil Forms

Another assumption in this type of argumentation that is difficult to maintain is the assumption that forms were equally abundant in all parts of the earth at the same time.

With the possible exception of the earthworm and the ant there is no form today which is even approximately universal in its distribution.

Yet the argument from the geological time table assumes that a form such as the trilobites — the "rock bugs" belonging to the same class as the modern crayfish and lobster — was universally distributed at a particular period of the earth's history and that therefore rocks containing a large number of trilobites must belong to a given geological period.

3. The Small Number of Fossils

Note, moreover, that the whole system is worked out on the basis of a relatively small number of fossils. This is but to be expected because of the slight chance of an organism's being fossilized and the slight chance of the discovery of an intact fossil. For instance, there are relatively few mammalian fossils from the entire Mesozoic era. All of the known Jurassic and Cretaceous mammalian fossils could be put into a small box. The fossil remains that we have are almost entirely tooth and jaw fossils.[36]

4. Forms That Have Not Evolved

Again, there are a number of forms which have not changed in the course of evolutionary history. Presumably the reason for evolutionary changes is the need for an improvement of the form. Presumably, too, all forms should feel this need to improve, because if a form did not improve, it would find itself unable to compete with other forms that had improved. And yet there are many, many forms which show no improvement at all in the course of evolutionary development. The brachiopod, *Lingula*, still alive today, has remained unchanged for several hundreds of millions of years. *Thyrsopteris*, a fern now living on Juan Fernandez Island, closely resembles Jurassic fossils.[37] The ginkgo, the sequoias, the living cycads, and the gnetales have changed but little since geological times.

Literally dozens of examples could be given of forms which are identical with, or very similar to, forms which are found as fossils in rocks supposedly millions of years old. The evolutionists have a special term for these. They speak of them as being bradytelic phyla, genera, and species. This very slow type of evolution is supposed to be associated with an adaptation to a stable environment, or with sessile growth, or with small size, or with nocturnal or secretive habits, or with great individual vitality, or with high fecundity, or with carrion-feeding, or with asexual reproduction, or with occupation of marginal ecological niches, or with long individual life spans. But, as Simpson points out, these same characteristics are found in forms that have evolved very rapidly.[38]

5. Differential Survival

Another problem is that of a differential survival of different forms. Evolutionists believe that it is possible to predict how long a given form will survive. But actual survival of forms does not match this expectation. To be sure, it is but to be expected that there will be a difference between the number expected to survive and those which actually survive. But the differences are so great that they are striking, to say the least. Among the pelecypods (the class to which the modern clam and oyster belong), for instance, a number of forms that should have died out many millions of years ago are still alive. Table 4 presents Simpson's calculations.

Geological Period	Genera Appearing in This Period	Approximate Expectations of Survival to Recent in Per Cent	Number of Expected Survivals	Number of Actual Survivals
Ordovician	33	0	0	1
Silurian	38	0	0	4
Devonian	54	0	0	4
Carboniferous	23	0	0	3
Permian	8	2	0	3
Triassic	68	3	2	20
Jurassic	56	6	3	16
Cretaceous	61	24	15	24
Tertiary	82	88	68	64

Table 4: Expected and Actual Generic Survivorship in the Pelecypods (Adapted from Simpson, George Gaylord. *Tempo and Mode in Evolution* [New York: Columbia University Press, 1944], p. 27)

Diver has studied the proportions of various forms of the snails *Cepaea nemoralis* L. and *C. hortensis* Mueller in shells of the Pleistocene age. He found that the proportions were practically the same as those found in colonies living today.[39] In this case, we should expect some change in the proportion of these in this long period of time, but it has not occurred.

6. Absence of Transitional Forms

Another problem is the absence of what are generally known as missing links — transitional forms — to show the development of the different phyla, classes, orders, etc. In mammals the earliest and most primitive known members of every order already have the basic ordinal characters. This is true of almost all orders of all classes of animals, both vertebrate and invertebrate. It is also true of the classes and of the phyla of the animal kingdom, and presumably it is also true of the plants. Simpson points out that the absence of these transitional fossils is a serious problem which cannot easily be dismissed. He says that in the larger groups — classes, orders, and phyla — transitional groups are not only rare, but practically absent.[40]

Merrell says that the gaps in the fossil record usually seem to occur at crucial stages where, if evolution is a gradual process, transitional forms connecting major groups ought to be found. He says that failure to find any transitional fossils has led many authorities to postulate a different evolutionary mechanism for the origin of higher taxonomic groups. But he believes that no special mechanism is demanded by the evidence.[41]

7. The Record of Plant Evolution

The fossil history of the plants presents a particular problem. This history is extremely fragmentary. Detached leaves, tree trunks, or bits of wood are all that have been preserved. And yet woody parts and leaf impressions are the least diagnostic of all plant parts. The flower parts, which are of great importance in plant taxonomy, are rarely preserved.[42] For many groups there are no fossils at all because of the lack of hard parts. Doubtless, then, a great many mistakes have been made in the study of plant fossils in spite of the very careful and often ingenious work that has been done by some investigators.

So far as the plant record itself is concerned, the first woody angiosperms (flowering plants) appeared in great abundance in the early Cretaceous period, supposedly about a hundred million years ago. For the next 40 or 50 million years differentiation occurred at a gradually decreasing rate. Since the Eocene epoch there have been few, if any, new genera. Most of our modern species date back at least to the middle of the Pliocene epoch. Some of our modern species have existed essentially in their present form since the Eocene epoch 40 or 50 million years ago, and a number have been

practically unchanged since the beginning or the middle
of the Miocene epoch, 20 to 30 million years ago.[43] Reid and
Chandler found that nearly all species of angiosperms found
in the lower Eocene London clay could be referred to living families and that most of them were close to, or identical
with, modern genera.[44]

In recent years several East Indian investigators have
described spores and wood fragments from the Middle and
Upper Cambrian of Kashmir, Spiti, and other Indian locali-
ties. Several scores of spore types have been recorded representing equisetalean plants, "other primitive pteridophytes," and the Pteridospermae. In 1949 Naumova reported
a considerable assemblage of spores from the Lower Cambrian blue clay of the Estonia-Latvia-Lithuania area which
are believed to represent bryophytes and pteridophytes. Andrews in discussing these finds says that while the authors
are insistent that preparations are free of contamination and
although we may accept the existence of pre-Silurian vascular plants, the occurrence of the pteridosperms in the
Cambrian is a matter that will require more substantial
proof.[45]

Stebbins believes that if spores of land plants existed
in strata of the Cambrian age, botanists will need to make
a radical change in their thinking about the evolutionary
history of the plant kingdom.[46]

The Fossil Evidence: *A SUMMARY*

In summary it should be said that the fossil evidence is
not as overwhelming as it first appears. To be sure, the
fossils do present a difficulty for us to which, in the present
state of knowledge, we do not know the full answer. There
is no doubt that many forms have become extinct in the
course of history, and the Bible record would not make
that impossible. It is possible, too, that there were great
climatic changes after or even before the Flood, and these
made it impossible for many animals to survive in the post-

diluvian world. Incidentally, Spencer refers to evidence among the echinoderms (starfish, etc.) which indicates a sudden catastrophe, such as the Flood. He says that much of the Paleozoic echinoderm material is found in thin beds which are isolated in great vertical masses of barren rock. These beds show all of the characteristics of an old sea bed which had been overwhelmed by a sudden catastrophe under conditions which have preserved the animal inhabitants very perfectly.[47] But we must recognize that none of these suggestions fully account for all the fossil observations we are able to make.

Evolutionists themselves recognize that they have problems and acknowledge the precariousness of the fossil evidence. Watson says that while paleontology is useful in studying the evidence of evolution in larger groups, the reasoning and evidence is precarious in dealing with small groups, such as species.[48] Huxley says that the material on which the paleontologist is forced to rely is unrepresentative. He points out that the chief groups which have yielded detailed results of past evolutionary change by means of fossils are the mollusks, the echinoderms, the brachiopods, the graptolites (slender plumelike animals belonging to the same phylum as the jellyfish), and the trilobites. Among the vertebrates, he says, we have many important fossils which he believes reveal the past history of the phylum, but for the most part they serve merely to show the general course of evolution and the broad relationships of the various groups. To show the restricted nature of the material on which the paleontologist relies, Huxley refers to the presidential address of Professor Hawkins to the Geology section of the British Association at Blackpool in 1936. Hawkins drew far-reaching conclusions as to the method and course of evolution on the basis of the echinoderms, mollusks, and brachiopods. No trends in vertebrates and no trends in land animals were discussed by him.[49]

Stebbins also calls attention to the restricted nature of

the fossil evidence. He says that the plant remains available from fossils are not only a minute but also a nonrandom sample. Nearly all the sites favorable for deposition were moist lowlands. Plants of uplands and dry climates have only rarely been preserved. Further, only certain types — the large woody species — have been preserved with any degree of frequency.[50]

Flower says that the fossil record is inadequate and our knowledge of it is incomplete. We have such anomalies, he says, as one Cincinnatian aglaspid, with no others known above the Trempealeauan; one Silurian piloceroid, with no others above the top of the Canadian; and the Mississippian Rayonnoceras with nothing connecting them with other actinocerodis in the Middle or Upper Devonian. Countless other examples of odd, seemingly isolated survivals could be added, he reports.[51]

Nilsson, a botanist, says: "My attempts to demonstrate evolution by an experiment carried on for more than 40 years have completely failed. At least, I should hardly be accused of having started from a preconceived antievolutionary standpoint." Later he says: "It may be firmly maintained that it is not even possible to make a caricature of an evolution out of paleo-biological facts. The fossil material is now so complete that it has been possible to construct new classes, and the lack of transitional series cannot be explained as being due to scarcity of material. The deficiencies are real, they will never be filled." [52]

Arkell and Moy-Thomas tell us that we simply do not know the true explanation of many paleontological relationships. They tell us that we are in the position of an observer who for the first time becomes aware of black men, white men, and mulattoes in the United States. From the mulattoes he might infer that the Negro and white populations are more closely related to each other than to their Negro and white forebears in Africa and Europe, or that there is a trend from black to white, or vice versa.[53] They believe that at best the paleontologist's results are hypothetical and more or less subjective.[54]

Davis goes so far as to say that the facts of paleontology conform equally well with other interpretations which he believes have been discredited by neobiological work. Among the other interpretations he mentions divine Creation, innate developmental processes, Lamarckianism, and the like. He believes that paleontology by itself can neither prove nor refute such ideas.[55]

Geographical Distribution

Another area in which the facts are difficult to reconcile with the Biblical record is that of the geographical distribution of plants and animals. As we indicated before, except for the earthworm and the ant there is no plant or animal which is even approximately universal in its distribution over the globe. Most are confined to somewhat limited areas, and in some cases the range is very narrow indeed. Plant and animal geographers distinguish six large areas of geographical distribution. They are:

Nearctic: Greenland and North America as far south as Mexico.

Palearctic: Europe and the northern part of Asia.

Neotropical: Central and South America.

Ethiopian: Africa, Madagascar, and the southern part of Arabia.

Oriental: The southern part of Asia, Malay States, Sumatra, Borneo, Java, Celebes, and the Philippines.

Australian: Australia, New Zealand, Tasmania, New Guinea, and the Pacific Islands.

Each of these geographical realms has characteristic plants and animals differing from those of other realms. Characteristic animals of the different realms are as follows:

Nearctic: Bowfin (*Amia*) and garpike (*Lepidosteus*); mud-
puppy (*Necturus*); rattlesnake; turkey and blue jay;
skunk, opossum, and raccoon.

Palearctic: certain species of magpie and pheasant; certain
species of deer, antelope, sheep, goats, moles, and oxen.

Neotropical: Certain species of hummingbird, the toucan,
the rhea; New World monkeys, llamas, sloths, armadillos,
anteaters, and peccaries.

Ethiopian: Lungfish (*Protopterus*); secretary bird; African
elephant, giraffe, zebra, several species of rhinoceros,
hippopotamus, gorilla, chimpanzee, several species of
baboon, and most lemurs.

Oriental: peacock, pheasant, jungle fowl; mouse deer, several species of rhinoceros, Indian tapir, Indian elephant,
tiger, some lemurs, gibbon, and orangutan.

Australian: lungfish (*Neoceratodus*); birds of Paradise, cas-
sowary, emu; platypus, kangaroos, and wallabies.

Biologists also distinguish different ecological zones —
forests, grasslands, deserts, etc. — in each of these broader
areas. Zones are even distinguished in the ocean. On every
shore there is a tidal zone, above water at low tide and
under water at high tide. Beyond this is the intertidal or
littoral zone, comprising the broad, gently sloping continental shelves. The seas over this zone, usually not more
than 100 fathoms deep, comprise the neritic zone. At the
edge of the continental shelf the ocean floor drops abruptly.
This expanse of the open ocean is divided into three zones:
the pelagic zone to a depth of 100 fathoms, the bathyal zone
to a depth of 1,000 fathoms, and the abyssal zone beyond
1,000 fathoms, where the sunlight never penetrates. The
littoral and neritic zones have the widest variety of plants
and animals. The deep ocean basins apparently form a barrier to the dispersal of forms living in these zones.

Peculiarities of Distribution

A number of striking things are apparent from any such survey of plant and animal geography and ecology. For instance, North America and South America differ very markedly in their large mammals. South America has a number of rather simple mammals, such as the anteater, the sloth, and the armadillo. Members of the camel family are found only in South America. Fossil camels, however, are found in North America, and Asia has camels today. It is believed that originally North America and South America were separate. The isthmus of Panama was submerged, and during this period North America and South America developed different plants and animals by evolution. At this time the camels crossed into North America from Asia by means of land connections across the Bering Sea. Later the isthmus of Panama emerged, making possible an exchange of plants and particularly of animals between North and South America. In this period the camel traveled down into South America. The Canadian porcupine and the opossum are believed to have traveled from South America to North America at this time. Still later camels became extinct in North America in the great mammalian destruction of the late Pleistocene epoch, but they did not become extinct in South America, where they still are found today.

Primitiveness of Southern Fauna

Another striking thing is the primitiveness of southern fauna (the term for all of the animals of a region) in general, but particularly of the fauna of the Australian zone. This zone is noted for the prevalence of the monotremes (egg-laying mammals) and marsupials (pouched mammals). One of the three genera of lungfish is known only from Australia. Except for the wild dog, which may have been introduced by early man, the rabbit, which was introduced in historical times, and some rodents, there are no placental mammals in Australia.

Peculiarities of Island Fauna

Some islands, too, are characterized by a peculiar fauna. Continental islands, such as the British Isles, have plants and animals quite similar to those of the nearby continents. Oceanic islands, however, which are separated from the continental masses by deep water and which are typically composed of igneous (volcanic) rock, ordinarily have unusual plants and animals. In general they have no land mammals except for bats. Most of the animals are those which can be carried on floating material or can be borne by the wind, such as snails, lizards, insects, and land birds. Plants, too, are quite different. Of Hawaiian plants, for example, 83 per cent of the species are found only on these islands.

Animal geographers report that a whole family of birds of 60 species occurs only on the Hawaiian Islands. Of the 260 species of birds on Madagascar, they tell us, half are found nowhere else. Forty per cent of the species of plants and 96 per cent of the reptiles on the Galapagos Islands live only there. Forty-three species of birds are known only from Jamaica; 74 species of birds only from the Bismarck Islands. Fifteen species of Greenland plants are found only there, and about 75 per cent of the New Zealand plants are found only there.

Areas from Which Certain Forms Are Absent

Another striking thing is the fact that there are large areas from which certain forms are excluded. There are no bears in Africa. New Zealand and Hawaii lack snakes; indeed, the Hawaiian Islands have only seven species of reptiles, and these are skinks and geckos. Australia and New Zealand lack placental mammals except for those which have been introduced. Though the Ethiopian region has the richest mammalian fauna, it lacks completely the monotremes and the marsupials.

Forms Limited to Small Areas

Still another striking thing is the fact that some species are limited to very small areas. That is particularly apparent in the snails. There are a number of instances in Hawaii, where species of these mollusks are confined to very small areas. Apparently they have been unable to travel farther. The snails of the genus *Partula* live in the bottoms of steep-sided mountain valleys. They can cross the bare, knife-edged ridges between the valleys rarely and only with difficulty. For that reason almost every valley has its own distinctive type or range of types. Other forms such as *Achatinella mustelina* also have very restricted ranges. The tendency today is to classify these types as varieties and races rather than as separate species.[56]

The range of the Kankakee mallow *Illiamna remota* occupies an island of only a few hundred square yards in the Kankakee River near Kankakee, Illinois, and a few hundred square yards on Peter's Mountain, Virginia. It has even been suggested that the latter colony is a distinct species.[57] Many insect species occupy only one or a few adjacent caves.

There is a species of violet that is known only from a few square yards in the Hawaiian Islands. Several species of trees there are found only on a 56-acre tract surrounded by lava. Plant geographers are very much concerned about the military development and industrialization of the Hawaiian Islands because some species with very limited ranges are being wiped out.

Geographical Distribution as an Evidence for Evolution

Evolutionists believe that these facts are evidence that evolution has taken place. They believe that species have evolved in almost all areas of the earth. Relatively simple forms or ancestral forms got to these areas in some way or another, and in the course of evolution the present species developed. In many cases forms are limited to restricted areas because they never succeeded in crossing some barrier.

Thus it is believed that Australia has been isolated at least since Permian times with a short-lived continental link at the end of the Cretaceous. This explains not only the presence of the marsupials but also the extraordinary scarcity of the late Paleozoic and Mesozoic land tetrapods which contrast strongly with other southern continents.[58] However, the present geographical distribution of animals is not necessarily believed to be an indication of the place of origin of a given species. It may very well be that a form has died out in the place of its origin and is known only in those places to which it migrated in the course of its evolutionary development.

Wherever the range is extremely limited as in the case of the snails, the violet, and the trees mentioned above, it is believed that either we have a species that is very young and has not had time to spread very far, or that its powers of migration or multiplication, or both, are very limited, or that it is approaching extinction. This last is regarded as a very rare phenomenon, since extinction is believed to occur rather abruptly.

Geographical Distribution and Special Creation

The evolutionist also believes that these facts cannot be explained on the basis of special creation. And we must admit that there is a problem here. It might be postulated that God created the plants and animals and placed them in the areas where we now know them. Australia and the oceanic islands have a peculiar flora and fauna, it might be argued, because God created that for them. However, the Flood makes such an explanation very difficult. Presumably all air-breathing animals that were not on the ark became extinct as a result of that cataclysm. Most plants, too, presumably perished, though it is possible that some of them survived as seeds, on rafts of vegetation, or in other ways. Huxley reports that the Gulf stream has transported seeds in its slow warm drift.[59]

But let us return to our problem. If only those animals on the ark survived, how did they achieve the present distribution? It is possible, of course, that they traveled by means of land bridges from Mount Ararat to the places where they are now found. The development of a land bridge, however, is not as easy as it sounds. It requires tremendous changes in the earth's crust. Heavier rocks, it is believed, must be replaced by lighter rocks if submerged areas are to rise.

At the same time the evolutionist has this same problem. He, too, wants land bridges to explain the migration of animals from one area to another. And if land bridges radiating from Mount Ararat to various parts of the world are difficult to erect, so are the land bridges of the evolutionist.

Some evolutionists have asked: "Why is it that there are no marsupials in Asia and along the Malay Peninsula, where they must have been found in their travels from Mount Ararat?" It is possible to suggest an answer. It may be that these forms have become extinct in Asia and along the Malay Peninsula. Possibly they were able to live in some of these areas for only a very short time and traveled almost immediately to those places included in their present range. The evolutionary scheme itself requires that animals have become extinct in many areas in which they once lived.

Indeed, in this case it requires that these same animals — the marsupials — have become extinct in these same areas. In late Cretaceous and early Tertiary times the marsupials were almost world-wide in their distribution, according to the evolutionists. However, the marsupials could not compete with the placental mammals when they arose, and so died out in all regions except those from which the placental mammals were excluded.[60]

Exceptions to Expected Plant and Animal Distributions

It should be pointed out, too, in considering the evidence from geographical distribution that not all of the earth's areas have the distribution that we would expect according to the evolutionary scheme. Islands often have a peculiar flora and fauna, but not always. On the island of Java, for instance, only a few of the 500 bird species are peculiar, and not a single bird genus is limited to Java. The animals of Madagascar, which is just off the coast of Africa, are most similar not to those of Africa, but to those of Asia. The animals of New Guinea are very similar to those of Australia, but quite different from those of other islands to the north and west which are almost as near as Australia. The animals of Sumatra are more like those of Borneo than like those of Java, though Java is closer to Sumatra than is Borneo.

Nor is there always the variation in insular species that we find in the snails of Hawaii and the turtles of the Galapagos Islands. Kinsey reports that in gall wasps the insular species are far less variable than the continental species. He believes this to be due to the fact that continental species are more common than island species. Yet the fact remains that their being insular species does not make for greater variability.[61]

Other peculiarities are also present. Lowndes reports that of the copepods (an order of the Crustacea) collected in the New Hebrides practically none of the species are endemic (limited to that area); indeed many are identical with British species. Yet they have relatively poor dispersal powers. The ostracods (another Crustacean order), which have relatively good dispersal mechanisms, are represented by a number of endemic forms. There are no endemic forms of spiders on the Scilly Isles, Lundy Island, or the Channel Islands. There is only one endemic form of *Hydracarina* on the Faroes Islands. There are no endemics (definite subspecies) of the myriapods on the Faroes, and no endemics of the mollusks on the Scilly Isles.[62]

Nonadaptive Nature of Differences Betweeen Supposedly Closely Related Species Living in Close Proximity

It is also true that many of the differences between species that are close to one another geographically are not adaptive. In other words, the differences between two such species are not such that they equip the two for their particular habitats. If these species have developed by evolution, then the differences between them should be adaptive. But the differences between the species of Hawaiian land snails are not adaptive. That is also true of the color polymorphism of the various races of *Peromyscus* (the deer mouse), and of the markings of *Buarremon inornatus* (one of the tanagers).[63]

Unexplained Limitations on the Ranges of Organisms

There are a number of cases in which a very limited geographical range cannot be explained on the basis of barriers or of the youth of the species. There is one species of toad found only in Texas, while another species of the same genus (*Scaphiopus*) is found in most of the Western plain states, the Rocky Mountains, and the Pacific Coast. One species of tree frog, *Hyla andersonii*, is found only in New Jersey and the Carolinas; another, *H. versicolor*, is found over most of eastern North America. There is a turtle found only in southwestern New Mexico and the adjoining regions of Mexico. Another species of the same genus (*Gopherus*) is found over most of the southern states.[64]

Other Explanations for Geographical Distribution

Theories and explanations for geographical distribution made by evolutionists have undergone changes from time to time. The continental drift theory was popular after it was first suggested by Wegener, then fell largely into disrepute, and recently has been revived. According to this theory there were at one time only two major land masses:

Gondwana centering around the South Pole and Laurasia in the vicinity of the equator. These masses gradually drifted northward, Laurasia splitting into North America and Eurasia and Gondwana splitting up to form Africa, South America, Antarctica, and the Arabian and Indian peninsulas. The drifting was very slow and not completed until the Tertiary. There is supposed to have been little drifting since Cretaceous times.[65] Recent studies on rock paleomagnetism have suggested that the poles have wandered considerably throughout the history of the earth, and this would seem to support the continental drift theory.[66] One of the main stumbling blocks has been the lack of a possible mechanism to initiate and maintain drift. Recently, however, the concept of spreading of the ocean floor has renewed for many the feasibility of drift. The hypothesis involves slow convection with the upper mantle by creep processes, drift being initiated above an upwelling, and continental fragments riding passively away from such a rift on a conveyor belt of upper mantle. This assumes movements of the order of a few centimeters per annum.[67]

Continental drift is invoked to explain geographical distribution since at one time organisms are supposed to have been able to move freely over the present continents when they were connected, but to have become isolated and separated when the continents drifted apart.

There are still some who question continental drift. Merrell says that the geological evidence for the split is not impressive and the theory poses about as many biogeographical problems as it solves.[68] MacDonald points out that the deep structure of continents places heavy restrictions on any theory of continental drift. A relative motion of the continents must involve the mantle to depths of several hundred kilometers; it is not possible, he says, to imagine thin continental blocks sailing over a fluid mantle.[69] Another theory that has been largely discarded is the age and area hypothesis of Willis. He believed that the size of the organism's range indicated the age of that particular species. Forms that had evolved in comparatively recent times, he believed, show only a restricted range. Forms that are distributed over much of the earth's surface are believed by him to be very old. Gaps in the range supposedly are due to the fact that in these parts of the range the organism became extinct.[70] This theory, too, has largely been discarded so far as species are concerned, though there are many who believe that it still fits larger groups. It is believed that a species may achieve rather wide distribution even though it is a "young" species and that, conversely, a restricted range does not indicate that the species is "young." Evolutionists have objected particularly to Willis' idea that endemic species (species limited to relatively small areas, such as the redwoods of the California coastal valleys) are young. Most evolutionists believe that these forms are usually relict forms that have died out over most of their range, which at one time was quite extensive.

NOTES

1. Davis, D. Dwight. "Comparative Anatomy and the Evolution of Vertebrates," *Genetics, Paleontology, and Evolution,* ed. Glenn L. Jepsen, Ernst Mayr, and George Gaylord Simpson (Princeton: Princeton University Press, 1949), p. 73.

2. Boyd, William C. *Genetics and the Races of Man* (Boston: Little, Brown, 1950), pp. 21 f.

3. Jenks, Albert Ernest. *Pleistocene Man in Minnesota, a Fossil Homo Sapiens* (Minneapolis: University of Minnesota Press, 1936).

4. Hrdlička, Aleš. "The Minnesota 'Man,'" *American Journal of Physical Anthropology,* XXII (1937), 198 f.

5. Dunkle, David H. "Review of 'On the Pectoral Fin and Shoulder Girdle of the Arthrodires' by Erik Stensiö," *Science,* CXXX (1959), 1402.

6. Cameron, Thomas W. M. "Southern Intercontinental Connections and the Origin of the Southern Mammals," *Evolution: Its Science and Doctrine,* ed. Thomas W. M. Cameron (Toronto: University of Toronto Press, 1960), p. 84.

7. Stebbins, G. Ledyard. *Processes of Organic Evolution* (Englewood Cliffs: Prentice-Hall, 1966), p. 134.

8. Ibid., p. 134.

9. Merrell, David. *Evolution and Genetics* (New York: Holt, Rinehart and Winston, 1962), p. 40.

10. Scagel, Robert F., Bandoni, Robert J., Rouse, Glenn E., Schofield, W. B., Stein, Janet R., and Taylor, T. M. C. *An Evolutionary Survey of the Plant Kingdom* (Belmont, Calif.: Wadsworth Publishing Co., 1966), p. 597.

11. Black, Craig C. "Middle and Late Eocene Mammal Communities: A Major Discrepancy," *Science,* CLVI (1967), 62–64.

12. Ehrlich, Paul R., and Holm, Richard W. *The Process of Evolution* (New York: McGraw-Hill, 1963), p. 259.

13. Deevey, Edward S. "Environments of the Geologic Past," *Science,* CXLVII (1965), 593.

14. Davis, p. 73.

15. Simpson, George Gaylord. "Some Principles of Historical Biology Bearing on Human Origins," *Cold Spring Harbor Symposia on Quantitative Biology,* XV (1950), 57 f.

16. Matthew, W. D. "The Pose of Sauropodous Dinosaurs," *American Naturalist,* XLIV (1910), 559 f.

17. Gregory, William King. *Evolution Emerging* (New York: Macmillan, 1951) I, 305 f.

18. Rensch, Bernhard. *Evolution Above the Species Level* (London: Methuen, 1959), p. 94.

19. Mayr, Ernst. *Systematics and the Origin of Species* (New York: Columbia University Press, 1942), p. 26.

20. Ibid., pp. 27 f.

21. Moody, Paul Amos. *Introduction to Evolution* (New York: Harpers, 1953), pp. 72 f.

22. Fell, H. Barraclough. "A Surviving Somasteroid from the Eastern Pacific Ocean," *Science,* CXXXVI (1962), 633.

23. McKenzie, Kenneth G. "Ostracod 'Living Fossils': New Finds in the Pacific," *Science,* CLV (1967), 1005.

24. Boyd, p. 324.

25. Simpson, George Gaylord. *Tempo and Mode in Evolution* (New York: Columbia University Press, 1944), pp. 158 f.

26. Carter, G. S. *Animal Evolution* (London: Sidgwick & Jackson, 1951), p. 272.

27. Ross, Herbert H. *Understanding Evolution* (Englewood Cliffs: Prentice-Hall, 1966), p. 73.

28. Barghoorn, Elso S., and Schopf, J. William. "Microorganisms from the late Precambrian of Central Australia," *Science,* CL (1965), 337.
Schopf, J. William, Barghoorn, Elso S., Maser, Morton D., and

Gordon, Robert O. "Electron Microscopy of Fossil Bacteria Two Billion Years Old," *Science*, CXLIX (1965), 1365.

29. *BioScience*, XVI, 2 (February 1966), 116.

30. Burdick, Clifford. "Microflora of the Grand Canyon," *Creation Research Society*, III (1966), 38–50.

31. Shull, A. Franklin. *Evolution* (New York: McGraw-Hill, 1951), p. 81.

32. Westoll, T. Stanley. "On the Evolution of the Dipnoi," *Genetics, Paleontology, and Evolution,* ed. Glenn L. Jepsen, Ernst Mayr, and George Gaylord Simpson (Princeton: Princeton University Press, 1949), p. 121.

33. Coon, Carleton Stevens. "Human Races in Relation to Environment and Culture with Special Reference to the Influence of Culture Upon Genetic Changes in Human Population," *Cold Spring Harbor Symposia on Quantitative Biology*, XV (1950), 247.

34. Knowlton, F. H. "Geology and Mineral Resources of Northwestern Alaska," ed. Philip S. Smith and J. B. Mertie Jr., *U. S. Geological Survey Bulletin* 815 (1930), pp. 222–224.

35. Stebbins, p. 137.

36. Gregory, pp. 353 f.

37. Stebbins, G. Ledyard Jr. *Variation and Evolution in Plants* (New York: Columbia University Press, 1950), p. 552.

38. Simpson, *Tempo*, p. 137.

39. Diver, C. "Fossil Records of Mendelian Mutants," *Nature*, CXXIV (1929), 183.

40. Simpson, *Tempo*, pp. 105–107.

41. Merrell, p. 43.

42. Stebbins, *Variation*, pp. 515 f.

43. Ibid., p. 526.

44. Reid, Eleanore Mary, and Chandler, Marjorie Elizabeth Jane. *The London Clay Flora* (London: British Museum, 1933), pp. 40–46.

45. Andrews, Henry N. "Evolutionary Trends in Early Vascular Plants," *Cold Spring Harbor Symposia on Quantitative Biology*, XXIV (1959), 217 f.

46. Stebbins, G. Ledyard. "The Synthetic Approach to Problems of Organic Evolution," *Cold Spring Harbor Symposia on Quantitative Biology*, XXIV (1959), 310.

47. Spencer, W. K. "Some Aspects of Evolution in Echinodermata," *Evolution*, ed. G. R. De Beer (Oxford: Clarendon Press, 1938), p. 287.

48. Watson, D. M. S. "The Evidence Afforded by Fossil Vertebrates on the Nature of Evolution," *Genetics, Paleontology, and Evolution*, ed. Glenn L. Jepsen, Ernst Mayr, and George Gaylord Simpson (Princeton: Princeton University Press, 1949), p. 61.

49. Huxley, Julian. *Evolution, the Modern Synthesis* (New York: Harpers, 1943), pp. 31 f.

50. Stebbins, *Variation*, p. 515.

51. Flower, Rousseau H. "Paleontology and Geology: A Review of *Time in Stratigraphy* by Alan B. Shaw," *Science*, CXLVII (1965), 1026.

52. Nilsson, Heribert. *Synthetische Artbildung* (Lund: Verlag C. W. K. Gleerup, 1953), pp. 1185, 1212.

53. Arkell, W. J., and Moy-Thomas, J. A. "Paleontology and the Taxonomic Problem," *The New Systematics*, ed. Julian Huxley (Oxford: Oxford University Press, 1940), pp. 401 f.

54. Ibid., p. 396.

55. Davis, p. 77.

56. Mayr, p. 35.

57. Ross, Herbert H. *A Synthesis of Evolutionary Theory* (Englewood Cliffs: Prentice-Hall, 1962), p. 122.

58. Glaessner, M. F. "Isolation and Communication in Geological History," *The Evolution of Living Organisms*, ed. G. W. Leeper (Victoria: Melbourne University Press, 1962), p. 248.

59. Huxley, Julian. *New Bottles for New Wine* (New York: Harper, 1957), p. 160.

60. Newman, H. H. *The Phylum Chordata* (New York: Macmillan, 1939), p. 388.

61. Kinsey, Alfred C. "An Evolutionary Analysis of Insular and Continental Species," *Proceedings of the National Academy of Sciences, Washington*, XXIII (1937), 5–11.

62. Robson, G. C., and Richards, O. W. *The Variation of Animals in Nature* (London: Longmans, Green, 1936), pp. 135–137.

63. Huxley, *Evolution*, p. 242.

64. Shull, pp. 71 f.

65. Ross, *Synthesis*, p. 301.

66. Ibid., p. 304.

67. Vine, F. J. "Spreading of the Ocean Floor: New Evidence," *Science*, CLIV (1966), 1405.

68. Merrell, p. 75.

69. MacDonald, Gordon J. F. "The Deep Structure of Continents," *Science*, CXLIII (1964), 928 f.

70. Willis, J. C. *Age and Area* (Cambridge: Columbia University Press, 1922).

7. Selection and Isolation

In this section we want to discuss two factors which are supposed to have played a very important role in evolution and in the development of the plants and animals that we now know: selection and isolation. We have had occasion to refer to both before: to selection in connection with Darwin's theory, and to isolation in connection with our discussion of the geographical distribution of plants and animals. The two are somewhat related at least in some of their aspects. In many cases organisms are supposed to have become isolated, and then natural selection is supposed to have worked, producing new forms.

Selective Breeding as Practiced by Man

Darwin was particularly impressed with the results of selection as practiced by man. It is a well-known fact that man by selective breeding has developed races of plants and animals that are quite different from their original wild ancestors. In fact, in some cases the wild ancestor has not yet been identified. By selective breeding man has also been able to "tailor" plants and animals to meet his needs. Some breeds of cattle, for instance, have been developed for milk production; others have been developed for their meat. Some breeds of chickens have been developed for egg production; others, again, for their meat.

Darwin believed that nature itself practiced an analogous selection on plants and animals in their natural environment. It was in this connection that he and his apologists spoke of overproduction, struggle for existence, variation, and survival of the fittest.

Variation in Wild Forms

For selection to operate, a great deal of variation is necessary. It might be well to discuss for a moment the amount of variation available in nature. For some time it was thought that wild type stocks were remarkably uniform, that there was practically no variation in nature. This, of course, would destroy much of Darwin's argument. In recent years it has been demonstrated that there is a great deal of variation in wild plants and animals. Most individuals examined, for instance, have been shown to contain at least one recessive mutation. We know now that a large number of wild forms are highly polymorphic and highly variable.

However, it does not appear that even this variation approaches the variety of forms found in domesticated species.[1] If this is true, then the analogy between natural and artificial selection loses some of its original force. In other words, there is not as much variety for natural selection to work on as Darwin assumed.

Is There Selection in Nature?

The second question to be considered is a more important one, and that is this: Does selection occur in nature? Darwin assumed that those varieties which had somehow acquired a favorable characteristic would be selected to survive over other members of the same species. Apparently he was thinking of selection largely as a matter of life and death. To him only those characters were favorable which prolonged the life of the individual. Today selection is no longer viewed in that way. It is rather obvious that a variation which will increase the fertility or prolong the reproductive period is just as important and perhaps even more important than one which lengthens the life of an animal or protects him against his enemies. And, of course, it must be admitted that selection could favor such characteristics just as well as those which lengthen the life of the individual.

Selection, therefore, is a very complex and complicated

thing. It is not easy to determine exactly how favorable a given characteristic is. For instance, in many cases there is a very high mortality rate in the early stages of the animal's life. For that reason characteristics which are favorable to the organism as an adult may help the cause of evolution very little if they are not favorable to survival in the early stages. Thompson and Parker, for example, found that in the case of the European corn borer, *Pyrausta nubilalis,* at least 90 per cent of the young larvae are killed off before any predators or parasites begin their attacks.[2] This means that favorable characteristics in the adult are not nearly so important as are favorable characteristics in the larvae.

Another striking thing is that in many cases mortality appears to be random. It is not possible to demonstrate that certain varieties are being favored over others. Often what determines which animal survives is not, let us say, the relative speed of the different members of the population, but rather which one is being chased by the predator. It is, of course, possible that selection works differentially among the survivors, and it is this point that selectionists stress. It may be, they tell us, that 99 per cent of the deaths are purely random, but selection can work on the 1 per cent where death is not random. However, it should be noted that in this case the group on which selection can work is a very limited one. If there is not as much variation as Darwin assumed and if selection can work on only a small number, then it may not be so important a factor as Darwin assumed.

Supposed Instances of Selection

There have been some studies which would seem to indicate that selection does occur and that it brings about changes in various populations. Let us look at some of these.

One of the classical ones is that of Weldon.[3] He and Thompson made a series of observations on a common species of crab, *Carcinus maenas,* in Plymouth Sound. A breakwater was constructed there which apparently led to an increase in the amount of silt in the water. Measurement of the carapace (the broad, hard shield of material covering the combined head and thorax) of crabs caught during a period of years after the building of the breakwater showed that the width of the carapace decreased relative to the length of the body. Weldon believed that the narrow carapace was correlated with smaller openings to the gill chambers and that this in turn reduced the amount of silt reaching the gills. Thus the increase in silt favored those animals with the narrow carapace. To test his conclusions further, crabs were caught, divided into two groups, and placed in aquaria. The first group was placed in aquaria containing clay silt in suspension. Those that died had a relatively wider carapace than those which survived. The second group was kept in clean water. After the first moult they were killed, and it was found that they had a relatively wider carapace — as would be expected in silt-free conditions according to Weldon's hypothesis.

Weldon's conclusions have been criticized by a number of men, including Cunningham, Vernon, Pearl, and Robson. They have pointed out that Weldon did not show that the amount of silt had increased in the period under consideration. He merely assumed that it had. Moreover, he did not take into consideration the possible effects of exceptional climatic conditions, such as occurred in 1893. They have also pointed out that while he assumed that a narrower carapace indicated narrower gill openings, he did not actually measure the entrance to the gill chamber itself. They have further pointed out that age may have an influence on the width of the carapace. Nor is any information given on controls from the wild population living in silt-free conditions. Robson and Richards conclude that the objections raised to Weldon's results are so serious that his study cannot be accepted as a good evidence for the efficacy of selection.[4]

Another study is that of Harrison.[5] He reported that in

one of the districts of Yorkshire a colony of the moth *Oporabia autumnata* was originally broken into two parts, one living in a coniferous forest and the other in a birch forest. The moths living in the birch forest were found to be paler in color than those living in the coniferous forest. Harrison believed that the paler forms living in the coniferous wood were more conspicuous to nocturnal birds and bats and were therefore eliminated. He reports that he found fifteen pairs of wings, which he believed to be the remains of moths attacked by predators, on the ground in the wood and that the majority of these were pale, even though in the total population the dark ones outnumbered the pale ones in a ratio of 25:1. Predators were numerous in the coniferous forest but very few in the birch forest, because the trees there were not well grown enough to afford cover.

Robson and Richards point out two criticisms of this evidence. First of all, there is a lack of definitely expressed evidence as to the frequency of enemies in the two woods. Secondly, only a small number of observations were made, and there is no definition of the term "majority" in the statement that the majority of the moth wings found were pale.[6]

Recent Developments Which Seem to Point to Selection

There have been some recent developments in plants and animals that appear at first glance to be occurring as a result of selection. It appears, for instance, that there has been an increase in melanism (dark color) in moths in industrial districts of England. The scale insect (*Aonidiella aurantia*), which has plagued the citrus growers of California, appears to have developed a resistance to cyanide gas which is used to exterminate it. Within the past few years we have been disturbed by the development of strains of micro-organisms which are resistant to the newer antibiotics, such as penicillin, aureomycin, and streptomycin. We have also found that insects, such as flies, have apparently been developing a resistance to DDT. Wheat rust strains

(*Puccinia graminis*) have developed which attack rust-resistant varieties of wheat.

These instances fit very well with the idea of selection. Dark color is thought to be an advantage to moths in areas where soot, smoke, and dirt are very common. It has been suggested that more light-colored moths are being eliminated than dark-colored moths, and this is bringing about an increase in the proportion of dark-colored moths. It would appear, too, that those micro-organisms which are susceptible to the effects of the antibiotics are being eliminated and that only those micro-organisms which in some way or other have developed a resistance to them are surviving. This same situation seems to hold true of flies: it would appear that those flies which are susceptible to DDT are being eliminated and only those which have some resistance to the agent are surviving. A similar situation obtains as to wheat rust; only those strains which can attack rust-resistant wheat varieties can survive.

Yet in view of our experience with other supposed instances of selection we should be very cautious in saying that these developments are actually the results of selection. Recent studies show that such caution is certainly in order.

For this theory to work, it is necessary that there be changes not only in the color of the British moths but also in their behavior. The dark variety are as vulnerable on unblackened patches of bark as are the white on the smoky backgrounds. In addition to developing the dark color, moths must develop the habit of settling on smoke-stained bark. There is some evidence that each variety preferentially chooses a background of its own color on which to settle where it is protected. Ehrlich and Holm report that there can be little doubt that under certain circumstances of stress the larvae of melanic moths are better able to survive, but they say that the most recent work on the subject indicates that the situation is more complex than was previously thought. In some recent experiments the expected deficiency of nonmelanic individuals was not found. In another experiment the results showed interbrood heterogeneity; while the offspring from some matings showed a significantly higher proportion of melanics, the offspring from others did not.[7]

Johnston, Bogart, and Lindquist report that resistance to DDT by flies is a very complex thing, apparently due to factors carried in the cytoplasm. They found that in one DDT-resistant strain, resistance declined until after nine generations resistance was little above that of the susceptible strain. However, on exposure to DDT, resistance increased. While they believe that selection was involved in the increase, they state that it is possible that selection alone did not account for all the increase in resistance, and they suggest that DDT itself may have stimulated the production of the particles necessary for the resistance.[8]

At a symposium on "The Origin of Drug Resistance and Related Problems" it was suggested that DDT-resistance may be a matter of adaptation. It may be that some stimulus produces hormones or enzymes which protect against DDT. An enzyme which removes hydrochloric acid from DDT in DDT-resistant flies has been demonstrated. This situation may be analogous to that in animals which tend to develop a white coat in winter but do not always develop one. It has been found that once a severe winter has induced the development of a white coat, whiteness recurs in subsequent seasons even though the temperatures remain moderate.[9] It may be that the factor for DDT-resistance is present but develops only after the flies have been exposed to DDT and then continues for a time.

More recent studies have shown a rather bizarre adaptation of micro-organisms to antibiotics. In extreme cases it may be found that a strain of bacteria requires an antibiotic that would result in the total destruction of another strain. The highly resistant bacteria apparently make obligate adjustments to the presence of the antibiotic, and when the antibiotic is absent the life processes are so disrupted that normal growth cannot take place.[10] Ross refers to a study by Sager, who found that one particular streptomycin-resistant strain of *Chlamydomonas* appears only when the forms are exposed to hypertoxic dosages of streptomycin. He believes the drug induces a mutation which is in some way linked to the drug itself. While he says that this is the only instance of such action known, be believes it nevertheless indicates the possibility of new discoveries and concepts with regard to the relation between environment and mutation.[11]

Selection Studies Classified

Robson and Richards, in their discussion of natural selection, divide the studies which are supposed to show selection into six groups. They find only three studies in which selection is probable, five studies in which the analogy with natural processes is doubtful, five studies in which other explanations are possible, eight studies in which the procedure is defective or the numbers too low, three studies in which selection is not found, and six studies in which the selective agency is unknown or doubtful. Some of the studies have been catalogued by them in more than one category.[12] They believe that at least a preliminary examination of the data shows that most workers have considered the deductive consequences of the natural selection theory rather than provided direct evidence for it. Only a small part of Darwin's own work, they say, dealt directly with the evidence for the theory of natural selection. They conclude that while natural selection cannot be disregarded as a possible factor in evolution, there is little positive evidence in its favor, there is much against it, and much that is still inconclusive. They do not believe that it can be regarded as the main causative agent in evolution.[13]

Cooper says much the same thing in reviewing White's *Animal Cytology and Evolution*. He feels that in White's book natural selection as a cause has been deduced from the effect, as is so often the case in the writings of modern evolutionists. The resulting arguments and conclusions, he says, are of course unconvincing.[14]

We should, therefore, be very hesitant in assuming that selection is acting in the various developments assigned to it. While it may be said that selection appears to be bringing them about, it is by no means certain that this is the case. Our experience in restudying and reanalyzing other supposed instances of selection should lead us to be very cautious.

The Contradictory Role of Selection

There are other aspects of the selection theory which deserve our attention. For one thing, the role played by selection is a self-contradictory one. The more intensive the selection, the fewer the varieties, and the fewer the species. The less intensive the selection, the more varieties and more species develop.[15] This phenomenon is common in both the plant and animal world. Huxley, for instance, tells us that among fish where predators are absent there are many species of fish, but where predators are present there are few species.[16] He cites the example of the cichlids which are found in all the great lakes of Africa. Where predators are present, as in Lake Albert, only four species are found. But in Lake Victoria, where predators are absent, over fifty species are found. In each case the fish found at present in the respective lakes are believed to have developed from a single species found in these lakes at the end of the Ice Age.[17]

This is only what we would expect, for intensive selection should eliminate all but the most favored individuals. Yet this role is one which slows down evolution and defeats the process which it is supposed to guide. For the fewer varieties and species there are, the slower evolution will proceed; and the less chance there will be for the organism to exploit a habitat which develops as a result of some climatic change.

Another thing that should be pointed out is that intensive selection may in itself result in the eventual elimination and extinction of an organism. It may become so highly adapted that it cannot survive even slight changes in its environment. Thus it may actually be committing suicide by becoming specialized. For that reason fitness is not favorable in a highly complex organism: rather flexibility is the coveted condition. Stebbins, for example, says that, while in organisms that are structurally or developmentally simple fitness is favored, with increasing complexity flexibility becomes the favored condition.[18] Survival seems to be favored by developing within the species a great deal of variety which is kept indefinitely. This variety is not to be reduced by natural selection choosing the most favorable forms, but it is to continue indefinitely.

The phenomenon of neutral polymorphism seems to support this idea. In this type of polymorphism the gene frequencies in wild populations remain remarkably constant over a long period of time.[19] If selection were operative, we would expect one gene to eliminate or at least to reduce the frequency of its allelomorph. Dobzhansky believes that polymorphism increases the fitness of the population as a whole, not by furnishing raw material for selection, but by making the population more efficient in exploiting a wide variety of environments. It is also better able to withstand irregular and sudden changes in the environment.[20]

Observations Which Cannot Be Explained on the Basis of Selection

There are also many observations which cannot be explained on the basis of natural selection. It may be argued of course that we simply do not know enough about these phenomena at the present time and that later observations may lead to a better understanding of them. But it is nevertheless true that at the present time they cannot be fitted into the scheme of selection. For instance, in England there are two shrews, *Sorex vulgaris* and *S. minutus*. They differ in that one is only half the weight of the other. They live in the same district, they feed on identical food, and, so far as can be ascertained, have the same habits and behavior. Both of these are relatively common. The differences between the two cannot be accounted for on the basis of natural selection.[21]

In plants an increasing asymmetry of the karyotype (the number, size, and form of the chromosomes) is considered to be the consequence of natural selection and evolution. Highly specialized forms which natural selection is supposed to have developed in the course of a long evolutionary history may be expected to have a very asymmetrical karyotype. Such an asymmetrical karyotype is found in *Cycas* (the cycads — evergreen plants with fernlike and palmlike leaves) and in the *Ginkgo* (the "living fossil") with broad, fan-shaped, forked, veined leaves). Yet *Pinus* (the pines) and *Taxus* (the yews), which are also supposed to be very specialized and to have a long evolutionary history, have a very symmetrical karyotype.[22]

The Problem of Small and Seemingly Insignificant Differences

Selectionists after Darwin spent a great deal of time in demonstrating the alleged selective value of small differences. In many cases no value could be demonstrated: then it was argued that survival value had to be there even if it could not be demonstrated.

There is a real problem here. It is certainly difficult to conceive of the selective value of the difference — the form of a single spot on the wings — separating *Hesperia pahaska* and *H. viridis* to which we referred in chapter 3. It is usually argued that there are physiological as well as morphological differences, but it must be admitted that the former have not been demonstrated.

This type of argumentation is still met occasionally

today. Carter believes that the black variant of the hamster (*Cricetus cricetus*) undoubtedly has some selective advantage, because it has spread over a large part of central Russia, though he says that we do not know the nature of the advantage.[23] Mather recognizes that some characters appear so trivial that to regard them as adaptations resulting from the past action of natural selection is little more than an act of faith. However, he argues that to regard them as so trivial as to be devoid of adaptive significance in the absence of observation and experimental evidence is equally an act of faith. He believes that the danger in such a case is at least as great, that it is just as dangerous to deny all adaptive significance as to insist upon it.[24]

Romer argues that evolution as seen in the fossil record must in its entirety be a study of continual adaptive processes, for he says that any feature of a mutational nature which becomes well enough established in a group to appear in the fossil record is surely sufficiently advantageous to be considered an adaptation, or at least it is associated with adaptive features in other structures or functions.[25] In other words, the characteristics must be advantageous, because only advantageous characteristics will be retained. The very fact that they are there proves they must have survival value.

Other Difficulties

Romer's statement is also of interest because it is often said that fossil series all show obvious selective trends. Apparently they do not. The studies of Rowe and Fenton, to which we shall refer, also indicate that selection is not always so evident. Some evolutionists insist, as does Romer, that it must be assumed even though it cannot be demonstrated. Many are frank enough to admit the problem. Carter says that much of the differentiation between species both in fossils and in forms extant today is apparently nonadaptive. He believes that this is characteristic of what he terms microevolution and what we would call the development of differences between members of the lower taxonomic categories — species and even genera.[26]

Mayr quotes Lerner as saying, "What we have learned so far about natural selection is obviously only the beginning. What remains to be learned is immeasurably more." He goes on to say that in spite of all the advances we have made, numerous unsolved problems remain, and he singles out four aspects of natural selection which he says raised doubts in his troubled mind. He lists first the selection of genes versus the selection of genotypes and points out that selection places considerable strain upon populations. Too rapid a rate of simultaneous selection against too many genes might eliminate the whole population. Second, he lists the measure of fitness. He believes that it is crucial to find an objective yardstick and ask whether it is not a basic error of methodology to apply such a generalizing technique as mathematics to a field of unique events such as organic evolution. The third aspect he discusses is the population as the unit of selection. He lists reproductive success as the fourth area in which he has some question. He believes that natural selection may be defenseless against certain genes which increase the rate of reproduction even though they are harmful in other ways.[27]

Harris believes that strictly speaking there is no selection but only the natural and inevitable survival of what can best adapt itself to its surroundings at the expense of what is less well adjusted. The agency of adaptation is not selection, he says, but what he calls the "auturgy of the living system," which exerts a constant nisus toward integration and order and protects the delicate structure of the organism both against the environmental changes and against its own internal mutations.[28]

Paleontological Data

Paleontological data are somewhat puzzling and contradictory in this whole area. Rowe lists a number of changes that took place in the sea urchin in an environment that was, as far as could be determined, unchanging.[29] On the other hand, Fenton studied changes in one of the brachiopods and found that, while the environment changed, the evolutionary changes in the brachiopod studied showed no correlation with these variations in the environment.[30]

The Role of Selection: *A SUMMARY*

In summary we shall have to say that the problem of selection is a very complex one. There are some facts which might be regarded as evidences for selection.

There is such a thing as selection, and there is such a thing as fitness in the sense of better or poorer adjustment to the environment in which the organism must live. But there are also many facts which do not fit the selection concept as it is applied to evolution. Most organisms seem rather well buffered so that they can adjust to some changes in the environment.

Types of Isolation

A second factor which is supposed to have played a very important role in evolution is isolation. It is believed that in consequence of being separated from one another, organisms have developed different characteristics and as a result have become separate species. The most common type of isolation thought of in this connection is geographical isolation. But there are also other types of isolation which are possible and which would be equally important in bringing about evolution by isolation. For instance, organisms may be separated from one another by sterility barriers. Even though living in the same general area, they may not interbreed because they are incapable of producing fertile offspring. Isolation may also be of an ecological character. Similar forms may occupy different parts of the same general habitat. For instance, one group of organisms may occupy

the air, another group may be a terrestrial group, and a third
group may be a subterranean group. Even though they are
found in the same general region, they are isolated because
they occupy different ecological niches. Similarly organisms
may also be separated by their food preferences. One, for
instance, may prefer buds and another leaves. Their feeding
habits may keep them from ever coming into contact with
one another. The role of isolation in evolution was first
emphasized by M. Wagner.[31] Today it is still assigned a very
important role in speciation.

Stebbins finds eight kinds of isolating mechanisms in
plants. They are as follows: (1) ecological or seasonal isolation. This occurs in organisms which are separated from one
another either by occupying different ecological niches or
by flowering at entirely different seasons. They need not be
incompatible and need not show a sterility to remain separate species, since it is rarely, if ever, possible for their
reproductive cells to meet. For that reason in these forms
incompatibility, hybrid inviability, and hybrid sterility are
weakly developed. As examples of this type of isolation he
lists the genera *Pinus* (the pines), *Quercus* (the oaks),
Larix (the larches), *Cistus* (the European rockroses), etc.
(2) The second group of plants are those which are highly
specialized for insect pollination, and in which mechanical
isolation is strongly developed. These include the Asclepiadaceae (the milkweeds) and Orchidaceae (the orchids).
They are forms which are especially adapted for pollination
by a specific insect. Other insects are unable to enter the
flower because of its structure. Only those insects which
carry the pollen from another member of the same species
are able to enter it. (3) Plants in which hybridization is
difficult or impossible under natural conditions. This is true
even when the species are very similar in external morphology. In these cases it appears that a genic sterility is the
chief cause for the isolation. Included in this group are
Solanum (the nightshades), *Lycopersicon* (the tomato), and

Datura (the Jimson weed). (4) Plants which apparently show a normal amount of difference between species in external structure, in crossability, in hybrid sterility, and in the structure of the chromosomes. In these, several types of isolating mechanisms are apparently operating with equal force. These include *Layia* (one of the composites), *Allium* (the onion), and *Lilium* (the lily). (5) The fifth group includes plants in which isolation seems to be due to a great deal of chromosomal differentiation. When crosses occur, the chromosomal behavior at meiosis is highly irregular in the hybrids. Allopolyploidy is quite common. Isolation in this case seems to be due to the structure of the chromosomes. (6), (7), and (8) These are plants in which there are differences in chromosome number. These include the polyploid series in *Rosa* (the roses), *Rubus* (the brambles), *Salix* (the willows), and *Viola* (the violets): the aneuploid series found in *Erophila* (the dill), *Carex* (the sedge), *Scirpus* (the bulrush), *Iris*, and *Stipa* (the feather grass): and apomictic forms, *Antennaria* (the everlasting), *Hieracum* (the hawkweed), *Arnica*, *Potentilla* (the cinquefoil), and *Poa* (the meadow grass).[32]

Presumably similar types of isolation should operate within animal populations. It should be clear, then, that different types of isolation may operate and that isolation involves more than mere geographical separation of forms.

It should be pointed out that evolutionists today believe that geographical and genetic isolation are far more important than other types of isolation in the formation of new species and in evolution. Ross discusses the suggestions that have been made about speciation by ecological isolation without the aid of geographical isolation and says that there is no good reason to suppose that the set of suppositions underlying such a model would work. The chief drawback, he says, is the lack of any apparent reason why, within the large network comprising the range of the species, individuals from one situation would not mingle with and mate with those from another unless the opposite ecological conditions were situated some distance apart, and in this case the genetic divergence of the populations would be the function of partial or complete geographical isolation, not ecological isolation.[33] He concludes that in both plants and animals the great bulk of present-day species owe their origin to geographic isolation and that the greatest number of species not created by geographic isolation are the result of allopolyploidy and genetic isolation.[34] Rensch says much the same thing and explains that ecological isolation can have only minor evolutionary effects. He believes that only in parasites does speciation by ecological isolation take place regularly, though he says that ecological isolation is frequently linked with geographical separation.[35]

Closely Related Species Living in the Same Area

One of the problems in connection with isolation as a factor in evolution is the problem of closely related species living in the same area. For many years it was assumed that this was not possible. According to evolutionary theory it simply could not be. Yet a number of instances have been discovered of closely related species which do live in the same general area. For instance, *Syrphus torvus* Ost.-Sack., *S. ribesii* L., and *S. vitripennis* Meig., three species of flies, occupy almost identical ranges and are often found together. The differences between the three forms are of no apparent adaptive significance, and since they occupy the same general areas, it is difficult to understand how they originated as separate species. It is generally believed that the cause of divergence in these animals is small inherited differences leading to sterility, but this is an assumption and nothing more. It has been suggested that the growth of these differences was fostered by their having been separated at one time into small discontinuous populations (the Sewall Wright effect), even though today they are found together, but there is no real evidence to support this suggestion.

The same problem exists with the grass moths *Crambus uliginosellus* Zell., *C. sylvellus* Huebn, and *C. pascuellus* L.[36]

Classifying Isolated Forms That Are Still Capable of Interbreeding

Another problem is the question of whether or not forms that are spatially or temporally separated but which are still capable of interbreeding are to be regarded as separate species. One of the generally accepted criteria for a species is sterility in crosses with other species. Shall forms which ordinarily do not interbreed but which are still capable of interbreeding be considered separate species?

We have referred to some instances of these in our discussion of "species."

Forms in Which Seasonal Isolation Can Be of Little Importance

At the same time there are many cases, though, in which seasonal occurrence appears to be of little or no importance in effecting isolation. Schubert reports that all thirty-three species of the dragon flies in the vicinity of Neustadt have overlapping periods with the possible exception of two species. These thirty-three species represent nineteen genera.[37] Richards has shown that among the flies of the family Sphaeroceridae most species are found throughout the year, and many of them seem to have no restricted breeding season.[38] In general it appears that the time of the appearance of the brood in insects has some relationship to the environment. In the north many insects have but one brood a year. Farther south they have in addition to their one brood a partial brood in which only a few individuals emerge. Still farther south there will be two complete broods a year, and still farther south even more than two complete broods a year. Thus forms isolated from one another by a seasonal occurrence in the north may not be isolated in the southern part of their range.

The Origin of New Species by Isolation

It should also be pointed out that there is considerable disagreement as to the ways in which these different types of isolation have arisen, of the significance of the various types of isolation for evolution, and of the relationship of the different types of isolation to one another. In general it is agreed that finally reproductive isolation must occur. In other words, the process of speciation is not complete until the organisms are incapable of interbreeding. And yet instances in which the development of sterility between two forms can be demonstrated are very rare. Huxley suggests only one. He refers to the two strains of maize which differ in only a single gene pair and which cannot cross. He believes that such occurrences are very uncommon, and he goes on to say that the evolutionary bearings of this fact are not clear.[39] It is clear, however, that geographical isolation in itself does not produce sterility. Nor is there any evidence that other types of isolation lead to sterility.

Stebbins points to the skunk cabbage (*Symplocarpus foetidus*) which is common in swamps throughout the eastern United States and is also found in several places in China. He believes that these two forms have been separated for millions of years. Yet he believes that there is probably more variation within the populations than there are differences between the two populations. He concludes that the separation of populations merely by distance is not enough to cause them to diverge and form different races. They must, he believes, be subjected to differential selection pressures; thus he believes that isolation and selection combined will cause the development of new species.[40]

In birds it is frequently said that ecological isolation leads to the development of new species. Forms that are closely related develop preferences for different ecological niches, and this gradually leads to the development of two or more new species. But Lack believes that ecological isolation in birds is primarily a result rather than a cause of speciation.[41] Their occupying different ecological niches does not result in the development of new species: rather the fact that they are separate species is the reason for their occupying different niches.

In birds Lack believes that there are no known subspecies or incipient species in the process of differentiation in adjacent habitats in the same region.[42] In other words, there is no evidence for the development of new species in habitats which vary only slightly from one another. All of the bird subspecies are isolated geographically, and Lack believes that geographical rather than ecological isolation is important in the development of bird species.

The Amount of Variability Found in Different Organisms

Another point to be considered is the amount of variability to be found in different organisms. Some species are said to be relatively stable, and thus provide little chance for the development of new forms even if they are geographically isolated. Other forms show a great deal of variability. This difference in variability may occur in closely related forms. Certain species of a genus may vary a great deal; others are quite constant. This is true also of the frequency with which geographical races occur. Robson and Richards point out that this makes it very difficult to study the effects of isolation, since isolation can work only on varieties within the species. If these do not exist, then isolation in itself cannot bring about evolution. They consider the relative stability of some species and the high degree of variability in others as one of the most curious and baffling problems of biology.[43]

The Adaptiveness of Differences Between Geographical Races

Still another point to be considered is whether the differences found in geographical races are actually adaptive.

In brief, is Race A particularly adapted to the habitat in which it is found, and is Race B particularly adapted to its habitat? It has been generally assumed that this is the case. But Watson says that it is probable that the differences between geographical races have only a statistical meaning and have no adaptive significance.[44] Huxley seems to agree with this statement, for he says that a great deal of the diversity produced by isolation is in a sense irrelevant to the main trends of evolution.[45] If the differences in geographical races have no real adaptive significance, it is hard to see how they play a part in the development of new species.

The Origin of Sterility by Isolation

The critical problem in any discussion of isolation is the mechanism whereby it can effect sterility and thus bring about the development of new species. Most of those who discuss isolation as a factor in evolution minimize the importance of sterility as a basis for recognizing species. Yet, as we have seen, it is one of the criteria set up by almost all who attempt to define the term. The truth of the matter is that there is little evidence to indicate that isolation per se brings about the development of sterility barriers. It is usually taken for granted and assumed, but there is no real evidence for the development of these barriers. Muller, for instance, believes that if two populations are geographically or ecologically isolated from one another for a sufficiently long period of time, differential and divergent processes of gene mutation will inevitably cause the formation of other types of isolating barriers, such as sterility.[46] Yet Stebbins points out that this is not necessarily true.[47] He refers to the two forms of the genus *Platanus* (the sycamore). *P. occidentalis* occurs in the eastern United States and *P. orientalis* in the eastern part of the Mediterranean region. They are widely separate geographically and the climates of the two habitats are quite distinct. Yet the artificial hybrid between them, *P. acerifolia,* is vigorous and highly fertile.[48]

In the animal world there is a race of the Gypsy moth (*Lymantria dispar*) which is supposed to have been isolated on the island of Hokkaido in northern Japan since the early Tertiary period, about 60,000,000 years ago. Yet this race has not developed into a new species in all that time.[49]

Stebbins also criticizes the suggestion of Dobzhansky that gene recombinations in the offspring of species hybrids may lead to the formation of individuals with discordant gene patterns, the destruction of which entails a decrease of the reproductive potential of the species whose members interbreed. Dobzhansky believes that the hybrids are sterile or at least less fertile. By interbreeding with another species an organism would be losing part of its reproductive potential. This would be an unfavorable characteristic, since it would reduce the net fertility of the organism. Thus genes which prevent hybridization would be favored by natural selection, since these would prevent the loss.[50]

Stebbins points out that there are many instances in which the hybrids are not inviable or weak: indeed, they may even have characteristics which are favorable under some conditions. Hybrids between two subspecies of *Potentilla glandulosa* (one of the cinquefoils), which are very different physiologically, are often very vigorous and have a high positive selective value under certain conditions.[51]

Some have suggested that sterility develops only where it is needed to conserve the reproductive potential. Where forms are not in contact they do not develop sterility, since it is unnecessary. Only where they are in fairly close contact does sterility develop to prevent the loss by interbreeding of different characteristics that have developed. However, there are not only examples of forms in close contact which are not intersterile but also many instances of hybrid sterility where the two forms were never in contact.[52] It should also be pointed out that there is no evidence for the development of these genetic barriers by means of a single gene mutation. In only one instance has the occurrence of such a process been suggested. That is the instance in maize cited by Huxley and referred to earlier.

It has also been suggested that the genic or chromosomal differences responsible for sterility may be associated or correlated with other characteristics of positive selective value. Thus it may be that the sterility is one of the side effects of a gene mutation which also governs the development of some favorable characteristic. Stebbins believes that there is no evidence for this hypothesis, since there are many favorable characteristics which are not associated with sterility.[53]

Huxley believes that ecotopic and ecobiotic isolation — a specialized sharing out of the environmental habitat — of closely related species leads frequently to the development of new species which have learned to exploit the habitat in different ways.[54] But Mayr states that ecological isolation of sympatric species — those occupying the same general habitat — is rather uncommon among animals.[55] Stebbins makes a similar statement with regard to plants. He says that available factual evidence points to the rarity of speciation without previous geographical isolation.[56] In other words, there is little evidence of what might be called sympatric speciation.

The Role of Isolation: *A SUMMARY*

Yet the crucial question remains: How can any type of isolation — geographical, ecological, seasonal, or the like — bring about a genetic isolation and the development of new species? Huxley says that the method by which such genetic isolation develops is by no means clear and presents a challenge to biologists.[57] And Stebbins has no really satisfactory suggestion as to how geographical isolation can bring about the development of genetic isolation and thus of new species. Robson and Richards are of the opinion that only in island populations is there any really convincing evidence that isolation affects the rate of evolution.[58] Until more evidence is forthcoming, we can afford to be somewhat skeptical about the role of isolation in bringing about changes in living organisms.

NOTES

1. Robson, G. C., and Richards, O. W. *The Variation of Animals in Nature* (London: Longmans, Green, 1936), pp. 190 f.

2. Thompson, W. R., and Parker, H. L. "The European Corn Borer and Its Controlling Factors in Europe," *U. S. Department of Agriculture Technical Bulletin* 59 (1928), 16.

3. Weldon, W. F. R. "Presidential Address, Section D," *British Association for the Advancement of Science 1898* (1899), pp. 887–902.

4. Robson and Richards, pp. 197–199.

5. Harrison, J. W. Heslop. "Genetical Studies in the Moths of the Geometrid Genus *Oporabia (Oporinia)*, with a Special Consideration of Melanism in the Lepidoptera," *Journal of Genetics*, IX (1920), 224 f.

6. Robson and Richards, p. 200.

7. Ehrlich, Paul R., and Holm, Richard W. *The Process of Evolution* (New York: McGraw-Hill, 1963), p. 130.
   Harris, Errol E. *The Foundations of Metaphysics in Science* (London: George Allen and Unwin, 1965), p. 238.

8. Johnston, E. F., Bogart, Ralph, and Lindquist, A. W. "The Resistance to DDT by Houseflies: Some Genetic and Environmental Factors," *Journal of Heredity*, XLV (1954), 177 to 182.

9. Gerard, R. W. "Experiments in Microevolution," *Science*, CXX (1954), 728–730.

10. Williams, George C. *Adaptation and Natural Selection* (Princeton: Princeton University Press, 1966), p. 267.

11. Ross, Herbert H. *A Synthesis of Evolutionary Theory* (Englewood Cliffs: Prentice-Hall, 1962), p. 81.

12. Robson and Richards, p. 212.

13. Ibid., pp. 309–316.

14. Cooper, Kenneth W. *Science*, CXXI (1955), 429.

15. Boyd, William C. *Genetics and the Races of Man* (Boston: Little, Brown, 1950), p. 150.

16. Huxley, Julian. *Evolution, the Modern Synthesis* (New York: Harpers, 1943), p. 323.

17. Huxley, Julian. *Man in the Modern World* (London: Chatto and Windus, 1950), p. 199.

18. Stebbins, G. Ledyard. *Variation and Evolution in Plants* (New York: Columbia University Press, 1950), p. 170.

19. Mayr, Ernst. *Systematics and the Origin of Species* (New York: Columbia University Press, 1942), p. 75.

20. Dobzhansky, Theodosius. "Human Diversity and Adaptation," *Cold Spring Harbor Symposia on Quantitative Biology,* XV (1950), 395.

21. Watson, D. M. S. "The Evidence Afforded by Fossil Vertebrates on the Nature of Evolution," *Genetics, Paleontology, and Evolution,* ed. Glenn L. Jepsen, Ernst Mayr, and George Gaylord Simpson (Princeton: Princeton University Press, 1949), p. 63.

22. Stebbins, p. 462.

23. Carter, G. S. *Animal Evolution* (London: Sidgwick and Jackson, 1951), p. 196.

24. Mather, Kenneth. *Human Diversity* (New York: Free Press, 1964), p. 5.

25. Romer, Alfred Sherwood. "Time Series and Trends in Animal Evolution," *Genetics, Paleontology, and Evolution,* ed. Glenn L. Jepsen, Ernst Mayr, and George Gaylord Simpson (Princeton: Princeton University Press, 1949), p. 103.

26. Carter, p. 47.

27. Mayr, Ernst. "Where Are We," *Cold Spring Harbor Symposia on Quantitative Biology,* XXIV (1959), 5 f.

28. Harris, p. 251.

29. Rowe, A. W. "An Analysis of the Genus *Micraster* as Determined by Rigid Zonal Collecting from the Zone of *Rhynchonella Cuvieri* to that of *Micraster cor-anguinum*," *Quarterly Journal of the Geological Society of London,* LV (1899), 494–546.

30. Fenton, Carroll Lane. "Studies in the Evolution of the Genus *Spirifer*," *Publications of Wagner Institute of Science,* II (1931), 71–75.

31. Wagner, M. *Die Entstehung der Arten durch räumliche Sonderung* (Basel, 1889).

32. Stebbins, pp. 234–236.

33. Ross, p. 182.

34. Ibid., p. 335.

35. Rensch, Bernard. *Evolution Above the Species Level* (London: Methuen, 1959), p. 50.

36. Diver, C. "The Problem of Closely Related Species Living in the Same Area," *The New Systematics,* ed. Julian Huxley (Oxford: Oxford University Press, 1940), pp. 312–317.

37. Schubert, Karl. "Die Odonaten der Umgegend von Neustadt O.–S." *Zeitschrift für Wissenschaftliche Insektenbiologie,* XXIV (1929), 178–189.

38. Richards, O. W. "The British Species of Sphaeroceridae (Borboridae, Diptera)," *Proceedings of the Zoological Society of London*, 1930 (1930), pp. 320–322.

39. Huxley, *Evolution*, p. 328.

40. Stebbins, G. Ledyard. *Processes of Organic Evolution* (Englewood Cliffs: Prentice-Hall, 1966), p. 90.

41. Lack, David. "The Significance of Ecological Isolation," *Genetics, Paleontology, and Evolution*, ed. Glenn L. Jepsen, Ernst Mayr, and George Gaylord Simpson (Princeton: Princeton University Press, 1949), pp. 302 f.

42. Ibid., p. 300.

43. Robson and Richards, pp. 137–140.

44. Watson, D. M. S., et al. "A Discussion on the Present Status of the Theory of Natural Selection," *Proceedings of the Royal Society of London* (B), CXXI (1936), 44 f.

45. Huxley, J. S. "Towards the New Systematics," *The New Systematics*, ed. Julian Huxley (Oxford: Oxford University Press, 1940), p. 11.

46. Muller, H. J. "Bearing of the 'Drosophila' Work on Systematics," *The New Systematics*, ed. Julian Huxley (Oxford: Oxford University Press, 1940), p. 256.

47. Stebbins, *Variation*, p. 241.

48. Sax, K. "Species Hybrids in *Platanus* and *Campsis*," *Journal of the Arnold Arboretum*, XIV (1933), 274–278.

49. Dodson, Edward O. *A Textbook of Evolution* (Philadelphia: Saunders, 1952), p. 270.

50. Dobzhansky, Theodosius. *Genetics and the Origin of Species* (New York: Columbia University Press, 1951), p. 208.

51. Stebbins, *Variation*, p. 243.

52. Ibid., p. 243.

53. Ibid., p. 244.

54. Huxley, *Evolution*, p. 284.

55. Mayr, *Systematics*, pp. 250 f.
    Mayr, Ernst. "Ecological Factors in Speciation," *Evolution*, I (1947), 263–288.

56. Stebbins, *Variation*, p. 238.

57. Huxley, *Evolution*, p. 284.

58. Robson and Richards, p. 139.

8. Suggested Mechanisms for Evolution

In any discussion of evolution the crux of the problem lies in the mechanism. It is possible to have all sorts of evidence that evolution has taken place, but before any theory can be considered reasonably complete some mechanism whereby such changes can be produced and can be inherited must be suggested. It is almost universally agreed that this mechanism must be found in the field of genetics, the science of inheritance. Any change which is not passed on from generation to generation cannot be of any importance in evolution. It is this defect in Lamarckianism which we have criticized, and it is because of this defect that Lamarckianism has largely been discarded. Conversely De Vries' claim to fame rests upon the fact that he suggested a mechanism whereby evolution could come about.

So much importance has been attached to the bearing of inheritance on evolution that the field of genetics has often been regarded as a laboratory experiment in evolution. No discussion of evolution would be complete today without a very careful and clear discussion of the bearing that genetics has on it.

Mendel, the Father of Genetics

The science of genetics is one of the relatively new branches of biology. Strangely enough, the initial research in this area was ignored for almost forty years after the work was published. The initial work was done by an Austrian monk, Gregor Mendel, in the Augustinian monastery of

Bruenn, Austria (now Brno, Czechoslovakia). In 1857 Mendel began his experiments on inheritance, working with the numerous varieties of the garden pea which seedsmen offered for sale. He carried out observations and experiments in the monastery garden for seven years. The choice of his material proved to be fortunate, and he was able to present his results to two meetings of the Natural History Society of Bruenn in the spring of 1865.

A great many men had attempted to study inheritance prior to the time of Mendel, but they had failed to use the technique he employed and, consequently, were unable to achieve the results he achieved. Mendel's work involved three new approaches. First of all, he used the statistical approach and counted the actual number of offspring of different types. Second, he studied single characteristics independently instead of studying the individual as a whole. Third, he kept accurate pedigree records of the members of successive generations.

Mendel's work involved opening the flower buds and removing the stamens — the parts of the flower that produce the pollen — to prevent self-pollination. He then fertilized these flowers artificially and prevented the access of insects to them by covering them. After many observations he developed a series of principles known as Mendel's laws.

Mendel's work lay unappreciated and almost unknown until the year 1900. In that year his principles were rediscovered and his paper unearthed by three different investigators — De Vries in Holland, Correns in Germany, and von Tschermak in Austria. Darwin was unacquainted with Mendel's work, or if he did know it he failed to appreciate its significance and developed a rather bizarre theory of pangenesis: he seems to have believed that environmental conditions rather than cross-breeding created new somatic variations. Since Mendel's time a great deal of work has been done in the field of inheritance, and much progress is still being made from day to day.

Drosophila as an Experimental Form

A great deal of this work has been done with the fruit fly, *Drosophila,* which is found wherever there is decaying fruit. A number of species of this form are known. Perhaps the best known of these is *D. melanogaster.* For some years

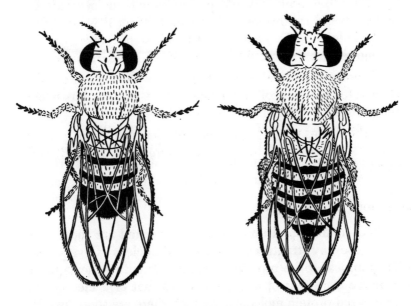

Figure 20. Drosophila melanogaster. This is the fruit fly, or vinegar fly, on which so many genetic studies have been conducted. The male is slightly smaller and has a darker tip on the abdomen. The male is to the left and the female to the right. (Redrawn from Shull's Heredity, McGraw-Hill, by permission)

the species now known as *D. simulans* was classified together with *D. melanogaster.* The two forms hybridize, but their hybrids are sterile.[1] They are so similar to one another that evolutionists cite them as instances where the expected character divergence between species has not developed. Similar resemblances are to be seen in *D. pseudoobscura* and *D. miranda,* which were also thought to belong to one species until Dobzhansky separated them by chromosome studies in 1935. Hybrids between these two species are also usually sterile, though Dobzhansky has found that hybrids between

D. pseudoobscura A and a race of *D. miranda* from Mount Whitney, Calif., show some degree of fertility.

Further studies of *D. pseudoobscura* have disclosed two races in this group, known as A and B. These probably never interbreed in nature, and White believes that if they did hybridize, the hybrids would probably be completely sterile under natural conditions.[2] *D. pseudoobscura* B is now generally known as *D. persimilis,* though some geneticists do not agree that this should be considered a separate species.

There are a number of other *Drosophila* species. We shall refer to some of them later. New species are being reported almost regularly.

Other forms which have been used successfully in genetic research in recent years include *Neurospora,* a mold, and various species of bacteria.

The Theory of the Gene

The fundamental units that are inherited are the genes. These are tiny structures found in the nucleus of every cell. They appear to be protein in nature. In size genes appear to range from that of a small virus to that of a medium to large-sized protein molecule. In fact, there are some investigators who believe that the viruses are genes which have in some way or other separated themselves from the chromosomes and nuclei in which they were originally found.

No reliable estimate can be given as to the number of genes to be found in an organism. It is generally believed that there are about 2,000 to 2,500 in the lily plant and 2,000 to 13,000 in *Drosophila,* with a probable number of 5,000. It is believed that the number of genes in man is somewhat higher. Huxley estimates it to be from four to six times larger than the number found in *Drosophila.*[3] Other estimates range from 5,000 to 120,000.[4] Spuhler on the basis of careful mathematical computations believes the number to be between 20,000 and 42,000.[5]

Chromosomes

The genes are believed to be arranged in a linear order on structures known as chromosomes. Today the genes are regarded as areas which can be delimited on the chromosome rather than as points on the chromosome as they were once pictured. Thus a gene today is regarded as an area of a chromosome which determines a specific trait. The chromosomes appear to be present as distinct bodies during all stages of mitotic activity but are readily visible in cells that are actively dividing.

While it is not possible to see a gene under an ordinary microscope, chromosomes can be seen. Their number is characteristic of the species. However, there appears to be no relationship between the number of chromosomes and the complexity of the species. Man, for instance, has 23 pairs of chromosomes, a total of 46. The fruit fly, *Drosophila melanogaster,* has four pairs, a total of eight. One of the roundworms, *Ascaris megalocephala univalens,* has only one pair of chromosomes. The crayfish, *Cambarus virilis,* has 200.

The highest chromosome number so far reported is that of a protozoan, a microscopic, single-celled radiolarian, which has about 1,600 chromosomes. The highest number recorded for a multicellular animal is 224, that of the geometrid moth, *Phigalia pedaria.*[6] In the Diptera (flies), the chromosome numbers are unusually low; in birds, the chromosome numbers are unusually high.

It might be pointed out that it is very difficult to count the chromosomes and that the chromosome numbers reported are not to be regarded as definitely established. For many years man was thought to have 48 chromosomes; today there is almost universal agreement that his chromosome number is 46.

There is a sharp gap in chromosome numbers between the marsupials and the placental mammals, the marsupials having much lower chromosome numbers. On the other hand, *Echidna,* a monotreme, resembles birds and reptiles rather than mammals in having a very high chromosome number.[7] This is usually believed to be due to the fact that the monotremes are relatively low on the scale of mammalian evolution and therefore have a chromosome number characteristic of the lower forms.

Chromosome Number in Supposedly Closely Related Species

A real problem in this connection is the fact that there are a number of instances in which supposedly closely related species have widely different chromosome numbers. Thus among the copepods of the Crustacea, *Cyclops strenuus* has 11 chromosomes, and *C. gracilis* has only 3. Similarly in the amphipods of the Crustacea, *Gammarus chevreuxi* has 13 chromosomes; *G. annandalei* has 27. Among the insects in the Trichoptera, *Limnophilus affinis* has 6 chromosomes; *L. stigma* and *flavicornis* have 30 chromosomes. In the Lepidoptera, in the Geometridae, *Biston hirtaria* has 14 chromosomes; *B. zonaria* has 56. Among the mammals, in the Rodentia, *Cricetus auratus* has 19 chromosomes; *C. griseus* has 7 chromosomes. All of these are haploid chromosome numbers. There is no really satisfactory explanation for these differences. It has been suggested that they may be instances of polyploidy, but White believes that this is doubtful, at least in many cases.[8]

The number of chromosomes in the plant world also varies. Corn has 20. The lily has 24. Tobacco has the same number as does man, 48. One of the ferns, *Pteris aquilina*, has 64.[9]

The Range of Chromosome Numbers

While there is some variation in the chromosome numbers of different organisms, the variation in chromosome numbers is limited. White says that it is not easy to explain why the range should be so restricted. There are also differences in the amount of variation in different groups. In some groups nearly all the species have the same chromosome number, while in others there is a great range of variation.[10] This, too, is not easy to explain. Williams says that it is remarkable how little we understand of the general significance of chromosome numbers even though they are a readily quantified aspect of a fundamentally important adaptive mechanism of almost all organisms.[11]

DNA

The most dramatic development in genetics and possibly in all biology has been the discovery of the structure and function of deoxyribonucleic acid, DNA, by Watson and Crick and other researchers. This material, found in the chromosomes, directs the synthesis of the various materials which make up protoplasm and in that way determines whether the individual will be mustard, mouse, or man. In most organisms DNA carries the genetic code; however, there are a few organisms in which RNA, ribonucleic acid, carries out this function. Complex molecules such as proteins are made of one or more linear chains of smaller units, the subunits of which are the amino acids. There are just 20 common kinds of amino acids. DNA seems to function by specifying which of the 20 amino acids occupies each site in the structure.

DNA is a double-stranded molecule built much like a ladder twisted around its longitudinal axis so that its sides form a long double helix. The twist, though of some significance to the physical chemist, seems to be unimportant so far as the genetic code is concerned, so that the biologically important aspects of DNA can be visualized by imagining an ordinary ladder in which the sides are made of a sugar phosphate and the rungs constructed of four nucleotides: adenine, thymine, guanine, and cytosine.

Adenine always hooks up with thymine, and guanine hooks up with cytosine. Sometimes the sequence is adenine-thymine, sometimes it is thymine-adenine, but the same two must always hook up together. It is as if a ten-inch rung is needed to bridge the distance between the two sides. Instead of being in one piece, each rung is built of two parts; some are built of six-inch and four-inch pieces, while others consist of seven- and three-inch pieces. Thus it does not matter whether you have a six- plus four-inch rung or a seven- plus three-inch rung. Furthermore, it does not matter whether the order is six plus four or four plus six.

The linear chain of the nucleotides is quite long. The shortest chain known is 5,500 nucleotides long; this is the chromosome of a small virus. In a larger virus the chain is known to be 200,000 nucleotides long. In a human cell we do not know how long the chains are; they may run the length of each of the chromosomes. But it is believed that the total length of all the chains is about 5 billion nucleotides.[12]

The genetic code therefore consists of four "letters" which we may represent as ATGC. It appears that these four letters are used by the cells in groups of three, called "codons." Since any one of the four letters can be in each of the three positions of the codon group, there are 64 varieties of codon, and these are used to spell out the instructional messages. Since there are only 20 commonly used amino acids, it would appear that more than one codon specifies a particular amino acid, and studies have indicated that that is actually the case. Some of the triplets may not code any of the amino acids; they may be nonsense syllables just as there are many combinations of letters in the English alphabet which are nonsense.

It is believed that along each chromosome the individual messages are ranged in a linear order. It would seem necessary that there be some symbol to indicate the beginning and end of a message: there is some evidence that in certain micro-organisms a specific codon is the signal for the beginning of a message and another codon the signal for the end of a message. Only one of the strands of the DNA ladder seems to be used in the genetic code, though both strands are used when the cell reproduces, each strand forming its complement so that a complete ladder is reproduced. For meaning, only the sense strand is read, and on it the messenger RNA is built. The messenger RNA carries the complementary code and serves as a template on which the amino acids are built up to form enzymes and proteins in the ribosomes. Thus the DNA directs the ribosomes to build up proteins from amino acids arranged in a certain sequence, and this determines the growth and development of the organism. RNA is believed to be a long, unbranched, single-stranded molecule. It does not seem to be built as a double helix or ladder and contains ribose instead of deoxyribose. Instead of thymine it contains uracil. Three kinds of RNA molecules are required for protein synthesis: messenger RNA, which transmits genetic information from the DNA molecule in the nucleus to the ribosomes; ribosomal RNA, which serves some function in connection with the ribosomes; and transfer RNA, which acts as an adapter to bring amino acids into line in the growing polypeptide chain in the appropriate place.

That DNA should direct the development of the organism is truly remarkable. It is believed that the amount of zygote DNA needed to specify all of the world's population would weigh only one-seventeenth as much as a postage stamp.

It might seem reasonable to expect that the amount of information could be simply measured by the amount of DNA in the zygote. Some studies indicate that this is the case. Simple Protista as the bacteria and Sporozoa have small amounts of DNA. The invertebrates are highly variable but with some association between the amount of DNA and the position on the phylogenetic scale. Among the vertebrates the only suggested trend is for reduction of DNA in the lungfish-to-bird sequence. Mammals have more than birds but not as much as amphibians; the frog exceeds man by a factor of more than two, the lungfish *Protopterus* ex-

ceeds by at least sixteen, and *Amphiuma* exceeds by more
than twenty-five.[13] Inconsistencies between the DNA content and the presumed level of evolutionary advance is
customarily explained by assuming a high level of genetic
redundancy in lower organisms. Williams suggests that all
organisms above a certain low level of organization, perhaps that of the simpler vertebrates, and beyond a certain
geological period, perhaps that of the Cambrian, may have
much the same amount of information in the nuclei. All
such organisms, he says, have quantities of DNA capable of
carrying an enormous amount of information, and he believes that evolution since the Cambrian is the history of
substitutions and qualitative change in the germ plasm, not
an increase in its total content. He says that evolution from
protist to man may have been largely the substitution of
morphogenetic instructions for a small portion of the biochemical and cytological instructions in the protist DNA.[14]
Dobzhansky says that various surmises to account for unexpected differences in the amount of DNA are equally un-
attractive, and he goes on to say that we can only conclude
that as yet no satisfactory explanation of the situation has
been reached.[15]

Is the code universal? That is, does the same DNA code
direct the selection of the same amino acid in all organisms?
Today the general feeling is that the code is universal or
at least close to being so.

It is possible, though, that the same genetic message
may be interpreted in different ways. The transfer RNA
from one organism may differ from that of another in relative response to some codons, and the cytoplasm in different organisms may respond differently to the same genetic
code. Williams refers to Fowler's work which showed that
to get normally proportioned frogs from both northern and
southern eggs, it was necessary that the nuclei be different,
not similar. Genetically similar nuclei in both would produce normal development in one and abnormal develop-

ment in the other.[16] Thus the cytoplasm may respond differently to identical letters of the genetic code. "Gift" means something entirely different in German from what these letters signify in English.

Some studies have been carried on to analyze the different amino acid sequences in the various enzymes and proteins in different organisms. The assumption is that the fewer the differences, the more closely related the organisms are. Thus cytochrome *c* is a chain of 104 amino acids in which the sequence in man differs from that in the horse by only 12 places, whereas it differs from that in the yeast by 39 places. This is interpreted as evidence that man is more closely related to the horse than to the yeast. Yet there are marked differences between the cytochrome *c* of *Neurospora* and the yeast even though the two organisms are included in the same class of the fungi. Jukes interprets this as an indication that the two groups are rapidly diverging and says it is also due to their rapid reproductive rates. In commenting on this, Williams says that this is debatable and possibly wrong on both counts.[17]

How the Genes Work

How do the genes work? We have learned a great deal through our studies of the role and action of DNA. We have, for instance, been able to explain the phenomenon of transduction, which at first was thought to be an evidence of an environmental effect. We know that the transfer of the DNA actually changes the genetic code, and this explains this unusual type of change in the bacteria.

One of the major problems today is the problem of gene inactivation. Only erythroblasts make hemoglobin, myoglobin is limited to muscles, and no collagen is found in white blood cells. Apparently every cell has the complete genetic code; yet cells are specialized in what they produce. The DNA code for the production of hemoglobin is present in every cell of the body; yet only the erythroblasts manufacture it. There must be some control which inactivates most of the genes in most cells. There is some evidence of such inactivation; in embryological development all of the genes on one of the "X" chromosomes in the female undergo inactivation. We can observe the giant chromosomes of *Drosophila* under the microscope, and there we notice certain enlarged regions, or "puffs." These puffed regions are believed to be chromosomal regions actively engaged in synthesizing the proteins needed for controlling the other activities of the cell at that moment. At any one time different tissues have different chromosomal puffs, while cells of one tissue will show different puffs at different times during the growth of the individual.

It is apparent that the genes and specifically DNA work through enzymes, antigens, organizer substances, and hormones. Thus they act chiefly by determining the rates of chemical processes that these substances control in the body.

Mutations: The Origin of Hereditary Differences

One of the very interesting problems, and also a very important problem for evolution, is that of the origin of these different kinds of genes. It is possible that God created some variation in Adam when He formed him out of the dust of the earth. In other words, it is possible that Adam was heterozygous (having one dominant and one recessive gene) for a number of characters. At the same time it is probable that a majority of the variations which we see in man, in the plants, and in the animals are the result of mutation. It was their existence which De Vries assumed. He coined the term even though he probably never saw a mutation.

These mutations occur spontaneously at a measurable rate. We have no idea at the present time what the cause or causes of natural mutation are, nor are we able to predict exactly when they will occur. However, we do know that they occur spontaneously, and we are even able to measure the rate at which they occur.

Our present understanding of the DNA code helps to understand how mutations may occur. Individuals suffering from sickle-cell anemia have hemoglobin which differs from normal hemoglobin in only one respect. It contains a unit of valine in place of a unit of glutamic acid. The RNA code (messenger RNA would be responsible for directing the development of hemoglobin) for valine is AUG, for glutamic acid UUG. Thus it may be that the production of sickle-cell hemoglobin arose from a change in which a certain A of the long code sequence for normal hemoglobin was replaced by a U.

A good example of such a natural mutation is the mutation responsible for the appearance of a breed of sheep known as the Ancon sheep. This first appeared in 1791 in

Figure 21. The Ancon Sheep. The ewe is in the center, the ram at the right. A normal ewe is on the left. Note the short, bowed legs. (Courtesy of *Life* Magazine. © *Time* Inc.)

the flock of Seth Wright, a New England farmer. He found a male lamb with remarkably short, bowed legs. Some of the fifteen ewes in Wright's flock were apparently heterozygous for the condition. When the Ancon ram was bred to these, Ancon offspring were produced. Of the fifteen lambs produced during the first season, two were of the new type. In succeeding years others were produced, and by breeding these to one another a pure-breeding Ancon variety was produced. Sheep of this breed are so short-legged that they are unable to jump over an ordinary stone wall or over a fence. This trait, of course, is an advantage to the farmer. In addition, their short legs limit their ability to run, so that they do not lose weight so readily as other sheep.

It might be pointed out in passing that this mutation, in keeping with our general experience with mutations, was actually a harmful one to the sheep. After all, it was disadvantageous to him not to be able to jump walls and not to be able to run fast. Such an animal would probably not survive long in a wild state. Moreover, this particular mutation also affected the reproductive rate. This effect was so pronounced that the breed became extinct in the 19th century. Interestingly enough, the mutation reappeared in the flock of a Norwegian farmer in 1925, and it has been possible to develop another Ancon variety from this sheep. This recurrence, too, is characteristic of mutations. Most of them appear several times in a period of years.

Mutation Rates

It is believed that mutations take place in the order of 10^{-5} (.00001) or 10^{-6} (.000001) per reproductive cell per generation. Because a given character is affected by a number of genes, it is believed that the frequency of new mutations affecting a single character may be of the order of 10^{-4} (.0001) or 10^{-2} (.01).[18] It is estimated that in *Drosophila* on the basis of a mutation rate of 10^{-6} a given gene will mutate once in about 40,000 years. However, because of the large number of genes it is believed that about one in every twenty germ cells will contain some sort of mutation. A large number of these mutations, however, will be lethal, killing the organism during its embryonic period, and this reduces the apparent number. Probably a large number, too, are so small that they escape detection.[19]

One mutation in man that has been carefully studied is that which brings about hemophilia, "bleeder's disease," in which the blood does not clot or the clotting time is abnormally long. As is the case in color blindness, the gene that controls this character is found on the sex chromosome and is inherited in a way similar to that of the gene for color blindness. Penrose and Haldane estimate that the normal allele of the hemophiliac gene mutates to hemophilia about once in fifty to one hundred thousand individuals per generation. This is a rate of between 1 and 2×10^{-5}.[20] More recently this rate has been revised, and it is now believed that the actual rate is about 3.2×10^{-5}. It is also believed that the male "X" chromosome mutates ten times as frequently as does the "X" chromosome of the female.[21]

Another estimate of mutation frequency in man is that made by Neal and Falls. They suggest that if man has 20,000 gene loci and if the average mutation rate is 2.6×10^{-5}, then the average total mutation rate ($2.6 \times 10^{-5} \times 2 \times 10^{4}$) is such that each diploid individual possesses one mutant gene not present in either parent.

However, this average figure is admittedly high. For one thing, in terms of animal life cycles this is a significantly higher rate than has ever been reported for any animal species. Then, too, the average reported is raised by figures for Pelger's nuclear anomaly, the frequency of which is 8×10^{-5}. The authors admit that this latter figure is not completely satisfactory.[22]

Muller's figure on the frequency of mutation is 0.1 to 0.5 per diploid individual compared with the 1.0 suggested by Neal and Falls.[23] Dobzhansky suggests a similar figure; he believes that 20 per cent of all humans carry newly arisen mutations.[24] Timofeeff-Ressovsky suggests an even lower rate. He believes that the total mutation rate per generation is of the magnitude of from 1 to 10 per cent. This would mean a rate of from 0.01 to 0.1 per diploid individual.[25] Winchester, who suggests a mutation rate of 5 per cent per generation for *Drosophila*, believes that the mutation rate in man is less than 10 per cent of the rate in *Drosophila*. He believes that in man the average gene is considerably more stable than in *Drosophila*.[26]

It must be admitted, then, that mutations occur and that their rate is apparently high enough to make possible a great deal of change.

The Cause of Mutations

Another very important problem is the mechanism by which these mutations occur. As was pointed out, we do not know what brings about the occurrence of mutations in nature. We only know that they do occur. In the laboratory we are able to produce mutations by various types of radiation — X ray, radium and radon, neutrons, and ultraviolet — by temperature changes, and by chemical agents.

By far the majority of the mutations produced have been produced by X ray. Organisms are exposed to a measured number of roentgen units and are then bred. Among the progeny of organisms so treated far more mutants are found than would ordinarily be expected. Often the X-ray dosage that is used is a sublethal dose, just under the dose that would be fatal. By using such a high dose a visible mutation rate of as much as 30 per cent has been obtained.

It appears that the rate of increase in mutations is in proportion to the dosage, as would be expected.[27] However, the mutation rate is independent of the wave length.

It has been suggested that mustard gas may be the source of spontaneous natural mutations. We know that mustard gas and related compounds may cause mutations. While it is very apparent that the cell rarely comes into contact with these compounds, it has been suggested that mutations may be caused by the production of these compounds within the cell as a result of various metabolic processes.[28] However, a large number of mutagenic agents active in microbial systems were found to be ineffective when tested with *in vitro* grown human cell lines.[29] In any case, it is rather evident that this cannot be the mechanism that brings about even a fair number of the mutations in nature.

Nor can natural radiation be the causative agent. Tests have been made to determine the actual amount of radiation to which an organism is subjected, and this has proved to be totally inadequate to cause mutations at the rate we know they occur. One type of radiation whose effects have been studied is cosmic rays. These rays are constantly entering our atmosphere from outer space. However, they are not abundant enough to bring about mutations at the rate at which they are known to occur. Moreover, it has been found that isolation from cosmic rays has no effect on the mutation rate.[30] Rensch says that according to our present knowledge it is improbable that spontaneous mutations are caused by ionizing radiations occurring under natural conditions.[31]

Nor is the amount of radiation from radioactive substances sufficient to cause mutations at the rate at which we know they are occurring.[32]

It must be stated, then, that at the present time we simply do not know what the cause of mutations in nature is, though Muller thinks that X rays, ultraviolet, and certain chemicals (such as mustard gas) may in their sum be inducing mutations at an appreciable rate.[33] We do know that they are occurring at a fixed measurable rate which differs in different organisms and in different genes of the organism. If it can be demonstrated that these actually bring about evolution, then the problem of the mechanism of evolution has been solved, and the problem of the cause of mutation remains for further scientific inquiry.

Most Mutations Lethal or Semilethal

The chief difficulty in the way of evolution by mutation is the fact that most mutations are either lethal or semi-lethal. Either they kill the organism outright — in which case they are said to be lethal — or they are harmful in some way, so that in the ordinary course of events they would be elimi-nated. These latter are said to be semilethal mutations. They include mutations in which the fertility rate is reduced, mutations which result in the loss of certain organs, and the like. The Ancon mutation is an example of a semilethal mutation. Winchester says that over 99 per cent of the muta-tions which have been studied in various forms of life are harmful in some degree.[34]

Supposedly Favorable Mutations

Some mutations, it is true, are believed to be helpful, and evolutionists argue that evolution takes place through these, even though they are very few. Let us examine some of these instances of supposedly favorable mutations. For instance, it has been reported that when purple eye and arc wing occur together in *Drosophila,* the viability rate is increased. Both "purple" and "arc" alone reduce the viability rate, so that flies with either of these mutations have a lower viability rate than the wild type flies. However, when these two are combined in a single individual, the viability rate is again increased.[35] Even this increase, however, does not bring the viability up to that of wild type flies. These latter, combining the results for both males and females, had an average life span of 39.47 ± 0.28 days. The "purple" flies had a life span of 24.54 ± 0.18 days. "Purple-arc" in combination increased the life span to only 33.71 ± 0.34 days. Muller points out, too, that this increase in viability may be due, not to the fact that these two genes in combination are favor-able, but rather to other factors. He points out that the stocks were not isogenic — identical for all genes except the two referred to, "purple" and "arc." This, he believes, suggests the possibility that other factors may be at work.[36]

Another mutation that is supposed to be favorable is one which abolishes phototropism, the tendency to fly toward a light, in *Drosophila* and which changes the body color to tan. Such flies would not be attracted to light which often leads to their death, and they would be at an advantage in dark surroundings. This mutation was first reported by McEwen in 1918. Nothing is said as to the effect of this gene on viability or of other possibly unfavorable effects of the gene.[37] Certainly these must be carefully studied before it can be stated that the mutation is a favorable one.

Rensch says that a small number of mutants show full or even increased viability or superiority in special fields of competition. Melanistic mutants of the moth *Ptychopoda sericata* show lower than normal mortality during development. He says that many other melanistic mutants show an increased viability.[38] On the other hand, as we pointed out earlier, most genotypes resistant to antibiotics are at some disadvantage in the absence of the antibiotic, and natural selection would oppose them.

Actually none of these "favorable" mutations have been examined carefully enough to warrant the conclusion that they are really beneficial. For one thing it is difficult to determine what is actually favorable for the organism. And it is also difficult to determine to what degree certain favorable characteristics outweigh other characteristics which may be unfavorable.

Nor do these "favorable" characteristics always behave as we would expect them to. For instance, we referred to the melanic forms of insects which have developed in some British manufacturing districts. These are usually regarded as evidence of an environmental adaptation which can be observed. Presumably they are better adapted to regions in which there is a great deal of smoke than are their lighter-colored relatives. Yet Ford points out that these forms which are supposed to be especially adapted to manufacturing areas have spread into regions outside the manufacturing areas.[39] We should not expect them to have any advantage here, and yet they have continued to spread. Certainly it is by no means certain that their dark color is responsible for their survival.

Ford points out, too, that in the geometrid moth, *Gonodontis bidentata,* the melanic or dark form (*nigra*) can emerge at a lower temperature than can the typical form. Yet the melanic form (which has almost completely replaced the typical form in the "dark" country of Lancashire) has not spread to the north, where its ability to emerge at a lower temperature should have a distinct advantage.[40]

There are some geneticists who question the appearance of any favorable mutations in the genetic work that has been done to date. Ford, for example, says that it appears highly doubtful that any mutations which have occurred have given rise to changes which could be of survival value in nature.[41] And Strandskov says that the variations produced by mutations bear no direct relationship to the requirements of the organism, though he believes that a very few mutations are favorable.[42] Muller discusses the matter from a little different angle and says that there is no relation between the kind of natural circumstances (e. g., type of climate or prevailing physiological state) under which given mutations arise and the direction of phenotypic change brought about by mutations. In other words, a change in environment does not seem to call forth mutations which adapt the organism to that environment. He goes on to say that there is no adaptive relationship between the two in the sense that the changes might tend to be of types that would be useful under the circumstances prevailing when they arose. In general, according to Muller, the natural mutations are sporadic, and one gets the same range under one type of conditions as under another.[43]

It is generally agreed, as we have pointed out, that mutations are almost always harmful. Muller, for instance, asks whether variations have a tendency to be adaptive and to further life. His answer is that the data on the actual occurrence of mutations show just the opposite. The vast majority of observed mutations, he says, are positively detrimental.[44] He believes, though, that this fact actually supports Darwin. And Ford says that of hundreds of mutations which have been studied in the various *Drosophila* species scarcely one has been found which does not lower the viability as compared with the wild type.[45] He further points out that mutations which have arisen in the laboratory are nearly always associated with some lowering of vitality as compared with wild type forms, and the more marked their effect, the more harmful does their action seem to be. Mutations, he says, appear to be concerned with the production of small superficial differences or with obviously pathological departures from the normal condition which could not, in any event, survive in a state of nature.[46]

Most Mutations Recessive

Closely related to the fact that most mutations are either lethal or semilethal is the fact that in most forms mutations are generally recessive to the wild type. This is significant because, in general, recessives have a lower viability than do their dominant alleles. Very often this difference in viability is striking. Sometimes it is associated with the fact that the recessive is obviously pathological. But this is not always the case. Even where the recessive gene is not obviously harmful it often reduces the viability and fertility rate to such a degree that it would soon be eliminated in nature. Any cursory examination of breeding data will show this striking reduction, and all geneticists recognize that this is the case.

A good illustration of how unfavorable recessives are is the study reported by C. Gordon. He liberated 36,000 *Drosophila melanogaster* in England, where they are not

normally found. This population contained originally 50
per cent of the recessive gene ebony (25 per cent were type,
25 per cent were homozygous "ebony," and 50 per cent were
heterozygous). After 120 days — a period representing five
or six generations — a large number of flies were caught and
examined. It was found that the frequency of the recessive
had fallen to 11 per cent.[47]

Harmful Dominants

But even the dominant mutations which occur are frequently harmful. Ford says that while a few so-called
dominant mutations have certainly occurred in *Drosophila*
and other forms, these do not in the least represent the production of normal dominant characters such as are to be
found in wild type as the alleles of recessive mutations.
Many of these genes, he says, though appearing to be dominant in the heterozygous condition, are not completely
dominant, and they are usually found to be extremely lethal
as homozygotes. He goes on to say that in the majority of
such instances the homozygous type is wholly inviable.
Later he goes so far as to say that it may be stated that no
mutation has ever occurred in the progress of genetic work
which is fully viable and which behaves as a dominant to
the wild type gene.[48]

The Gene Complex

One point that must be considered in connection with
mutations is the gene complex in which that mutation occurs.
This term refers to the sum total of the genes which the
organism possesses. The gene complex is an elaborately coordinated system, very delicately balanced. For that reason
any alteration is likely to be harmful. Indeed, it is believed
that this accounts for the fact that most mutations are harmful. No matter what change they effect, mutations are likely
to upset the delicate balance to some extent. It is also to
be expected that the larger the change, the more likely

it is to prove harmful. It is unlikely that a change of any magnitude will be helpful. It is far more probable that it will cause a tremendous upset within the gene complex.[49]

Sometimes the gene complex acts to eliminate an unfavorable characteristic. "Eyeless" in *Drosophila* is a recessive character resulting in a reduction in the size of the eyes. Sometimes they are completely absent. It also results, like most mutations, in a decreased fertility and a lowered viability. Morgan found that after inbreeding eyeless flies for a number of generations without artificial selection, practically all the flies had normal eyes and showed little reduction in fertility or viability. The "eyeless" gene, however, had not disappeared, for on outcrossing to wild type flies the original

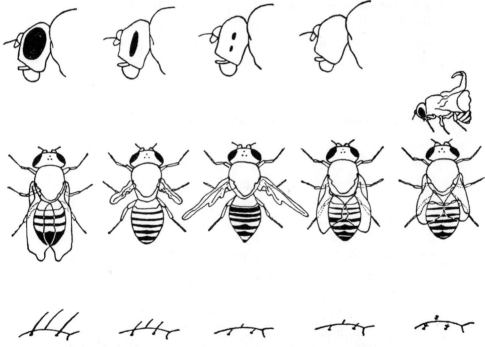

Figure 22. Mutations in Drosophila. The top line illustrates different eye mutants, the middle line different wing mutants, and the lower line different mutants in bristle shape. The illustrations to the left on the top and lower line illustrate the normal or "type" condition. (Redrawn from Goldschmidt's Understanding Heredity, Wiley, by permission)

characteristics of the "eyeless" stocks reappeared. In fact, there was an even greater variability in the condition.[50] It is believed that these phenomena are due to modifiers. By a selection of the most favorable gene complex the combinations making for "eyeless" were eliminated. Thus the gene complex served to preserve and maintain the *status quo*. It acted to eliminate the changes brought about by the "eyeless" mutation.

Ross believes that the primary influence restricting change is physiological. A change must act harmoniously in relation to the rest of the gene complex because of the many chemical pathways involved in duplicating the organism. Thus, the fact that a change is possible chemically does not necessarily mean that it will produce a balanced genetic system and that it will actually result in a permanent change in the organism. Genetic changes which are effectively introduced into a living population are restricted by the physiological framework into which they must fit.[51]

The Genetic Control of Development and Metabolism

It is believed that the genes function by producing enzymes which in turn control a series of steps resulting in the final structure or chemical substance. Thus substance A is changed to substance B in the presence of enzyme A, substance B to substance C in the presence of enzyme B, substance C to substance D in the presence of enzyme C. Any mutation is likely to result in the production of an enzyme which is unable to catalyze one of the steps of the process. The net result will be a structure imperfectly formed or not formed at all or a necessary chemical substance such as an enzyme or hormone not produced. This is what happens when a defective sickle-cell hemoglobin is produced. It is also what happens in the case of the diabetic who is unable to synthesize insulin.

Phenocopies

In this connection the phenomenon of phenocopies must be considered. This refers to the fact that changes similar to those effected by mutation are sometimes produced by the environment. Goldschmidt found that by exposing *Drosophila* larvae to a temperature between 35° and 37° C. for short periods at definite stages of their development he was able to bring about modifications of the wings and other organs similar to certain well-known mutations. These changes, however, are not hereditary. Probably the phenomenon is rare outside the laboratory. However, it is possible that some changes regarded as mutations are actually changes of this sort.

The Origin of Dominance

Another problem to be considered is the origin of dominance. Various theories have been suggested to account for this phenomenon, but none is completely satisfactory. It is very striking that most of the wild type genes should be dominant over mutants. Ford suggests that dominance may be a gradual development. He believes that at first the favorable character is recessive, then it becomes intermediate in its effects, and finally it becomes a dominant. He refers to the character known as "crinkled-dwarf" in Sea Island cotton. The character itself is a recessive, but when it is crossed to other mutant stocks, various degrees of dominance appear. He believes that this is due to the fact that the other stocks are not as strong and are not equipped to resist its dominance.[52]

Fisher has also suggested a way by which dominance may develop. He believes that the mutant and its normal allele are not the only genes which can alter the characteristics which they affect. He believes that natural selection will favor modifier genes which cover up the effects of new harm-

Figure 23. Phenocopies. At the top is a genetically rumpless fowl. This characteristic will be transmitted to the offspring. At the bottom is a phenocopy of rumplessness. In this case the trait will not be transmitted to the offspring. (From Sinnott, Dunn, and Dobzhansky's *Principles of Genetics*, McGraw-Hill, by permission)

ful genes. This would mean that eventually the new gene would no longer exert its characteristic effect when present, while the normal wild gene would still be able to act as usual, even when paired with one of the new mutants in a heterozygous state. Thus the new gene would be transformed into a recessive.[53] This particular theory has been criticized by Wright and by Haldane.[54]

Still another suggestion for the origin of dominance has been the theory of increasing potency, according to which a gene recurs with different potencies. Under favorable environmental conditions and with maximum strength it might appear as a dominant. Suppressor and enhancer genes are also supposed to play their part in the origin of dominance.[55]

In any case, it is clear that at the present time we have no idea as to how dominance develops or why certain few mutants are dominant and others recessive.

Position Effects

Another phenomenon that has been widely studied in this connection is that known as the "position effect." Here the effect of a gene is changed by its being surrounded by genes different from those which normally surround it. Thus in the normal sequence of genes ABCDEFG gene "C" has a certain effect. If, however, the sequence is altered by a chromosomal rearrangement such as one of those to which we shall refer in the next section, and the sequence becomes ABCFEDG, then the effect of the gene "C" will be somewhat different. Thus it is possible for the effect of a gene to be different even though it does not mutate.

However, these position effects are rather uncommon. While they do have striking effects when they occur, they probably occur so rarely that they can hardly contribute to the progress of evolution.[56] This is true in animals and especially in plants. Stebbins says that the position effect in plants is so uncommon that it has relatively little importance in plant evolution.[57]

The Likelihood of Selective Value in Mutations

Another question to be discussed is the likelihood of a mutation having real selective value. It may be that mutations occur and perhaps even with a fair degree of frequency. The question still remains: How many, if any, have a selective value? How many are really helpful to the organism? Fisher believes that the probability of any mutation being favorable to the organism is inversely related to the size of the mutation.[58] In other words, the smaller the mutation, the more likely it is to be favorable; and, conversely, the larger it is, the more likely it is that it will be harmful. This, of course, fits with our present concept of the gene complex to which we referred earlier. As we stated then, this delicate balance is easily upset. The larger the change, the more likely it is to be upset. Any mutation which upsets this complex will in its totality be harmful even though it does bring about some favorable characteristics. It is only reasonable to believe that the smaller the mutation, the less likely it is to upset the balance of the gene complex, and the more likely it is to be favorable *in toto*. This idea is quite generally accepted. Fisher is not the only one who believes that this is the case. Muller, for instance, also points out that those mutations which have smaller effects should on the whole be less harmful than those with marked effects. He believes that the smaller ones, therefore, have a better chance of getting established in the course of evolution than do the larger ones.[59]

In this connection a statistical measure of selective value has been worked out. It is known as the coefficient of selection, and is calculated as follows: Gene "A" and its allele "a" should occur in the same number of individuals in each generation, assuming that the frequency of the two genes in the general population is the same. If, however, selection favors "A" over "a," they will not continue to be equally frequent, but "A" will become more common than "a." In the generation following the one in which they are equally frequent, "A" will occur in n individuals and "a" will occur in $(1-s)n$ individuals. In this case s is the coefficient favoring "A." Complete selection, where s equals 1.00, occurs where the alternative is wholly lethal.

Most biologists feel that very small selection coefficients

have been responsible for evolutionary development, but Ehrlich and Holm disagree. They say that only recently biologists have begun to realize that very large selection coefficients may be the rule rather than the exception.[60]

Fisher has calculated the chances of survival of a given gene under neutral and favorable conditions.[61] It is presented in Table 5.

Number of Generations	Probability of Survival	
	No Advantage	$s=0.01$
1	0.6321	0.6358
3	0.3741	0.3803
7	0.2095	0.2175
15	0.1127	0.1217
31	0.0589	0.0687
63	0.0302	0.0409
127	0.0153	0.0271
Limit	0.0000	0.0197

Table 5: Chances of Survival of an Individual Gene

This table clearly indicates that in the course of time a neutral gene, one which has no advantages over its allele, will probably be eliminated. We are not too surprised at this result, and it has no real bearing on the problem of evolution, since we are concerned particularly with the survival of favorable genes. However, it is very striking that only 197 out of 10,000 favorable genes with a survival advantage of 1 per cent will survive. In other words, the probability is that even if the mutation is slightly favorable, it will be eliminated. Haldane agrees at least in principle with Fisher's conclusions and says that even if a mutation confers some favorable quality, the chances are strongly against its survival in the species.[62]

Coefficients of .01 corresponding to the 1 per cent advantage in Table 5 are said to have been demonstrated. Yet Wright believes that most of the mutations which have been important in evolution have had a much smaller selective coefficient than it is practical to demonstrate in the laboratory.[63] This would indicate that even fewer than 197 of 10,000 favorable mutants in nature will survive.

Other calculations confirm the fact that the chance of survival of a favorable gene is very slight and also indicate that it would take a very long time for a favorable gene to increase appreciably its frequency in the population. Boyd reports that if a dominant gene had a selective advantage of 0.1 per cent its frequency in the stock would increase from 5 per cent to 50 per cent (equally abundant with its allele) in slightly less than 3,000 generations, a period corresponding to between 60,000 and 70,000 years in man.[64] In all this time it would not have resulted in the formation of a new species; it merely would have become as common in the population as its allele. Even this assumes that its frequency at the beginning of the period was already 5 per cent. He also calls attention to a table reporting the time required for a given change in the per-cent frequency of a gene having a selective advantage of 0.01 (1 per cent), which we have reproduced as Table 6.[65]

DOMINANT GENE		RECESSIVE GENE	
CHANGE IN FREQUENCY FROM	No. OF GENERATIONS	CHANGE IN FREQUENCY FROM	No. OF GENERATIONS
0.01– 0.1	230	0.01– 0.1	900,230
0.1 – 1.0	231	0.1 – 1.0	90,231
1.0 –50.0	559	1.0 – 3.0	6,779
50.0 –97.0	3,481	3.0 –50.0	3,481
97.0 –99.0	6,779	50.0 –99.0	559
99.0 –99.9	90,231	99.0 –99.9	231
99.9 –99.99	900,230	99.9 –99.99	230

Table 6: Time Required for a Given Change in the Per-Cent Frequency of a Gene Having a Selective Advantage of 0.01 (1 per cent). Modified from K. Pätau

This means that a gene having a selective advantage of 1 per cent (and this is a greater advantage than most mutations which Wright believes have been important in evolution have had) would completely replace its allele in somewhat more than 1,001,741 generations — a fantastically long time. For the gene even to gain equality with its allele would take 1,020 generations if the gene were dominant, and 1,000,721 generations if the gene were recessive.

Carter says that the rate is so slow in recessives as long as the mutation is rare that it is doubtful whether it is fast enough to give an effective basis for differentiation even on an evolutionary scale of time. He says that this difficulty is real in the evolution of animals with a long life history and possibly in all evolution. A possible solution he finds in the fact that mutations occur repeatedly, but even this fact, he says, does not remove the whole difficulty. Another possible solution, according to Carter, is the possibility that some recessives may develop into dominants.[66]

Carter's own figures for the spread of a mutation which he has taken from Haldane are only slightly different from those which we have quoted. He believes that a recessive gene with a selective advantage of 0.1 per cent would increase in frequency in a population from 0.001 per cent to 1 per cent in 309,780 generations. It would go from 1 per cent to 50 per cent in 11,624 generations, from 50 per cent to 99 per cent in 4,819 generations, and from 99 per cent to 99.999 per cent in 6,920 generations. The speed of the spread of a dominant would be just the opposite. It would go from 0.001 per cent to 1 per cent in 6,920 generations; from 1 per cent to 50 per cent in 4,819 generations, etc.[67]

It is clear, then, that if a recessive mutant is to play any important part in evolution, its initial frequency must be rather high. This can come about only if the mutation rate is a very high one.

Wright refers to another aspect of this. His calculations are reproduced in Table 7.[68]

Population Size	Advantage of Homozygous Recessive 0.01	No Advantage (Neutral Gene)	Disadvantage of Homozygous Recessive 0.01
10	0.05	0.05	0.05
50	0.013	0.01	0.007
200	0.0057	0.0025	0.0003
800	0.0027	0.0006	0.00000

Table 7: Chance of Fixation of a Recessive Gene (Chance of Its Replacing Its Allele)

This indicates rather clearly that the possibility of a beneficial gene's becoming fixed is inversely related to the size of the population. It also indicates that in a large population a harmful gene will be eliminated and a gene which is neutral has little chance of survival. Indeed, it is only in a small population that neutral genes and harmful genes can survive. We shall have more to say on this particular topic when we discuss the Sewall Wright effect or genetic drift.

Also to be considered in this connection is that most of these studies have been based either on mathematical models or on laboratory experiments, and there is still some question as to whether mutations do produce qualities which actually have selective value in nature. Barnicot says that although the evidence provided by laboratory experiments may enable us to imagine the ways in which some attributes could have adaptive value in nature it may be very difficult to show by field observation what actually occurs.[69] We come back again to the concept of the gene complex. The studies that have been made have concentrated on improvement in one trait and have implied that evolution may come about through an accumulation of small improvements. But an improvement in one trait may upset the balance of the gene complex. Ehrlich and Holm use the analogy of an airplane. They say that we can try to improve the airplane by making the motor more powerful, but this would do little good if the increased speed would tear out the wings. The problem might be solved by strengthening the fuselage or the structural members of the wings. But this would not help if it made the airplane too heavy to get off the ground. They say there is a limit to how much one factor alone can be modified before the "working combination" is seriously disrupted.[70] Oparin points out that a particular organ can arise and become perfected only by the evolutionary development of the organism as a single whole.[71] Harris points to a number of instances where a series of changes would be necessary before the particular quality would be of any value to the individual.[72]

Mortality Rates and the Survival of a Given Gene

The mortality rate in different forms has a significant effect on the chance of random elimination. Those forms in which the mortality rate is very high are likely to lose the individual possessing the favorable characteristic. It appears that in man the mortality rate is 10 per cent (considering abortion and infant mortality rates). In mammals, however, under the most favorable conditions, the mortality rate appears to be about 90 per cent. In other animals the mortality rate appears to be 99 per cent in most terrestrial species except for species with special life cycles, such as the blister beetles. In these the rate is probably 99.9 per cent. This same mortality rate — 99.9 per cent — is believed to exist in many marine animals, and in many it may go as high as 99.9999 per cent.[73]

The Possibility of the Simultaneous Occurrence of a Number of Favorable Mutants

In view of these figures it should be rather evident that the chance of a favorable mutation surviving is very slight. It is also evident that those mutants which do survive will probably have only a very slight effect on the form, since mutants with large effects are almost always lethal. It might be asked whether it is not possible for a number of favorable mutants — individually small but in aggregate significant — to occur in a single individual. However, it appears that this is unlikely when we examine the possibility of this occurring. It has been calculated that if the mutation rate were .00001 (1 in 100,000 — an average mutation rate) and if the occurrence of each mutation doubled the chance of another mutation occurring in the same cell, the probability that five simultaneous mutations would occur in any one individual would be 1×10^{-22} (.0000000000000000000001). This means that if the population averaged 100,000,000 individuals and if the average generation lasted but one day, such an event (the appearance of five simultaneous mutations in one individual) would be expected once in every 274 billion years.[74]

Mutations and Pre-adaptation

We have referred to the obvious lack of relationship between mutants and the environment in which they develop. To account for this it has been suggested that organisms may be developing mutations which will be of use under future environmental conditions. This theory is known as pre-adaptation. It assumes that the organism develops a large number of mutations which are neutral or even harmful under the conditions in which they develop, but which are advantageous to the organism when conditions change. In other words, mutations supply a great deal of variety with which natural selection works not today, but at some future period in the earth's history. Or we might say that mutation provides the organism with a reservoir of potentially favorable variations which protect it against changes in the environment.

Rensch gives as an example of pre-adaptation the white mutant of *Drosophila* which is more resistant to higher and lower temperatures than the normal type and which he believes is favored during strong shifts of climatic conditions and in possible migrations and expansions into different climatic areas.[75]

Yet natural selection must work now and with the materials at hand. Darwin and his followers always assumed that natural selection worked with variation developing within the organism at the present time level. Moreover, it is hard to believe that selection would not act against neutral or harmful mutations to eliminate them before the environmental changes favorable to them appeared.

Romer questions the whole idea of pre-adaptation. He says that he doubts very much that development actually precedes utilization.[76] There are many geneticists who share these doubts. They recognize the problem of explaining how neutral or unfavorable characters can be retained until circumstances make them favorable.

Heterozygosity and Polymorphism

Usually associated with the idea of pre-adaptation is the concept that many organisms are highly heterozygous. Presumably the trait best adapted to some future environment is recessive and is less desirable in the present environment. The organism is protected against the undesirable effects of this recessive because the recessive is covered by the dominant allele; yet it is also available for the changed future environment.

Instances are also cited where the heterozygote has a higher viability or fertility rate than either homozygote. An oft-cited example of this is the sickle-cell gene. In the homozygote state it causes sickle-cell anemia which results in the death of most of its victims. Yet the gene seems to persist at a rather high frequency in the human stock, even though it is usually lethal when homozygous. It has been found that individuals heterozygous for the sickle-cell gene are more resistant to malaria than individuals who are homozygous for the gene producing the normal type of hemoglobin. Thus it has often been argued that the heterozygous condition has a marked advantage in the malarial regions of Africa and that this is the reason why the gene has been preserved in the human stock even though when homozygous it is lethal. Dobzhansky refers to evidence that heterozygous carriers of Tay-Sachs disease, infantile amaurotic idiocy, show a reproductive advantage of about 6 per cent:[77] this, it is suggested, is another example of where the heterozygote has an advantage over both homozygotes.

Also to be considered in this connection is the fact of

hybrid vigor. For some reason or other, outbreeding seems to be most desirable in most species and close inbreeding seems to result in undesirable traits. This is used as an evidence that heterozygosity is a desirable condition and provides a measure of fitness.

Stebbins believes that the evolutionary significance of heterozygote superiority in natural populations goes beyond the mere maintenance of adaptive fitness conferred by hybrid vigor. He believes that in complex organisms like higher animals and plants, adaptation to new environments requires the establishment of an entire gene complex involving scores of genes. When a change in the environment takes place, the most successful population will be the one which can most quickly alter its gene pool to take advantage of the change. Adjustment can be very rapid if there are some genes among those already existing in the gene pool which can immediately shift the population toward a new adaptive peak. Consequently, he says, those evolutionary lines which will have the greatest success in the long run will be those having a large store of concealed or partially used genetic variability. He believes that heterozygosity is a sort of genetic insurance in evolution.[78] Species showing a great deal of heterozygosity are likely to be highly polymorphic; that is, there is likely to be a wide variety of traits within the species.

Careful studies of the sickle-cell situation show that there are marked disadvantages to the heterozygous state which may well cancel out the demonstrated greater resistance to malaria. Barnicot refers to a study in which it was shown that heterozygotes for the sickle-celled gene do not concentrate their urine as much as normal controls. It is not known whether this condition persists under the conditions of strenuous work in heat, where a strong antidiuretic effect is normally manifested, but Barnicot believes the evidence indicates this genetic difference would probably be a distinct disadvantage in an arid climate.[79]

There are a number of geneticists who question the value of heterozygosity in evolution. Williams says there is no support for a general conclusion that heterozygosity has value as a biotic adaptation either by allowing evolutionary responses to changing conditions or by increasing tolerance to long-term changes or in any other way.[80] He believes that organisms would be better off so far as survival is concerned by being divided into a number of ecologically differentiated populations, each largely homozygous for different alleles rather than a single extensively heterozygous population.

Very often it is argued that the retention of an undesirable gene in the germ plasm is in itself evidence of some adaptive superiority. Essentially this is the argument behind the sickle-cell phenomenon, and it is believed that the discovery of the superior resistance to malaria of individuals heterozygous for the sickle-cell gene supports this conclusion. Stebbins argues in much the same way in discussing the large number of albino seedlings in orchard grass. He reports that from 5 to 48 per cent of the individual orchard grass plants are heterozygous for the albino genes and says that since such individuals would usually produce some lethal offspring and so would have a lower reproductive capacity than individuals free of such lethals, they could be kept in a population only if they were adaptively superior to individuals homozygous for the normal alleles. He goes on to say that the strong correlation of the percentage of heterozygotes with the soil on which the plants grew gives further support to the hypothesis that these plants remain in the population because of their adaptive properties.[81]

There are other very real problems with heterozygosity and polymorphism. Mayr expresses puzzlement over why phenotypic polymorphism is so widespread in certain groups of animals while other families are singularly uniform and says that even among closely related species one may be highly polymorphic and another completely uniform. He says that the only answer we can give at present is the very lame one that different organisms meet the challenge of the environment in different ways.[82]

Carson believes that individuals at the edge of the species range show homozygosity and that heterozygosity is characteristic only of the center of the population; yet it is at the edge of the species range that new environments present themselves for exploitation. He says that species in *statu nascendi* show homozygosity as opposed to heterozygosity and doesn't believe that heterozygosity is the source of new species in evolution. He points out, moreover, that organisms which depend heavily on heteroselection have limited futures. He says that such an organism is definitely restricted in long-term potential. Relying on vigor produced by heteroselection is a self-limiting process which cannot lead to novelties. He believes it would be going too far to say that progressive evolution has ceased in such forms, but he believes it may be so slow as to be essentially as closed to future change as if the species had substituted asexual reproduction for sexual.[83]

Burns reports spermatophore counts in the wild females of *Papilio glaucus* which show that monomorphic nonmimetic males mate less frequently with the mimetic female morph than with the nonmimetic morph, and he believes that female dimorphism in this species cannot be maintained by heterozygous advantage.[84]

There are many forms in which heterozygosity is impossible, and these seem to get along very well. Ehrlich and Holm say that many plants have genetic systems that seem to enjoy almost complete homozygosity from which they appear to suffer not at all. They believe that the relationship between fitness, heterozygosity, and outbreeding is not well understood as yet and that it cannot be assumed that all organisms maintain developmental and genetic homeostasis through outbreeding and heterozygosity.[85]

Reverse Mutations

Another fact to be considered in connection with mutations and evolution is the occurrence of reverse mutations. At one time it was thought that evolution was irreversible. Once the direction of evolution had been established, it continued to proceed in that direction. In fact, evolutionists had a law, known as Dollo's law, which stated that evolution is irreversible.

However, all this has now changed, and it is now believed that evolution is reversible. Romer says that there is not only strong evidence from recent forms of the reversibility of evolution but that the paleontological evidence is conclusive. He believes that the idea of the irreversibility of evolution can no longer be accepted.[86]

There is no doubt, too, that reverse mutations — mutations which change a character back to its original or wild type condition — occur in organisms, so that Dollo's law can hardly be regarded as having a genetic basis. Muller goes so far as to say that most mutations in *Drosophila* are reversible in direction and that very often the reverse mutation appears to reconstitute precisely the original gene.[87] Huxley reports that in guinea pigs a stock has been developed with four toes on the hind feet. The normal guinea pig has only three toes on its hind feet. It is believed to have evolved from a four-toed stock and to have lost its fourth toe millions of years ago. The development of this fourth toe again is believed by Huxley to indicate definitely that reverse evolution may occur.[88] It would be interesting to know how paleontologists would recognize such a form, if fossilized, as a modern form. Might they not regard it as an early stage in guinea-pig evolution?

Not only do these reverse mutations occur, but they occur rather frequently. Table 8 shows the results of a study of frequency of reverse mutations in *Drosophila*.

MUTATION	FORWARD		REVERSE	
	NO. OF GAMETES	NO. OF MUTATIONS	NO. OF GAMETES	NO. OF MUTATIONS
+to forked	43,000	11	44,000	15
+to pink eye	52,000	1	58,000	9
+to eosin	69,500	9	72,000	3
eosin to white	69,500	28	54,000	0
+to bar	69,500	0	9,000	8

(+=wild type)

Table 8: Mutations in Drosophila

Modified from Blum, Harold F. *Time's Arrow and Evolution* (Princeton: Princeton University Press, 1951), p. 148

It should be pointed out that these results may be unusual and that the rate is perhaps unusually high. Ordinarily, the reverse mutation rate is probably lower than these data would indicate, though according to Blum these data are perhaps the only data available for a careful study of the problem.

Some have suggested that apparent reverse mutations are actually mutations at entirely different gene loci; however, careful analysis has established the existence of true reverse mutations.[89]

There are many geneticists and evolutionists who believe that in spite of these reverse mutations, evolution never really reverses itself. They believe that it would be inconceivable for conditions to be exactly the same at two different times. Muller, for instance, concludes that real reversibility in evolution does not occur.[90] Blum doubts that the mutations reported are strictly reversible changes,[91] though Muller, as we pointed out, believes that reverse mutations often reconstitute the original gene. Evolutionists question whether it is possible for exactly the same genes to come together in one organism. And yet they do not find it difficult to believe that the most desirable aggregate of genes can come together in response to the needs of natural selection.

What are the implications of reverse mutations for the theory of evolution? Certainly they increase the problem.

For evolution will move very slowly indeed if it moves forward three steps and then takes two steps backwards. It reduces the amount of variation available to natural selection. For those mutations which are reverse mutations do not provide variety; instead, they cancel out existing variety. They slow down the rate at which evolution can occur.

Restrictions on the Direction of Mutation

Another point to be considered are the restrictions on the direction of mutation. Changes do not occur in all directions, but only in a limited number of directions. For instance, green is rare in adult butterflies. There have been no mutations to blue in woodpeckers; there have been no mutations to red or yellow or green in the plumage of gulls; and there have been no mutations to red in penguins.[92]

Oddly enough in this connection the ingenious studies of Dr. Levick seem to indicate that the Adélie penguins prefer red to all other colors. He found that sitting penguins steal stones from one another's nests. He then colored stones various colors to see which ones the penguins would steal. He found that the red stones were most widely distributed in penguin nests, and he concluded that this indicated a preference for red.[93] Yet no mutation to red has ever occurred in penguins. Apparently nature missed a bet here, for a male penguin who developed some red in his coat pattern would undoubtedly, according to theories of sexual selection, have been preferred by the females. Imagine what a sensation a male who developed a red necktie to go with his black and white formal would have created!

The chemical nature of DNA restricts the direction of mutation in that only certain new bondings or breaks can be made in a complex biological compound without destroying it.

Someone has compared these restrictions to the wheel of fortune in a well-managed casino which betrays a strong urge to stop at certain numbers and to avoid others. But the fact that there are such limitations restricts the directions that evolution can take, and it also limits the ability of an organism to adapt itself to its environment, for the necessary mutations may not even be possible.

It also appears that whenever variation in a new direction becomes established, the chance of further advance in that same direction is increased. Huxley believes that once an evolutionary trend has begun, much greater changes are necessary to switch the stock over to some other mode of life than to improve the arrangements for the existing mode of life.[94] It almost seems as if a sort of orthogenesis is occurring in spite of the evidence against it.

Blum also speaks of evolution as being channeled along certain paths, but not in the sense of orthogenesis. He believes that the most convincing evidence for this is derived from homology and analogy.[95] One wonders why it is so far fetched to believe that these similarities are attributable to a common basic plan in the mind of the Creator.

Mutation Suppressors

Other restrictions on mutations also seem to exist. Sturtevant and Shapiro believe that in the course of time the mutation rate is gradually reduced through the selection of mutation suppressors, at least in well-established and well-adapted species.[96] In brief, as time goes on, the rate of mutation decreases, so that evolution is a sort of self-limiting process. It automatically slows itself down and even stops.

Restrictions Imposed by Parthenogenesis

It is also recognized that in parthenogenetic species such as *Habrobracon* (a parasitic wasp in which males develop from unfertilized eggs), evolution will take place more slowly. Recessives which are in any way unfavorable should be eliminated almost at once. In diploid individuals, recessives may be balanced by their dominant alleles and the organism shielded from their ill effects. But this cannot occur in forms with male haploidy (those forms, such as *Habrobracon,* in which the males develop from unfertilized eggs). For in these, recessive mutations show up in the males at once. It is difficult enough for mutations to become established in a diploid stock. It is even more difficult for these to become established in a stock in which parthenogenesis occurs.

Additional evidence of this effect can be seen from observations made on the relative number of mutants found on the sex chromosome in forms such as *Drosophila* compared with the number of mutations to be found on the autosomes. Gordon and Dubinin report that the incidence of mutant genes in the sex chromosome of wild-caught individuals is low compared with their incidence in the autosomes.[97] It is believed that this is due to the fact that recessive genes in the autosomes do not exert their effects except when homozygous (occurring in a double dose). This cannot occur unless two individuals are heterozygous (carrying one dominant and one recessive gene) for the gene mate, which rarely happens. Sex-linked mutations, on the other hand, exert their influence immediately in the male.

One would expect that forms in which male haploidy occurs would show little evolutionary progress. Yet the Hymenoptera (ants, bees, and wasps) are widespread and are usually regarded as a high and successful type. Indeed many zoologists consider them to be the most highly developed of the invertebrates.[98]

Mutation and the Origin of Sterility

Another problem is whether sterility between forms can develop by mutation. We have referred to this problem before and have called attention to one case in maize in which there are two strains which are thought to differ in a single gene pair and which will not cross. It is assumed that in this case sterility has been brought about by this single gene difference. Huxley says that such occurrences appear to be very uncommon, and that at the present time the evolutionary significance of this is not clear.[99]

We are not even certain that this is the actual way in which this sterility developed. It is merely assumed that this difference is responsible for the sterility. There is certainly a difficulty involved in this suggested mechanism, for unless several of the mutant kind are produced at once, the mutant form will necessarily die out. If only one of the mutant type is produced, there will be no form with which it can breed, and it will be lost.

Mutations as a Mechanism for Evolution: A SUMMARY

In summary we must say that mutations appear at first glance to supply a very promising mechanism for evolution. It does look very much as if this may be the mechanism for supplying the variety on which natural selection may work. A more careful analysis of this phenomenon, however, shows a great many problems and casts serious doubt on the idea that mutations supply the necessary mechanism for evolution. For one thing, most mutations are either lethal or semilethal. There is real doubt that any are really favorable. The chance, moreover, that a mutation will be preserved in the stock, even if favorable, is very slight. Mathematical calculations show this very clearly. Reverse mutations, which seem to occur rather frequently, would certainly slow down evolution. Moreover, there are many restrictions on mutations: restrictions on the direction of mutation, mutation suppressors which reduce the mutation rate, restrictions imposed by parthenogenesis, and the like.

Some evolutionists have themselves recognized these problems, and while they are reluctant to cast aside mutations as a mechanism for evolution, their fairness has forced them to point to the problems involved. Stebbins says that most point mutations affect the genotype so slightly that they can have very little effect on the evolution of self-fertilized forms.[100] Thus mutations cannot be a mechanism in this group of plants. MacBride says that laboratory mutations are no proof whatsoever that mutations had anything to do with the formation of species.[101] Elton thinks that mutation rates do not seem to be sufficient to account without discriminate spread for the origin of ecologically adaptive features in species.[102] R. A. Fisher goes so far as to say that the explanatory content of a theory of evolution only reaches its absolute zero with the mutation theory.[103] Huxley says that no one holds any longer to the notion that species in higher animals arise by a single mutation or even in a few steps. Evolution, he believes, consists in the accumulation and integration of many and mostly small genetic changes.[104] He also says that it must be admitted that the direct and complete proof of the utilization of mutations in evolution under natural conditions has not yet been given.[105] Carson says that one of the great dilemmas in modern evolutionary theory is that most of the mutations found repeatedly within such populations as those of the different *Drosophila* species do not constitute the kind of differences which distinguish species.[106]

Harris believes that it is impossible for evolution to have taken place by mutation in the time assigned to it. He says that we must assume that present-day living organisms are the products of purely random mutations and the equally random shuffling of genes in the gene complex and that we must further assume that selection has simply prevented the survival of countless others. This means that the incredibly complicated and superbly well-adjusted mechanisms of the mammalian body must have been assembled by pure and uninfluenced chance *within a period of less than 3 billion years*, which he regards as an improbability which cannot reasonably be entertained. He believes that selection could easily reduce the size of the assemblage of organisms to one which could be accommodated even on so limited an area as the surface of the earth, but it could not

limit the time needed for the occurrence by chance of so
vast a number of precisely and minutely adapted modifications. He discusses the development of the eye by small
random mutations and says that while the necessary mutations could certainly occur and could occur successively, the
probability of the mere chance occurrence of any one of
them is exceedingly small. Furthermore, that they should
occur one by one *in the right order,* even if interspersed
with disadvantageous modifications, is less probable still.
He says that, even though not impossible, the degree of
improbability of the series taken as a whole surely necessitates a time scale beyond any that is applicable and even
beyond any that is available.[107]

Medawar says that the main weakness of modern evolutionary theory is its lack of a fully worked-out theory of
variation, that is, of candidature for evolution, of the forms
in which genetic variants are proffered for selection. We
have, therefore, no convincing account of evolutionary
progress, he says; that is, of the otherwise inexplicable tendency of organisms to adopt even more complicated solu-
tions of the problems of remaining alive.[108] Ehrlich and
Holm quote Norbert Wiener as saying that it is very difficult
to study the interaction of two systems with different rates
of time course. This is true, he says, when we attempt to
understand history on the basis of day-by-day human behavior or when we try to understand phylogenetic history
on the basis of individual gene changes in contemporary
organisms.[109] Hooton believes that there are problems in
a theory of multiple spontaneous variations transmitted by
heredity and miraculously selected through surviving generations in such a way as to simulate direct morphological
adaptation. He states that a complete dependence upon
such a theory of evolution involves incredible absurdities.[110]
He believes that other factors must play a part. Lindsey
says that evolution has not been haphazard but directly
adaptive at every step. He believes that it is scarcely logical

to believe that it has come as a result of haphazard genetic changes or random mutations with an assumed preadaptive value.[111]

Goldschmidt is outspoken in his condemnation of mutations as a mechanism for evolution. He believes that at most they can bring about changes within the species. The sub-species and varieties formed, says he, are neither incipient species nor models for the origin of species. He characterizes them as diversified blind alleys. Only by changes involving whole chromosomes, to which we shall refer below, does he believe that real evolution can take place.[112] In commenting on Goldschmidt's views Mayr says the fact that some geneticists can come to conclusions diametrically opposed to those of other geneticists is striking evidence of our ignorance of the actual facts.[113]

Types of Chromosomal Change

A second mechanism for the development of variation involves whole chromosomes. A number of types of changes are possible. These can be divided into two general types: changes in the number of chromosomes and changes in the number or arrangement of genes within a chromosome. All of these changes may be classified as follows:

I. Changes in the number of chromosomes

    A. Changes involving whole sets

        1. Haploidy or monoploidy: each chromosome represented only once instead of twice

        2. Polyploidy: each chromosome represented more than twice. This includes triploid individuals, in which each chromosome is represented three times; tetraploids, in which each chromosome is represented four times; octoploids, in which each chromosome is represented eight times; etc.

        a. Autopolyploidy: a polyploid derived from a single diploid individual

      b. Allopolyploidy or amphiploidy: a polyploid derived from a hybrid between two diploids

B. Changes involving the number of chromosomes in a set: heteroploidy or aneuploidy

    1. Monosomics: organisms which have lost one chromosome from one set

    2. Polysomics: organisms which have gained one or more chromosomes in a set. This includes trisomics, which have gained one chromosome in one set; tetrasomics, which have gained two chromosomes in one set; etc.; also double trisomics, which have gained one chromosome in two sets; etc.

II. Changes in the number or arrangement of the genes within a chromosome

A. Changes in number

    1. Deficiency or deletion: loss of one or more genes. ABCDHIJ

    2. Duplication: addition of one or more genes. ABCDEFGEFGHIJ

B. Changes in arrangement

    1. Translocation or segmental interchange. This involves an exchange of parts between non-homologous chromosomes to form two new chromosomes. If the original chromosomes were ABCDEFGHIJ and KLMNOPQRSTUV, then the new ones might be ABCDEFRSTUV and KLMNOPQGHIJ

    2. Inversion. Within the chromosome a block of genes may become rearranged. If the order were ABCDEFGHIJ, by inversion it might become ABCHGFEDIJ

All of these changes have been demonstrated and are

known to take place. It is also known that they bring about marked changes within the organism. If this mechanism will work, it is a mechanism for bringing about sudden, marked changes within the species. These changes are of a much greater magnitude than those brought about by mutation. They are just as sudden and abrupt and accomplish a great deal more. Goldschmidt believes that this is the only mechanism by which changes of the magnitude demanded by evolution can take place.

Haploidy

Haploidy can probably be dismissed rather quickly as a possible mechanism for evolution. It occurs regularly in the alternation of generations in plants, where one generation reproduces asexually and is diploid and the next generation reproduces sexually and is haploid. In addition, the males of some species of animals are regularly haploid. In other cases where it occurs it is distinctly an abnormal condition, definitely harmful to the organism. Haploid plants, for instance, are smaller than their diploid relatives, and their cells have a volume about half that of the diploid cells.[114] They can hardly be regarded as a means of improving the stock; their occurrence is definitely harmful.

Polyploidy

There is no doubt that polyploidy, and particularly tetraploidy, has been the means of producing what are ordinarily regarded as new species. We have referred to the occurrence of some of these forms before. They do not interbreed with their parent forms, and they are fertile when bred among themselves. In general they meet the criteria which have been set up for good species. That this mechanism is important is indicated by Mayr's statement that polyploidy is the only proved mechanism of instantaneous speciation in sexually reproducing organisms.[115] And Stebbins says that polyploidy is one way, and perhaps the only way, in which an interspecific barrier can arise in one step and thus give an opportunity to a new line to evolve independently and to diverge from the parental type.[116]

It is also apparent that this mechanism is a rather common one. Stebbins reports that typical allopolyploid species have been synthesized in forty or more instances. He reports, too, that between 50 and 100 naturally occurring species have been analyzed and appear to be autopolyploids.[117] This number is smaller than the number suggested at one time. Many of the forms thought to be the result of autopolyploidy are now believed to be the result of hybridization.[118]

The Origin of Polyploids

How is polyploidy brought about? It appears that most cases are due to abnormal cell division of one sort or another. Instead of germ cells undergoing reduction division, so that they have only the haploid or monoploid number of chromosomes, the germ cells receive the diploid number, usually as a result of both sets of chromosomes going to one cell and the other cell receiving none at all. Such an abnormal germ cell, if an egg, is then fertilized; or if a sperm, it fertilizes an egg. If the other gamete which it fertilizes or by which it is fertilized is a normal haploid gamete, the zygote is triploid. If, by chance, it meets another diploid gamete, the zygote is tetraploid. An octoploid results when this abnormal situation occurs in a form that is already tetraploid.

Polyploidy may also develop as a result of an irregular mitosis (ordinary cell division). Instead of one set of chromosomes going to one pole and the other set to the other pole in anaphase and telophase, both sets go to one pole.

The Production of Polyploids

Various ways have been employed to bring about such abnormal cell division — both abnormal reduction division and abnormal mitosis — in the laboratory. Sometimes tissues have been irritated to produce abnormal types of cell division. Most of the cases of chromosomal doubling, however, have taken place as a result of treating a plant with colchicine, an alkaloid drug derived from the corm of *Colchicum autumnale,* the autumn crocus. A great many polyploids have been produced in this way. The drug interferes with the metabolism of nucleic acid, one of the major constituents of the chromosomes. The prophase, or first stage, of mitosis is apparently normal in colchicine-treated cells, but the spindle fibers — thickenings which draw the chromosomes to the ends of the cells — are either partially absent or missing entirely, so that two sets of chromosomes go to a single daughter cell.

What causes natural polyploidy is as much a mystery as the cause of natural mutations. Presumably abnormal cells are produced from time to time in various forms, and these result in the formation of natural polyploids.

The Effects of Polyploidy

What are the effects of polyploidy? In other words, what changes does this mechanism bring about? For one thing, it is generally observed that polyploidy results in some degree of gigantism. Polyploids are larger than their diploid relatives.

It has also been suggested that polyploids are better able to stand severe climates. They are therefore especially adapted to unfavorable habitats. But this idea has not stood up. Stebbins believes that this statement cannot be made as a generalization.[119] It is true that the number of polyploids increases as one goes north or to higher altitudes. But Stebbins believes that this is without significance. It is also true that in some cases it appears that polyploids have a wider geographical range than what are assumed to be their diploid ancestors, but Stebbins points out that this is by no means universal.[120] Polyploids are also believed to possess

Figure 24. Effects of Polyploidy. All these apples are of the McIntosh variety. Those at the top are diploid; those at the bottom are tetraploid. The tetraploids are almost twice as large as the diploids. (Courtesy U. S. Department of Agriculture)

a wider range of tolerance for climatic and edaphic conditions: they can stand wider ranges of temperature and water supply than can their diploid ancestors. Stebbins believes, though, there are other ways, too, in which plants can adapt themselves to new habitats.[121]

Stebbins points out other differences. Polyploidy tends to decrease osmotic pressure, though this does not always happen and cannot be regarded as a generalization. This in itself would be an unfavorable characteristic, since a plant with a high osmotic pressure is able to get more water from the soil than a plant with low osmotic pressure. Desert plants typically have a high osmotic pressure. Conversely plants that grow in wet places usually have a low osmotic pressure. Autopolyploids in general also show a lower growth rate than do their assumed diploid ancestors. They flower later than do the diploids. Both of these characteristics appear to be unfavorable characteristics. However, polyploids flower over a longer period of time. This, presumably, is a favorable characteristic. In polyploids the amount of branching is reduced, and the leaves are usually thicker. Under some conditions these characteristics might be favorable; under other conditions they would be unfavorable.[122]

The Reduced Fertility of Polyploids

In general polyploids have a lower reproductive rate than do their diploid relatives. This is especially marked in triploids, but also appears in tetraploids. Ross points out that all triploid species of animals reproduce parthenogenetically and that triploids and other odd *n* plants occur as isolated perennial individuals in many groups but as with the animals never form bisexual populations.[123]

This reduction in fertility in triploids is due to the fact that apparently only those gametes are viable which receive one or two complete sets of chromosomes. For example, if the monoploid number of chromosomes is nine, a triploid will contain 27. In meiosis, or reduction division, these may be distributed in any fashion, but only those gametes which receive each of the nine original chromosomes or a pair of each of the nine original chromosomes show a fairly normal viability and fertility. If one or more chromosomes is missing, or if one or more is duplicated while the others occur singly, the gamete is likely to be inviable. This is due to the fact that, as we have pointed out earlier, the gene balance is extremely complex and extremely delicate. Adding a chromosome has the effect of adding a whole set of genes; subtracting a chromosome has the effect of subtracting a whole set of genes. Such an addition or subtraction is likely to upset the balance to such a degree as to make the gamete inviable.

This inviability is not restricted to triploids. Tetraploids, too, show a marked reduction in viability and fertility. It is, of course, more likely that in meiosis in these there will be an equal division of the chromosomes, but even here there is a good chance that the division will not be equal and the resulting gamete will be inviable.[124] For that reason the reduction in fertility is not surprising. Stebbins reports that the reduction in pollen and seed fertility in autopolyploids as compared with their supposedly diploid ancestors ranges from 5 per cent to 20 per cent in some maize to almost 100 per cent in an autotetraploid of *Gossypium herbaceum,* one of the cottons.[125] In other words, the latter is almost completely sterile. He does not believe that this is due to an irregular segregation at meiosis as we have suggested above and as has been suggested by a number of investigators, but he believes that it is due to the effect of certain specific genes or gene combinations. In maize the effect is, he believes, largely physiological. In *Antirrhinum* (the snapdragon), *Dactylis* (the orchard grass), and *Lolium* (the darnel), it seems to be due to a lagging of the chromosomes at later stages of meiosis. Other investigators, too, report facts which seem to suggest genic rather than cytological effects.

The significant point is the loss of viability and fertility regardless of its cause. This can hardly be an important method of evolution if it results in the formation of inviable and partially sterile forms. For that reason it is generally agreed that chromosomal mutations can ordinarily survive only if the individual is capable of perpetuating itself in some other way. Tetraploid plants can survive, for instance, if they reproduce by clones, stolons, rhizomes, bulbs, or "winter buds." Gustafsson has shown that among the perennials polyploid species are more common in forms with effective methods of vegetative reproduction than in forms with other methods of reproduction.[126] Polyploid forms might also survive in animals in hermaphrodite and parthenogenetic species.[127]

It should be noted that in some instances polyploids do appear to regain their fertility after several generations.

It appears that some eventually become stabilized and are able to reproduce at a normal rate. Fertility in polyploids may sometimes be restored by alterations in the chromosomal structure which eliminate the association of chromosomes from the two parents. Or fertility may be restored by gene mutations which suppress or counteract the physiological disharmonies of chromosomes from the two different parents which are responsible for their failing to pair at meiosis.[128]

One way in which this first condition can come about is through a failure of the chromosomes to separate at mitosis. In this way each chromosome is double, so that there are homologs for the chromosomes from the two different parents. It is generally assumed that this is the most common way in which allopolyploids regain their fertility. However, it is apparent that this is not the only way in which recovery of fertility can be accomplished, since there are some instances in which complete fertility has returned and constant true breeding lines have developed from sterile interspecific hybrids without a doubling of the chromosome number.[129] Yet unless polyploids have an effective means of vegetative reproduction, they are likely to die out before these changes take place and they can regain their fertility and viability.

Polyploidy Limited Almost Exclusively to Plants

Another important difficulty in the way of polyploidy being an important mechanism for evolution is the fact that it is limited almost exclusively to the flowering plants. Only one polyploid is known among the gymnosperms (the conifers).[130] Multiple sets of chromosome numbers have been reported in some genera of the algae, and this might indicate polyploidy in these forms. Polyploidy is rare or possibly even absent in the fungi. Most cases of polyploidy in the flowering plants are found in the perennial herbs. Only a few cases are reported in the woody plants.[131]

Darlington believes that the almost complete absence of
polyploidy in the gymnosperms and its comparative rarity
in the woody plants is due to the fact that it is mechanically
impossible where the chromosomes are large relative to the
cell size.[132]

Polyploidy occurs in *Paramecium*, a protozoan. It is very
rare in the multicellular animals. White says that it is extremely rare, possibly even rarer than is generally believed.[133] There is some indication of polyploid species in
the hermaphroditic Mollusca (shelled animals, such as the
clam and the oyster) and Annelida (segmented worms).
The polyploid races of animal species, such as *Solenobia*
(a psychid moth) and *Trichoniscus* (the sow bug), are usually parthenogenetic.[134] Other examples from the parthenogenetic arthropods are also reported. Haldane suggests that
there may be polyploids in the Lepidoptera (*Lycia*). He
reports that the only artificial animal allopolyploids have
been developed in this group (in *Pygaera* and *Saturnia*).[135]
Slack claims that polyploidy occurs in the Heteroptera (true
bugs), but White doubts that this is the case.[136] There is
some evidence of polyploidy in the weevils and among the
fish in the Salmonidae. Stebbins refers to this latter as the
first example of a sexual polyploid complex.[137] All of these
are apparently cases of autopolyploidy. White says there
are no well-authenticated instances of allopolyploidy in the
Metazoa.[138]

Wallace points out that for an animal polyploid species
to survive successfully, a complicated combination of rare
events — hybridization and doubling of the chromosome
number — would have to occur simultaneously in each of
two individuals, one male and one female, living in the
same neighborhood. Furthermore, these two individuals
would have to choose each other as mates in preference to
normal individuals of the parental species living in the
same region, and their offspring too would have to prefer
one another and mate brother and sister for a number of

generations. Animal species then could adopt polyploidy, he believes, only as a consequence of coincidence of four, five, or six extremely rare events.[139]

It has been suggested that the reason for the rarity of polyploidy in animals which reproduce sexually is the fact that sex is determined by either the homogametic or heterogametic condition. In the heterogametic sex (male in mammals, female in birds) the two like sex-chromosomes of major value would tend to segregate from one another. The result would be the production of few or no gametes having the normal ratio of sex chromosomes to autosomes. As a result polyploidy in sexually reproducing animals is almost impossible.[140] This is one of the reasons why Mayr says that while polyploidy is the only proved mechanism of instantaneous speciation in sexually reproducing organisms, and while it is common among plants, it is of no significance in animals.[141]

Polyploids and Kinds

In any case, polyploids are certainly not new kinds in the sense in which the word is used in Genesis. Stebbins says that the species originating by polyploidy are for the most part very similar to their diploid ancestors, both in their external morphology and in their preferences for certain ecological niches. Or else, in the case of allopolyploids, he says, they contain recombinations of characteristics found in their ancestors.[142]

The Origin of Natural Polyploids

Stebbins points out that it is difficult to decide in what way natural polyploids have originated. It might seem at first glance that it should be very easy to determine whether the polyploids originated from a single diploid species or from a cross between two diploid species. And yet no single criterion can be used to decide whether the form has arisen from a fertile species or from a sterile interspecific hybrid.

Types of Polyploidy

Nor can all forms be classified as autopolyploids or allopolyploids, for this classification, according to Stebbins, fails to recognize all of the patterns of cytogenetic variation which polyploids produce. Stebbins suggests at least four categories: autopolyploids, segmental allopolyploids, true or genomic allopolyploids, and autoallopolyploids. The first two conditions occur in triploid or tetraploid forms. The third is to be found in forms that are tetraploid or that have an even higher multiple of the diploid number. The last is to be found in forms that are hexaploid or more.

Another term used by Stebbins is amphiploid. He defines this as a polyploid which has arisen after hybridization between two or more diploid species normally separated by barriers of hybrid sterility. This covers the last three groups plus the aneuploids, which we shall discuss later.[143]

We have defined autopolyploids earlier. Ehrlich and Holm believe that strict autopolyploids are rare in nature.[144] Segmental allopolyploids are those forms containing two pairs of genomes (sets of chromosomes) which possess in common a number of homologous chromosome segments or even whole chromosomes, but differ from one another in another group of genes or chromosome segments. In a sense this is an unstable condition and ordinarily changes either in the direction of a typical autopolyploid or of a typical allopolyploid. Such a form usually produces partly fertile hybrids when it is backcrossed to one of the parental species. It is this type of development that we have in introgressive hybridization, to which we shall refer later.

A true or genomic allopolyploid is fully fertile and constant from the start. It is also strongly isolated and is not fertile in crosses with its relatives. These are usually tetraploids or hexaploids but may even contain four different sets of chromosomes, as in the grass *Bromus carinatus*.

Autoallopolyploids are forms which have resulted from a chromosomal doubling following a cross between two separate species. These may be AAAAAABB or AAAABBBB. The origin of these is usually so complex, according to Stebbins, as to defy analysis at present.[145]

Polyploidy and New Ecological Niches

Stebbins believes that the chief external factor making possible or favoring the establishment of polyploidy is the availability of new ecological niches. In other words, there must be some new habitat to exploit; otherwise there will be no advantage to the polyploid. For if it develops in the same habitat as its diploid ancestor, it will have to compete with already-established diploids and will be at a disadvantage. For that reason Stebbins believes that polyploidy has an advantage only when new environmental conditions arise suddenly.[146]

Polyploidy and Recessive Characters

Autopolyploidy restricts the evolutionary function of recessives. In most cases the recessive condition does not appear unless all four recessive genes are present. In other words, a single dominant will result in the appearance of the dominant character. There are only a few cases in which three recessives are dominant over a single dominant. Most mutations are recessive, and this can only mean that in polyploids they will have little chance of showing themselves. In a diploid they are able to make themselves felt in the offspring of a cross in which both parents carry the recessive. In a tetraploid, however, they can appear only in the offspring of parents which carry two recessives and then only as the result of a combination in which both the egg and the sperm have those two recessives.

Polyploidy and Progressive Evolution

Stebbins believes that the long-continued evolution needed to differentiate genera, families, orders, and phyla appears to have taken place chiefly on the diploid, or at least on the homoploid, level in those forms which have had a polyploid origin. The little evidence that exists for evolution by means of polyploids, he feels, is a bit hazardous at present and not too impressive. He says that even with this evidence it does not appear that progressive evolution is furthered by polyploidy. He points out that none of the trends in floral specialization which have been so important in plant evolution are caused or promoted by polyploidy. And he concludes that polyploidy does not originate a major new departure. Indeed, he says, polyploidy is a complicating force rather than one which promotes progressive evolution. The species originating by polyploidy he characterizes as being for the most part very similar to their diploid ancestors in external morphology and in ecological preferences, or else they contain recombinations of the characteristics found in those ancestors.[147]

Cameron believes that polyploidy is an evolutionary dead end and that ultimately polyploids will succumb as a result of their inability to go back to the diploid condition and because genetic variation seems to be hampered by the high number of chromosomes.[148] Ehrlich and Holm say that such mechanisms as polyploidy are often considered disadvantageous from a very long-range view. However, they argue that since they are extremely common in both plants and animals, they must have some selective advantage.[149]

The Multiplication of Chromosomes

It should be pointed out that chromosome number cannot be doubled indefinitely without harmful results. Auto-octoploids, for instance, are nearly always so abnormal as to be sublethal. It appears that for each species there is an optimum chromosome number, and that any increase beyond this optimum number is actually harmful.[150] Ross points out that there is an apparent limit to the extent of polyploidy compatible with viability and fertility, and he believes this is probably associated with increasing problems of physiological adjustment when too many genes affect the same processes.[151]

Other Chromosomal Changes

Chromosomal changes other than polyploidy are actually of little importance so far as evolution is concerned. They are so harmful that they cannot possibly be the means by which evolution has occurred. However, it has been suggested by some investigators that under some circumstances evolution may have occurred by types of chromosomal changes other than polyploidy. It has been suggested, for instance, that changes in the chromosome number have come about by the gradual addition or subtraction of single chromosomes. This results in aneuploid forms.

a. Reduction in the Number of Chromosomes

Chromosome reduction can take place only if there is a loss of a centromere, the fixed point where the spindle fiber attaches to the chromosome in cell division. Most instances of aneuploidy represent a decrease in chromosome number.[152] The number of chromosomes is determined by the number of centromeres. It is believed that the regions of the chromosome near this point are relatively inert. It is possible for chromosomes to be lost only if the centromere and the inert regions near it are lost. Chromosome number cannot be decreased by an end-to-end fusion of single chromosomes. Other genes near the distal portions — the far ends — of the chromosomes which have lost their centromeres attach themselves to other chromosomes in a sort of translocation and if only the inert material is lost, the chromosomal balance is not disturbed.[153]

These can survive only if the amount of material lost is negligible or insignificant, and in that case the amount of evolution accomplished by this mechanism is also negligible or insignificant. It should also be pointed out that this type of evolution involves a loss and not a gain.

b. The Addition of Chromosomes

More important from a theoretical standpoint is the addition of single chromosomes. Many evolutionists have concluded that much of the process of evolution has been the addition of chromosomal material by this method. Muller believes that the establishment of such repeats is the only effective means of gene increase in evolution except for polyploidy. He admits, though, that because of the gene imbalance brought about by aneuploidy there will be a certain amount of selection against the new type at first and that it can survive only in cases where the effects of genetic drift outweigh those of selection.[154]

Yet it is very striking that many of the so-called lower forms have a higher chromosome number than do the higher. The crayfish, *Cambarus virilis*, for instance, has 200; man has only 48; the shield fern, *Aspidium*, has 72; the onion, *Allium*, has only 8. And not only is this true, but in many cases the actual size of the chromosomes is greater in the so-called simple forms than in the more highly developed ones. Stebbins, for instance, points out that the most archaic types of land plants, the Psilotales and the Ophioglossales, have larger chromosomes than the majority of flowering plants. He says that plant physiology provides no evidence in favor of the hypothesis that progressive evolution has been accompanied by a regular increase in the number of gene loci found on each chromosome.[155]

It is also true that within certain groups the supposedly most primitive forms have the highest chromosome numbers. This is the case in *Crepis*, the hawk's-beard. It is believed that here evolution has been marked by a reduction in chromosome number, one chromosome at a time.[156]

According to Stebbins, there is no experimental evidence for evolution by an increase in chromosome number of the order suggested above, though it is believed that this occurred.[157] Ehrlich and Holm say there are numerous examples suggestive of progressive increase in chromosome number but unfortunately little experimental evidence.[158] White says that there is little evidence for a reduplication of one whole chromosome at a time in animals, except in a few very special cases.[159] In other words, there is little or no evidence that evolution has occurred by adding one chromosome and then a second chromosome to the chromosomal complex. Polysomics can occur only in a very abnormal type of cell division. They cannot be produced by a simple transverse fragmentation of the chromosomes, since this will not result in additional centromeres. Any increase must involve either a duplicate chromosome or at least a duplicate centromere-bearing fragment.[160] Testrasomics are usually unstable, and they normally lose their identity by crossing with their normal relatives.[161]

White believes that the formation of supernumerary chromosomes is the chief method by which chromosome number has increased. A supernumerary chromosome is one which is absent in some individuals of the species altogether without noticeably affecting the appearance of the organism. The genetic properties of this chromosome are so slight that individuals possessing several or none at all are fully viable and differ, if at all, in ways so insignificant as to escape notice. Presumably, too, the effects of this chromosome are so slight as not to affect the delicately balanced gene complex. It is thought that these represent duplications of regions present elsewhere in the chromosome set. It is postulated that these arise from normal chromosomes by the deletion of all or nearly all of the euchromatic parts (the typical gene-bearing portions of the chromosome), so that the centromere, the telomeres, and the inert regions are left behind. Usually the same number of supernumerary chromosomes is present in each cell, but it is possible to have a variation in number in different cells of the same gonad.

There is little information on the distribution of supernumerary chromosomes in wild populations. In maize it is known that there may be as many as 25 without any genetic effect. It is thought that subsequent to the appearance of such a supernumerary chromosome active parts of other chromosomes may be translocated to it, and it may become a permanent part of the chromosome set.[162]

It should be pointed out that there is no evidence that these supernumerary chromosomes are anything else than an abnormal temporary situation in the cell. There is no indication either that active parts of chromosomes ever become translocated to such a chromosome. Indeed it is difficult to believe that they could be translocated without upsetting the gene complex.

Of both these methods of evolution — evolution by adding or by subtracting whole chromosomes — Stebbins says that such types are partly sterile and genetically unstable. For that reason he believes that they are of relatively little significance in evolution. He also points out that they are very rarely found in nature.[163] White says that in animals the genic balance is probably so delicate that trisomics inevitably show a much lower viability and that the effect is even more pronounced in tetrasomics.[164]

Deficiencies and Duplications

What has been said about the addition or subtraction of whole chromosomes applies also to the addition or subtraction of parts of chromosomes — deficiencies and duplications. They are ordinarily harmful to the organism. Both are very likely to upset the delicate gene balance. Huxley, for instance, says that while deficiency is not an uncommon occurrence in laboratory stocks of *Drosophila*, it is probably of little evolutionary significance either in *Drosophila* or in other forms, because homozygous deficiencies are usually lethal.[165] White points out that in wild populations of *Drosophila* deficiencies and duplications are hardly known at all, though in *D. ananassae* races or strains may differ in respect to small duplications and deficiencies at or very close to the ends of the chromosomes. He says that it is difficult to understand how net losses or gains of genetic material could become established in the course of evolution unless they were very small or involved inert regions. Any other change is likely to upset the delicate gene balance. Yet White believes that this has happened.[166]

Stebbins says much the same thing. He, too, points out that deficiencies are usually lethal or semilethal when homozygous.[167]

Chromosomal Re-arrangements

There remains to be discussed the possibility that re-arrangements may be the mechanism for evolution. These include translocations and inversions. It should be pointed out that this type of change is rather rare, presumably because in most cases it is completely lethal. N. P. Dubinin and his associates report that in many thousands of chromosomes from the wild populations of several *Drosophila* species which they examined they found only 35 sectional re-arrangements. Thirty-three of these were paracentric inversions (inversions which did not include the centromere), one was a small shift, and one was a small translocation.[168] In another study Dubinin, Sokolov, and Tiniakov report that they found eight different paracentric inversions in 34,515 chromosomes of wild type *Drosophila*. These occurred in 525 chromosomes, or 1.5 per cent of those examined.[169] White reports that a total of 21 different inversions are known in the third chromosome of the two *D. pseudoobscura* races. He, however, feels that this is a very unusual condition. A similar situation is known only in *azteca*. He regards this situation as difficult to explain.[170]

The Harmful Effects of Re-arrangements

It is true, of course, that these re-arrangements do change the organism and often in a striking way. The changes are much more marked than those to be seen in gene mutations.

Some *Drosophila* studies have indicated that heterozygotes of various inversions possess greater vigor than their respective homozygotes and that the proportions of the various gene re-arrangements vary in cyclic fashion during the year.[171] Yet, as we have pointed out, they are almost always harmful changes, as are also those brought about by mutation. Stone and Griffen were able to alter *Drosophila melanogaster* considerably by a translocation. They succeeded in translocating the small fourth chromosome to the "X" chromosome. Males thus became hemizygous. However in doing this the viability was considerably reduced.[172]

Muller says that only those re-arrangements can survive which involve a breakage of one or more chromosomes in at least two points, together with a union of the pieces so formed by their broken ends in a new order leaving the originally free ends, or telomeres, still free and leaving one spindle fiber attachment, or centromere, on each chromosome. This limits drastically the number of re-arrangements that can survive. In *Drosophila* Muller believes that this condition is met only by those inversions which are confined to a given chromosome arm and to a lesser extent by exchanges between virtually whole arms.[173]

Stebbins calls attention to another harmful effect by pointing out that while inversions do alter the genetic mechanism they do so in such a way as to produce more constancy and fitness at the expense of flexibility. Thus the organism is not able to meet even relatively minor changes in the environment. He also points out that by themselves they rarely, if ever, produce the isolation barriers necessary for separating species.[174]

Huxley points out that large re-arrangements are not only much rarer than gene mutations, but they can hardly ever repeat themselves as happens with gene mutations. This latter is important, since repeated mutations are thought to be one of the ways of increasing the frequency of a new gene in a population and keeping it from dying out. However, by their very nature it is almost impossible for two identical re-arrangements to occur.[175]

Moreover, the re-arranged section is genetically isolated from its normal homolog. This means that organisms possessing it cannot interbreed freely, or in some cases cannot interbreed at all with related forms which do not have it. Thus, so long as it remains rare, it does not have the same plasticity as a normal form, because it is not capable of free interbreeding with the rest of the population.[176] It is handicapped, then, as Stebbins points out, if adaptive change is demanded.

Furthermore, because of the peculiar behavior of sectional re-arrangements, when the reproductive cells are produced at meiosis, inevitably a certain proportion of the gametes will have an unbalanced gene complement. This can only give rise to inviable offspring and reduce the fertility rate significantly. This inviability is particularly marked with translocations and with pericentric inversions, those which include the centromere.[177]

Even where the translocation is a homozygous one, there is usually a significant lowering of viability and fertility. Dobzhansky reports the results indicated in Table 9.[178]

Chromosomes Involved	No. Tested for Viability	Per Cent Viable	No. Tested for Fertility	Per Cent Fertile
I and II	57	52.6	23	91.3
I and III	71	42.2	30	90.0
I and IV	14	100.	13	100.
II and III	120	15.8	19	100.
II and IV	33	69.6	17	88.2
III and IV	37	48.6	18	88.8

Table 9: Viability and Fertility of Homozygous Translocations in Drosophila

Huxley concludes that sectional re-arrangements are rarely, if ever, the sole cause of evolutionary diversion. He says that for one thing they have little prospect of becoming established. Then, too, he says, their presence in noninterbreeding groups is normally accompanied by numerous single gene differences which are themselves often responsible for much of the group incompatibility. He believes that they can, therefore, be regarded only as secondary agents in bringing about speciation.[179]

White says much the same thing. He says that it is now clear that most kinds of re-arrangements cannot cause speciation in a single step. They may, he believes, furnish a basis on which isolating mechanisms are subsequently built up, but they cannot themselves serve as isolating mechanisms.[180]

Chromosomal Patterns in *Drosophila*

It is interesting to note that in *Drosophila* the number of different gene sequences or chromosomal patterns is greater in species with a restricted distribution, as *D. pseudoobscura*, than in species whose distribution is worldwide, such as *D. melanogaster, D. funebris, D. simulans,* and *D. hydei.* We would expect the opposite to be the case, since a wider distribution should make usable a wider variety of chromosomal patterns. Genic variation does agree with this expectation: worldwide species are more varied than those whose distribution is more limited. But variety of chromosomal patterns is different from what we would expect. White explains this as being due to the fact that many of these forms owe their present wide distribution to human agencies.[181] But if this is the case, why has it not affected genic variation in the same way?

Chromosomal Similarities and Dissimilarities

In this connection it might be well to refer briefly to chromosomal similarities and dissimilarities. We have seen that evolutionists make much of various kinds of homology. Some attempts have also been made to compare chromosomal structure, but these have not been too successful or too promising. Huxley believes that the gross morphology of the chromosomes throws little light on evolutionary relationships. In *Drosophila melanogaster,* for instance, the haploid chromosome complement consists of two "V's," one rod (the "X" chromosome), and one dot (the small fourth chromosome, or microchromosome). *D. willistoni* has no microchromosome. It has two "V's" and one rod. The "X" chromosome is a "V." *D. virilis* has five rods and a microchromosome. *D. immigrans* has one "V" and three rods.[182] However, these similarities do not agree with other studies of the relationships of the various *Drosophila* species, and one wonders whether these similarities are minimized because they do not agree with other evolutionary ideas.

Muller also concludes that chromosomal relationships do not agree with other studies of relationships. He points out that *Drosophila simulans* and *D. melanogaster* are least alike of the five pairs of closely related forms of *Drosophila* in regard to the morphological character of their chromosomes, but they are most alike in regard to sectional re-arrangements. *D. virilis* and *D. americana* are least alike in the metaphase chromosome picture but are most alike in respect to fertility in crossing. He also points to striking serological differences in *D. hydei.*[183]

Muller further refers to the opinions of Spencer, who listed the species of *Drosophila* in groups and compared them as follows:

A — *pseudoobscura* A and B

B — *pseudoobscura* and *miranda*

C — *melanogaster* and *simulans*

D — *virilis* and (*virilis*) *americana*

E — *azteca* and *athabasca*

The order of similarity between these groups in different characteristics, Spencer believed to be the following:[184]

Morphological and physiological characteristics:
    A B E D C

Salivary chromosome structure: C A=D B E

Metaphase chromosome structure: A=C=E B D
Hybrid fertility: D A C=B=E
Psychology and sex reactions: A B E D C
Geographical Distribution: C B A E D

NOTES

1. White, M. J. D. *Animal Cytology and Evolution* (Cambridge: Cambridge University Press, 1948), p. 140.
2. Ibid., p. 142.
3. Huxley, Julian. *Evolution, the Modern Synthesis* (New York: Harpers, 1943), p. 50.
4. Strandskov, Herluf H. "Genetics and the Origin and Evolution of Man," *Cold Spring Harbor Symposia on Quantitative Biology*, XV (1950), 2.
5. Spuhler, J. N. "On the Number of Genes in Man," *Science*, CVIII (1948), 279 f.
6. White, p. 153.
7. Ibid., p. 160.
8. Ibid., pp. 175–178.
9. Mavor, James Watt. *General Biology* (New York: Macmillan, 1948), p. 708.
10. White, pp. 153 f.
11. Williams, George C. *Adaptation and Natural Selection* (Princeton: Princeton University Press, 1966), p. 133.
12. Sinsheimer, Robert L. *The Book of Life* (Reading, Mass.: Addison-Wesley, 1967), p. 14.
13. Dobzhansky, Theodosius. "Evolution of Genes and Genes in Evolution," *Cold Spring Harbor Symposia on Quantitative Biology*, XXIV (1959), p. 16.
14. Williams, p. 42.
15. Dobzhansky, p. 16.
16. Williams, p. 64.
17. Williams, Curtis A. "The Ascension and Apotheosis of DNA," *Science*, CLV (1967), 308.
18. Muller, H. J. "Redintegration of the Symposium on Genetics, Paleontology, and Evolution," *Genetics, Paleontology, and Evolution*, ed. Glenn L. Jepsen, Ernst Mayr, and George Gaylord Simpson (Princeton: Princeton University Press, 1949), p. 423.
19. Winchester, A. M. *Genetics* (Boston: Houghton Mifflin, 1951), p. 228.

20. Penrose, L. S., and Haldane, J. B. S. "Mutation Rates in Man," *Nature*, CXXXV (1935), 907 f.

21. Haldane, J. B. S. "The Mutation Rate of the Gene for Haemophilia, and Its Segregation Ratios in Males and Females," *Annals of Eugenics*, XIII (1947), 270.

22. Neel, James V., and Falls, Harold F. "The Rate of Mutation of the Gene Responsible for Retinoblastoma in Man," *Science*, CXIV (1951), 419–422.

23. Muller, H. J. "Our Load of Mutations," *American Journal of Human Genetics*, II (1950), 169.

24. Dobzhansky, Theodosius. *Mankind Evolving* (New Haven: Yale University Press, 1962), p. 50.

25. Timofeeff-Ressovsky, N. W. "Mutations and Geographical Variation," *The New Systematics*, ed. Julian Huxley (Oxford: Oxford University Press, 1940), p. 77.

26. Winchester, p. 228.

27. Oliver, C. P. "The Effect of Varying the Duration of X-ray Treatment upon the Frequency of Mutation," *Science*, LXXI (1930), 44–46.

28. Auerbach, C., Robson, J. M., and Carr, J. G. "The Chemical Production of Mutations," *Science*, CV (1947), 243–247.

29. Szybalski, Waclax. "Chemical Reactivity of Chromosomal DNA as Related to Mutagenicity: Studies with Human Cell Lines," *Cold Spring Harbor Symposia on Quantitative Biology*, XXIX (1964), p. 157.

30. Rajewsky, B. N., and Timofeeff-Ressovsky, N. W. "Höhenstrahlung und die Mutationsrate von *Drosophila melanogaster*," *Zeitschrift für Induktive Abstammungs- und Vererbungslehre*, LXXVII (1939), 488–500.

31. Rensch, Bernhard. *Evolution Above the Species Level* (London: Methuen, 1959), p. 6.

32. Shull, A. Franklin. *Evolution* (New York: McGraw-Hill, 1951), p. 144.

33. Muller, H. J. "Radiation Damage to the Genetic Material," *American Scientist*, XXXVIII (1950), 33–59.

34. Winchester, p. 290.

35. Gonzales, Bienvenido Maria. "Experimental Studies on the Duration of Life. VII. The Influence upon Duration of Life of Certain Mutant Genes of *Drosophila melanogaster*," *American Naturalist*, LVII (1923), 289–325.

36. Muller, H. J. "Bearings of the 'Drosophila' Work on Systematics," *The New Systematics*, ed. Julian Huxley (Oxford: Oxford University Press, 1940), p. 196.

37. McEwen, Robert Stanley. "The Reactions to Light and to

Gravity in Drosophila and Its Mutants," *Journal of Experimental Zoology,* XXV (1918), 88–90.

38. Rensch, p. 5.

39. Ford, E. B. *Mendelism and Evolution* (London: Methuen and Co., 1949), p. 105.

40. Ibid., p. 100.

41. Ibid., p. 44.

42. Strandskov, p. 8.

43. Muller, "Redintegration," p. 424.

44. Muller, H. J. "The Method of Evolution," *Scientific Monthly,* XXIX (1929), 488.

45. Ford, p. 37.

46. Ibid., pp. 43 f.

47. Gordon, Cecil. "An Experiment on a Released Population of *D. melanogaster,*" *American Naturalist,* LXIX (1935), 381.

48. Ford, p. 44.

49. Huxley, p. 115.

50. Morgan, T. H. "Variability of Eyeless," *Carnegie Institute of Washington Publication* No. 399 (1929), pp. 139–168.

51. Ross, Herbert H. *A Synthesis of Evolutionary Theory* (Englewood Cliffs: Prentice-Hall, 1962), p. 94.

52. Ford, pp. 52 f.

53. Fisher, R. A. *The Genetical Theory of Natural Selection* (Oxford: Clarendon Press, 1930), pp. 48–69.

54. Winchester, p. 294.

55. Boyd, William C. *Genetics and the Races of Man* (Boston: Little, Brown, 1950), p. 51.

56. White, p. 60.

57. Stebbins, G. Ledyard. *Variation and Evolution in Plants* (New York: Columbia University Press, 1950), p.84.

58. Fisher, pp. 38–41.

59. Muller, "Redintegration," p. 424.

60. Ehrlich, Paul R., and Holm, Richard W. *The Process of Evolution* (New York: McGraw-Hill, 1963), p. 310.

61. Fisher, p. 76.

62. Haldane, J. B. S. "The Equilibrium Between Mutation and Random Extinction," *Annals of Eugenics,* IX (1939), 400 to 405.

63. Wright, Sewall. "The Statistical Consequences of Mendelian Heredity in Relation to Speciation," *The New Systematics,* ed. Julian Huxley (Oxford: Oxford University Press, 1940), p. 178.

64. Boyd, p. 144.

65. Ibid., p. 146.
66. Carter, G. S. *Animal Evolution* (London: Sidgwick and Jackson, 1951), p. 217.
67. Ibid., p. 180.
68. Wright, Sewall. "Comment," *Journal of Heredity*, XXXIII (1942), 333 f.
69. Barnicot, N. A. "Climatic Factors in the Evolution of Human Populations," *Cold Spring Harbor Symposia on Quantitative Biology*, XXIV (1959), 126.
70. Ehrlich and Holm, p. 152.
71. Oparin, A. I. *The Origin of Life on the Earth* (New York: Academic, 1957), pp. 260 f.
72. Harris, Errol E. *The Foundations of Metaphysics in Science* (London: George Allen and Unwin, 1965), pp. 238 f.
73. Buzzati-Traverso, Adriano. "Genetic Structure of Natural Populations and Interbreeding Units in the Human Species," *Cold Spring Harbor Symposia on Quantitative Biology*, XV (1950), 16.
74. Simpson, George Gaylord. *Tempo and Mode in Evolution* (New York: Columbia University Press, 1944), pp. 54 f.
75. Rensch, p. 5.
76. Romer, Alfred Sherwood. "Time Series and Trends in Animal Evolution," *Genetics, Paleontology, and Evolution*, ed. Glenn L. Jepsen, Ernst Mayr, and George Gaylord Simpson (Princeton: Princeton University Press, 1949), p. 106.
77. Dobzhansky, Theodosius. "Changing Man," *Science*, CLV (1967), 411.
78. Stebbins, G. Ledyard. *Processes of Organic Evolution* (Englewood Cliffs: Prentice-Hall, 1966), p. 56.
79. Barnicot, p. 122.
80. Williams, *Adaptation*, p. 143.
81. Stebbins, *Processes*, p. 42.
82. Mayr, Ernst. "Where Are We," *Cold Spring Harbor Symposia on Quantitative Biology*, XXIV (1959), 9.
83. Carson, Hampton L. "Genetic Conditions Which Promote or Retard the Formation of Species," *Cold Spring Harbor Symposia on Quantitative Biology*, XXIV (1959), 90 f.
84. Burns, John M. "Preferential Mating versus Mimicry: Disruptive Selection and Sex Limited Dimorphism in Papilio glaucus," *Science*, CLIII (1966), 551.
85. Ehrlich and Holm, p. 171.
86. Romer, pp. 109 f.

87. Muller, H. J. "Reversibility in Evolution Considered from the Standpoint of Genetics," *Biological Reviews,* XIV (1939), 276.

88. Huxley, pp. 501 f.

89. Merrell, David J. *Evolution and Genetics* (New York: Holt, Rinehart and Winston, 1962), p. 212.

90. Muller, "Reversibility," p. 276.

91. Blum, Harold F. *Time's Arrow and Evolution* (Princeton: Princeton University Press, 1951), p. 149.

92. Huxley, pp. 517 f.

93. Huxley, Julian. *Man in the Modern World* (London: Chatto and Windus, 1950), p. 95.

94. Huxley, *Evolution,* pp. 498 f.

95. Blum, pp. 179 f.

96. Sturtevant, A. H. "Essays on Evolution. I. On the Effects of Selection on Mutation Rate," *Quarterly Review of Biology,* XII (1937), 464–467.
    Shapiro, N. J. "The Mutation Process as an Adaptive Character of a Species," *Zoological Zhurnal* (Moscow), XVII (1938), 592–601.

97. Gordon, Cecil. "The Frequency of Heterozygosis in Free-Living Populations of *Drosophila melanogaster* and *Drosophila subobscura,*" *Journal of Genetics,* XXXIII (1936), 55.
    Dubinin, N. P., et al. "Experimental Study of the Ecogenotypes of *Drosophila melanogaster,*" *Biologicheskii Zhurnal* (Moscow), III (1934), 202–206.
    Dubinin, N. P., et al. "Genetic Constitution and Gene-Dynamics of Wild Populations of *Drosophila melanogaster,*" *Biologicheskii Zhurnal* (Moscow), V (1936), 970 f.

98. Duncan, Carl D., and Pickwell, Gayle. *The World of Insects* (New York: McGraw-Hill, 1939), pp. 4, 238.

99. Huxley, *Evolution,* p. 328.

100. Stebbins, *Variation,* p. 426.

101. MacBride, E. W. "Mutations and Variations and Their Bearing on the Origin of Species," *Proceedings of the Linnaean Society of London,* CL (1937), 228.

102. Elton, Charles. "Animal Numbers and Adaptation," *Evolution,* ed. G. R. De Beer (Oxford: Clarendon Press, 1938), p. 134.

103. Fisher, R. A. "The Measurement of Selective Intensity," *Proceedings of the Royal Society of London* [B CXXI (820)] (1936), p. 59.

104. Huxley, *Evolution,* p. 371.

105. Ibid., p. 116.

106. Carson, p. 95.

107. Harris, pp. 232–235.
108. Medawar, Sir Peter. "A Biological Retrospect," *BioScience* XVI, 2 (February 1966), 94.
109. Ehrlich and Holm, p. 71.
110. Hooton, Earnest Albert. *Up from the Ape* (New York: Macmillan, 1946), p. 77.
111. Lindsey, Arthur Ward. *Principles of Organic Evolution* (Saint Louis: Mosby, 1952), p. 346.
112. Goldschmidt, Richard. *The Material Basis of Evolution* (New Haven: Yale University Press, 1940), pp. 183, 205 f.
113. Mayr, Ernst. *Systematics and the Origin of Species* (New York: Columbia University Press, 1942), p. 65.
114. Sinnott, Edmund W., Dunn, L. C., and Dobzhansky, Th. *Principles of Genetics* (New York: McGraw-Hill, 1950), p. 426.
115. Mayr, Ernst. "Speciation and Systematics," *Genetics, Paleontology, and Evolution*, ed. Glenn L. Jepsen, Ernst Mayr, and George Gaylord Simpson (Princeton: Princeton University Press, 1949), p. 285.
116. Stebbins, *Variation*, p. 308.
117. Ibid., p. 308.
118. Ibid., p. 316.
119. Ibid., pp. 342 f.
120. Ibid., p. 347.
121. Ibid., p. 349.
122. Ibid., pp. 304 f.
123. Ross, p. 198.
124. Scagel, Robert F., Bandoni, Robert J., Rouse, Glenn E., Schofield, W. B., Stein, Janet R., and Taylor, T. M. C. *An Evolutionary Survey of the Plant Kingdom* (Belmont, Calif.: Wadsworth Publishing Co., 1966), p. 5.
125. Stebbins, *Variation*, pp. 305 ff.
126. Gustafsson, Ake. "Polyploidy, Life-Form, and Vegetative Reproduction," *Hereditas*, XXXIV (1948), 1–22.
127. Hogben, Lancelot. "Problems of the Origins of Species," *The New Systematics*, ed. Julian Huxley (Oxford: Oxford University Press, 1940), p. 276.
128. Stebbins, *Variation*, p. 331.
129. Ibid., p. 286.
130. Haldane, J. B. S. "The Nature of Interspecific Differences," *Evolution*, ed. G. R. De Beer (Oxford: Clarendon Press, 1938), p. 83.
131. Stebbins, *Variation*, pp. 300 f.

132. Darlington, C. D. *Recent Advances in Cytology* (Philadelphia: Blakiston, 1937), p. 84.

133. White, p. 183.

134. Dodson, Edward O. *A Textbook of Evolution* (Philadelphia: Saunders, 1952), p. 360.

135. Haldane, "The Nature of," pp. 83 f.

136. White, p. 183.

137. Stebbins, *Variation*, pp. 366 f.

138. White, p. 305.

139. Wallace, Bruce. *Chromosomes, Giant Molecules, and Evolution* (New York: Norton, 1966), p. 42.

140. Muller, H. J. "Why Polyploidy Is Rarer in Animals Than in Plants," *American Naturalist*, LIX (1925), 346–353.

141. Mayr, Ernst. "Speciation," p. 285.

142. Stebbins, *Variation*, p. 359.

143. Ibid., p. 286.

144. Ehrlich and Holm, p. 190.

145. Stebbins, *Variation*, pp. 318–335.

146. Ibid., p. 358.

147. Ibid., pp. 359–366.

148. *Evolution: Its Science and Doctrine*, ed. Thomas W. M. Cameron (Toronto: University of Toronto Press, 1960), p. 121.

149. Ehrlich and Holm, p. 207.

150. Levan, Albert. "Plant Breeding by the Induction of Polyploidy and Some Results in Clover," *Hereditas*, XXVIII (1942), 245 f.

151. Ross, Herbert H. *Understanding Evolution* (Englewood Cliffs: Prentice-Hall, 1966), p. 131.

152. Ehrlich and Holm, pp. 184 f.

153. Stebbins, *Variation*, pp. 445 f.

154. Muller, "Bearings," p. 221.

155. Stebbins, *Variation*, pp. 80 f.

156. Ibid., p. 447.

157. Ibid., p. 451.

158. Ehrlich and Holm, p. 186.

159. White, p. 183.

160. Stebbins, *Variation*, p. 446.

161. Ibid., p. 452.

162. White, pp. 119–123.

163. Stebbins, *Variation*, p. 77.

164. White, p. 184.

165. Huxley, *Evolution*, p. 89.

166. White, pp. 105–107.

167. Stebbins, *Variation*, p. 78.

168. Dubinin et al. "Experimental Study," p. 166.
Dubinin et al. "Genetic Constitution and Gene-Dynamics,"
p. 939. Quoted in Huxley, *Evolution*, p. 363.

169. Dubinin, N. P., Sokolov, N. N., and Tiniakov, G. G. "Intraspecific Chromosome Variability," *Biologicheskii Zhurnal*
(Moscow), VI (1937), 1050.

170. White, pp. 100–103.

171. Ross, *Synthesis*, p. 102.

172. Stone, Wilson S., and Griffen, A. B. "Changing the Structure
of the Genome in *Drosophila melanogaster*," *University of
Texas* (Austin) *Publication* No. 4032 (1940), pp. 208–217.

173. Muller, "Bearings," p. 257.

174. Stebbins, *Variation*, pp. 420 f.

175. Huxley, *Evolution*, p. 362.

176. Muller, "Bearings," pp. 217 ff.

177. Huxley, *Evolution*, p. 362.
Muller, "Bearings," pp. 217 ff.

178. Dobzhansky, Theodosius. "Position Effects on Genes," *Biological Reviews*, XI (1936), 366.

179. Huxley, *Evolution*, p. 333.

180. White, p. 99.

181. Ibid., p. 10.

182. Huxley, *Evolution*, p. 365.

183. Muller, "Bearings," pp. 223–250.

184. Ibid., p. 248.

9. Human Evolution

One area of evolution which has attracted considerable interest but which has supplied few facts and few data is the area which deals with the evolution of man. Not so many years ago there was considerable interest in the suggestion that man had descended from the monkey. And in popularizing evolutionary theories many proponents of evolution made that very statement. As a matter of fact, no evolutionist seriously entertains the idea that man descended from a monkey or from an ape. Instead, evolutionists believe that man and the monkey or man and the ape have had a common ancestor. It is believed that this ancestral stock divided and that monkeys, apes, and man today represent different branches of this stock. At the same time, if we were to see the purported common ancestor of man and the ape, we would probably classify him as an ape.

The Scarcity of Human and Prehuman Fossils

One of the problems in connection with human evolution is the fact that there are very few human and prehuman fossils. A number of explanations have been advanced for this scarcity. For one thing, it has been suggested that man originally was a tropical organism and that under tropical conditions of high heat and humidity decay sets in so rapidly that fossilization rarely, if ever, occurs. This would also account for the fact that there are also very few primate fossils, since all of the primates other than man are essentially tropical animals.

Yet it is generally agreed that man has occupied other habitats too. The fact that we find some human fossils in regions that were not tropical is itself an evidence of this truth.

Another explanation for absence of fossils is that man developed the custom of burying his dead very early in his evolutionary history. Burying the dead is a distinctly human practice. Indeed it is a clear indication that man is different from other organisms and not similar to them.

Measures of Evolutionary Development

a. Brain Capacity

Many of the comparisons that are made between man and the other primates and between supposedly prehuman fossils and man as we know him today are made on the basis of brain capacity and of dentition (tooth structure and arrangement). It is believed that an increased brain capacity indicates a higher development on the scale of evolution, since it is believed that the evolution of the primates and of man in particular has come through development of his brain.

But there are problems in the study of brain capacity. It is true, of course, that in these forms we do find a gradual increase in brain capacity. The mean brain capacity of the gorilla, for instance, is 549 cc. (there are about 16 cubic centimeters in a cubic inch); for the various *Pithecanthropus* fossils it is 900 cc.; for modern man the variability ranges from 800 to 2,000 cc.[1] Sklerj points out that this variability presently found in modern man covers all the range from *Pithecanthropus* to modern man. He also points out that the Neanderthalers had a brain size which averaged somewhat larger than that of modern man.[2]

Yet brain size and cranial capacity are in themselves only relative, and the data are meaningless unless they are compared with the actual weight of the whole organism. If we compare only absolute weights, it is possible to prove that men are more intelligent than women, since the average man's brain weighs more than does the average woman's brain. However, when we compare the weight of the brain with the weight of the rest of the body, we find that a woman's brain constitutes the same per cent of her body weight as does a man's brain.

Another factor to be considered is the age of the individual. A child's brain is smaller than that of an adult, but this is no indication that he is relatively less intelligent.

Schultz says that for comparative purposes the absolute size of the brain and the cranial capacity in fossil primates will remain meaningless until we have gained more information about the general body size and the age and growth rates in extinct forms.[3]

Even when we compare brain size with body weight, we do not always get the answers that we want. The brain weight of the South American squirrel monkey *Saimiri* or *Chrysothrix sciureus* is $\frac{1}{17}$ of the total body weight. Man's brain weighs approximately $\frac{1}{35}$ of his total body weight.[4] Certainly no one would argue on this basis that the squirrel monkey is more highly developed than man.

Actually, the important consideration is the number of folds and convolutions in the brain. It is difficult if not impossible to study these in a fossil form. And so Mayr says that the size of the brain can hardly be regarded as a criterion of intelligence. He is very hesitant to use brain size as any sort of criterion in the genus *Homo*. It is misleading, he says, to believe that the *Homo* stage is reached when the brain capacity reaches 700 to 750 cc. He points out, as we have above, that brain size is correlated to some degree with general body size and that size of brain itself is no criterion of intelligence.[5]

Bennett, Diamond, Krech, and Rosenzweig sum up the problem by saying that in the last century the size and weight of the brains in men were measured in an effort to discover the differences that might relate to the degree of intellectual attainment. While at first the results were encouraging and it was found that the more capable had larger brains than the inferior, it was soon realized that men in different stations in life often differed in health and nutrition as well as intellect, and it was recognized that the former factors might also affect brain weight. It was also discovered that there were striking exceptions to the general relation: idiots were found with large brains and geniuses with small brains. Consequently the suggestion was made that evolution involved the development of additional neural interconnections or chemical changes of the brain. The difficulty of working with such factors discouraged research, they say, and the problem largely reverted to the realm of the speculative.[6]

Dobzhansky believes that cranial capacity and brain size are not reliable criteria of "intelligence" or intellectual abilities of any kind. He not only points out that the cranial capacity of the Neanderthal race was equal to or even greater than that of modern man but also points to the paintings found in the Altamira and Lascau caves: these artists may well have been no less talented than Picasso. He believes, though, that not all of their contemporaries could paint equally well or were equally talented and intelligent.[7]

b. Tooth Structure

The second criterion that is frequently used for classifying fossil primates is the tooth structure. But this type of study also has its problems. There are many supposedly primitive primates and fossil humans which have teeth larger than those which we find in men today. Does this indicate gigantism? Or are these large teeth in an ordinary-sized jaw? Hooton criticizes very severely conclusions that are reached from teeth and tooth structure. He says that recent paleontological discoveries of both human and ape remains in which teeth are accompanied by skull bones and other skeletal parts indicate that classifying an organism and making inferences as to the degree of evolution achieved on the basis of teeth alone is most precarious. He believes that early human types may have had some teeth that are indistinguishable from those of apes and vice versa. Dentitions that at one time would have been confidently assigned to early humans, he says, have now been found in the crania of apes.[8]

The Path of Human Evolution

How do the evolutionists believe man has developed? Which were the ancestors common to him and to the other primates? As might be expected, there is considerable difference of opinion as to how man has developed. However, there is general agreement among evolutionists that he, like all other organisms, did develop from simpler forms. Let us see what paths this development is supposed to have taken.

In a later section we shall discuss the origin of the vertebrates and of the mammals. At this point we want to discuss man's supposed development from the early mammalian stocks. It is generally thought that the preprimate stocks, those which gave rise to man and the other primates, were probably very close to the existing tree shrews and belonged to the order Insectivora.[9] These are relatively simple mammals, not at all so highly developed as the rodents or the perissodactyls, such as the horse. It is interesting that the primates are considered to be still relatively simple animals in some respects. Their excellence is supposed to lie in the superior development of their brains. It is believed that the earliest known primates lived in the early Paleocene and late Cretaceous periods.[10]

The Classification of the Primates

It might be well at this point to discuss the classification of this order, the Primates, to which man is supposed to belong. Today they are usually divided into two suborders, the Prosimii and the Anthropoidea. The Prosimii are further divided into three infraorders and into six families: the tree shrews which are found in the East Indies, Malaya, the Philippines, Borneo, and Sumatra; the lorises, pottos, and bush-babies found in Africa, Southeast Asia, and the Philippines; the tarsiers found in the East Indies and the Philippines; the indris, sifakas, and avahis; the aye-aye; and the lemurs. All three of the latter families are restricted to Madagascar and the Comoro Islands off the southeast coast of Africa. Until recently the tree shrews were classified as insectivores rather than as primates, but today they are believed to be primates.

The Anthropoidea are divided into three superfamilies: the Ceboidea, the Cercopithecoidea, and the Hominoidea. The Ceboidea include all the living primates of Central and South America: the New World monkeys such as howlers, capuchins, spider monkeys, squirrel monkeys, and marmosets. The Cercopithecoidea are the monkeys of Europe, Africa, and Asia such as the macaques, Barbary apes, baboons, mandrills, drills, langurs, and guenons. The Hominoidea contain two families; the Pongidae or Anthropoid apes, and the Hominidae or man. Two of the Anthropoid apes are found in Africa, the chimpanzee and the gorilla. The other two, the orangutan and the gibbon, are found in Southeast Asia and the East Indies.

Figure 25. A Lemur. Note the long, bushy tail. (Courtesy Chicago Natural History Museum)

Figure 26. A Tarsier. Note the large eyes. The animal is nocturnal. (Courtesy Chicago Natural History Museum)

Man is usually regarded as being most closely related to the Cercopithecoidea or Old World monkeys. He has only two premolars on each side of the jaw, whereas the New World monkeys have three. The bony auditory canal which is present in man and the Old World monkeys is absent in the New World monkeys, and this, too, places man among the Old World monkeys.

There is, however, no complete agreement even on this point. F. W. Jones, for instance, believes that man did not have any Cercopithecoidean ancestors. He believes that the stock which developed into man was separated even before the Cercopithecoidea were differentiated.[11] It is interesting to note that there are no fossil Cercopithecoidea in the Western Hemisphere and no fossil Ceboidea in the Eastern Hemisphere.[12] It should be noted that it is not easy to say which of these forms is really the most primitive. The marmosets are classified among the Ceboidea, most of which have a prehensile tail that they are able to use as a fifth foot. However, the marmosets of the family Hapalidea have a bushy nonprehensile tail. In addition to the nonprehensile tail these monkeys have a very straight profile; indeed, their profile is straighter than that of any primate except man.[13] This, too, would seem to be an advanced character. Yet at the same time they have claws on all of their digits except the great toe; this is a primitive character. Moreover, their thumb is not opposable, another primitive character.

The index of cephalization also creates a problem in the study of relationships. Jerison reports that the index for man is 0.92. For the monkeys it is 0.41, and for the great apes it is 0.29. The index of cephalization is believed to give a numerical indication of the level of brain evolution. Animals with a high index of cephalization, such as the primates, are those generally regarded as rather intelligent: those with intermediate values, such as the ungulates and carnivores, as being moderately intelligent; and those with low values, such as the rodents, as being relatively unintelligent. Thus it might appear that in this respect man is more closely related to the monkeys than he is to the great apes. Jerison believes that this is due to the fact that there has been a special type of evolution in the direction of additional cerebral tissue, the weight of which is independent of body weight.[14]

Early Primate Fossils

The earliest anthropoid ape fossil is found in Lower Oligocene formations. The earliest Old World monkeys are found in the same deposit, so that as far as the fossil record is concerned, they appear to have been contemporaneous.[15] However, it is generally believed that monkeys did develop before the anthropoid apes, but that their fossil record has not yet been discovered.

Of more direct significance for human evolution were the East African Miocene apes known as *Proconsul*, which are represented by three "species." This group of apes was equal in size to the modern siamang gibbons.

Man Diverges from the Primate Stock

Most authorities believe that man himself started as a small ground ape and developed from this form. Many of the resemblances between man and the tree-dwelling apes are believed to be due to convergence, possibly through the development of parallel mutations, rather than because of descent from a common ancestor. It should be pointed out, though, that one difficulty in the way of assuming that man started out in this way is the fact that a small ape would have had little chance of survival. Hooton calls attention to this problem.[16] He himself believes that man had attained approximately human size before he became a terrestrial biped. Thus when he became man, he was already bigger than the monkeys but not as big as the giant apes. Others believe that man started out as a tree-dwelling anthropoid who grew in size and weight to such an extent that he could no longer live in trees.

Kraus believes that man began to diverge from the Pongid stock during the Miocene epoch, about 26 million years ago. He thinks he developed from either a terrestrial or arboreal ape, no longer represented among the living primates, to a terrestrial biped with a relatively expanded brain, manlike dentition, and a very simple cultural inventory.

Kraus believes that there is a 25-million-year period during which there are no fossils, and he believes that it is surprising that in this vast expanse of time not one fossil has been found which is thought representative of the hominid line. There are fossil primates in Asia, Africa, and Europe during this period, but scientists are generally agreed that these represent lines of adaptive radiation that have become extinct. It seems most peculiar, Kraus believes, that we find the skeletal remains of the evolutionary failures and that not a single fossil has been discovered of the successful line which led to modern man.[17]

It is difficult to explain what constituted man's early superiority if not size. Some have suggested that as he began to differentiate from his anthropoid relatives, he developed very quickly the typical human brain, which enabled him to survive. However, the fossils on which the evolutionists are so dependent for their story of human development would indicate that this brain development was a gradual process. And Clark indicates his belief that the development of man's brain was a gradual one by saying that the differences in the brain size between apes and man were attained after full human status had been achieved in limbs and trunk, just as differences in dentition developed after full human status had been achieved.[18]

Today it is generally believed that the factor which differentiated man and the apes was the development of a culture represented by tools and marked by an ability to communicate. The study of cultural artifacts is as complicated as the study of fossils, and because of all the difficulties Kraus says that claims as to the time, place, origin, and course of evolution of the modern human races must be regarded for what they are: ofttimes fanciful excursions into the unknown far beyond the limits of evidence.[19]

Man's Method of Evolution

Man presents a great many other problems for the evolutionist. Indeed, as we shall see, his method of evolution is supposed to have been entirely different from that of other organisms. Huxley believes that he developed in a sort of reticulate evolution by means of various recombinations and that he is the only organism that developed in this way.[20] The problem with man is to explain the fact that he is so remarkably uniform. Man is a fairly numerous species. He is found in all parts of the earth. And yet all human beings are very much alike. In spite of racial differences man is much more uniform than the average natural species.

A great many people believe that man developed by outbreeding. They believe that the usual barriers to breeding between members of the same species isolated geographically or in some other way were absent. This has resulted in a distribution of new mutants throughout much of the human race. There has been a continual mixing of the genes, and it has not been possible for sterility barriers to develop. Huxley says that in man there has been no polyploidy, no formation of especially stable races, but instead the progressive increase of migration and crossing has led to a progressive increase in general variability. This has resulted in a single worldwide species instead of the usual adaptive radiation, which leads to many intersterile species.

Differences Between Man and the Primates

Let us look at some of the differences between man and his supposed anthropoid relatives. As Christians we would say that the most important difference is that only man has a soul. It is not difficult to assemble a long list of other differences. Some are minor, and some are striking. One of the most striking is the permanent bipedal locomotion — the ability to walk on two feet rather than on all fours — which not only is characteristic of man but also is a distinctive characteristic of his. It is not found in any of the apes,[21] but it is found in man after infancy.

Hewes reports observations on wild chimpanzees in which in three cases the animals, normally quadrupedal, were observed walking or running bipedally while carrying food. However, the maximum distance over which bipedal locomotion while carrying food was observed was thirty meters.[22] There was a time when it was believed that man originally walked on all fours and that the consequences of his presently erect posture are flat feet, pain in the back, and a dropping of the viscera. However, Lawton points out that during World War II it became apparent that lying down was an equal hazard, and we entered an era in which attention was focused on problems of bed rest. As a result of changes in our approach, it was found that a number of complications following surgery and after delivery were re-

lated to recumbency and inactivity, and today early ambu-
lation of the surgical patient has become quite common.
He believes that some of the problems of weightlessness that
we have encountered in our space program are due to the
fact that our astronauts are recumbent rather than upright.[23]

The human nose has a prominent bridge and a well-
developed elongated tip, which is lacking in the apes. Man
has a median furrow in his upper lip. This is lacking in the
apes. The lips of man are outrolled so that the mucous membrane is visible as a continuous red line. Man has a chin;
apes do not. The dental arch in the apes is U-shaped with
the canines projecting sharply at the base of the U. In man
the jaw is smaller and the dental arch is parabolic. Man
lacks the diastema or gap found in the upper and lower
dental arches in apes. The apes lack the forward convexity
of the spine known as the lumbar curve. Only man has it.

The great toe in man is not opposable to the other toes;
apes have thumbs on their feet as well as on their hands.
Man's foot is arched both transversely and in an anterior-
posterior plane. His toes are short, the first toe being frequently the longest and not divergent. Man's body is relatively hairless. It is also completely devoid of "feelers" or
tactile hairs. Man's brain is two and one-half to three times
as big as the brain of the largest ape, the gorilla, and his
brain is also relatively the largest. The canine teeth in man
project only slightly, if at all, beyond the level of the other
teeth. All of the apes have projecting canines.[24] The head
of man is balanced on top of the spinal column. That of all
the nonhuman catarrhines is hinged in front rather than
on top.[25]

Man shows a very long period of postnatal growth. Man
has the greatest weight at birth in relation to body weight
in adult life. Yet man shows the least degree of maturation
at birth, being far more helpless and far more dependent on
his parents than are any of the apes. Only in man do we
have wavy and curly hair. Ischial callosities are absent in

man. The *os centrale* disappears earliest in man as an independent bone. Rarely do the nasal bones fuse in man, and when they do, this fusion occurs very late. In man the facial sutures between the maxillary and premaxillary bones disappear earlier than in any of the anthropoids. The great fontanelle closes latest in man. Man has an *ossicula mentalia*. He also has a true inguinal ligament and a transverse metatarsal ligament between toes I and II. These are all lacking in the anthropoids.

The structure of his kidney is unique. He has the highest total number of vertebrae. He has the highest average number of thoracolumbar and coccygeal vertebrae. He has the longest cervical and lumbar regions in the spine. In man there is less approximation between the thorax and pelvis than in the anthropoids. Man lacks the penis bone found in the anthropoids. There is also the least increase in the average stoutness of the trunk when he is compared with the anthropoids. Man has the lowest shoulders and the lowest placed nipples. Compared with the anthropoids, he shows the greatest average relative length of the lower limbs and the shortest average relative length of the upper limbs. He has by far the lowest intermembral index. He has by far the longest thumb in proportion to the length of the hand and also relatively the longest free portion of the thumb. His hand is characterized by the straightness of the fingers when the palm is extended.

The position of the pelvis in relation to the longitudinal axis of the trunk is unique. The direction of the *fossa iliaca* is unique. He is characterized by the equality of the sexes with regard to the size of the canine teeth. Man has the shortest relative length of the phalangeal portions of fingers II to V. He is characterized by a complete permanent adduction of the hallux. He has the shortest height of the face in relation to trunk height and in relation to the size of the brain part of the head. He has the shortest height of the pelvis in relation to the trunk height and the breadth of the ilium. He has the greatest enlargement of the sacral surface of the ilium.[26]

There are also chromosome differences that deserve attention. Today it is believed that the chromosome number in·man is 46. The chimpanzee and the gorilla are believed to have 48; the gibbon, 44. The ruffed lemur and several species of marmoset are believed to have 46. While there are many similarities between the chromosomes of these primates and man, there are also two distinct differences. The rhesus monkey, the pig-tailed macaque, and the Guinea baboon lack the chromosome pair with median centromeres, which is the largest pair in man. In addition their "Y" chromosome is much smaller than the human "Y." [27]

Man is the only creature who weeps and sheds tears when he is emotionally disturbed.[28] The 24-hour clock by which the organism alternates periods of activity and inactivity and other forms of behavior is particularly well developed in the primates, but in man this clock no longer manifests itself by sharp, alternating 12-hour periods of activity and inactivity. In primates survival is believed to depend on ability to adjust to these alternating 12-hour periods; in man survival depends on his ability to free himself from the 24-hour routine in order to function at more even levels for longer periods throughout the entire 24 hours.[29] In monkeys and apes adult males never provide food; in man this is a major responsibility. Monkeys and apes have a rather small territory, and man has a large territory. Monkeys provide no shelter at all, and apes only temporarily nest; man provides houses, shelters, and fire.[30]

Finally only man is teachable in the true sense of the word. Indeed, Dobzhansky and Montagu believe that the most important evolutionary trend in the human species is that toward a genetically determined educability — the ability to learn from experience and the ability to modify one's environment accordingly.[31] Other animals can be trained: the pig-tailed macaque has been regularly and extensively trained for picking coconuts and other fruits in southeast Asia but it cannot be educated. Hooton says that perhaps the most important reason why the anthropoid apes do not behave like human beings is that they are not really teachable.[32] This contributes to another unique and important characteristic of man — his possession of a culture, cumulative tradition, the capacity for transmitting experience and the fruits of experience from one generation to another. To do this, he must develop language and be articulate.

This list is certainly a striking one. It is true, of course, that there are a great many similarities to the anthropoids. But there are also differences, and it is out of keeping with scientific objectivity to stress the similarities without even mentioning the differences.

Man's Closest Relatives

Which of the anthropoids does man resemble most closely? A great many comparisons have been made. So far as the number of thoracic segments of the spinal column is concerned, the Old World monkeys, the orangutan, and man ordinarily have twelve. The gibbons and the African apes have thirteen. The number of lumbar segments averages as follows: lower catarrhines, seven; the gibbon and man, five; the orangutan, four; the chimpanzee and gorilla, less than four. In the number of bones in the sacrum monkeys average three; gibbons average four plus; and the great apes and man average five plus. The number of the vertebrae in the tail region averages 4.2 in man, and it averages from 2.4 to 2.7 in the Asiatic anthropoids. The lumbar region forms well over 40 per cent of the trunk height in Old World monkeys, 37 per cent of the trunk height in man, 31 per cent in the gibbons, and from 22 per cent to 27 per cent in the great apes. The Old World monkeys have from seven to nine pairs of ribs attached directly to the sternum. The apes and man average between six and eight, the great apes having a lower average than man.[33]

It is apparent from these comparisons that in some characters man is more like the monkeys than he is like the apes, to whom he is supposed to be more closely related. He and the orangutan, for instance, have twelve ribs as do the Old World monkeys, whereas the African apes have thirteen. The average number of vertebrae in the tail region is considerably greater in man than in the Asiatic anthropoids. Certainly there are as many resemblances to the lower primates in these comparisons as there are to the higher primates.

In some characteristics there are striking resemblances between man and the chimpanzee. The chimpanzee, for instance, presents some of the varieties of skin color found in man. In different geographical races of these anthropoids some individuals are completely black; others are completely brown; and in still others, the face, hands, and feet are black, but the remainder of the body is white or brown.[34] While this variability does not approach the variability found in man, it is striking that only the chimpanzee shows this particular characteristic.

The chimpanzees can also be divided into tasters and nontasters. Like man, some of them apparently experience a bitter taste from PTC (phenylthiocarbamide). To other chimpanzees the compound is tasteless. This would seem to indicate a rather close relationship to man. Some have suggested that the difference between taster and nontaster was present in the primate stock even before there was a separation between chimpanzees and man. Others have suggested that this condition has developed as the result of parallel mutations in both forms.[35]

On the other hand, the adult human foot resembles most closely the foot of the gorilla.[36] And in other characteristics, too, man seems closest to the gorilla. Schultz has analyzed fifty-seven characters found in man and the anthropoid apes.

Figure 27. A Chimpanzee. Many evolutionists believe that this is man's closest relative. Note how long his arms are. (Courtesy Chicago Natural History Museum)

In twenty-three of these man resembles most closely the gorilla. In fifteen he resembles most closely the gibbon or siamang. In twelve he resembles most closely the chimpanzee, and in seven he resembles most closely the orangutan.[37]

Simpson believes that it is clear that man is most closely related to the chimpanzees and gorillas, which he believes are in turn closely related. He believes that man's relationships to the chimpanzee and gorilla are about equal, although gorillas may have become somewhat more specialized with respect to the common ancestry.[38]

Oreopithecus and Dryopithecus

Let us look now at the various prehuman and early human fossils. In discussing these we shall present the geological dating suggested by the geologist and anthropologist. Already in the 19th century, fossils of a primate now known as *Oreopithecus bambolii* were found in lignite beds believed to date from the Upper Miocene and Lower Pliocene in Italy. *Oreopithecus* is believed to have been an arboreal brachiator about the size of a chimpanzee who did not walk erect. Some have suggested that he was a hominid, but it is generally believed today that he was not in the line of the later pongids and hominids although related to them.[39]

Dryopithecus was originally uncovered in the Siwalic Hills of India; other dryopithecine material has been found in Europe and China. He is believed to date from the Middle Miocene and Lower Pliocene. He has well-developed, projecting canines that are apelike rather than hominoid.

Homo habilis and Zinjanthropus

Two of the most recent finds have been those of *Homo habilis* and *Zinjanthropus* which Leakey discovered in the Olduvai Gorge in Tanganyika, East Africa. *Zinjanthropus* was the first to be found and was discovered in 1959 together with fragments of a child's skeleton. Leakey estimated that *Zinjanthropus* lived about 600,000 years ago, but two University of California scientists, Curtis and Everndon, using potassium-argon dating techniques, examined the volcanic tuff in which the bones were found and arrived at an age of 1,750,000 years for the *Zinjanthropus,* and the age is now believed to be uncertain.[40] In commenting on the dating Straus and Hunt say: "Because some of the Olduvai Gorge dates are inconsistent, some must be inaccurate: they may all be. Until further tests determine which materials give dependable dates, we do not know which dates are accurate. Until this is learned, the indicated ages must be taken *cum grano salis.*" [41]

The *Zinjanthropus* finds include a very complete cranium with all sixteen upper teeth and the wisdom or third molar still in the process of erupting. The cranial capacity of *Zinjanthropus,* the "nut cracker man," was about 530 cc. His teeth are even larger than those of *Australopithecus robustus,* to which we shall refer later.

In spite of his huge teeth, Leakey originally thought he was hominid. The child, found in the same beds, was thought to be more like man than *Zinjanthropus* himself. Today most anthropologists believe that *Zinjanthropus* should be properly classified as *Australopithecus boisei,* and it is generally thought he was not directly related to man.

Homo habilis was discovered later in the same bed and at the same level as *Zinjanthropus,* and Leakey considers him to have been a contemporary of *Zinjanthropus.* His dental features are much more like those of modern man: the molars are much narrower than those of *Australopithecus.* The remains are rather sparse. In reconstructing the skull from the parietal bones Tobias thought he had a brainbox capacity between 642 and 724 cc.[42] The teeth of *Homo habilis* do not show the wear patterns of a gritty diet. Primitive stone tools have been found associated with him, and *Homo habilis* measurements are proportionate to those of modern man.

The type or standard *Homo habilis* fossil consists of a lower jaw with teeth, an upper molar tooth, an incomplete cranial vault, and a set of hand bones. This form was definitely a juvenile; the state of eruption of the teeth and the incomplete growth and ossification of bones show this. In addition to this type form, the remains of four other specimens of *Homo habilis* have been found, and at present there is a total of some forty teeth, two tolerably complete lower jaw bones and fragment of a third, parts of a pair of upper jaw bones, varying portions of the brain cases of four skulls, hand bones of two individuals, foot bones, and a collar bone. The type specimen was actually found 35 centimeters (a little over a foot) below *Zinjanthropus*. Potassium-argon dating suggests ages of from 1.75 to 1.65 million years for the two levels in the lower half of Bed One at Olduvai Gorge from which these specimens were taken. *Homo habilis* is believed to have been a pigmy-sized hominid about four feet tall with a relatively large cranial capacity, reduced and narrow teeth, and a number of marked hominid features in his hip bones. One of the specimens is taken from Bed Two, which is believed to be 750,000 years later, and in this specimen the hominizing trends have been carried still further. Primitive stone implements have been found in Bed One in conjunction with *Homo habilis*. Originally they were thought to have been the work of *Zinjanthropus*, but it is now believed that they were actually produced by *Homo habilis*.[43]

Probably the greatest significance of the *Homo habilis* finds is the fact that it now appears that man diverged from other anthropoids much earlier than it was once thought. It seems clear that *Homo* diverged from *Australopithecus* as early as the Upper Pliocene or first part of the Lower Pleistocene. Montagu suggests that *Homo habilis* is actually an early pithecanthropine and thus an early representative of *Homo erectus*.[44]

The whole picture has been complicated by two very recent finds. Patterson and Howells report the finding of a hominid humeral fragment from the Early Pleistocene in northwestern Kenya. Potassium-argon dating of the lava overlying the lacustrine sediments in which the fossils were found indicate that the lava is 2.5 million years old, and it is believed that the sediments in which the fossils were found were the same age. They found the well-preserved distal end of a left humerus which they believe to be the earliest Pleistocene hominid yet found. This discovery, too, serves to confirm the antiquity of man.[45]

Leakey reports a still earlier find which he calls *Kenyapithecus africanus*, which he dates as being 20 million years old using the potassium-argon method, and which he believes to be the very oldest representative of the hominids.

The *Pithecanthropus* Fossils

The first important prehuman fossils to be discovered were those which were found on the island of Java. These are generally known as *Pithecanthropus erectus* fossils, now referred to as *Homo erectus*. They are supposed to date from the Pleistocene epoch, about 500,000 years ago. The first of these was discovered in 1890 by a Dutch Army physician by the name of Dubois. It is also known as the "Trinil man." Oddly enough, Dubois started out in his explorations without any indication that he might find fossils of man on the island of Java. Within a few years after beginning his exploration he had found a skull cap, a lower jaw, two separate molar teeth, a premolar, and a femur. The

Figure 28. A Gorilla. Some evolutionists believe that this rather than the chimpanzee is man's closest relative. Note how he walks on his knuckles. (Courtesy Chicago Natural History Museum)

femur was found 50 feet away from the head parts, and a number of investigators have expressed doubt as to whether it belonged with the head parts. The brain cavity is estimated at 914 cc. — intermediate between the anthropoid ape and man. The jaw and the teeth are partly apelike.

After Dubois' original work a number of expeditions were made to Java to find additional fossils, and Dubois himself did further exploratory work. As a result, the following forms of *Pithecanthropus* or of closely allied humanoid forms have been found: (1) The skull cap of Trinil (Dubois, 1891), known as *Pithecanthropus* I; (2) Mandible of Kedung Brubus (Dubois, 1890), *Pithecanthropus,* Mandible A; (3) Juvenile skull of *Homo modjokertensis* (Geological Survey, 1936); (4) Mandible of Sangiran (von Koenigswald, 1936), *Pithecanthropus,* Mandible B; (5) Skull of Sangiran (von Koenigswald, 1937), *Pithecanthropus,* Skull II; (6) Skull, fragment of Sangiran, juvenile (von Koenigswald, 1938), *Pithecanthropus,* Skull III; (7) Maxilla and skull fragment of Sangiran (von Koenigswald, 1939), *Pithecanthropus,* Skull IV, *P. robustus,* Weidenreich; (8) Mandible of Sangiran (von Koenigswald, 1939), *Meganthropus paleojavanicus,* female (possibly ape); (9) Mandible of Sangiran (Von Koenigswald, 1941), *Meganthropus paleojavanicus,* male.[46]

Dubois himself has pointed out that the ratio of brain mass to the length of the femur in *Pithecanthropus* is exactly what it would be if a gibbon's cranium would be enlarged to that of *Pithecanthropus.* He believed that *Pithecanthropus* may have been a giant gibbon and not an ancestor of man.[47] Weidenreich, however, does not agree with Dubois. He believes that *Pithecanthropus* is actually a prehuman form.[48]

Pithecanthropus I, as mentioned above, consisted of a skull cap, three teeth, and a left femur. The cubic skull content has been calculated to be about 914 cc. Dr. G. S. Mueller, Jr., believed that the teeth of *Pithecanthropus* I were those of a fossil orangutan, and Hooton is inclined to agree.[49] Nor is too much to be made of the brain capacity. A very small-brained pigmy today may have a brain capacity of only 900 cc.

In the case of *Pithecanthropus* II most of the skull vault is present except for the right side of the frontal bone. However, the skull is broken up. Von Koenigswald offered a reward for each fossil brought in to him, and it is possible that the natives broke up the skull deliberately in order to collect several rewards. Some thirty fragments have been recovered. It has a cranial capacity of only 750 cc. and is believed to be the skull of a female.

Pithecanthropus mandible B was collected in the absence of von Koenigswald. It consists of the greater part of the right half of the mandible. The second premolar and all three molars are preserved in their sockets. The molars increase in size from the first to the third. This is not the case in modern man.

Pithecanthropus IV consists mostly of the posterior half of the skull. It includes also the more posterior part of the base of the skull and an upper jaw, the maxilla, with all the teeth in place except the incisors and the last two molars on the left side. The teeth are huge and the molars increase in size from front to back. The back of the head has been caved in, apparently by a blow with a club or a stone weapon.

The juvenile skull cap, *H. modjokertensis,* is believed to be that of an infant of eighteen months.

In general it is believed that *Pithecanthropus* was an erect-walking primate. He apparently had primitive stone implements, since these are found in the same geological stratum. Kraus suggests that if a *Pithecanthropus* child were born and raised in the modern world, he would fare no better or no worse than a randomly selected *Homo sapiens* infant.[50] Perhaps he was not as primitive as early anthropologists suggested.

Meganthropus and the Problem of Gigantism

Von Koenigswald gave the name *Meganthropus* to two of the fossils listed above because of the giant size of the teeth. Weidenreich believes that these giant forms were ancestral to the smaller ones.[51] He believes that gigantism has often been the precursor of a more average-sized race. He points out that gigantism has occurred in other groups of animals.

However, not all anthropologists agree that this has been the case. Some have pointed out that the huge mammals of the Tertiary period are not believed to have been the ancestors of the small mammals of today. Nor were the dinosaurs the ancestors of the small reptiles of today. There are many anthropologists who believe that man is a descendant of pigmy ancestors. It is interesting in this connection to note that the Bible itself speaks of giants in the early days of the earth (Gen. 6:4).

Other Javanese Finds

Another Javanese find was made along the Solo or Bengaway River in central Java at Ngandong. Eleven fossil skulls and two tibia were found. These were found in 1931 after interest in the search for human remains had returned to Java once more. The original *Pithecanthropus* finds were made in Java, but when subsequent expeditions found very little, interest turned to Europe. By 1930 interest had focused itself again on Java, with the result that these forms were found. The bases of the skulls had been smashed in. It appears that the brains of these unfortunates had been eaten by cannibals and their skulls dumped in this one place. Primitive implements were found along with these. The cranial capacity of these skulls ranged from 1160 cc. to 1316 cc. It is thought that these represent a stage in evolution above *Pithecanthropus*. They are believed to be below the Neanderthal man, however.[52]

Australopithecus

Another early form is the man-ape from South Africa, whose exact status still remains to be clarified. It has been called *Australopithecus africanus*. It is represented by a fossil brain cast and an incomplete skull found in a limestone fissure at Taungs near Kimberley in the Transvaal. The skull is small in size, resembling that of a young chimpanzee, but the brain itself is relatively large, and the parietal area seems to have been well developed. In this same cave Dart, who discovered *Australopithecus,* found a number of baboon skulls. These were broken open, and it appears as if the brains of these baboons had been eaten.

The brain case has only a frontal bone, and it is not quite complete. The fossil has 20 milk teeth and four permanent teeth — first molars. Three other forms which are apparently similar have been found. They have been called *Plesianthropus transvaalensis, Paranthropus robustus,* and *Paranthropus crassidens.* Today they are all classified as *Australopithecus. Zinjanthropus* is also regarded as *Australopithecus.* All of these lack the brain overgrowth that is specifically human.[53] Mayr believes that some of the forms are age or sex stages of a few related tribes. He does not believe they are as dissimilar as generally believed.[54] The brow ridges are massive, not unlike those in the chimpanzee and gorilla, but in details of their architecture they are remarkably close to man. There are several interpretations of the functional significance of these brow ridges, and until this is understood we cannot determine their real significance.[55]

Kraus does not believe that the lack of definite association with cultural materials should be interpreted as an indication that they were without culture. He suggests that they did have a rudimentary culture. He says that the widely scattered and profuse remains of these throughout South Africa indicates they adapted successfully to their environment, and he doubts this would have been possible if these erect bipedal hominoids were without language and culture.[56]

It is noteworthy that the jaws and teeth of *Australopithecus* far surpass those of *Homo sapiens* in size, but that the several femora, or thighbones, all are smaller than those of man today. There are some who believe that the teeth belong to a race of giants and that the femora belong to a race of pigmies, so that both giants and pigmies were present at that particular time.[57] It has also been suggested that the femora may belong to women, while the jaws and teeth are those of men.

Washburn, however, points out that large teeth do not necessarily mean large bodies. He believes that it would be possible for small forms or average-sized forms to have large teeth.[58] Weidenreich, as we have pointed out, believes that modern man is the descendant not of pigmies but of such supergiants as *Meganthropus*, the giants represented by the *Australopithecus* teeth, and the *Gigantopithecus* to which we shall refer. He believes that man has diminished in stature but has kept the absolute brain size of his giant ancestors. Weidenreich himself is of the opinion that *Australopithecus* is not in the human line, but belongs to a special group which has preserved some of the original characters of the common stock from which both man and the anthropoids originated.[59] Oakley is more or less of the same opinion. He does not believe that *Australopithecus* is one of the ancestors of man. Rather he believes that he is a collateral of the immediate forerunner of *Homo*.[60]

Observe also that these very primitive South African hominids lack certain simian features usually considered primitive. These are such characteristics as powerful canines, large incisors, the sectorial form of the first lower premolar, an exaggerated development of the supraorbitals, a simian shelf, and powerful brachiating arms for swinging from trees. Mayr believes that this is due to the fact that the great apes

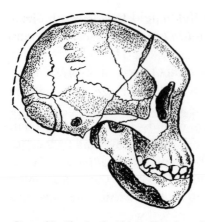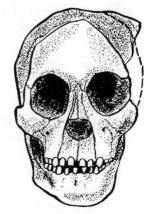

Figure 29. The South African Man-Ape, *Australopithecus africanus*. The brain cast has lost its covering bones, except for the frontal bone which is nearly complete. The dotted lines indicate where these covering bones would be expected to be. (Redrawn from Hooton's *Up from the Ape*, Macmillan, by permission)

acquired these characteristics after the hominids had branched off from the ancestral stock.[61]

The time at which the Australopithecines lived is a problem since at present it seems they were contemporary with *Homo habilis* and *Homo erectus*.[62]

Gigantopithecus

Gigantopithecus is known from a series of teeth found in China. In 1935 G. H. R. von Koenigswald reported that he had purchased a huge lower third molar in a drugstore in Hong Kong. This exceeded in size the largest gorilla third molar, and he believed it represented a new species called *Gigantopithecus*. Later he obtained a worn upper second molar and still later another third molar. In some way or other these had gotten into the apothecary trade of China where they are used as medicine. Indeed, fossils, known in the Far East as "dragon bones," are common ingredients of a number of medicines. Von Koenigswald believed these large teeth indicated a group of giants, though, as we have pointed out, Washburn does not believe that large teeth necessarily mean large individuals. Weidenreich, however, still considers *Gigantopithecus* the largest and most primitive member of the human race. He believes that it is even ancestral to *Meganthropus* found in Java.[63]

Sinanthropus

A number of other fossils have been found in China. The first of these was discovered near Peking around 1922. This find consisted of several teeth. Later a lower jaw and finally a number of skulls were found. The site of these discoveries was a partially collapsed cave used as a dwelling near the village of Choukoutien, 37 miles southwest of Peking. These fossils are frequently known as the Peking man, or *Sinanthropus*.

In 1938 the *Sinanthropus* collection consisted of 38 fossils. Most of these were represented by teeth, jaw fragments, and odd bits of skulls. Only six skulls have the vaults more or less completely preserved. Forty per cent of the finds seem to represent children up to 14 years of age. Three skulls may belong to adults under 30, three to people between 30 and 40, and one seems to be that of a really old woman. It is thought they date from about 360,000 years ago, the latter part of the Mindel (Elster) glaciation.[64]

Today it is generally believed they should be classified as *Homo erectus*. The cranial cavity varies from 850 cc. to 1,300 cc. with the average of 1,075 cc. The forehead is receding, but there is a distinct bump on the frontal bone that is missing in *Pithecanthropus*. There is a prominent ridge running down the middle of the skull, a characteristic found today in Eskimos and Australians. The nasal index (breadth of nasal aperture to the height of the nose) averages 57.2. This is unusually broad and compares with modern Negroes. Apart from the teeth and skull fragments there are only a few skeletal remains. These include seven pieces of femora (thighbones), two of humeri (upper armbones), one broken clavicle (collarbone), and an isolated wrist-

FOUND IN A CAVE NEAR PEKING, CHINA

PEKING MAN AND CHOPPER TOOLS
(SINANTHROPUS PEKINENSIS)
200,000 YEARS OLD

FOUND ALONG THE SOLO RIVER, JAVA

JAVA MAN
(PITHECANTHROPUS ERECTUS)
200,000 YEARS OLD

Figure 30. Pithecanthropus, the Java Man, and Sinanthropus, the Peking Man. Note the comparisons with modern man. (Courtesy Chicago Natural History Museum)

bone. Interestingly enough, the deposits in which these were found abound in animal remains, though there are these very few human remains. It is also interesting to note that the femora found in Java at Trinil appeared to be more modern than those of *Sinanthropus*.[65]

The skulls appear to have been bashed in. Some think that the presence of skulls only indicates that these were the trophies of head-hunters. This would also account for the fact that there are very few human remains but many animal remains. Weidenreich thinks that *Sinanthropus* was the ancestor of the modern Mongoloids.[66] He believes, too, that he was a contemporary of *Pithecanthropus*. The two are supposed to represent the same level of evolution but different regional or racial variations of that stage.

Recently Pei Wenchung, a Chinese anthropologist, reported the discovery in western China of a fossil skull from the Late Pleistocene age which he believed to be more than 10,000 years old. It is definitely *Homo sapiens*. While this discovery has not yet been fully evaluated, it is significant that modern man should have lived so long ago in China. This is the oldest *Homo sapiens* discovered to date in China.[67]

The Piltdown Man

Turning to Europe, we find there a number of supposedly human and prehuman fossils. One of the most controversial, recently disclosed to be a complete hoax, is that of the Piltdown man (or woman), also known as *Eoanthropus dawsoni*, or the Dawn man, discovered by Charles Dawson and Sir Arthur Smith-Woodward in 1912. It was found in a gravel pit along the side of the road in a lane leading up to Barkham Manor, an English farmhouse. The age of this fossil was variously estimated by geologists and anthropologists at from 200,000 to 1,000,000 years. The dating was made difficult by the possibility that the remains, which were found near the surface, may have been moved. The fragments included the larger part of the left side of the frontal bone, almost the whole of the left parietal bone, two thirds of the right parietal, most of the lower part of the occipital bone, almost the entire left temporal bone, the nasal bones, the right half of the mandible, and a lower canine tooth. The bones were very thick, and it has been suggested that this may be a pathological thickening. It is possible that their appearance was brought on by a condition similar to acromegaly today.

In addition there was a lower jaw with the second and third molars intact. This was almost indistinguishable from the jaw of a chimpanzee. The chin region did not jut out but fell away as in the apes.

Ever since its discovery, *Eoanthropus* has been the center of controversy even among anthropologists and evolutionists themselves, though in the popular press it has been represented as an important and significant prehuman fossil find. Its sex has been in dispute. Some have suggested that it is the fossil of a male; others have insisted that it is the fossil of a female. Another controversy has been over its brain capacity. Smith-Woodward assumed a brain case capacity of 1,070 cc. Keith in his reconstruction believed that he (or she) had a brain capacity of 1,500 cc. Later the two got together and suggested a brain capacity of 1,358 cc. This is approximately the average brain capacity for European females today. Keith, however, believes that the skull is that of a male.

The chief problem of *Eoanthropus* is that we have here a large and noble-browed skull and an almost apelike jaw. From the beginning of the controversy there have been those who have insisted that the jaw is that of a chimpanzee or of an orangutan. Others, however, insisted that the two must belong together, since there was no evidence of apes in Britain during the Pleistocene epoch, the period from which the cranium was supposed to date. Weidenreich insisted that the jaw and skull could not belong together.[68] Hooton, however, saw no difficulty in believing that the skull and jaw belonged together.[69]

A few years ago the newly discovered fluorine technique of dating organic remains was applied to *Eoanthropus*. The first studies indicated that the mandible and skull were contemporaneous, if they did not belong together. Both appeared to date from the third interglacial period. This was a later dating than the one originally proposed: generally it was assumed that the Piltdown man came from the first or at the latest the second interglacial period.[70] Dr. Birdsell, in evaluating this first fluorine evidence, said that it presented a more embarrassing problem than *Eoanthropus* did in its prefluorine chronology.[71]

Since that time further studies have been made by Drs. Weiner, Oakley, and Clark. These have led to the conclusion that the lower jaw and canine tooth are those of a modern anthropoid ape, deliberately altered so as to resemble a fossil. Dr. Weiner was able to demonstrate experimentally that the teeth of a chimpanzee could be altered by a combination of artificial abrasion and proper staining so as to appear similar to the molars and canine teeth ascribed to *Eoanthropus*. Careful study of the specimen itself showed that the wear on the teeth was produced by an artificial filing down, resulting in surfaces unlike those produced by normal wear. Microscopic examination showed fine scratches, such as might be produced by an abrasive. X-ray examination showed that there was no deposit of secondary dentine, as would be expected if the teeth were worn down naturally before the individual's death. Refined methods of fluorine analysis indicate that while the cranium is a true fossil, the jaw and teeth are not. It appears that these have been artificially stained to match the cranium. Weiner, Oakley, and Clark concluded that the distinguished paleontologists and archeologists who took part in the excavations at Piltdown were the victims of a most elaborate and carefully prepared hoax, concocted with extraordinary skill. Their opinion has been generally accepted today.[72]

Further studies have indicated the extent of the hoax to be even greater than was at first believed. Not only has it become very evident that the teeth were deliberately altered, but Weiner has also demonstrated that the chin region of the broken lower jaw resembles that of an orangutan. Clark believes that the fragments of the so-called "turbinal bone" (one of the bones of the nasal cavity) are actually those of a small limb bone of some animal. Radiometric assays of the vertebrae by Bowie and Davidson indicate that the fragments belong to the Recent rather than the Pleistocene epoch. The other vertebrate remains from the Piltdown site give a remarkably wide range of radioactivity. The teeth of *Elephas* differ from any British mammalian bones of the Tertiary or later age so far studied and resemble a specimen from Tunisia. The hippopotamus teeth and some of the beaver bones are quite unlike any other British or foreign Tertiary fossils examined.

Although the gravel and loam from the site and from nearby ground water are low in sulfate content, mixtures of apatite and gypsum were found in the Piltdown cranium, and gypsum was found in many of the other Piltdown specimens. Gypsum is a sulfate mineral and is believed to have been produced when the apatite was treated with weak iron alum in an attempt to produce the full brown color characteristic of a fossil.

The black coating on the teeth is believed to be paint, identified by Werner and Plesters as probably Vandyke brown. The organic content of the Piltdown mandible is that of fresh bone: intact collagen fibers characteristic of fresh bone were found in the mandible, but not in the brain case. The flint "paleoliths" are all, according to Oakley, artificially stained. The worked elephant bone could not have been carved while fresh. The hippopotamus molar tooth is low in nitrogen and fluorine and is matched only by cave deposit material which is found, for example, in Malta. From the total evidence it appears that the Piltdown bones and teeth were assembled from a wide variety of sources, some of them outside Britain itself.[73]

It is worth nothing that the fraud was pointed out by scientists who did not hesitate to call the attention of the scientific world to this fraud. However, it is also interesting that the fraud was not uncovered earlier even though the

Piltdown man was examined carefully by the most competent scientists of the day.

The Swanscombe Skull

Another skull found in England is the Swanscombe skull, which was found on the south side of the Thames River between Dartford and Gravesend. Several gravel pits are found here, the best known of which is the Barnfield Pit. On June 29, 1935, Dr. A. T. Marston of Clapham found a fossilized human occipital 24 feet from the surface. Nine months later he found a left parietal at the same depth but 8 yards farther back. It is believed that the two bones belonged to the same individual. The finds were carefully examined by geologists, archeologists, and anthropologists from the Royal Anthropological Institute. They reported that the industry (tools, weapons, etc.) in the layer in which the skull was found is Middle Acheulean, the name applied by anthropologists to the supposed second interglacial period. The animals found with it are those of what geologists have called the Middle Pleistocene epoch and represent an interglacial type.

It is believed that the skull, the associated animals, and the archeological materials represent the second or Mindel-Riss interglacial period, the great interglacial period. The bones differ from modern remains of *Homo sapiens* only in the breadth of the occipital and in the great thickness of both bones. The Swanscombe skull is, therefore, believed to be older than any other European skulls except the Heidelberg man. It is possible that even this belongs to the second interglacial period, but it is even more probable that it comes from the first interglacial period. The Swanscombe skull appears to be that of a female who died in her early twenties. She had a cranial capacity of 1,325 cc. The very striking thing is that these bones, in spite of their apparent age, appear so similar to those of modern man. Because of the apparent age Stewart hesitates to classify the Swanscombe skull *Homo sapiens.* He admits, though, that the evidence points in this direction, but he suggests caution.[74] Hooton, however, says that there is no denying the conclusion that Swanscombe is either a mid-Pleistocene *Homo sapiens* or something so close to it that the differences are zoologically inconsiderable.[75]

The Galley Hill Man

Another British fossil is that of the Galley Hill man, which was found by workmen at Galley Hill, some miles below London. It was found eight feet down in the gravel and about two feet above the chalk. It seems to represent a male about 50 years old and about 5 ft. 3 in. tall. The Galley Hill man is thought to have had a brain capacity of about 1,350 cc. Some think that this represents a burial, since the various bones were found close together. It is believed that the Galley Hill man was a contemporary of the possessor of the Swanscombe skull. The bones of the Galley Hill man were excavated before they could be examined by competent geologists, and there are some who question whether it dates from the period assigned to it. However, the finding of the Swanscombe skull tends to authenticate the Galley Hill find.[76]

Two other British skulls which may date from this period are the London skull and the Bury St. Edmunds skull.

The Heidelberg Man

Another very famous European find is the Heidelberg man, found in 1907 by the owner of a sand pit six miles southeast of Heidelberg, near the village of Mauer. The find consists of a well-preserved lower jaw with all the teeth in place. It was found at a depth of 82 feet. It was first described by Dr. Otto Schoetensack. The jaw is a very large jaw. It is thick, deep, and chinless. Indeed, the chin falls away as it does in the ape. Yet the teeth are ordinary in size. It has been dated as belonging to the Pleistocene epoch, probably the first interglacial period. This interglacial period is supposed to have occurred between the Mindel I, 476,000 years ago, and the Mindel II, 435,000 years ago. Hooton,

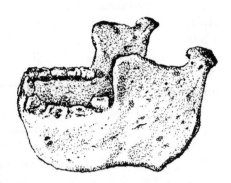

Figure 31. The Heidelberg Jaw. Note how the chin falls away. (Redrawn from Hooton's Up from the Ape, *Macmillan, by permission)*

though, questions whether the stratigraphic and paleontological evidence justifies such a precise dating.[77] The Heidelberg man is believed to be a crude pre-Neanderthal man.

Other European Skeletal Finds

Another series of European skeletal finds is that made in the Grotte des Enfants near Mentone on the Italian Riviera at Grimaldi. These were discovered by an expedition financed by the Prince of Monaco. They were discovered between 1895 and 1902. The cave got its name from the fact that the skeletons of two children were found in its upper strata. The cave is choked with layers of debris over thirty feet thick. About 29 feet from the top, at the level of the lowest hearth, a grave containing two skeletons was found. The first of these was that of an old woman, and the second was that of a boy 15 or 16 years of age. Both had been buried. Both of these skeletons are said to have pronounced Negroid characteristics. The woman is believed to have had a cranial capacity of 1,375 cc. and the boy one of 1,580 cc. Some believe that these were the ancestors of the Bushmen of South Africa, but others dissent from that opinion. They are definitely *Homo sapiens.*

A recent discovery in France is that of the Fontéchevade man. These remains were found in the department of Charente in France. They are believed to date from the last interglacial period, the Riss-Würm. Unfortunately, the skulls are incomplete. The more complete one consists of a left parietal, the upper half of the right parietal, and the upper part of the frontal. Vallois believes that we have here well-dated specimens. He believes that this is the first time that human remains definitely antedating the Neanderthal remains have been found in Europe. He believes that the Fontéchevade man is very similar to the Swanscombe form. The cranial features are less primitive than those found in fossils of the succeeding period, which was supposed to be more advanced culturally — the Neanderthal man of the Mousterian Age (the age which is supposed to have followed the Acheulian Age).[78]

The Rhodesian Man

Other fossil men beside *Australopithecus* have been found in Africa. Perhaps the best known of these is the Rhodesian man found in a cave at Broken Hill in Rhodesia. This find was made about sixty feet below the ground level by T. Zurgelaar, a miner. It includes a skull, a left tibia (shin bone), parts of the left femur, a sacrum, portions of the two pelves, and a part of an upper jaw. The pelves, the sacrum, and the leg bones belong to a man about 5 ft. 10 in. tall. The other bones may be those of a woman. Except for the skull, the bones are in no way remarkable, and it is possible that the skull does not belong with the bones at all. It is extraordinarily apelike. The brow ridges are enormous, and it has a low forehead. It resembles a great deal a present-day gorilla. The brain case is inferior even to that of *Pithecanthropus*. It has a cranial capacity of about 1,305 cc., quite small for so large a skull. Most anthropologists rank it below the Neanderthal man. The teeth are large but of human proportions. The canines are reduced to the level of

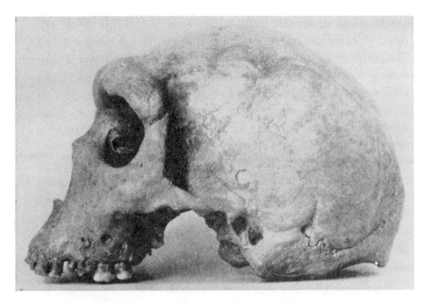

Figure 32. The Rhodesian Skull. Note the large brow ridges and the low forehead. (Courtesy British Museum, Natural History)

the other teeth, a human characteristic. The third molars are reduced and degenerate. Ten of the fifteen teeth in the upper jaw have been affected by decay; evidently the Rhodesian man failed to see his dentist twice a year. Keith, the anthropologist, calls attention to the fact that acromegaly, an endocrine disturbance of the pituitary gland, sometimes causes changes similar to those found in the Rhodesian skull.[79]

Other African Finds

Other African fossils include those discovered by Prof. Raymond A. Dart of the University of Witwatersrand, Johannesburg, South Africa; Dr. Robert Broom of the Transvaal Museum, Pretoria; and their co-workers. Dart's first find was made in 1925, when he reported the discovery of *Australopithecus*.

Dr. Broom was responsible for the finding of *Plesianthropus* and *Paranthropus*. Later he found the well-preserved skull of an old female; parts of two huge jaws, the teeth of which were larger than those of von Koenigswald's *Meganthropus;* a small pelvis in which the ilia were transversely widened; and several other parts of skeletons. Dart meanwhile secured a number of jaws and teeth from a form which he has called *Australopithecus prometheus.* This *Australopithecus* was supposedly a fire maker, as the species name indicates. Present-day anthropologists are of the opinion, however, that *Australopithecus* did not use fire, and they regard it as unfortunate that the species name *prometheus* was assigned. All of these African finds of Dart and Broom combine apelike brains (from 450 cc. to 650 cc.) with teeth of human or near-human pattern. The jaws are rather large and the cheek teeth massive. These latter are even larger than those of the Heidelberg man.[80]

Another African man is the so-called Boskop man. In 1913 workmen digging a ditch near Boskop in Transvaal came across mineralized bones in the subsoil four and one-half feet below the surface. Only a few skull fragments and the long bones of the legs were found. The Boskop man had a very large skull capacity — about 1,630 cc. He stood about 5 ft. 6 in. high. The teeth and mandibles resemble those of the modern Bushmen. The face is small and short, and the teeth are reduced in size. The Boskop man is said to date from the Middle Stone Age and is definitely *Homo sapiens.* He is thought to be one of the ancestors of modern Negro types.[81]

Still other African fossils include those found in a rock shelter at Alfalou Bou Rhummel on the Mediterranean Coast, thirty km. east of Bougie, Algeria. These include the scattered remains of about forty-eight individuals of both sexes, representing all age groups. Six fairly complete skeletons were recovered. These apparently were the victims of a massacre. Farther down, the skeleton of an adult male and the skull of a child were found. These are believed to have some Negroid features, and are definitely *Homo sapiens.*

The skeleton of the adult male referred to resembles the Combe-Capelle man — a Cro-Magnon specimen — and is apparently a Galley Hill type.

Still another African fossil is the Asselar man found in the middle of the Sahara Desert, about 400 km. northeast of Timbuktu. The skeleton was found by a French scientific expedition in 1927. It is believed that this is the skeleton of a drowning victim. It is thought to date from the Upper Pleistocene epoch. The skeleton is undoubtedly Negroid. However, it is more like the Bushmen, Hottentots, and southern Bantus than like the Negroes found in that particular area today. Again it is definitely *Homo sapiens.*

Another African skeleton is the so-called Oldoway man. This was found in 1913 as a fossilized human skeleton at the Oldoway Gorge in Tanganyika. It supposedly dates from the Lower Pleistocene epoch, but it, too, is clearly *Homo sapiens.* Another interesting fact is that the lower incisor teeth have been chipped or filed, a custom which is still practiced by Africans today. The position of the skeleton indicates that it was buried.[82] Its antiquity has been questioned, but Dr. L. S. B. Leakey believes that it is of great antiquity.[83] It is not a Negroid skeleton but appears to be that of an individual belonging to a tall, slender Hamitic white race of East Africa.

In 1932 Leakey made other excavations nearby on the southern shores of the Kavirondo Gulf of Victoria Nyanza at a place called West Kanam. Here he found a number of examples of *Homo sapiens* in what was supposed to be Lower Pleistocene rock. The geological age of these finds has been questioned by some authorities, but Hooton is inclined to believe that the Pleistocene dating of these finds is correct, and that it will someday be confirmed. He believes that there is good reason for assuming that these deposits are quite ancient and that the finds resemble closely modern types.[84]

In 1933 Prof. T. F. Dreyer made a number of finds while

carrying out excavations at a site at Florisbad, a warm lithium spring about 25 miles north of Bloemfontein. His finds include the frontal region of a skull, except for the left supraorbital portion, the top of the left parietal bone, and parts of the left side of the face and the nose. The frontal region is flat and receding, and yet it is definitely *Homo sapiens*.[85] The remains are believed to date from the Middle Stone Age. The oldest deposit in the spring dates from the Middle Pleistocene epoch. The Florisbad finds have many Australoid features.

From 1935 to 1938 a number of finds were made on the northeast shore of Lake Eyasi (Najarasa) in Tanganyika Territory. The human bones were smashed into small pieces and include only skull fragments. At least three skulls are represented. There is also a loose molar tooth. This form has been called *Africanthropus* and is believed to be closely related to *Pithecanthropus* and *Sinanthropus*. *Africanthropus* has been restored and reconstructed. However, Hooton does not believe that these restorations are correct, and he believes that a great deal of imagination has gone into the restorations which have been made.[86]

North American Finds

Not too many human and prehuman remains have been found in America. The most important of these is the Folsom man found near Lubbock, Tex. He is supposed to be about 10,000 years old and is believed to have been a bison hunter.[87]

Another human fossil was found by a group of workmen ripping up a road with a grader at Pelican Rapids, Otter Tail County, Minn. They discovered a bone dagger and a skeleton on June 18, 1931. Further excavations were made in 1932. This find is believed to date from the Late Pleistocene epoch, about 20,000 years ago, the time of the retreat of the last glacier. It might be noted that recently some have placed the retreat of the last glacier at 12,000 years ago. It represents a young woman about 15 years old. The cranial capacity of the skull is about 1,345 cc. The teeth are unusually large, and the third molars are larger than the second molars. The skull shows a great many Mongoloid features, but it is clearly of *Homo sapiens* stock.[88]

It is generally agreed that the earliest remains of man found in America do not differ essentially from those of recent Indians.[89]

Australian Finds

A number of skeletal remains have been found in Australia. One of the best known is the Keilor skull, one of two skulls found a mile north of Keilor village, ten miles north of Melbourne, Australia. Only one of the two skulls has been described in detail. It supposedly dates from the Pleistocene epoch and had a cranial capacity of 1,593 cc., a very high cranial capacity. It appears to combine Australian and Tasmanian features. The fact that this has a large brain size is particularly interesting, since this sort of evidence seems to indicate that a decrease in brain size has occurred. Coon is one who believes that such a decrease has occurred in the recent evolution of *Homo sapiens*.[90] If this is the case, it is a strange development, since man's evolution is supposed to have centered in the development of a larger brain.

Another Australian skull is the Talgai skull. This was found in 1884 at Talgai Station in Queensland, but it did not come to scientific notice until 1914. It is thought to belong to the Pleistocene epoch and to be that of a boy of about 14 or 15 years. An early reconstruction pictured a simianlike human being with enormous, caninelike projecting teeth. Further studies indicate, however, that the canines, although large, did not project unduly and that the palate, although large, was quite human in shape.

Still another famous Australian skull is the Cohuna specimen. This skull was publicized by Mackenzie and Keith and was originally said to represent a very primitive form. In fact, in some features it was supposed to be more primitive than heretofore observed in man. Careful studies, however, would seem to indicate that the skull is not unusual and that all its features are well within the range of modern aboriginal Australian skulls.[91]

The Neanderthal Man

The first group of fossil men of which there are a fair number of skeletons is the Neanderthal man. The first of these Neanderthal men was found in a cave in a valley called the Neanderthal in Germany. It is located near Duesseldorf. The first find was made in 1856. The Neanderthal man is

Figure 33. A Neanderthal Family. This restoration represents a cave-dwelling Neanderthal man and his family. He is supposed to have lived in Europe about 100,000 years ago. It is generally agreed that he is to be classified as *Homo sapiens* as is also modern man. (Courtesy Chicago Natural History Museum)

believed to have reached his peak development in Europe from about 200,000 years ago to 115,000 years ago. He is supposed to have disappeared completely about 72,000 years ago. This is believed to correspond to the period from the latter part of the third interglacial period to the advancing stage of the fourth glacial period. Remains of the Neanderthal man have been found in Jersey, France, Belgium, Germany, Czechoslovakia, Jugoslavia, Spain, Italy, Russia, the Rock of Gibraltar, Palestine, and Uzbek in the U. S. S. R.

The Neanderthal men were once portrayed as semi-erect, stooped, apelike individuals, but it is now known that many of them walked erect. One author is criticized for flogging a dead horse when he depicts the classic Neanderthal man as a "semi-erect degenerate ape-like fellow with a prehensile great toe who shuffled along like a chimpanzee." Straus says this ancient paleoanthropological calumny has been exposed and abandoned by serious students. The stooped and semi-erect position found in some of them is due to their having suffered from some bone disease.[92]

Wells says that the twin complex of osteoarthritis and osteophytosis was common among the Neanderthal men. The jaw was especially prone to be attacked, and since the joint was often affected at an early age in Neanderthals, we can assume that they fed on a rough, perhaps uncooked, diet and put their jaws to vigorous use in gnawing bones, cracking nuts, and champing roots. The La Chapelle skeleton also had extensive vertebral changes, and these were destined to have far-reaching effects because it was the reconstruction of this specimen which encouraged the view that the Neanderthals groped their way through a hundred thousand years of prehistory in a semi-erect position. It is clear that the La Chapelle man did walk with a pronounced stoop as many old men with his degree of spinal curvature do today, but it is unfair to the rest of the Neanderthalers to judge them by this singularly pathological example. Wells believes that there is ample evidence that they were an erect and lissome people.[93]

The Neanderthal man seems to have had a well-developed culture and was interested in religion. It is among the Neanderthalers that we find the first real evidence of the interment of human remains. Some of the Neanderthalers are found in intentional burials, their skeletons either flexed or extended, sometimes with the bones of animals arranged nearby in a way suggesting the modern custom of some primitive peoples in providing the dead with food for their journey into the other world.[94]

It is very easy to regard the Neanderthal man as a very primitive individual, especially since the stooped, arthritic La Chapelle reconstruction looks apelike. Yet such judgments are relative: so-called primitive people can survive under environmental conditions which would quickly wipe out most civilized men. Kraus says that our Neanderthaloid ancestors would have had a chuckle over our helplessness under such severe environmental conditions.[95]

Two definite types of Neanderthal men have been described. The first of these is the so-called conservative type, with a flattened-down brain case, a bun-shaped protuberant occiput, a marked projection of the jaws, and practically no chin. The bones of the postcranial skeleton in the conservative type show many ape features.

The second type is the so-called progressive type. Representatives of this type have a laterally compressed and higher cranial vault. They also show a lower attachment of the neck muscles and a submedium to fair development of a bony chin. Other skeletal features are approximately those of primitive but anatomically modern forms of man.

The height of the conservative type is estimated at about 5 ft. 1 in. to about 5 ft. 5 in. The cranial capacity is at least that of Europeans today. The classical example of the conservative type is the "Old Man of La Chapelle-aux-Saints," found in 1908 in a small cave in France. He seems to have had a cranial capacity of about 1,600 cc. The brain was apparently long, broad, and low. The pattern of convolutions was crude and rather simple. On the whole he appears to have been massive and primitive, yet distinctly human. He is believed to have had an intelligence only slightly lower than that of some primitive men today.

The Ehringsdorf skull may be taken as an example of the progressive Neanderthalers. It was dug out of a quarry near Weimar, Germany, in 1925. It is thought to date back to the third or last interglacial period, about 130,000 years ago. Weidenreich thought that this skull was that of an adult female, but Keith thinks that it belongs to a youth about eighteen years of age. The individual to whom it belonged met a violent death, and it has been suggested that he or she may have been the victim of cannibals. The cranial capacity appears to be about 1,480 cc. In this and in other progressive Neanderthal skulls the bones are thin, the vault is high and gable-roof shaped, the forehead is moderately high, and in general the skeleton seems very similar to that of modern man.

Complete skeletons of Neanderthal men were found in two adjoining caves in Mount Carmel in 1931–32. The remains of ten progressive Neanderthalers were found in the first of these caves. The second contained the remains of conservative Neanderthalers. In the progressive Neanderthalers the men were tall, and the women short or medium in height. In these the brain was better developed than that of most progressive Neanderthalers. For that reason the Mount Carmel skeletons are sometimes regarded as representing the next step in human evolution after the Neanderthal man.

There are two opinions as to the significance of this progressive Neanderthal type. Some people believe that it represents the next step in evolution beyond the conservative Neanderthal type. Others believe that the progressive type represents a hybrid between Neanderthal man and some variety of *Homo sapiens*. Hooton believes that the Neanderthal stock may have been an ancestor of one type of human, such as the Australian aborigines, but he does not believe that the Neanderthal man is the only ancestor of modern man.[96] McCown believes that the Neanderthal races were a subspecies (a race or variety) of *Homo sapiens*. He does not believe that the Neanderthal man gave rise to modern man.[97]

Kraus says that there is general agreement that the chronologically early Neanderthaloids are morphologically closer to *Homo sapiens* than the chronologically younger forms. This creates some real problems and results in what he regards as bizarre interpretations on the part of human paleontologists. One theory holds that the early Neanderthaloids evolved into the classical Neanderthaloids in Europe, whereupon the latter became extinct by one means or another. A second contends that the fate of both groups in Europe remains a mystery at the present time, but the Neanderthaloids in Western or Central Asia evolved into modern man. A thin hypothesis would have the early Neanderthaloids radiating into two branches, one leading to the classical Neanderthaloids in Europe and the other into *Homo sapiens* in the Near East.[98]

It should be emphasized that in any case the Neanderthal man is distinctly human. There is no question that he is *Homo sapiens*. McCown, for instance, says that he wishes to emphasize that while the Neanderthal pattern is distinctive, it seems to him impossible for anyone to hold any longer to the view of a morphological hiatus between modern man and the Neanderthal population.[99]

The Cro-Magnon Man

Another well-known early human form is the Cro-Magnon type. The first of these was discovered in the small rock shelter of Cro-Magnon in the little village of Les Eyzies in France. This rock shelter was excavated by Lartet. He found human remains in the highest strata of the deposit, far back underneath the overhanging wall of the cliff. These consisted of a skull and some other bones of an old man. A short distance away he found parts of the skeletons of four

Figure 34. Prehistoric Men. Restorations of *Pithecanthropus*, the Piltdown man, Neanderthal man, and Cro-Magnon man from left to right. The Piltdown man is now known to be a fraud. (Courtesy American Museum of Natural History)

other individuals. It is believed that the type of man discovered here lived in various places in western Europe throughout the three upper Paleolithic, or Old Stone Age, periods.

Typical of this group is the "Old Man of Cro-Magnon." He is believed to have been about 5 ft. 6¼ in. tall. His forearms were rather long compared with his upper arms, and his shins were long relative to his thighs. These are often referred to as Negroid proportions, and while they do not occur in modern Europeans, they are found in the taller groups of American Indians and in other races not ordinarily considered to be Negroid. One of the best preserved skeletons of this period was discovered at Combe-Capelle in 1900.

The Cro-Magnon people had massive skulls. The brain case of the "Old Man of Cro-Magnon" had a capacity of about 1,660 cc. The forehead was broad and of a moderate height. Most of the Cro-Magnons had larger brains than the average modern man, and this was true of at least some of the Neanderthals.

Hooton does not believe that the Cro-Magnon race is a race in our sense of the word. He points out that in order to establish that a given type constitutes a race the individuals attributed to it must show a certain homogeneity in crucial racial features. They must vary less in their bodily characteristics than do random individuals selected from assorted racial groups. This is not true of the Cro-Magnons. Not a single feature shows a reasonable consistency. For instance, they are often said to have been giants, but some of them are of medium height or even short. They are said to have had dolichocephalic skulls (longer than broad), flattened on the crown, and to have had short, broad faces. Some of them, however, had round heads, and quite a few had long faces. Some people have suggested that the Cro-Magnon men became the ancestors of modern Eskimos. Hooton, however, doubts this.[100] It should, however, be pointed out once more that the Cro-Magnons are definitely *Homo sapiens.*

Human Fossils Evaluated

a. Their Small Number

What shall we say about these human and prehuman remains? First of all, it is very striking that we find relatively few of these. Most are represented by one or two series of bone remnants. Boyd says that any idea that human prehistory can be reconstructed from an examination of fossil remains is a will-o'-the-wisp. He points out that there simply are not enough fossil bones.[101]

Heberer says that despite all the progress made in primate paleontology especially since the end of World War II, documentation is still sparse and more material is needed.[102] Jepson is reported as having said at a 1965 Symposium on Time and Stratigraphic Problems in the Evolution of Man: "What we need are more competent fossils. We have plenty of competent anthropologists but not enough specimens." [103]

b. Their Fragmentary Character

Another striking thing is the fragmentary character of most of these fossils. There are few complete skulls and even fewer complete skeletons. Often the entire find is represented by a piece of the skull or by a jawbone. Certainly any reconstruction based upon such fragmentary remains is extremely precarious. Dobzhansky says it goes without saying that virtually all fossil finds are fragmentary and that investigators often submit to the temptation of speculating on the basis of scanty bone fragments.[104] Hooton calls attention to this by saying that when we recall the fragmentary condition of most of these fossil skulls and when we remember that the faces are usually missing, we can readily see that even the reconstruction of the facial *skeletons* (italics his) leaves room for a great deal of doubt as to details. To attempt to. reconstruct the soft parts, he points out, is an even more hazardous undertaking. The lips, the eyes, the ears, and the nasal tip leave no clues on the underlying bony parts. Hooton says that you can model on a Neanderthal skull either the features of a chimpanzee or those of a philosopher. He concludes by saying that the alleged restorations of ancient types of man have very little, if any, scientific value and are likely only to mislead the public.[105]

c. Dating Human Remains

Another problem is that of dating these human remains. We have pointed out the difficulty of dating fossils in general. The same problems apply also to the dating of human fossils. And, indeed, the problem is multiplied by the custom that man has had of burying his dead. It is quite possible that a human fossil found in a given stratum did not die at the period in which that stratum was laid down. He may have been buried in that stratum much later. There is some evidence that some of the fossils which we have found represent burials. We have referred to the fact at times that a given fossil may represent a burial. Hooton says that it is very difficult to establish the geological age of chance finds of human remains coming out of the gravel pits, railway cuttings, and other commercial excavations, particularly because the bones are usually removed before they have been seen *in situ* by qualified archeologists and geologists. Only these, he believes, can judge whether the bones were introduced into the deposit after it was laid down or whether they were contemporaneous with the stratum. Even when there is no question of burial or any other intrusive agency, he says, the geological age of the layer in which the bones occur is often debatable or indeterminate.[106]

This fact has often been used to discredit the finding of specimens of *Homo sapiens* in supposedly early layers. Because of the possibility of burial, the man who has been interested in discounting the high antiquity of *Homo sapiens* finds has always had the advantage. However, the Swanscombe skull, Hooton says, is clearly a Pleistocene skull.[107] If this is true, then certainly some of the previous finds whose antiquity was discounted are probably of great age, too, and *Homo sapiens* himself is of great antiquity.

d. The Problem of Scattered Remains

Another problem is that of determining whether scattered remains belong to one individual or whether they belong to several different people. It is rarely possible to be certain that a given skull belongs with a given skeleton. Strangely enough, many investigators insist that bones found by them in widely scattered areas belong to the same individual while they doubt that scattered fragments discovered by someone else can belong to one person. Hooton comments on this strange inconsistency.[108]

e. The Precariousness of a Classification Based Only on Skeletal Remains

Another thing to be considered is the precariousness of classification based upon skeletal remains alone. We know that the skeleton is very easily affected by environmental changes, either external or internal. It is quite possible that some of these fossil men represent human beings whose skeletal structure has in some way or other been altered from the normal. Earlier we referred to the case of M. Tillet, known professionally as "The Angel." We also called attention to Keith's suggestion that acromegaly sometimes causes changes similar to those found in the Rhodesian man. The Neanderthal man is another example of this.

f. Classifying Human and Prehuman Remains

Another problem is that of classifying these fossil remains. Usually they are named without any regard to other fossil finds. Weidenreich is quoted as saying that it has been customary and still is to give generic and specific names to each new type found without very much concern for its relationship to other types formerly known.[109] This tendency is, of course, understandable. Each man is interested in gaining for himself the honor of discovering a new form. And the more unusual the form is, the more attention it will gain for him. For that reason, he is likely to overemphasize and even exaggerate its unique characteristics. But understandable as this tendency may be, it is confusing and misleading. And it is not scientific.

Not only is there a tendency to ignore relationships, but there is also a tendency to multiply the number of genera and species. This, too, is understandable. But it is appalling to taxonomists, who, because they have no direct interest, are likely to be more objective in classifying these forms.

Simons says high physical and dental variability in man and apes has long been known, but this was not taken into account by the majority of past and recent describers of fossil hominoids. Since the late 19th century the oversplitting of known varieties of hominoids, he reports, has produced approximately three genera and countless species.[110] Dobzhansky says that a minor, but rather annoying, difficulty for a biologist is the habit human paleontologists have of flattering their egos by naming each find a new species if not a new genus. This causes not only a needless cluttering of the nomenclature, he believes, but is seriously misleading because treating as a species what is not a species beclouds some important issues.[111]

Today it is almost universally agreed that both the Cro-Magnon and Neanderthal races are *Homo sapiens*. Mayr expresses himself as agreeing that this is the case.[112] Stewart says that the total variability represented by the various Neanderthal specimens does not appear to exceed that of present-day man.[113] Dobzhansky, commenting on Stewart's statement, says that it is now clear that the Neanderthaloids and the so-called *sapiens* type were at no time two reproductively isolated species, but rather component races of a single species.[114] Elsewhere he expresses the same opinion.[115]

Recent Classifications of Human Fossils

Mayr reduces all fossil men to one genus and three species. He believes that all of them should be classified in the genus *Homo*. He places the Java man and the Peking man in one species, which he calls *Homo erectus*, and the various South African ape-men (*Australopithecus africanus*, *Australopithecus prometheus*, *Plesianthropus transvaalensis*, *Paranthropus robustus*, *Paranthropus crassidens*) in a second species, *H. transvaalensis*. All other fossils, he believes, belong to *Homo sapiens*.[116] It should be pointed out that most anthropologists exclude *Australopithecus* from the ancestors of man and reject the name *Homo transvaalensis*.

Weidenreich goes still further. He believes that the anatomical evidence offers no alternative but to unite all of the known human fossils and modern man in a single species, *Homo sapiens*.[117] While he suggests that the South African forms may constitute a separate species not in the human line, *Pithecanthropus* and *Sinanthropus* are definitely included in *Homo sapiens*.[118]

Kraus says that since no one has succeeded in showing a constellation of trait distribution curves wherein *Homo erectus* and *Homo sapiens* overlap by less than 25 per cent, it would appear that there is really no firm basis for disputing Weidenreich's thesis that all hominid forms from the beginning of the Pleistocene to the present represent a single species. Kraus believes that all erect bipedal, culture-producing hominoids can properly be subsumed under the single genus *Homo* and the single species *sapiens*, and he thinks that these forms should be given three names: *Homo sapiens pekinensis*, *Homo sapiens erectus*, and *Homo sapiens prometheus*.[119] Certainly this reduction to one species or even to one genus and three species (*Homo habilis*, *Homo erectus*, and *Homo sapiens*) is striking. Perhaps the problem of fossil men is not so troublesome a one after all.

NOTES

1. Hooton, Earnest Albert. *Up from the Ape* (New York: Macmillan, 1946), p. 159.
2. Sklerj, Bozo. "Comments," *Cold Spring Harbor Symposia on Quantitative Biology*, XXIV (1959), 215.
3. Schultz, Adolph H. "The Specializations of Man and His Place Among the Catarrhine Primates," *Cold Spring Harbor Symposia on Quantitative Biology*, XV (1950), 46.
4. Gregory, William King. *Evolution Emerging* (New York: Macmillan, 1951), I, 467.
5. Mayr, Ernst. "Taxonomic Categories in Fossil Hominids," *Cold Spring Harbor Symposia on Quantitative Biology*, XV (1950), 116.
6. Bennett, Edward L., Diamond, Marian C., Krech, David, and Rosenzweig, Mark R. "Chemical and Anatomical Plasticity of the Brain," *Science*, CXLVI (1964), 610.
7. Dobzhansky, Theodosius. "Changing Man," *Science*, CLV (1967), 410.
8. Hooton, p. 278.
9. Ibid., p. 66.
10. Van Valen, Leigh, and Sloan, Robert E. "The Earliest Primates," *Science*, CL (1965), p. 743.
11. Jones, Frederic Wood. *Hallmarks of Mankind* (Baltimore: Williams and Wilkins, 1948), pp. 32, 44 f.
12. Schultz, p. 37.
13. Gregory, p. 471.
    Hooton, p. 18.
14. Jerison, Harry J. "Brain to Body Ratios and the Evolution of Intelligence," *Science*, CXXI (1955), 448 f.
15. Hooton, p. 278.
16. Ibid., p. 135.
17. Kraus, Bertram S. *The Basis of Human Evolution* (New York: Harper and Row, 1964), p. 253.
18. Clark, Wilfrid E. Le Gros. "New Paleontological Evidence Bearing on the Evolution of the Hominoidea," *Quarterly Journal of the Geological Society of London*, CV (1950), 225–264.
19. Kraus, p. 339.
20. Huxley, Julian. *Evolution, the Modern Synthesis* (New York: Harpers, 1943), pp. 353 f.
21. Schultz, p. 38.
22. Hewes, Gordon W. "Hominid Bipedalism: Independent Evi-

dence for the Food-Carrying Theory," *Science,* CXLVI (1964), 417.

23. Lawton, Richard W. "Biological Aspects of the Space Program," *The Science Teacher,* XXXIII, 7 (October 1966), 21.

24. Hooton, pp. 38 f.

25. Schultz, p. 46.

26. Schultz, Adolph H. "Characters Common to Higher Primates and Characters Specific for Man," *Quarterly Review of Biology,* II (1936), 450.

27. *Science,* CXXI (1955), 381.

28. Montagu, Ashley. "Natural Selection and the Origin and Evolution of Weeping in Man," *Science,* CXXX (1960), 1572.

29. Richter, Curt P. "A Hitherto Unrecognized Difference Between Man and Other Primates," *Science,* CLIV (1966), 427.

30. Dobzhansky, Theodosius. *Mankind Evolving* (New Haven: Yale University Press, 1962), p. 164. Kraus, p. 17.

31. Dobzhansky, Th., and Montagu, M. F. "Natural Selection and the Mental Capacities of Mankind," *Science,* CV (1947), 587–590.

32. Hooton, p. 158.

33. Schultz, "The Specializations," pp. 40 f.

34. Ashley-Montagu, M. F. "A Consideration of the Concept of Race," *Cold Spring Harbor Symposia on Quantitative Biology,* XV (1950), 327.

35. Boyd, William C. "Three General Types of Racial Characteristics," *Cold Spring Harbor Symposia on Quantitative Biology,* XV (1950), 235 f.

36. Schultz, "The Specializations," p. 43.

37. Schultz, "Characters Common," p. 449.

38. Simpson, George Gaylord. "The Biological Nature of Man," *Science,* CLII (1966), 473.

39. Simons, Elwyn L. "Some Fallacies in the Study of Hominid Phylogeny," *Science,* CXLI (1963), 888.

40. Seaborg, Glenn T. "Science and the Humanities: A New Level of Symbiosis," *Science,* CXLIV (1964), 1200.

41. Straus, William L., Jr., and Hunt, Charles B. "Age of Zinjanthropus," *Science,* CXXXVI (1962), 295.

42. Tobias, P. V. "Cranial Capacity of Zinjanthropus and Other Australopithecines," *Nature* (London), CXCVII (1963), 743–746.

43. Tobias, Phillip V. "Early Man in East Africa," *Science,* CXLIX (1965), 22–33.

44. Montagu, Ashley. "Homo habilis," *Science,* CXLIX (1965), 918.

45. Patterson, Bryan, and Howells, W. W. "Hominid Humeral Fragment from Early Pleistocene of Northwestern Kenya," *Science,* CLVI (1967), 64–66.

46. Hooton, p. 289.

47. Dubois, Eug. "On the Gibbonlike Appearance of *Pithecanthropus erectus," Koninklijke Akademie van Wetenschappen te Amsterdam,* XXXVIII (1935), 578–585.

48. Weidenreich, Franz. *Apes, Giants, and Man* (Chicago: University of Chicago Press, 1946), p. 27.

49. Hooton, pp. 289 f.

50. Kraus, p. 282.

51. Weidenreich, pp. 60 f.

52. Hooton, pp. 348–351.

53. Ibid., pp. 281–288.

54. Mayr, p. 112.

55. Kraus, p. 226.

56. Ibid., p. 285.

57. Gregory, p. 491.

58. Washburn, S. L. "The Analysis of Primate Evolution with Particular Reference to the Origin of Man," *Cold Spring Harbor Symposia on Quantitative Biology,* XV (1950), 74.

59. Weidenreich, p. 22.

60. *Science,* CXIX (1954), 863.

61. Mayr, p. 111.

62. Kraus, p. 223.

63. Weidenreich, pp. 60–62.

64. "Age of Peking Man," *Science,* CXXXI (1960), 1511.

65. Hooten, p. 303.

66. Weidenreich, p. 84.

67. *Science,* CXXI (1955), 492.

68. Weidenreich, p. 23.

69. Hooton, p. 311.

70. Oakley, Kenneth P., and Hoskins, C. Randall. "New Evidence on the Antiquity of Piltdown Man," *Nature* (London), CLXV (1950), 379–382.

71. Birdsell, Joseph B. "Discussion," *Cold Spring Harbor Symposia on Quantitative Biology,* XV (1950), 107.

72. Straus, William L., Jr. "The Great Piltdown Hoax," *Science,* CXIX (1954), 266–268.

73. *Science,* CXX (1954), 366 f.

74. Stewart, T. D. "The Problem of the Earliest Claimed Representatives of *Homo sapiens*," *Cold Spring Harbor Symposia on Quantitative Biology*, XV (1950), 101.

75. Hooton, p. 363.

76. Ibid., pp. 363 f.

77. Ibid., p. 317.

78. Vallois, Henri V. "The Fontéchevade Fossil Men," *American Journal of Physical Anthropology*, n. s., VII (1949), pp. 357 f.

79. Hooton, pp. 339–346.

80. Gregory, pp. 485–487.
    Straus, William L., Jr. "Fire and the Australopithecines," *Science*, CXX (1954), 356 f.

81. Hooton, pp. 394–396.

82. Ibid., pp. 388 f.

83. Leakey, L. S. B. *The Stone Age Races of Kenya* (London: Oxford University Press, 1935), pp. 121–124.

84. Hooton, pp. 389 f.

85. Ibid., p. 396.

86. Ibid., pp. 347 f.

87. Sellards, E. H. "Age of Folsom Man," *Science*, CXV (1952), 98.
    Libby, Willard F. *Radiocarbon Dating* (Chicago: University of Chicago Press, 1952), pp. 82, 103.

88. Hooton, pp. 405–407.

89. Stewart, p. 97.

90. Coon, Carleton Stevens. *The Races of Europe* (New York: Macmillan, 1948), pp. 24, 27, 31, 267.

91. Hooton, p. 357.

92. Straus, W. L., Jr. "Review of L. S. Palmer's 'Man's Journey Through Time,'" *Science*, CXXXI (1960), 220.

93. Wells, Calvin. *Bones, Bodies, and Disease* (New York: Praeger, 1964), p. 62.

94. Kraus, p. 273.

95. Ibid., p. 279.

96. Hooton, p. 338.

97. McCown, Theodore D. "The Genus *Palaeoanthropus* and the Problem of Superspecific Differentiation Among the Hominidae," *Cold Spring Harbor Symposia on Quantitative Biology*, XV (1950), p. 92.

98. Kraus, p. 245.

99. McCown, p. 92.

100. Hooton, pp. 365–373.

101. Boyd, William C. *Genetics and the Races of Man* (Boston: Little, Brown and Co., 1950), p. 324.
102. Heberer, Gerhard. "The Descent of Man and the Present Fossil Record," *Cold Spring Harbor Symposia on Quantitative Biology*, XXIV (1959), 235 f.
103. "Problems of Evolution," *Christianity Today*, X, 8 (Jan. 21, 1966), 411.
104. Dobzhansky, *Mankind Evolving*, p. 171.
105. Hooton, p. 329.
106. Ibid., pp. 358 f.
107. Ibid., p. 363.
108. Ibid., p. 303.
109. Mayr, p. 109.
110. Simons, p. 880.
111. Dobzhansky, p. 171.
112. Mayr, pp. 112 f.
113. Stewart, p. 105.
114. Dobzhansky, Th. "Discussion," *Cold Spring Harbor Symposia on Quantitative Biology*, XV (1950), 106.
115. Dobzhansky, Th. "On Species and Races of Living and Fossil Men," *American Journal of Physical Anthropology*, n. s., II (1944), 265.
116. Mayr, pp. 112–115.
117. Weidenreich, p. 3.
118. Ibid., pp. 22, 30.
119. Kraus, p. 331.

10. Special Types and Various Forms of Evolution

In this section various special methods and modes of evolution will be considered. Then the descriptions of the various paths evolution is supposed to have taken will be summarized. These various special methods are supposed to have played a part in evolution, either a major part in the evolution of one particular group or a minor part in evolution in general. Often these various methods are supposed to have worked together with mutations or chromosomal changes or with one another; this is the essence of the currently accepted synthetic theory.

Hybridization

The first of these is hybridization, which is believed by some to have played a significant part in evolution. Hybridization is usually applied to crosses between different varieties of the same species.

There is no doubt that hybridization does provide a considerable variation potential. If we assume ten thousand loci in the monoploid number in man, for example, and if there are two alleles at each locus, then the number of possible genotypes for human population would be approximately $3^{10,000}$. No one questions that hereditary differences provide infinite variety. It is for this reason that, except for identical twins, identical triplets, and the like, there are probably no two human beings with exactly the same hereditary background. And we would say that this is the

382 Genes, Genesis, and Evolution

mechanism which God has provided to make possible a great deal of variety. It would be a dull world, indeed, if the entire human race were a race of identical twins, with the same likes and dislikes, abilities, interests, and the like. A similar variety is possible and no doubt exists in plants and animals.

It has been suggested that this variety is a means of providing materials for natural selection. In other words, evolution has progressed by utilizing the varieties available within the species. It is usually assumed that mutation is the source of this variety, but for an analysis of variation or hybridization itself as a factor in evolution the source of the variation is not important. The particular significance of hybridization in evolution is that it may provide a rapid increase in the size of the gene pool from which natural selection may quickly sort out entirely new adaptive gene complexes for adaptation to a new habitat.

Nothing New Added by This Process

Our chief criticism of this method of evolution is that nothing new is added by this process. Hybridization merely provides a new combination of the characters already present. It does not make for anything new within the species itself. It certainly is not a mechanism by means of which new *kinds* are developed. True, hybridization can bring about the development of a wide variety of sub-species and types within the species itself, but it goes no farther. And it is the development of new forms beyond the specific level that is the critical problem for evolution. Simpson, for instance, says that evolution on the basis of existing variability is a self-limiting process that cannot proceed beyond the specific level.[1] Mayr believes that hybridization, instead of promoting speciation, accomplishes just the opposite. He believes that it eliminates the gap which previously existed between two populations or two subspecies.[2] Certainly this fact, if true, limits the importance of hybridization as a mechanism for evolution.

Introgressive Hybridization

A special type of hybridization is introgression or introgressive hybridization. This involves the introduction of genes from one species into the gene complex of another species by a crossing of the two species and then a backcrossing to one of the parents. Polyploidy as it occurs in nature is most often associated with some sort of hybridization either between species or between different subspecies or races of the same species.[3] Often there will be a great deal of crossing and backcrossing resulting in what is usually known as a hybrid swarm.

But even this does not bring about real evolution. Stebbins points out that it merely produces a convergence between previously more distinctive species. He says that by its very nature it is not a means of producing new morphological or physiological characteristics and for that reason cannot be a mechanism for progressive evolution.[4] He is of the opinion that in most cases hybridization and introgression play their part in plant populations when old habitats are disturbed and new ones opened by human activity.[5] Most botanists agree that this is the case. Hybridization is believed to be much more important in plants than in animals. White says that the evidence for evolution by introgression in animals is very meager.[6] And Mayr characterizes it as a theoretical process which in animals is not well supported by facts.[7] Yet Stebbins believes that it has probably played a larger role in animal evolution than many zoologists think it has. He recognizes that animals have a much more complex pattern of development which is controlled by equally complex and highly integrated sequences of gene action so that the proportion of successful recombinations which can segregate in a hybrid progeny is much lower. He thinks that in animals hybridization is especially significant in hybrids between subspecies and closely related species in which hybrid inviability and sterility may be only weakly developed.[8]

The Necessity of Vegetative Reproduction in Introgression

Introgressive hybridization can play an important part only in plants with an efficient means of vegetative reproduction. In many cases the hybrid is itself sterile and can survive only if it is able to propagate itself vegetatively. But this type of reproduction is in itself a very conservative type of reproduction. Little evolution is possible so long as there is dependence upon vegetative reproduction.[9]

Often, too, in introgressive hybridization as a result of breeding back to one of the parents, most of the genes of the other parent are eventually lost. This loss seems to be due to the fact that the parent plants produce a great deal of viable pollen while the hybrid itself produces very little. In this case the new characteristics that have been introduced will slowly be lost.[10] White believes that it is unlikely that introgressive hybridization has been of much importance in speciation. He, too, believes that the foreign genes would soon be diluted.[11]

Complex Heterozygosity

Another phenomenon that is supposed by some to have played a part in evolution is complex heterozygosity as illustrated in the case of the various forms of the evening primrose, *Oenothera*. It is thought that these plants are almost permanent hybrids or permanent heterozygotes. It appears that in most "species" each plant produces two types of gametes, differing not in a single gene but in very many closely linked genes. The set of genes carried in a given complex is constant and is held together throughout the life cycle. Each of the species of *Oenothera*, according to this hypothesis, contains two of these gene series or gene complexes, and at meiosis each separates from the other as a single entity. Thus *Oenothera lamarckiana*, one of the species, is composed of a gene complex called *gaudens* containing genes for green buds, nonpunctate stems (lacking white dots), white nerves, broad leaves, and red flecks on the rosette leaves (the leaves forming a circle at the base of the plant); and *velans*, containing genes for red-striped buds, punctate stems, narrow leaves, white nerves, and no red flecks on the rosette leaves. Thus *lamarckiana* is a *gaudens-velans* complex. Half of its pollen grains and half of its eggs contain the *gaudens* gene complex, and the other half contain the *velans* complex.

Self-fertilization should result in three types of offspring: *gaudens-gaudens, gaudens-velans,* and *velans-velans.* The first and the third are believed to die out because of balanced lethals which they contain. The *gaudens* complex is believed to contain a recessive lethal, the dominant normal allele of which is found in *velans;* and *velans* is believed to contain another recessive lethal, the dominant normal allele of which is to be found in the *gaudens* complex. Thus the zygote which is formed by a *gaudens-gaudens* fertilization contains two recessive lethals and dies. The same is true of the *velans-velans* combination. Only the *gaudens-velans* combination can survive. This theory seems to be borne out by the fact that about half of the fertilized ovules either fail to produce seeds or produce seeds which are not viable.

Other species of *Oenothera* are made up of different complexes. Thus *Oenothera biennis* is an *albicans-rubens* combination, and *Oenothera muricata* is a *rigens-curvans* combination.

It is thought that this heterozygosity can lead to the development of new types, and that this sort of development may have played a part in evolution. However, here again there are definite limitations on the amount of change possible. Not only is the amount of change limited, but actually no new characters are being introduced: we have only a recombination of characters already present. Stebbins believes that this complex heterozygosity has never led to anything more than a multiplication of races or of species within a subgenus.[12] And Darlington calls this mechanism an evolutionary blind alley.[13]

Preadaptation

Another theory is that of preadaptation, which is associated chiefly with Cuénot.[14] He believed that mutations adapt the organism not to life as it is now, but to life as it will be sometime in the indefinite future. Today it is believed that preadaptation is usually followed by post-adaptation, which further adapts the organism to its new environment. Heterozygosity and polymorphism, which we have discussed in chapter 8, is often suggested as a mechanism for preadaptation.

A number of examples of preadaptation have been cited. For instance, in the moth *Ephestia kühniella,* the mutation to brown color is accompanied by a reduction in egg number and in length of life and also by a markedly higher heat tolerance. It is believed that this is an example of a mutation which will enable the animal to survive if it should come into a habitat in which the temperatures are markedly higher.[15]

It should, however, be pointed out that in this case the brown mutant would be wiped out rather quickly unless it happened to come into circumstances where it could make the most of its favorable characteristic. Under ordinary conditions a form in which the number of eggs was reduced would be selected against, and it would soon die out. Only if the temperatures changed rather rapidly could the moth make the most of this mutation. Thus preadaptation could not occur very much sooner than the change in the temperature conditions.

Another example of such preadaptation is the situation reported by Lamoreux and Hutt. They found that White Leghorn chickens are markedly more resistant to Vitamin B_1 deficiency than two other breeds.[16] This particular characteristic would be an advantage under conditions where the diet was not balanced and Vitamin B_1 was deficient or absent. Once more, however, there is always the possibility that the breed might be eliminated before it has an opportunity to take advantage of this favorable characteristic. Naturally we must deal with characteristics present at this very time level. We pointed this out earlier in connection with our discussion of mutations, and the criticisms mentioned there apply to the whole idea of preadaptation.

The idea of preadaptation has some of the aspects of teleology, which is in general disfavor in biology today. One writer speaks of natural selection as being "endowed with an unparalleled gift, the automatic property of foresight." He believes that it is impossible to imagine sexual reproduction as a result of a gradual accumulation of changes, each one of which had value as an adaptation. Williams criticizes this point of view and believes that sexual reproduction has evolved gradually.[17]

Quantum Evolution

Another type of evolution is what has been called quantum evolution. This is an explosive type of evolution, a sudden shifting to a new type of adaptation. It consists of three phases. First there is an inadaptive phase in which the group loses the equilibrium of its ancestors or collaterals. These, presumably, were or are well adapted to the habitat in which they have lived. They have made the necessary changes, have developed desirable mutations, and they are now well fitted for the environment in which they find themselves. The organism which is undergoing the first phase of quantum evolution, however, loses this fitness, and develops a large number of varieties, most of which are poorly adapted to the environment.

The second phase is the preadaptive phase. In this there is a great selective pressure, and the group moves toward a new equilibrium. Many populations that go through the first phase and lose their adaptation to the environment do not make this step toward a new stability, but merely become extinct. It is at this stage, too, that the organism moves into a new adaptive zone. This new zone must be empty or only sparsely or marginally occupied, so that the form experiences little or no competition. This situation is necessary because the new form cannot meet strong competition from forms already well entrenched in a given ecological niche. Often the new habitat is open because the previous inhabitants have died out.

The third stage in quantum evolution is an adaptive phase, in which the organism reaches a new equilibrium with its environment. In this stage it develops the stability which it had before undergoing this quantum evolution.[18]

Quantum evolution is used to account for the sudden outbursts of evolution that geological history is supposed to show. Those periods in which different forms are supposed to have evolved rapidly are believed to have been instances in which quantum evolution was occurring and the organism was jumping in to exploit a new habitat. Evans, for instance, believes that the idea of gradual and continuous evolution is insufficient to explain all of the observed facts of the evolutionary development of leafhoppers. He believes that in addition to gradual and continuous development evolutionary changes occurred more rapidly during the Paleozoic than subsequently and that the steps which have given rise to some of the higher categories of leafhoppers may have been initiated by abrupt and not gradual evolutionary change.[19] This theory also helps to meet Goldschmidt's particular problem. Goldschmidt believes that evolution occurs in big jumps rather than in small steps. Mutations provide a mechanism only for small step evolution, and for that reason he has more or less rejected mutations as a mechanism for evolution. Quantum evolution would make possible "big jump" evolution as the organism begins to exploit an entirely new habitat. The theory also assumes a certain amount of preadaptation.

The chief difficulty with this theory is the probability that the organism would become extinct before it had gained a foothold in the new habitat. Simpson, who is the particular champion of this theory, believes that in most cases the organism becomes extinct before entering the second step of quantum evolution. He also points to the fact that the organism can gain a foothold in the new environment only if that particular habitat is empty or only sparsely or marginally occupied. This type of evolution would require an almost complete absence of selection pressure during most of its steps.

The Sewall Wright Effect: Genetic Drift

Another supposedly very important factor in evolution is the Sewall Wright effect, also known as genetic drift. This involves changes which are supposed to develop within the species because of the population size. Emphasis is laid not so much on the individual as on the population as a whole. In recent years much research has been carried on in the field of population genetics, and much research is being carried on today in this area. It is believed, for instance, that in a small population harmful genes or accidental characteristics of no survival value may easily become fixed. For instance, if the population is a small one, any mutation has a good chance of becoming fixed in that population. Sewall Wright believes that this is the way in which nonuseful characters have appeared in various species. In a very small population a large number of the organisms will be eliminated by random causes rather than by selection. It is very possible that among the survivors a large number will be found who possess nonadaptive characteristics — characteristics which are neutral or even harmful. Thus this nonadaptive character will become fixed in the population even though selection would ordinarily eliminate it.

Wright believes that this solves the problem of the origin of nonuseful characters which Eimer and his coworkers attempted to solve by orthogenesis. In a small population the guiding factor in evolution is believed to be mutation pressure rather than selection. "Mutation pressure" refers to the number and kinds of mutations that occur.

But it should be pointed out that this does not really solve the problem of the origin of nonuseful characters. This accounts for the origin of nonuseful characters only in those populations which are small and in which there is a high mutation rate. There are many nonuseful characters which have appeared in populations which have apparently always been large, and in which the mutation rate is not unusually high. Stebbins, who believes that the Sewall Wright effect is the chief source of nonadaptive differences between populations, races, and species, points out that these can arise in this way only in small populations that are breeding rapidly. He believes that genetic drift rarely, if ever, occurs in the higher plants.[20]

Conversely, according to the Sewall Wright effect, in very large populations there is a limit on the amount of free gene interchange that is possible. Because of the large number of individuals in the population, it is simply not possible for a free interchange of genes to occur. Thus in a very large population a favorable gene might be eliminated merely because it would not have an opportunity to gain a foothold in the population. Large populations tend toward a genetic equilibrium unfavorable for rapid and sustained progressive evolution.[21]

According to Sewall Wright, the most favorable population for evolution by natural selection is a medium-sized population or, even better, a large population divided into several small subpopulations partially isolated from one another. In the latter situation — a large population divided into several smaller subpopulations — random fixation will tend to establish in each subpopulation characteristics which, while they may be of no immediate selective value, may enable the subpopulation to develop gene combinations with a new type of adaptive value. This is believed to have occurred many times in the history of man.[22] These valuable genes or gene combinations may be transferred from one subpopulation to another by occasional migration followed by hybridization. This migration, it is believed, would probably be due to a sort of migration pressure where a group in the subpopulation would be forced by a lack of food or some other pressure to leave the habitat and migrate.[23]

Thus very large populations may differentiate rapidly, but their sustained evolution will be at a moderate or a slow rate and will be mainly adaptive. Populations of medium size provide the best conditions for sustained progressive and branching evolution, adaptive in its main lines but also accompanied by inadaptive fluctuations, especially in characters of little selective importance. Small populations will be virtually incapable of differentiation or branching and will often be dominated by random, nonadaptive trends.

Small populations are peculiarly liable to extinction. It is believed that this is the reason why relatively small populations often become extinct very rapidly. At the same time genetic drift is postulated as a way of protecting small populations against extinction. It is believed, for instance, that the population may reach a precariously low point, may be poorly adapted to its immediate environment and therefore close to extinction. Under these circumstances it is believed that adaptive genetic mutons which are recessive and might be swamped in the larger population could by a rare coincidence of mating suddenly become homozygous and thus phenotypically effective, in this way saving the small population.[24] Thus Sewall Wright believes that the elementary process in evolution is a change in the gene frequency and not mutation itself.[25]

Population Fluctuations

Also playing a part in the population effect is the fact that natural populations undergo a considerable fluctuation in their size. At one time it was thought that the size of wild populations remained rather constant. It was often said that every pair of animals today will be represented by a single pair of animals in the next generation, even though they may produce a large number of offspring. But it is now known that there is considerable variation in the size of populations from time to time. These facts were first reported by Elton, and the existence of such population fluctuations is generally accepted today. In fact, it seems as if many, if not most, wild animals undergo cycles, during the course of which the population goes from one extreme of a relatively large population to another extreme of a relatively small population. The exact reason for these population fluctuations is not fully understood. No doubt food abundance, resistance to disease, fertility rates, etc., are involved.

It is believed that at different periods during the cycle different parts of the Sewall Wright effect will make themselves felt. Thus it is believed that at the lowest point in a population cycle certain nonadaptive characters may become fixed in the population. Later the effects of a medium-sized and a large-sized population will be felt. In that way over the course of several of these cycles considerable change could occur in a natural population.

H. D. and E. B. Ford report observations which seem to indicate that this change occurs. They carried these observations out on an isolated colony of *Melitaea aurinia,* a butterfly, for thirteen years. The colony had been observed previously for thirty-six years. During this time the colony, which was an isolated one, experienced an extreme diminution in numbers. This was followed by a rapid increase until finally a sort of equilibrium was reached. During the period of rapid increase, variability was extreme. Forms appeared that could almost be regarded as pathological freaks. This excessive variability decreased when the numbers became stabilized once more, but the new modal representative type was distinctly different from that found during the previous stable period.[26] Presumably when stability was reached, natural selection was able to exert its influence once more, and variability decreased. It is not clear from the report exactly how different the new modal type was. Nor is it clear whether this difference was the result of mutants preserved at the low period or the result of mutants preserved at the period of rapid increase.

Haldane does not believe that variation is promoted by having mutant individuals preserved during a low period of fluctuating numbers. He concludes that the chance of a mutation becoming established in such a way is so remote as to be of no practical significance.[27] E. B. Ford says that the increase in variation reported in the observations on *Melitaea* was so rapid and the changes so marked that it is unlikely that the factors postulated were wholly responsible for them.[28]

Because of fluctuations in population size the effective size of a population may be smaller than its apparent size. The effective size refers only to sexually mature individuals who are capable of interbreeding. It is possible to have in a population a large number of juveniles who have not yet reached the reproductive age or a large number of adults who are past the reproductive age. Neither of these add to the effective size of the population. Also there may be a great many more mature individuals of one sex than of the other sex, and this preponderance may reduce the

effective size of the population. In monogamous species the
effective size of the population is governed by the number
of the less common sex. If there are wide variations in the
number of offspring reaching maturity left by different
parents, the effective number may also be reduced. So far
as the Sewall Wright effect is concerned, the effective size
of the population in a population which undergoes more or
less definite cycles in numbers is determined by the phase
in which the number is smallest.[29]

Genetic Drift and Evolution

Now, what has this to do with evolution? Certainly the
phenomena with which Wright worked and to which he
called attention will reduce the effectiveness of natural
selection in many cases and will reduce the rate of progressive evolution. Selection acts very rapidly in an intermediate population with an intermediate gene frequency,
but it acts much more slowly in very large populations and
very small populations. This is confirmed by the experiments of H. V. Harlan and M. L. Martini. They worked
with a number of varieties of barley (*Hordeum*). The most
successful types increased in number rapidly and evenly
throughout the experiment. Those of intermediate adaptive
value rose rapidly at first, reached a rather low peak, and
then declined rapidly. Toward the end of the experiment,
however, the rate of this decline slackened. The unsuccessful types declined rapidly at the beginning and then more
slowly, so that toward the end there were still some of the
unsuccessful types present.[30]

Presumably the elimination of those barley types of intermediate adaptive value and of the unsuccessful barley types
was due to natural selection. At the beginning of the experiment the number of plants present constituted a small
population. In this small population barley plants of intermediate selective value were able to increase. Again, at
the end of the experiment, in a large population, they con-

tinued to survive even in competition with the successful varieties. Selection was not able to eliminate them. Only when they reached their maximum number in the medium-sized population were they eliminated at a rapid rate, presumably by selection. The unsuccessful types were also able to survive toward the end of the experiment in the very large population. Thus natural selection was somewhat limited. It was ineffective in a small or a large population and worked only in an intermediate population.

It is difficult to say at exactly which point selection begins to make itself felt. Wright believes that it is effective when Ns=0.5 ("N"=population size, "s"=coefficient of selection). Thus in a population whose effective size is 5,000, selection will have an effect even if the selective advantage, or coefficient of selection, is only 0.01 per cent.[31]

Yet genetic drift and population fluctuations would certainly seem to impose a limitation on the effectiveness of natural selection. Genetic drift can operate only in intermediate populations or in large populations separated into smaller subpopulations. This means, too, that often success itself will be a self-limiting factor. As the population becomes very large, it reduces the effectiveness of natural selection in promoting its evolution. Only where isolation plays a part in producing subpopulations can natural selection continue to be effective after the population has become a fairly large one.

There is at least one problem that the Sewall Wright effect does not solve. If it is correct that small populations favor uniformity and nonuseful characters, why is it that cyclic species, as a consequence of the periodic reductions to low points in number of individuals, have not become particularly pure genotypically in comparison with those forms in which these cycles do not appear? Elton feels that this is a curious thing.[32] It would seem logical that those species which undergo the cycles should be much purer genotypically than species which do not undergo these reduction cycles, for at the low point in the cycle most of the variability should be eliminated. However, we do not find any appreciable difference in the amount of variety found in forms which undergo a periodic reduction in numbers and in those in which the numbers are relatively stable.

It should be pointed out that Ford is of the opinion that genetic drift is of little importance in evolution. He believes that the evidence indicates it is of no significance in evolution where the population consists of 1,000 individuals or more. Colonies of smaller size, he believes, are not permanent and become extinct before there can be any real evolution.[33] It cannot be effective in them either.

Williams lists a series of conditions which must coincide before genetic drift can be effective and says that he can see no hope of achieving any reliable estimate of how frequently the necessary conditions have been realized. He is, however, convinced that the frequency of such combinations of circumstances must be relatively low and the combinations quite temporary when they do occur.[34] Stebbins believes that at present no example of differentiation between populations is known which can be ascribed solely or principally to this factor. He believes that selection in combination with genetic drift may be significant.[35]

The General Course of Evolution

Let us look at the course that evolution is supposed to have taken. Today most evolutionists believe that evolution has been a branching process rather than a straight-line process. They deplore the misconceptions that the so-called phylogenetic trees have produced in the minds of many people. According to this latter pattern there is a straight-line development from simple organisms to man.

In many cases phylogenetic trees have been drawn for individual organisms. Perhaps the best known of these is the history of the horse. Actually, however, as we have seen, the history of the horse shows branching rather than a straight-line tree. And a form such as the rhinoceros shows no trunk whatsoever but rather a straggling bushy effect.[36]

Parallelism and Convergence

In the course of this branching development, a distinction is made between parallelism and convergence. Parallelism refers to a type of evolution in which two separate species are evolving along a parallel line. These have diverged from a common ancestor but have continued to develop along a parallel line. Not only have they a similar heritage, but they also live in a habitat which is similar. Thus *Drosophila melanogaster* and *D. simulans* are believed to be examples of parallel evolution.

By convergence is meant the development of similar characteristics in two forms which had radically different ancestors. This convergence is believed to be due to the fact that the two organisms are living in very similar habitats. Thus the wolf and the Tasmanian wolf (*Thylacinus cynocephalus*), a marsupial, are supposed to have developed similar characteristics by convergence. Their ancestors were presumably quite different, but they find themselves living in similar habitats and occupying the same ecological niche, which each of them goes about exploiting. Because they must exploit the same ecological niche, they develop similar characteristics even though their ancestors were quite different.

Huxley's Summary

Huxley has attempted to summarize the various means of the development of new species in his *Evolution: The Modern Synthesis*.[37] It might be well to discuss these at some length. Most of these methods of speciation have been discussed earlier, and it would be repetitious to restate the various difficulties in the way of evolution by these various methods. However, we do want to summarize these

Figure 35. The Tasmanian "Wolf," *Thylacinus cynocephalus.* This animal is a marsupial, but it is very much like a wolf. It and the wolf are supposed to have developed similar characteristics by convergence. (Courtesy of New York Zoological Society)

methods to give a broad overview of the various ways in which evolution is believed to have occurred.

Huxley refers to four different modes of speciation: successional, divergent, convergent, and reticulate. In each case he points out the way in which the groups are isolated, how fast they separate into new species, how fast morphological differences appear, and what sort of barriers there are to interbreeding between the new forms.

1. Successional Speciation

In successional speciation he believes that the groups have been isolated by time, that one species has given rise to another species in the course of time. These new species separate gradually, and their morphological differences develop gradually. Since they are separated by time, it is not possible to analyze their barriers to fertility. They cannot possibly interbreed because they are separated by time barriers.

2. Divergent Speciation

Huxley believes that there are eight kinds of divergent evolution. In this method of speciation one species has gradually divided into two or more new species. In three of these types of divergent evolution the isolation is a spatial one, and in five the isolation is genetic.

a. *Spatial Isolation*

(1) Geographical Isolation. — The first kind of spatial isolation is geographical isolation. As the name indicates, organisms are separated by geographical barriers, such as land masses, bodies of water, mountains, and the like. This type of isolation is believed to have been important especially in birds. The Canada and Oregon jays, the mourning warbler and MacGillivray's warbler, and the common chickadee and the Carolina chickadee (though these latter two Huxley considers to be a borderline case) are supposed to be examples of this type of speciation. Huxley believes that there are a few examples of this type of isolation among plants, such as the gentians, but not very many. There are also a great many examples of this type of speciation among the mammals and fish. Several species of squirrels and deer mice are supposed to have developed in this way. The common red fox is also supposed to be an example of this type. Originally the Old World fox and the New World fox were classified as separate species, but today they are regarded as subspecies. These two subspecies show a number of differences. Silver fox, a variety of the New World red fox, is due to a gene found only in the Canadian population. For that reason the silver fox is unknown in Europe.

In general it is believed that the wider the range of the organism and the fewer the barriers, the fewer the number of species in a genus, and the smaller the number of subspecies within the species. This is to be expected, since geographical barriers are supposed to be responsible for the development of species and subspecies. Thus, among the large birds which presumably have a rather wide range and few barriers to interbreeding, 54.5 per cent of the species are monotypic (lacking in subspecies), and of those species which are polytypic the average number of subspecies is only 1.6 per species. In contrast to this among the small nonmigratory birds only 29.6 per cent of the species are monotypic, and polytypic species show an average of 7.2 subspecies per polytypic species.

In this type of isolation the species separate gradually, presumably because of the gradual accumulation of genes which make for sterility. Visible differentiation is also a gradual process. These differences are believed to have developed as a result of isolation itself. Huxley believes

Figure 36. Varieties of the Red Fox, *Vulpes fulva.* Although these varieties are quite different, they all belong to the same species. (Courtesy Chicago Natural History Museum)

that it is extremely unlikely that the mutations of two isolated groups will be the same. He believes, too, that non-adaptive or accidental differentiation may occur where the isolated groups are small (the Sewall Wright effect).

It might be expected that the sterility barriers would be weaker between forms that are geographically isolated than between those whose distribution areas overlap. In short, if species are to retain their identity, they must develop sterility barriers over against closely related species having a contiguous or overlapping range; otherwise they will soon lose their identity. They will not, however, find it necessary to develop such sterility barriers over against closely related species which are widely separated from them geographically. This explanation is advanced to explain the fact that widely separated forms that have been classified as separate species will often interbreed and produce fertile offspring when artificially hybridized. However, there has been only one real study of this phenomenon. The relationships of the different races of *Drosophila miranda* and *D. pseudoobscura* have been studied. The aversion which *D. pseudoobscura* has to pairing with *miranda* is strongest near the areas where *miranda* occurs. This seems to fit with the theory. But there are also some exceptions. *D. pseudoobscura* from Oaxaca in southern Mexico displays a very strong sexual isolation from *miranda* though they are separated geographically by several hundred miles. Other Mexican races do not show nearly this same degree of sexual isolation though they may be closer together.[38] White believes that a great many more studies of this phenomenon are needed and that caution is in order in identifying the isolating mechanism.[39]

We have discussed this type of evolution in connection with our discussion of the geographical distribution of plants and animals and also in connection with isolation itself as a factor in evolution There we have pointed out some of the difficulties.

(2) Ecological Isolation. — A second type of isolation which Huxley believes has resulted in divergent speciation and the production of several species from a single parental species is ecological isolation. He points out that actually this type of isolation overlaps with geographical isolation. He distinguishes three types of ecological isolation: ecoclimatic, ecotopic, and ecobiotic. By ecoclimatic isolation he refers to instances in which two species replace each other within the same main area as one goes from lower to higher altitudes. He mentions the ptarmigan and red grouse, the twite and the linnet, the ring-ouzel and the blackbird, the mountain and the common hare, the black and the common redstarts, and the alpine and the common lady's mantle. He believes that this same type of ecoclimatic divergence may occur when the habitats differ in that the one is a maritime and the other an inland region, and he gives several examples to illustrate this view.

By ecotopic isolation he refers to instances in which the adaptation is primarily to distinct local habitats. As an example he mentions the two subspecies of song sparrow that are found in the San Francisco Bay area. One of these lives in the salt marshes; the other, on dry hillsides. He also mentions the example of the two subspecies of caribou, one of which lives in the woodland and the other on barren grounds.

By ecobiotic isolation Huxley refers to adaptation primarily to distinct modes of life. This type of separation is due frequently to food preferences. He points to the case of the greater and lesser spotted woodpeckers, which differ in size — apparently, he says, because of differences in the food taken. He also points to the different kinds of finches. The goldfinch prefers thistle heads; the bullfinch prefers fruit buds; the hawfinch prefers berries and green peas; and the crossbill prefers pine seeds. He points to several examples among the predatory birds. The peregrine preys on ducks and pigeons; the merlin preys on smaller birds; the buzzard preys on rabbits, mice, and small animals; the kestrel preys on voles and insects; the sparrowhawk preys on small birds; the hobby preys on dragon flies and swallows; and the osprey preys on fish.

Huxley believes that as a result of ecological divergence the new species separate gradually. He believes that differentiation develops gradually, but he points out that distinctive characters are frequent. The barriers to fertility, he believes, are developed largely as a result of selection. This method of speciation we have discussed under the general heading of isolation, and there we have pointed out some of the difficulties. It might also be noted that Mayr believes ecological divergence without geographical isolation to be impossible.[40]

(3) Biological Isolation. — The third method of spatial isolation referred to by Huxley is biological. Actually he believes that this is a special form of ecobiotic divergence. He thinks that it comes about as a consequence of a divergent adaptation of separate groups of parasites or of plant-eating animals to particular hosts or food plants. For instance, he calls attention to the fact that there are two subspecies of the apple fly. One of these attacks apples; the other attacks blueberries and huckleberries. There are also two subspecies of the ermine moth. One of these feeds on apples; the other, on the hawthorn and the blackthorn.

Huxley believes that with biological isolation the separation of new species is a gradual process. He believes, too, that the visible differentiation is gradual, but there are few distinctive characters. This is in contrast to the results of ecobiotic isolation. As a result of this latter type, there are usually easily discernible distinctive characters, but with biological isolation there are usually few distinctive characters. The barriers to fertility, he thinks, come about largely as a result of selection. This method of isolation has also been discussed under the general heading of isolation as a factor in evolution.

b. *Genetic Isolation*

A second general type of isolation is genetic isolation. Five types of genetic isolation are possible: genic, asexual segregation, segmental interchange, inversion, and auto-polyploidy. Huxley believes that this sort of isolation has been of less importance than the other types of divergence. He does, however, believe it has been of tremendous secondary importance in effecting sterility in some way or other in forms that have been isolated by geographical or ecological factors.[41]

(1) Genic Isolation. — Genic isolation is apparently a very uncommon thing. The only example cited of this particular type of isolation is the one to which we referred earlier, the two strains of maize which will not cross and which apparently differ in only a single gene pair. In this type of speciation the separation into new species would be very abrupt. The visible differentiation, however, would be gradual. The barriers to fertility would be present automatically, since the essence of this type of isolation is the development of an immediate sterility.

(2) Asexual Segregation. — The second type of genetic isolation, asexual segregation, develops as a result of an interbreeding of two good species. The hybrids are, of course, sterile, but under some conditions they can continue to exist because they are able to reproduce asexually. Much of Luther Burbank's work consisted in the development of new forms of this type. In this type of evolution the new species would, of course, develop abruptly; by its very nature a hybrid is sterile and cannot be bred back to the parent species. Similarly, the visible differentiation in this type of evolution would be abrupt. The hybrid would have characteristics of both parents and would be quite different from either parent. Huxley believes that further differentiation would occur subsequent to the initial cross by gene mutation. The barriers to fertility would be present automatically, since the hybrid could not be crossed back to

either parent. This type of evolution includes introgressive hybridization. This method alone could hardly be an important method of evolutionary divergence, since hybrids are sterile.

(3) Translocations. — The third method of genetic isolation depends upon the development of translocations. In some cases there are reciprocal translocations, where the two nonhomologous chromosomes trade parts. In other cases the translocation might be a nonreciprocal one, whereby a piece of one chromosome only would become detached and be attached to a nonhomologous chromosome. Huxley believes that this type of development may lead to a system of balanced lethals such as is believed to exist in the evening primrose (*Oenothera*). It is believed that a similar situation exists in the Jimson weed (*Datura*). In this genus there are a number of different types which are not visibly distinct. The separation of the new species is believed to be a gradual process, and the visible differentiation is also supposed to be a gradual process. Indeed, there are ordinarily few distinctive characteristics. The barriers to fertility are believed to be partially present automatically. As we pointed out when we considered this as a mechanism for evolution, the development of a translocation is usually lethal.

(4) Inversions. — A fourth type of genetic isolation is believed to be brought about by inversion. This is believed to be the mechanism by which *Drosophila melanogaster* and *D. simulans* separated from each other. For a long time these two forms of the fruit fly were not recognized as separate species. It was thought that where crosses proved to be sterile, the individuals were themselves sterile. Later it was found that they were two separate and good species which were so similar morphologically that they were confused with one another. It is postulated that these two species became separated as a result of an accumulation of inversions in their chromosomes.

Like segmental interchanges, inversions are usually lethal. Nevertheless, evolutionists believe that new species develop in this way. They are supposed to separate gradually, and the development of visible differentiation is also supposed to be a gradual process. It should be pointed out that morphological divergence has not occurred between *Drosophila melanogaster* and *D. simulans* even though they are separate species. As noted above, they are so similar morphologically that for many years they were thought to belong to the same species. In forms evolving in this way there are few distinctive characteristics. The barriers to fertility are believed to be partly present automatically.

(5) Autopolyploidy. — The last type of genetic isolation listed by Huxley is autopolyploidy. This is the sort of development that arises when the chromosome number in some abnormal way is doubled. Such polyploids are sterile when crossed with their diploid parents. The separation of the new species is usually an abrupt one, but it may also be a gradual one. Visible differentiation appears gradually. The barriers to fertility are present automatically because of the incompatibility of the chromosome numbers. This mechanism, too, has been discussed earlier.

3. Convergent Speciation: Allopolyploidy and Aneuploidy

The third general mode of speciation is a convergent speciation. In this type we have two separate groups coming together. This mode is in contrast with divergent evolution in which a single group splits into several species. There are two types of this convergent speciation. In one type isolation occurs by allopolyploidy — the doubling of the chromosomal number following a cross between two separate species. In the other type isolation occurs by allopolyploidy followed by autopolyploidy — chromosomal multiplication first by a cross between two separate species and then a doubling which does not involve a cross with another species. The result is an aneuploid, in which some types of chromosomes are represented more often than others in the total chromosomal complement. In both these types the separation into new species is an abrupt one.

A number of instances of allopolyploidy have been referred to earlier. As examples of the type of aneuploidy producing a convergent evolution Huxley mentions different strains within the violet, *Viola kitaibeliana; Dahlia merckii* compared with other species of the genus *Dahlia;* and some of the hawk's-beards, *Crepis.* In both these types visible differentiation is supposed to be abrupt at the beginning. Later, however, other differences develop gradually. The barriers to fertility in both cases are believed to be present automatically.

4. Reticulate Speciation

a. *Convergent-Divergent Speciation*

A fourth general method of speciation is the reticulate method. Here Huxley distinguishes two submodes of speciation: convergent-divergent and recombinational. The first of these brings about isolation chiefly by genetic means. In this group he would place the many polyploid complexes, such as we have in the roses, the brambles, the willows, and the hawthorns. This type of evolution is supposed to be complicated by a combination of polyploidy and various methods of asexual reproduction. The result is a network of closely related forms. Much of the reproduction in these genera is asexual, and the result is that it is difficult to distinguish between species and varieties. In general, there is an absence of sterility barriers between related species. Huxley believes that new species, however, are separated abruptly and that visible differentiation appears abruptly. However, he points out that sterility barriers are almost entirely absent.

Convergent-divergent evolution is so complex and complicated that it defies analysis even by the evolutionists themselves. At the present time it is simply not possible to determine how many species of roses, brambles, willows, and hawthorns there are. Actually in these forms there are probably only a few "kinds," though there are thousands of varieties and subspecies. Mayr says that this mechanism can be almost disregarded as a method of evolution in animals. He says that it is possible only where successful hybridization can occur and that hybridization occurs only exceptionally in animals.[42]

b. *Recombinational Speciation*

The chief example of recombinational evolution is said to be man himself. What little isolation there is, is a geographical isolation, and this type of isolation is reduced by a considerable amount of migration. Since this type of evolution does not result in new species, it is not possible to speak of the separation of new species. Instead of a visible differentiation there is an increased variability within the species. And, of course, there are no barriers to fertility. Recombinational evolution by its very description does not result in the development of new species, and it is actually only a description of the way in which variation within the species occurs.

It might be pointed out that the degree of variability found in man, which is supposed to have resulted from this recombinational evolution, is not unique. Schultz says that there is not only as much variability in the anthropoid apes as in man, but he believes there is vastly more intraspecific variability in the anthropoids.[43]

Boyd's Summary

Another summary of the various ways in which evolution is supposed to have occurred is given by Boyd. He lists four main evolutionary mechanisms — mixture, mutation, selection, and genetic drift.[44] By mixture he has in mind what we have described as hybridization, and, as we have pointed out, this does not produce new species. The other three:

mutation, selection, and genetic drift we have discussed in detail, and Boyd's analysis is merely presented to show once more how some evolutionists believe evolution to have occurred by a combination of various mechanisms.

Stebbins' Summary

Stebbins recognizes five basic types of processes in evolution: gene mutation, changes in chromosome structure and number, genetic recombination, natural selection, and reproductive isolation. He believes the first three provide the genetic variability without which change cannot take place and that natural selection and reproductive isolation guide populations of organisms into adaptive channels. In addition he believes there are three accessory processes which affect the working of the five basic processes. These are migration of individuals from one population to another, hybridization between races or closely related species, and chance acting in small populations.[45]

All of these — the summaries of Huxley, Boyd, and Stebbins — present the modern synthetic theory of evolution which was first popularized by Huxley. It is also referred to as Neo-Darwinism, since it employs essentially Darwinian principles modified in the light of our modern understanding of genetics. It should also be pointed out that, as we have noted earlier, a number of Darwinian principles are understood differently from the way in which Darwin understood them. For instance, evolutionists today have an entirely different understanding of fitness, survival, and the struggle for existence than that which Darwin had.

Evolutionary Rates

It might also be well to say something about the rate at which evolution is supposed to have taken place. Simpson distinguishes three types of evolutionary rates. The first of these he calls a horotelic rate. This might be called the standard evolutionary rate. In it one finds a very prominent mode, and the frequency of evolutionary rates falls off steeply on each side. According to this type of evolution there is a slow evolution at first, followed by a very rapid evolution, and that, in turn, by a slowing down again of the evolutionary rate.

A second type of evolution he has called bradytelic evolution. This might be called a slow type of evolution. According to it, bradytelic forms evolve at a rate much slower than the normal.

The third type of evolution is tachytelic evolution. Here the rate of evolution is faster than normal. In this group we have forms that are evolving very, very rapidly, much more rapidly than at the average rate.[46] Such evolution is sometimes called "explosive" evolution. It is believed to have occurred in forms such as the belemnites — one of the fossil cuttlefishes — and the terebratuloid brachiopods. These are found in a single broad zone. Indeed, numerous forms resulting from the "explosion" may be found in a single bed and show little indication of variety in their habits. At present the "why" of such explosions is little understood.[47] Rensch believes that the evolution of new animal groups is often inaugurated by a phase of explosive radiation, though he recognizes that there are numerous cases in which a period of rapid splitting occurs after a long and steady development over several geological epochs.[48]

There is no doubt, according to evolutionists, that rates of evolution do vary. Simpson, for instance, gives the following rates of evolution determined by an examination of the fossil history of the forms.[49]

	AVERAGE NUMBER OF GENERA PER MILLION YEARS
Hyracotherium-Equus	.18
Chalicotheriidae	.17
Triassic and Earlier Ammonites	.05

Table 10: Rates of Evolution

The Problem of Bradytelic Evolution

The particular type of evolution that causes difficulty is slow evolution. It is hard to understand how some forms should find it possible to evolve more slowly than other forms. They should be subject to the same selection pressures to which other forms living at the same time are subjected. And yet for some reason or other they do not seem to find it necessary to evolve as rapidly as the other forms.

Simpson believes that a number of factors may make slow evolution possible. He lists a low mutation rate, long life span, and asexual reproduction as factors that have been suggested as slowing down the rate of evolution. However, he concludes that none of these is of any real importance in slowing down the rate of evolution. Indeed, he says that indirect evidence opposes that idea.[50] He also suggests that large-sized populations may be an important factor in slowing down the rate of evolution. This view agrees, of course, with the genetic drift ideas of Sewall Wright. He pointed out that necessarily in a large population the rate of evolution will be slow, since the chance of a mutation becoming established is rather slight and the amount of gene interchange possible in a large population is restricted.

Simpson also suggests that at the time these various forms stopped evolving they consisted of a large breeding population or were progressive and relatively high types, so that they were able to coast for a long time without evolving. However, as he points out, only a few individuals of *Latimeria,* the fossil fish, have ever been found, so that it is hardly likely that the population of *Latimeria* is large enough to stop its evolution. The same thing might be said of *Sphenodon,* the lizardlike reptile noted for its nonfunctional third eye, the population of which is so small that it is almost extinct. It is also hard to believe that these forms were far enough along at the time when their evolution stopped that they could afford to stop evolving.

Mayr says that there are two explanations for bradytelic

evolution, both of which are somewhat dubious. One is that this type of evolution occurs in stable habitats where selection itself is a conservative factor. Mayr points out that all species associated with these surviving species at former geological periods have since become extinct or have changed drastically. This, he believes, deprives this explanation of probability. The other hypothesis is that the lack of change is due to an enormous stability of genetic material in these species which results in an incredibly low rate of mutation. Mayr, however, says this postulate does not explain why the replication of the genetic material should be so nearly errorless in a few exceptional types of organisms when there are rather well established mutational rates of definite magnitudes in the vast majority of organisms. He believes that the rates of mutations in these are of the same order of magnitude as in other organisms but the developmental homeostasis is so highly developed as to prevent completely the phenotypic appearance of the concealed genetic changes.[51]

Absence of Correlation Between Rate of Evolution and Length of Generation

Another difficulty in connection with evolution rates is the fact that there should be a direct correlation between the rate of evolution and the length of generations. But this does not appear to be the case. Opossums have short generations, but are thought to have evolved slowly. In fact, they are thought by many evolutionists to be the most primitive of the mammals, even more primitive than the monotremes. Elephants have long generations, but they are believed to have evolved rapidly. Invertebrates in general have shorter generations than vertebrates, but they are believed to have evolved more slowly than the vertebrates.[52]

NOTES

1. Simpson, George Gaylord. *Tempo and Mode in Evolution* (New York: Columbia University Press, 1944), pp. 34 f., 42.

2. Mayr, Ernst. *Systematics and the Origin of Species* (New York: Columbia University Press, 1942), p. 270.

3. Stebbins, G. Ledyard. *Variation and Evolution in Plants* (New York: Columbia University Press, 1950), p. 301.

4. Ibid., p. 279.

5. Ibid., p. 270.

6. White, M. J. D. *Animal Cytology and Evolution* (Cambridge: Cambridge University Press, 1948), p. 217.

7. Mayr, p. 74.

8. Stebbins, G. Ledyard. *Processes of Organic Evolution* (Englewood Cliffs: Prentice-Hall, 1966), p. 127.

9. Stebbins, *Variation*, p. 293.

10. Anderson, Edgar. *Introgressive Hybridization* (New York: Wiley, 1949), pp. 54–56.

11. White, p. 227.

12. Stebbins, *Variation*, p. 430.

13. Darlington, C. D. *The Evolution of Genetic Systems* (Cambridge: Cambridge University Press, 1939), p. 92.

14. Cuénot, L. *La Genèse des Espèces Animales* (Paris: Félix Alcan, 1911).

15. Strohl, J., and Köhler, W. "Experimentale Untersuchungen über die Entwicklungsphysiologie der Flügelzeichnung bei der Mehlmotte," *Verhandlungen, Schweizerische Naturforschende Gesellschaft,* CXV (1934), 367–372.

16. Lamoreux, W. F., and Hutt, F. B. "Breed Differences in Resistance to Deficiency of Vitamin B1 in the Fowl," *Journal of Agricultural Research,* LVIII (1939), 307–316.

17. Williams, George C. *Adaptation and Natural Selection* (Princeton: Princeton University Press, 1966), p. 128.

18. Simpson, pp. 206–217.

19. Evans, J. W. "Evolution in the Homoptera," *The Evolution of Living Organisms,* ed. G. W. Leeper (Victoria: Melbourne University Press, 1962), p. 259.

20. Stebbins, *Variation*, p. 146.

21. Simpson, p. 95.

22. Strandskov, Herluf H. "Genetics and the Origin and Evolution of Man," *Cold Spring Harbor Symposia on Quantitative Biology,* XV (1950), 9.

23. Wright, Sewall. "Breeding Structure of Populations in Relation to Speciation," *American Naturalist*, LXXIV (1940), 232–248.

24. Simpson, pp. 70 f.

25. Wright, Sewall. "The Statistical Consequences of Mendelian Heredity in Relation to Speciation," *The New Systematics*, ed. Julian Huxley (Oxford: Oxford University Press, 1940), p. 164.

26. Ford, H. D., and Ford, E. B. "Fluctuations in Numbers and Its Influence on Variation in *Melitaea aurinia*," *Transactions of the Entomological Society of London*, LXXVIII (1930), 345.

27. Haldane, J. B. S. *The Causes of Evolution* (London: Longmans, Green, 1932), p. 138.

28. Ford, E. B. *Mendelism and Evolution* (London: Methuen and Co., 1949), p. 78.

29. Wright, "Statistical Consequences," pp. 170 f.

30. Harlan, H. V., and Martini, M. L. "The Effect of Natural Selection on a Mixture of Barley Varieties," *Journal of Agricultural Research*, LVII (1938), 189–199.

31. Simpson, p. 82.

32. Elton, Charles. "Animal Numbers and Adaptation," *Evolution*, ed. G. R. De Beer (Oxford: Clarendon Press, 1938), p. 134.

33. Ford, E. B. "Early Stages in Allopatric Speciation," *Genetics, Paleontology, and Evolution*, ed. Glenn L. Jepsen, Ernst Mayr, and George Gaylord Simpson (Princeton: Princeton University Press, 1949), p. 313.

34. Williams, p. 112.

35. Stebbins, *Processes*, p. 76.

36. Romer, Alfred Sherwood. "Time Series and Trends in Animal Evolution," *Genetics, Paleontology, and Evolution*, ed. Glenn L. Jepsen, Ernst Mayr, and George Gaylord Simpson (Princeton: Princeton University Press, 1949), p. 107.

37. Huxley, Julian. *Evolution, the Modern Synthesis* (New York: Harpers, 1943), p. 148.

38. Dobzhansky, Th., and Koller, P. Ch. "Sexual Isolation Between Two Species of *Drosophila:* A Study in the Origin of an Isolating Mechanism," *Genetics*, XXIV (1939), 97 f.

39. White, p. 227.

40. Mayr, p. 199.

41. Huxley, p. 339.

42. Mayr, p. 280.

43. Schultz, Adolph H. "The Specializations of Man and His Place Among the Catarrhine Primates," *Cold Spring Harbor Symposia on Quantitative Biology*, XV (1950), 49.

44. Boyd, William C. *Genetics and the Races of Man* (Boston: Little, Brown and Co., 1950), pp. 131—159.
45. Stebbins, *Processes,* p. 2.
46. Simpson, p. 147.
47. Romer, pp. 114 f.
48. Rensch, Bernard. *Evolution Above the Species Level* (London: Methuen, 1959), p. 112.
49. Simpson, p. 17.
50. Ibid., pp. 137 f.
51. Mayr, Ernst. "Where Are We," *Cold Spring Harbor Symposia on Quantitative Biology,* XXIV (1959), 13.
52. Simpson, pp. 62 f.

11. Evolutionary History of Plants and Animals

In this section we want to consider the general evolutionary history of the earth. Here we are not concerned with the relationship of development to geological age but rather with the course that evolution has supposedly pursued and with the assumed general relationships and interrelationships of various organisms. Throughout the chapter we shall use the terminology of the evolutionist to describe how he believes these forms developed. We shall also use his dating and chronology.

The General Course: From Simple to Complex

To begin with, we may make a few general statements with regard to the course that evolution is supposed to have taken. In general it is believed that development has been from the simple to the complex, though, of course, there are many instances in which this has not been the case. It is also believed that life originated in the water and more specifically in the sea, rather than in fresh water. In general, too, it is believed that plants are simpler and presumably prior to animals. This supposition is, of course, necessary also because of the fact that only plants can carry on photosynthesis. All animals are necessarily dependent on plants for their food.

The First Living Things

The first primitive organism is generally believed to have been a very simple organism like *Euglena*. This single celled organism is capable of carrying on photosynthesis — a plant characteristic — and it also shows an animal characteristic in that it is capable of locomotion. A great many evolutionists believe that the first organisms were simple forms showing both plant and animal characteristics and that from these simple organisms, still represented by the Protista, the plant and animal kingdoms developed.

Yet these organisms are not necessarily simple. Willmer calls attention to the fact that even in the bacterial cell all the main oxidative systems found in higher animals are already represented. Cytochrome and haem are there. Polysaccharides are formed and used for capsule formation. Carbohydrates are metabolized in ways very similar to those found in higher organisms. Adenosinetriphosphate already holds its key position, and proteins are both formed and used for food. He says that even in the simplest protozoan living, most of the main framework for living matter has already been laid down and that the only major advance has been that brought about by the combined activity of several cells.[1] Stebbins, however, believes that there are marked differences between the simple organisms and the more complex ones. He believes that the differences between the prokaryote cell possessed by bacteria and blue-green algae and the eukaryote cell found in all higher organisms constitute the sharpest gap between major groups of organisms which exist anywhere in the world of life. He points out that organelles are absent in the prokaryotes apart from the cellular membrane and are present in the eukaryotes, that there is a completely different organization of the chromosomes and the mechanism for cell divisions, and that there are profound differences between the bacteria and eukaryote organisms in their mechanisms for genetic recombination.[2]

Plant Evolution

The Place of Plant Origins

A great many evolutionists believe that plants began as salt water forms, probably similar to the algae which make up plankton today. But evolutionists are by no means agreed on this statement. Gregory believes, for instance, that the plant kingdom started its career in fresh water and that ability to live in salt water as well as the ability to live on land came later.[3] Coulter agrees, but points out that there are many uncertainties in determining and describing these primitive forms.[4] Fungi are a real problem; some evolutionists believe that they had a completely different evolutionary origin from other plants and therefore, taxonomically speaking, should not be regarded as plants at all.[5]

The Evolution of Algae and Bryophytes

In any case, *Euglena,* or a form very similar to it, is supposed to have given rise to the other algae. The bryophytes are believed to have been derived from one of the green algae, probably from a tide-flat dweller for whom land adaptations would be advantageous. Some evolutionists believe that the bryophytes in turn gave rise to the vascular plants (ferns and seed plants) through forms similar to the hornworts. Others believe the vascular plants are derived directly from the green algae. The hornworts show a more prominent sporophyte generation than do most of the bryophytes, a characteristic which would seem to foreshadow the condition found in the vascular plants. However, since vascular plants existed already in the Silurian period and bryophytes are unknown as fossils until the Pennsylvanian period, most evolutionists believe that the bryophytes are a terminal group, a side branch of the green algae, which did not give rise to higher forms.[6]

The Origin of the Vascular Plants

Today it is generally believed that the vascular plants were derived from a green alga that lived in the tide flats and that had branching filaments. As the land was elevated, the tide pools became isolated and dried up. Most of the plants dwelling in these tide pools died. In a few, however, some of the branches penetrated the ground and became transformed into a root system. Other branches straightened out, leaving a main stem, or trunk, with branches.

The earliest of the vascular plants are believed to have been the Psilopsida, represented today by two living genera, *Psilotum* and *Tmesipteris*. The living forms are confined to the tropics. The Psilopsida are supposed to have given rise to the three remaining pteridophyte groups, the Lycopsida (the ground pines and club mosses), Sphenopsida (the horsetails), and Pteropsida (ferns). These are not believed to have evolved from one another, but are said to have had separate psilopsid ancestors. Both the Lycopsida and Sphenopsida are believed to be terminal groups, not giving rise to higher forms. The gymnosperms or conifers are supposed to have developed from the Pteropsida, or ferns, through the seed ferns. It is thought that they may have arisen in the Pennsylvanian period.[7]

The Sudden Appearance of the Flowering Plants

One of the big problems of plant evolution, and especially of the evolution of flowering plants, is the fact that the latter appear so suddenly in the geological record. As we pointed out earlier, they appear in great variety and abundance in the late Cretaceous period. Darwin called their origin an "abominable mystery," and most evolutionists today still agree. It is generally assumed that they must have originated earlier, not because fossils have been found, but because it is inconceivable that they should have originated so suddenly. Sprague says that apart from the Caytoniales, which occupy a rather isolated position, the earliest angiosperms recorded in the fossil state belong largely to recent families and genera. He also points out that fossils afford no clue to the interrelationships of the families.[8]

Scott says much the same thing. He points out that the fossil history of the flowering plants shows no sign of a beginning, for with few exceptions all the specimens can be referred to families still existing.[9]

Animal Evolution

The Rarity of Transitional Forms

The evolution of animals has been studied in much greater detail, but even here we are confronted once more by the absence of intermediate forms or missing links. We have the various clusters of organisms which we classify into the different phyla, but the bridges between the phyla are lacking, and most of the suggestions that have been made are sheer speculation. Indeed, so rare are these intermediate forms that when a form like *Peripatus*, which is supposed to be a link between the annelids and the arthropods, is found, it is widely hailed.

Another famous link is *Seymouria* from the Permian of Texas, an animal that is structurally intermediate between amphibians and reptiles so that paleontologists cannot agree on which group should claim it. *Seymouria*, however, is contemporary with many true reptiles so that it cannot be the actual ancestor of that group.[10]

The Origin and Evolution of the Protozoa

In general it is assumed that animal life began with the protozoa, relatively simple one-celled organisms. Presumably these could not have existed without plants, since all animals today are dependent upon plants. For that reason it is generally believed that a form similar to *Euglena* was the link between the plants and the animals.

The first of the true protozoa is imagined to have been a form similar to the modern heliozoa or radiolaria. The former are spherical one-celled organisms surrounded by a gelatinous matrix or a sort of latticelike case. They have many fine, radiating strands of protoplasm known as pseudopods, which lead to the name "sun animalcules." The radiolaria are somewhat similar to the heliozoa, but their cytosome is separated into an inner and an outer portion by a central capsule, and they have a skeleton of silica or of strontium sulfate.

The well-known *Amoeba* is believed to be a degenerate descendant of these forms. All of the other protozoa are also supposed to have developed from the heliozoa or radiolaria. In many of the protozoa of different classes the spores are supposed to resemble this simple radiolarian or heliozoan type.

There are some reports of radiolaria in pre-Cambrian rock, but there is no real evidence of their existence in the Proterozoic and Archeozoic rocks. In Cambrian rocks the protozoa make up but 0.4% of the fauna, but this is believed to be no real key to their abundance. Most of them are believed to have left no record in the rocks. Typical foraminifera, another of the shelled protozoa similar to the *Amoeba,* are known only from late Paleozoic rocks of the Carboniferous period. Since they are shelled and should leave fossil remains, it is generally believed that they did not originate until this time.[11]

Sponge Evolution

The sponges are supposed to have developed from a specialized type of protozoa known as the Choanoflagellata. These are flagellates belonging to the same class as does the modern *Euglena.* Each of these single-celled individuals has a long lash, or flagellum, surrounded by a funnel or delicate protoplasmic collar. It is believed that groups of these animals came together and gradually developed into simple sponges. From these the many kinds of sponges that we know today have evolved. The sponges are said to be off the main line of evolution.[12]

At the same time the sponges are believed to display the skeleton key to basic blastula formation, which in many other groups has made possible other new developments. This skeleton key in the sponges, Willmer believes, unlocks the basic pattern upon which most embryonic forms are constructed. He says that the essential features of blastula formation which are seen in the sponges can later be recognized, although with considerable modification, in the development of many other organisms, and he believes that the primitive metazoan from which eventually all the various phyla of both the Parazoa and Metazoa have emerged was an organism not unlike that which can be seen today in the free-living blastula of the calcareous sponge.[13]

The Origin of Skeletal Armor

One of the problems of the early forms is the development of skeletal armor. A great many evolutionists have held that armored forms are derived from naked, free-swimming forms. They have assumed that animals without protection came first and that only later did a skeleton develop in response to the need for protection. This also fits with the general concept of development from simple to complex.

Gregory, however, believes that the reverse is the case. He believes that as the number of cells increased some were brought into contact with the immediate environment. This favored the development of a cuticle, or limiting membrane. This in turn resulted in a difference in osmotic pressure, which then led to the deposition of heavier materials in the skin. Thus armored forms developed very early, and naked forms evolved from these. He further believes that a skeleton is necessary as a fulcrum on which to base the contractile forces of muscular tissue.[14]

The Coelenterates

The coelenterates are believed to have developed directly from the Protozoa or from a form which also gave rise to the early sponges. These latter have not yet reached the tissue level of organization. While it is true that the sponges have two layers of cells, the one in contact with the environment and the other lining the digestive tract, these are not true tissues. The coelenterates, however, have advanced to this stage. Essentially they are considered to be organisms which have never gone beyond the gastrula stage in embryological development. They lack a middle layer of cells, the mesoderm, but they do have an ectoderm and an endoderm.

One of the unusual characteristics of the coelenterates is the fact that they have stinging cells. These are nettle threads which contain a poisonous substance. They are supposed to have developed from the trichocysts of such protozoa as *Paramecium*. Another striking characteristic of this group is the fact that they show a sort of alternation of generations. In many of them there is one stage in which the organism reproduces asexually and another stage in which it reproduces sexually. This is similar to the alternation of generations in plants except for the fact that the coelenterate has the diploid number of chromosomes throughout its life cycle, both in the asexual and sexual phase. Only the eggs and sperms are monoploid. Fossil coelenterates are found from the Cambrian period onward.[15]

The Comb Jellies

The comb jellies (ctenophores) are believed by some to be links between the coelenterates and the flatworms. They are more complex and more highly organized than the coelenterates. Like the jellyfish they have long trailing tentacles and a pair of balance organs. They secrete an adhesive material to entangle small animals, which are then conveyed to the mouth.[16] They and the coelenterates are the only animals which have a basic radial symmetry. True stinging cells are lacking in the comb jellies. The comb jellies are rather abundant in warm seas, though some of them also occur in temperate regions. Most of them live close to the surface, but a few live at great depths. A number of them are luminescent and emit light at night. One of them is flattened and is able to crawl out on the ground like a flatworm. Buchsbaum, however, does not believe they are the connecting links between the coelenterates and flatworms.[17]

The Flatworms

In the flatworms the mesoderm appears for the first time. This is the third germ layer that is found in all of the higher organisms. The flatworm shows a bilateral symmetry, characterized by an anterior and a posterior end, a dorsal and a ventral surface, and a right and a left half; and also a better-developed nervous system. Some of the flatworms are free-living, but many are parasites. The parasites are supposed to represent a higher stage of evolution than the free-living forms. They are supposed to have evolved from free-living forms which developed the parasitic habit and then lost organs that they no longer needed.

The Roundworms

The flatworms are believed to have given rise to the roundworms, the first group to show a tube-within-a-tube type of body structure. Between the outer tube, or body wall, and the inner tube, or digestive tract, there is a cavity known as the coelom, though the coelom of roundworms is not considered a true coelom. Some of the roundworms are free-living, and some are parasites. One of the roundworm groups, the arrowworms (*Sagitta* and *Spadella*), is suggested as one of the ancestors of *Amphioxus*. Gregory, however, believes that the resemblance is due to convergence and that it is a superficial resemblance.[18]

Annelid Evolution

The roundworms are believed to have given rise to the marine annelids (segmented worms). In these we find a fairly advanced type of aquatic locomotion brought about by a series of oarlike projections known as parapods. These function in both locomotion and respiration. The particular advance of the segmented worms is the development of segmentation. These worms are divided into a large number of segments, or metameres. Each metamere has a part of most of the systems of the animal. The common earthworm belongs to this group and is thought to have evolved from marine annelids which invaded the soil along the shore and gradually became highly specialized. In the course of evolution they lost their parapods, so that earthworms do not have these.

The annelids show the general type of nervous system found in many other groups of invertebrates, including the trilobites, the arthropods, and *Peripatus*. This latter is the famed link between the annelids and arthropods to which we referred earlier.

Peripatus

Peripatus is found in South Africa, Australia, New Zealand, South America, and the West Indies. It lives in moist habitats, such as rotting logs, crevices of rock, and

Figure 37. Peripatus. This animal is supposed to be a link between the worms and arthropods. It has characteristics of both. (Courtesy Ward's Natural Science Establishment, Inc.)

under stones. It is represented by 10 genera and over 70 species. At the present time it is usually classified as an arthropod, because it has a tracheal system, the type of respiratory system found in the insects. It also has specialized appendages that are modified as jaws.

The internal organs of *Peripatus* are arranged in a way that is very similar to the arrangement found in the annelids. The excretory organs, or nephridia, are paired and found in each segment. In addition there are cilia in the reproductive organs — an annelid characteristic. The animal is believed to be very close to a fossil form dating from the Middle Cambrian period found by Walcott and named *Aysheaia*.[19] The latter is believed, though, to have been a marine form.

Evolutionary Sidelines

a. *The Mollusks*

Before discussing the generalized history of the arthropods, we shall refer briefly to the evolution of the mollusks and a few other forms. These forms are believed to be off the main course of evolution. However, fossils of mollusks are very prominent in the various rocks, and a great deal of evolutionary theory is based on their fossil history. Some say that the mollusks represent the end of one of the three great lines of evolution, the other two being the vertebrates and the arthropods.

In comparison with other invertebrates, several important features are either lacking completely or are poorly developed in the mollusks. For one thing, locomotion is not very highly developed. While many of them are able to swim, crawl, climb, or dig, none of them develop the jointed structures which we call legs. Then, too, the mollusks seem to have missed a bet in failing to develop segmentation. While in some cases the shell is divided into a series of segments, the nervous system is not so divided.

Another significant characteristic missing from these animals is the concentration of important organs at the anterior end. Not all mollusks have a head, and in those that do there is no important concentration of organs in the head. In some cases the head is used as a foot for locomotion. It is thought that possibly the muscles which are now used for locomotion were at one time used to pull the head back into the shell. These original mollusks, it is surmised, were sedentary; but when they discovered that these muscles could also be used for locomotion, the "head foot" was used for that purpose.

The origin of the mollusks is still very obscure in so far as evolutionists are concerned. The various classes were present already at the beginning of the fossil record in the Cambrian period. In many characteristics they are similar to the annelids and arthropods. Their mesoderm, for instance, originates in a way that is similar to these forms. The free-floating larval stages are similar to the free-floating larval stages of the annelids. The dominant structure in the mollusks is a highly variable and adaptable mantle, the skinlike tissue found under the shell. It is this mantle which, in turn, produces a wide variety of shells.

b. *The Brachiopods*

Another group that is off the main line of evolution is the phylum brachiopods. These are also called the lampshells because of their resemblance to an old Roman lamp. They resemble superficially the bivalves like the clam and oyster. However, the shell of the brachiopod is hinged at the side instead of at the top. The dorsal valve is usually smaller than the ventral valve. It is believed that these are among the oldest of the sedentary animals that have built for themselves protective shells. The larvae of the brachiopods are free-swimming and have cilia. They resemble somewhat the larvae of some of the annelids, mollusks, and echinoderms. Embryologically there is said to be a faint resemblance to the echinoderms and chordates.

These forms were very numerous and very diverse in Paleozoic times. They are supposed to have descended from free-swimming organisms which had a bilateral symmetry but were asymmetrical in a dorsoventral plane. Their ancestors are also believed to have had a rudimentary head provided with eyespots. Their evolution is believed to be

the history of the transformation from a motile to a fixed
mode of life.

c. *Bryozoa*

Still another phylum that is believed to be off the main
line of evolution is the Bryozoa or Polyzoa. These are often
known as the moss animalcules. It is thought by some that
these developed from a primitive brachiopod stock which
evolved into a colonial organism. They are not known
until the Ordovician period. Some evolutionists, however,
suggest that they are related to the stock from which the
annelids developed, because their larvae resemble somewhat the larvae of certain of the latter.

d. *The Rotifers*

Still another group that is thought to be off the main
line of evolution are the rotifers. These are sometimes
known as the wheel animalcules. Although they are microscopic, they are multicellular. While some evolutionists
have believed that they are related to protozoa like the
Paramecium, others believe that they are more closely
related to the worms. Their larvae are free-swimming and
also have cilia. In these ways they resemble the annelids.

e. *The Echinoderms*

A final group supposed to be off the main line of invertebrate evolution but thought by many to be very important
in the evolution of the vertebrates is the phylum Echinodermata. These include the starfishes, the sea lilies, the sea
cucumbers, and the sea urchins. It is believed that they are
built up on a basic radiate plan with five arms or sides or
other main subdivisions. They have developed a highly
differentiated system of sacs or outgrowths from the primitive digestive tract. Their larvae are bilaterally symmetrical
and free floating. Some of these resemble rather closely the
larvae of the acorn worm, which is supposed to be related to
Amphioxus. The earliest echinoderms were covered with a
thin coat made up of lime plates. Many of these were per-

forated with small pores, leading to little tubes in the plate. Possibly these were used to draw in sea water. They are assumed to have begun in a small way as saclike animals, feeding on minute organic matter, which was ingested by the lashing of cilia, and gradually developed into the great variety of echinoderms which we know today. Fossils of the sea lilies are very common.

The Arthropods

The arthropods are generally regarded as the highest of the invertebrates, though some consider the mollusks equally well developed. The earliest of the arthropods were presumably the trilobites. These are found already in the lower Cambrian rocks. They are so common that they are often known as "rock bugs." Already the earliest of these had large and well-developed heads, large paired eyes, and a great many body segments. Each of these segments bore a pair of undifferentiated appendages. These are believed

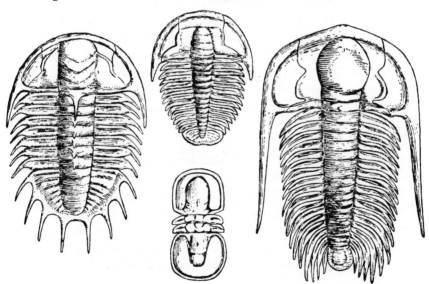

Figure 38. Typical Cambrian Trilobites. These are so common as fossils they are often called "rock bugs." They were similar to the modern crayfish. (Redrawn from Pirsson and Schuchert's *Textbook of Geology, Part II. Historical Geology*, Wiley, by permission)

to have been similar to the parapods of the annelids, but they were jointed. Their head was covered with a dorsal shield. While some evolutionists have held that the trilobites were ancestral to the modern crustaceans, most evolutionists believe that the trilobites and crustaceans are parallel offshoots of a primitive pre-Cambrian annelid stock. The mollusks are regarded as a peculiarly specialized side branch of this stock, while the trilobites and other arthropods are regarded as the progressive descendants of this stock. While the mollusks developed a skeleton of lime, the trilobites went on to develop a skeleton of chitin.

The trilobites, in turn, are believed to have given rise to forms that might be characterized as primitive horseshoe crabs and scorpions. The former are still represented by five living species. One advance which soon appeared was the ability to pass through successive molts. The crustaceans and many insects cast off their old skin as the body increases in size and emerge with a new one. The mollusks cannot do this. They simply secrete a new, enlarged extension of their shell. The ability to molt and the jointed appendages enabled the arthropods to evolve much more rapidly than any of the mollusks except the squids.

The horseshoe crabs, or limulids, are believed to have developed into the eurypterids, which are now wholly extinct, and these in turn are supposed to have developed into the scorpions. In the course of time, these forms gave up the exposed gills of the trilobites and developed covered "book gills" which can be used for respiration on land.

The spiders are believed to be a highly specialized side branch of the scorpions. Their particular evolutionary specialization was the development of the ability to spin a web. This ability, it is generally recognized, is not a matter of intelligence, but is rather a matter of instinct.

The Origin of Insects

At one time it was thought that the trilobite stock also gave rise to the insects, but a great many evolutionists today are of the opinion that insects developed directly from the pre-Cambrian annelid stock.[20] De Beer suggests that they originated from the larvae of some myriapod forms by a retention of juvenile characters.[21] In any case the typical insect has condensed the many segments of the annelid into a complex head; a thorax divided into three parts and bearing three pairs of legs and the wings, if any are present; and a segmented abdomen which lacks legs.

One of the noteworthy developments here is the development of wings. These are said to have developed from two pairs of expanded dorsal plates. It is thought that originally they may have been auxiliary respiratory organs, and the veins which we find in them may at one time have been respiratory tubes.[22] The wings themselves have undergone a great deal of evolution. In some cases one pair has become massive and leathery, as in the beetle; in others one pair has become vestigial, as in the mosquitoes; and in still other forms one pair has disappeared completely, as in some of the other Diptera.

Even more striking than the development of wings has been the development of instinctive behavior in the insect, a characteristic developed to a very high degree in these forms. The origin of the complex habits culminating in the societies of the wasps, ants, termites, and bees is still a real problem for the evolutionist. Many are so intricate and involved that it is difficult to accept the suggestion that they have developed in steps. It would almost seem that they would have to develop all at once. It is hard to believe that they would have any value when partly developed. Indeed, they probably would have been disadvantageous. Yet it is also hard to believe that these developed suddenly.

The Problem of Vertebrate Origins

In passing on to the evolution of the vertebrates, we find that one of the difficult problems of the evolutionists is the problem of explaining their origin. At first glance it seems rather obvious that these must be derived from invertebrate

ancestors. It would also seem very reasonable that these
should have been derived from some of the arthropods, since
these presumably represent the highest of the invertebrates.
However, there is a tremendous gap between the highest
invertebrate and the lowest vertebrate. None of the invertebrates have anything which remotely resembles the
vertebral column, which is one of the outstanding characteristics of the vertebrates.

Furthermore, the body plan of the invertebrates is quite
different from the body plan of the vertebrates. For one
thing, the annelids and arthropods have a ventral nerve
cord. The vertebrates all have a dorsal nerve cord. The
invertebrate nerve cord is solid; the vertebrate nerve cord
is hollow. The invertebrate heart is dorsal; the vertebrate
heart is ventral. Indeed, it would seem that a vertebrate is
in many ways an invertebrate turned inside out. And at
one time it was seriously suggested that the vertebrates
were derived from an invertebrate which became attached
to a rock in a swiftly moving stream. Gradually, according
to this hypothesis, the force of the water turned the invertebrate inside out to produce the vertebrate body plan.

Theories of the Origin of the Vertebrates

At the present time there are a number of theories as
to the origin of the vertebrates. These are discussed in
detail by Gregory.[23] We shall summarize them here.

a. *The Coelenterate Theory*

There is, first of all, the coelenterate theory. According
to this theory *Amphioxus,* supposedly the primitive pre-
vertebrate, was derived from a coelenterate, such as *Hydra*
or a jellyfish, by the addition of a third layer of cells.

Amphioxus is a tiny, fishlike organism lacking a backbone or vertebral column. It does, however, have a notochord, a rod of cells extending the length of the animal,
which gives support to the soft tissues. It can swim about

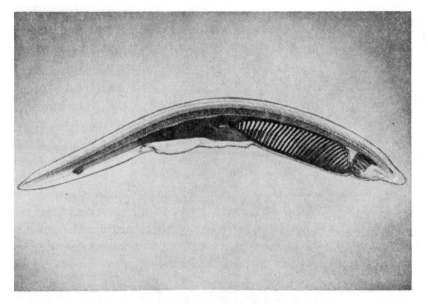

Figure 39. Amphioxus. Most evolutionists believe that this was among the earliest, if not the earliest, of the prevertebrates. Length, two and one-half to three and one-half inches. (Courtesy General Biological Supply House)

by fishlike undulations of the body, but usually it is found buried in the sandy bottom with only the anterior end protruding. In this way it feeds by drawing into its mouth a steady current of water, from which it strains microscopic organisms.

In addition to the notochord, *Amphioxus* has a dorsal nerve cord which contains a minute canal. The animal lacks a heart. Its blood is pumped by rhythmic contractions of the ventral aorta. The blood passes posteriorly in the dorsal blood vessel and anteriorly in the ventral blood vessel. This is the condition found in the vertebrates. It is just the opposite of the condition found in the invertebrates.

Many evolutionists look upon *Amphioxus* as a relatively primitive chordate. It is supposed to exemplify many of the ancestral conditions. According to the coelenterate theory, *Amphioxus* is believed to have developed this third layer of cells because it came into contact with the substratum and attempted then to creep forward. This theory suggests that the vertebrates separated from the invertebrate stock at a very early stage. It eliminates the necessity of accounting for the great differences in body plans, because according to this theory the invertebrate and vertebrate stocks were already separate before the nerve cord and heart developed in either.

b. *The Flatworm Theory*

Another theory derives the vertebrates from the flatworms. It has been suggested that the long proboscis and sheath of the flatworm developed into the vertebrate notochord. This theory, however, does not account for the intricacies found in even the earliest vertebrates.

c. *The Annelid-Arthropod Theory*

A third theory looks for the origin of the vertebrates in the annelids (segmented worms) and arthropods (crustacea, insects, and the like). All three groups show metamerization (division of the body into segments) and a segmental nervous system. In addition, the annelids and arthropods have a nerve ring and dorsal ganglia which may be regarded as a primitive brain. Those who support this theory have also pointed out that in the vertebrate embryo the anterior end of the digestive tract is connected with the brain cavity, and resembles to a certain degree the condition in the two invertebrate phyla in which the tube from the mouth pierces the circumesophageal nerve connectives.

d. *The Arachnid Theory*

Another theory would relate the vertebrates to the arachnids, or spiders. Patten has suggested that the higher arthropods and the vertebrates possess in common a complex head formed by the coalescence of enlarged nerve segments. The theory is supported by a series of comparative diagrams, which at first seem rather striking. But, according to Gregory, Patten's method consisted in supporting his main hypothesis by assuming a host of implied hypotheses and by citing analogies in assumedly similar cases. While it is true, according to Gregory, that Patten has shown how a primitive eurypterid might have been transformed into a vertebrate, there is a definite lack of real transitional stages showing that it did happen in that way.

e. *The Ammocoetes-Limulus Theory*

Still another theory is the so-called *Ammocoetes-Limulus* theory. Gaskell suggested this theory starting with a comparison of the horseshoe crab, the scorpions, other arthropods, and the various vertebrates. He compared particularly the cranial nerves of the larval lamprey with those of the scorpion, of the horseshoe crab, and of other arthropods. He was also impressed with the resemblances between the Paleozoic eurypterids and the ostracoderms. This theory, too, is rejected by Gregory and by most evolutionists today.

f. *The Neotenous Larva Theory*

The neotenous larva theory depends upon tracing the relationship not through adult stages, but rather through the larvae. Garstang and De Beer believe that the echinoderms and the vertebrates had a common ancestor whose adults were less specialized than the adults of the existing echinoderms and whose larvae resembled those of the existing echinoderms. Gregory points out that this theory lacks evidence.

g. *The Echinoderm-*Tornaria *Theory*

Another theory is the echinoderm-*Tornaria* theory. This depends upon a comparison between the echinoderms and the vertebrates, especially with regard to their free-swimming larvae, and the fact that the most primitive echinoderms as to form might be compared to the acorn worms (the acorn worm is a simple chordate), which have begun to settle down to a sedentary life.

This theory is the most widely accepted today, though there is little about the adults to suggest relationship between the two phyla. Because of striking larval similarities, especially in the mode of development of the coelom or body cavity, it is believed today that some echinoderms gave rise to a group of Protochordates of which the acorn worm is a survivor and that this group in turn gave rise to the vertebrates.

h. *Eclectic Theories*

According to this theory the various distinguishing characteristics of the vertebrates are not to be found in any single invertebrate form, but are to be looked for in different invertebrate forms. Gregory calls this an eclectic theory, since it is built upon a number of theories. Thus the vertebrates belong to what is known as an enterocoelic superphylum. This group is entirely different from the annelids and arthropods. The vertebrates are more closely related to the echinoderms than to any of the other invertebrates. They are believed to have originated from organisms resembling the echinoderm larvae by neoteny, a retention of juvenile characteristics.[24] The resemblances which they show to various other invertebrate groups are believed to be due to convergence. The fact that the earliest known vertebrates, the ostracoderms, have lost all indisputable external resemblance to the echinoderms is believed to be due to the fact that a great deal of evolution occurred during a sort of free-swimming larval stage, when there were no skeletons to leave fossils.

The vertebrates began as food sifters and gradually developed into predators. *Amphioxus*, according to this theory, is an archaic but specialized vertebrate. The next stage above *Amphioxus* is represented by the larval stage of the lamprey eel. Predation in the vertebrates developed not as a consequence of the fact that their ancestors were predators, but from the food-sifting habit of their ancestors. The notochord is believed by Gaskell to be derived from the ventral groove of the primitive arthropods. Gregory, however, holds that it is an entirely new organ evolved by primitive chordates.[25]

Perhaps the extreme of this composite or eclectic theory is reached in an attempt to find all vertebrate characteristics in some invertebrate group. It is doubtful that those who suggest this are really serious. First of all, it is hard to believe that the vertebrates are derived from all of the invertebrates and that they have taken characteristics from each of the groups. Moreover, many of the tissues and structures are not homologous and show only general analogies to vertebrate types. Then, too, the theory does not fit the general ideas of evolution portrayed by the various phylogenetic trees. These all assume a trunk or branching arrangement. None suggests the extreme type of convergence that this theory postulates.

In all of these theories of the origin of the vertebrates there are many problems and gaps. The absence of missing links is even more pronounced here than in the supposed evolution of other forms. The chordates are quite different from other forms, and there is simply no denying that. The suggestion that the chordates have developed by more or less convergence from a large number of different forms, that they have incorporated into their body plan characteristics from almost all of the invertebrate phyla, is one which tests one's credulity as we have indicated above. It requires a great deal of imagination and faith to believe that this has actually taken place. Hooton says that all of these suggestions are complicated, obscure, and dubious.[26]

Parallel Evolution Suggested

For that reason there are some biologists who believe that the evolution of the chordates has paralleled the evolution of the invertebrates. Instead of the former arising by descent from the latter, the two groups are believed to have evolved along in parallel paths. In short, animal life started out in two different forms: an invertebrate protozoan which gave rise to the various invertebrates, and a vertebrate, similar to *Amphioxus,* which gave rise to the wide variety of vertebrates we know today. Thus the difficulty of relating vertebrates to ancestral invertebrates is avoided.

However, in solving one problem this merely creates another. For there are no primitive vertebrates found as fossils in early rock strata. There are no chordates in Cambrian rock, except for the possible fish scale referred to earlier. And the first found are not protochordates, such as *Amphioxus,* but are vertebrates — fish. These are found in Silurian rock. It is also difficult to believe that life originated in two different forms: explaining the origin of life in one form presents enough of a problem. For these reasons the idea of separate origins of vertebrates and invertebrates has never been too popular.

Early Chordate Evolution

a. Amphioxus *to the Ascidians and Ostracoderms*

Even in studying vertebrate evolution there is no real agreement as to the course which evolution has taken. Two general paths are suggested. Some have suggested that the primitive chordates gave rise to *Amphioxus.* From *Amphioxus* two types developed. The first of these became a mere side branch and developed into the modern ascidians, such as the sea squirt. The second type to develop from *Amphioxus* was the primitive fish type, apparently similar to the ostracoderms. These were on the main line of evolution, and these gave rise to modern fish.

b. Ostracoderms *to* Amphioxus *to* Ascidians

The second general path of evolution of the vertebrates that has been suggested pictures the basic chordates developing into primitive fish, such as the ostracoderms. These primitive fish gave rise to *Amphioxus* and the related cephalochordates, and these in turn gave rise to the ascidians. Gregory believes that this latter theory is the more likely one.[27]

Armor vs. Thin-Skin in the Early Fish

It is generally agreed that the most primitive of the vertebrates are the fish. But here again there is no general agreement as to which type of fish actually came first. Some have suggested that the first fish were more or less naked or thin-skinned. This idea has been supported by the finding of a fossil ostracoderm by Dr. E. I. White of the British Museum. The fossil, which he named *Jaymoytius kerwoodi* and which he later restored, lacked armor and had a very thin skin. The internal skeleton was apparently cartilaginous. The fossil was found in. the late Silurian shale of Lanarkshire.[28]

Others, however, have insisted that the first fish were well-armored forms. Stensiö supports this view, and Gregory is inclined to agree. They point out that armor is not necessarily an indication of degeneration but may very well represent the primitive condition. While it is true that according to evolutionary theories the dinosaurs developed armor toward the end of their existence, this, according to those who support this view, is not necessarily true of fish. For that reason many believe that heavily armored forms, such as the ostracoderms, were ancestral even to *Amphioxus*.[29]

The Ostracoderms

The name "ostracoderm" means "shell-skin" and refers to the fact that these had a head and trunk covered with a hard bony shell or shield. They were only a few inches long and are believed to have been very sluggish, spending most of their time on or near the bottom. Apparently they were poor swimmers, since they were not streamlined like modern fish and had only a lop-sided tail for power. They had no real jaws, but choked in floating food particles by a pumping action of their throat. A few of them were rather active and almost fishlike.

The Origin of the Cyclostomes

The ostracoderms are believed to have given rise to several groups, one of which is represented by the modern lamprey eel and its relatives (the cyclostomes). These ani-

Figure 40. An Ostracoderm, *Cephalaspis.* Now extinct, they are believed to have been among the first of the chordates. Both head and trunk were covered with a hard bony shell or shield. (Redrawn from Neal and Rand's *Comparative Anatomy,* Blakiston, by permission)

mals have a round, jawless, sucking mouth and a rasping tongue for drawing blood and getting food. They lack bone and have only a cartilaginous skeleton. They are serious parasites in oceans and lakes.

The Origin of the Elasmobranchs

A second branch of the ostracoderms gave rise to the modern elasmobranchs. These are the modern sharks and rays. They, too, have a cartilaginous skeleton. There is considerable dispute among evolutionists as to whether the ancestral fish were bony, and cartilaginous forms developed from these; or whether the ancestral fish were cartilaginous, and bony fish developed from these. It has generally been assumed that cartilage is older than bone, since at the present time, it is found in forms which are generally considered less highly developed than forms which have bones. However, there are a number of evolutionists who believe that bone may be older than cartilage and that the elasmobranchs may have developed from bony forms.[30] The sharks and rays have jaws, which the cyclostomes lack.

The First Bony Fish

The oldest representative of the bony fish is the *Cheirolepis*, which dates from the Middle Devonian Period of Great Britain. Presumably it developed from a third branch of the ostracoderms. It was well streamlined, sharklike, with a large predatory mouth and a single dorsal fin. It had complex jaws similar to those of the acanthodians, which are supposed to have been the ancestors of both the elasmobranchs and the bony fish. The particular advance of this form was the arrangement of the surface plates of the head, which was quite similar to the arrangement found in the ganoid and teleost fish. Oddly enough, the early bony fish of the Devonian period had lungs.[31]

The Crossopterygians

Contemporaneous with the *Cheirolepis*, which is classified as a paleoniscoid, there arose the crossopterygians, or lobefins. These, too, are believed to have developed as a branch from the primitive ostracoderms. The earliest of these was the *Osteolepis* from the Middle Devonian period of Europe. It was a small sharklike predaceous fish. Its body was covered with a special type of scale known as ganoid scales. This group underwent a separate type of evolution.

The Paths of Fish Evolution

During the long ages of the Devonian, Mississippian, Pennsylvanian, and Permian periods the fish stock is believed to have branched and rebranched into many so-called families, in which there was a wide variety of body form, jaws, and dentition. Gradually, it is believed, early stocks gave rise to more advanced types.

The first of these were the armored holostean ganoids, in which the skeleton is more fully ossified. The gar pike is supposed to be a descendant of the ancient Holostei.

A second supposed derivative from the paleoniscoids were the Amiidae. The modern descendant of this group is believed to be the bowfin, a North American fresh-water fish.

The third group supposed to be derived from the paleoniscoids were the teleost or the modern fish. The earliest of these were the leptolepids, which were slight, elongated, herringlike fish with a large mouth and small teeth. They were probably plankton feeders like the modern herring. The old paleoniscoid stocks, it is thought, were gradually replaced during Permian and Triassic times by these progressive derivatives of theirs. This older, conservative stock is represented today by the sturgeons and spoonbills. These modern representatives are characterized by a skeleton which is largely cartilaginous. In addition, they have lost most of their scales.

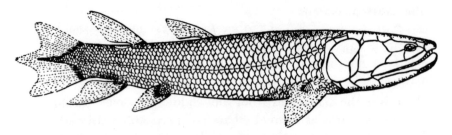

Figure 41. A Crossopterygian, *Eusthenopteron*. It is believed that originally these had lungs and that they gave rise to the amphibians. Later they lost their lungs. Also the coelacanths are crossopterygians. (Redrawn from Raymond's *Prehistoric Life*, Harvard, by permission)

The teleosts in the course of their evolution are believed to have developed into most of the modern forms of fish as we know them. Many of their orders were well differentiated already by the Upper Cretaceous. In general they have come to develop more and more bone and less and less cartilage.

Modern teleost fish occupy all sorts of habitats; indeed, the variety of types is astounding. Some live in fresh water; others are almost exclusively marine. Some species, as the salmon, spend the earliest part of their lives in fresh water, live as adults in salt water, and return to fresh water to spawn. Others, such as the eel, have a life cycle that is almost the opposite. They begin their lives in salt water, live as adults in fresh water, and return to the salt water to spawn.

Cave Fish

Much interest has centered in the development of the various types of cave fish, which typically are blind. It has been suggested that these swam into caves from nearby streams. In a cave eyes are useless. Eventually the power of vision is believed to have deteriorated, and it was lost. Originally this type of development was explained on what was more or less the Lamarckian principle of deterioration through disuse. Today their development is usually explained on the basis of so-called "loss mutations" — mutations which cause such a loss. Ordinarily this loss would result in the extinction of the individual, because he would be unable to compete. However, in a cave the loss of visual power is not missed, and so the individual continues to survive.

One problem is to explain why these fish should swim into the darkness of a cave. It has been suggested that the blind cave fish came originally from forms that normally shunned light and lived in corners and holes. Thus evolution from a light-shunning fish to a cave-dwelling fish was not too

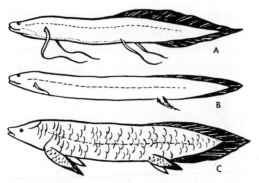

Figure 42. Lungfishes. Although it is believed that these were at one time very common, there are only three genera extant today. A. the African lungfish. B. the South American lungfish. C. the Australian lungfish. (Redrawn from the *Guidebook to the John G. Shedd Aquarium* by permission)

great a step. It was believed that these light-shunning fish were more likely to enter caves and that it was easy for them to lose their visual powers through the occurrence of a few "loss mutations."

However, Huxley points out that *Anoptichthys jordani,* a blind cave fish found in Mexico, seems to be rather closely related to *Astyanax fasciatus,* a large-eyed, open-water form. With large eyes and ordinarily living in open water, it would be unlikely to wander by accident into a cave.[32]

The Choanata: Fish with Lungs

The Choanata form a separate group of fish. Originally these are all believed to have had paired lungs. Some of their descendants, the dipnoans, have kept the paired lungs. Others, the crossopterygians, have lost their paired lungs. The two forms are quite different, but Romer believes that they are linked together in a general group which he calls the Choanichthyes, or Choanata. They have a few characteristics in common, but they have marked differences in skull and dentition. These differences are believed by evolutionists to indicate a very remote common source from which there was an early divergence.

The lungfish at one time were very numerous. The first of these, *Dipterus,* appeared in the Devonian period, and they were very prominent at that time. Even these Devonian ancestors of the dipnoans are believed to have been very specialized forms. At the present time there are three genera and five species of lungfish. One of these lives in Australia, where it inhabits quiet pools that become stagnant during the dry season. At this time it is able to rise to the surface and is able to live in this stagnant water by taking air into its lungs. A second genus lives in South America. It inhabits swamps, and in the dry season retires to what amount to burrows, or nests, lined with mucus. A third genus, of which there are three species, is found in central Africa. Here during the dry season it burrows in the mud, where its mucus dries to form a cocoon with a tube, used for respiration, leading to the mouth of the fish. Casts of lungfish burrows of the Lower Permian have been discovered, indicating that ancient lungfish aestivated just as modern lungfish do.[33]

The Origin of the Amphibians

In spite of the fact that the lungfish appear to be the logical ancestors of the amphibians, evolutionists today derive the amphibians from the crossopterygians. They believe that the evolution of the dipnoans has led toward an eellike and almost limbless form rather than toward a well-limbed, land-living, four-footed form, represented by modern amphibians.[34]

Latimeria, of which over thirty specimens have been taken, is a crossopterygian, so that the crossopterygians, as well as the dipnoans, are still represented by living forms today.

Evolutionists are by no means satisfied with present theories for the origin of the amphibians. Hooton points out that the paired fins of fish do not in any detail resemble the limbs of land animals. He believes that between fish and amphibians there are still serious paleontological and anatomical gaps.[35]

Amphibian Evolution

The earliest known amphibian fossils come from the Upper Devonian of eastern Greenland. It is believed that the crossopterygians lost their lungs after the amphibians had developed from them, so that these early air-breathing crossopterygians developed fore and hind limbs suitable for walking on land from the strong muscular paddles with which they were equipped. At first these paddles were of very little value in moving about out of water.

Some of these early wrigglers multiplied their vertebrae and reduced their fins to vestigial organs. These became the ancestors of the serpentiform amphibians found in the coal fields of Ohio and in the Lower Permian period rocks of Europe. Others developed small but well-formed pectoral and pelvic fins, and these are believed to have evolved into the modern newts, salamanders, and mud puppies.

The Origin of the Reptiles

Typical amphibians spawn in the water and pass through an aquatic stage with external gills. Reptiles, on the other hand, lay their eggs on the land, and the embryonic stages are passed generally within a large egg. Most of the amphibians are believed to have drifted off into side branches, and only the earliest and most primitive amphibians gave rise to the reptiles. We have referred to *Seymouria* from the Permian of Texas, an animal that is structurally intermediate between the amphibians and reptiles. The reptiles began to lay eggs very early. The stem reptiles, or cotylosaurs, differed from the typical amphibians also in avoiding the flattening of the skull and the shortening of the ribs. However, many of the basic features of the earliest amphibians are believed to have been retained in the skeleton.

The first of these reptiles are believed to have moved

with a sort of Australian-crawl method of swinging the arms and legs quickly forward and slapping the wide feet down at the beginning of each stride. These reptiles are believed to have given rise to the modern mammals. The reptilian stock itself, however, developed into a number of branches which led to the fishlike ichthyosaurs, the bat-winged pterosaurs, the tuatara, the lizards, the snakes, the crocodiles, the dinosaurs, and the plesiosaurs. Gradually it is believed to have evolved also into the birds.

Reptile Characteristics

The Mesozoic era has been called the Age of the Reptiles, for it was at this period that the reptiles are supposed to have dominated the earth. And of the reptiles the most important in this period were the dinosaurs. All of the other reptiles of the period were subservient to these. They were exclusively lung breathers, and had a large egg which they may or may not have laid before hatching.

Dinosaurs

The dinosaurs are thought to have developed from the cotylosaurs through the thecodonts, crocodilelike reptiles, that also gave rise to the pterosaurs and the crocodiles.

Ordinarily we think of the dinosaurs as being rather large animals. Actually, though, some of the earliest and least specialized of these, supposedly from the Upper Triassic, were not much larger than roosters except for their long, lizardlike tails.[36] It is generally believed that, like our modern reptiles, they were cold-blooded. While they were apparently as active as many warm-blooded animals today, the tropical climate in which they lived presumably made a constant temperature mechanism unnecessary.

The minimum recorded size, that of *Compsognathus*, was about 2½ feet, with a bulk about that of a modern domestic cat. Some footprints found in the Connecticut Valley indicate an even smaller size: possibly only half the size of *Compsognathus*.[37] The largest dinosaur thus far discovered is the *Gigantosaurus* of East Africa, whose over-all length was probably about eighty feet. It is thought to have weighed about forty tons. This weight is considerably less than that of some of the great whales, which are alive today, and which may weigh as much as 125 or 150 tons.

The dinosaurs appear to have been almost worldwide in their distribution, though thus far no dinosaurs have been found in New Zealand. Some were carnivorous; others were herbivorous. Some lacked teeth entirely, and we do not know what their diet was. They are divided into two groups: the Saurischia and the Ornithischia. The Saurischia were more crocodilian; the Ornithischia more birdlike.

The Saurischia

The earliest known dinosaurs were the Saurischia. They appear to have walked or to have run on their hind legs, the front part of their bodies being balanced by a long, slender tail. Evolutionists believe that their front legs gradually decreased in size so that these were not used for locomotion but for grasping. Most of these were carnivorous.

The most fearful of these was *Tyrannosaurus*, who reached a length of forty-seven feet and in bulk must have been larger than the biggest elephants today. He is supposed to have weighed eight or ten tons. The head was about four feet in length and contained powerful jaws bearing teeth from three to six inches long. In addition, the animal had great eaglelike claws on the hind feet and possibly on the front feet as well. The front legs were very short and apparently could not even reach the mouth so that they could not have been used in feeding.

Tyrannosaurus is placed in the suborder Carnosauria. Another of the saurischian suborders was the Coelurosauria and still another the Sauropoda. These latter had a very complex backbone, built in such a way as to give a maximum of strength with a minimum of materials. The limb bones, on the other hand, were very massive, with wrinkled ends, as though the joints were formed largely of cartilage. This

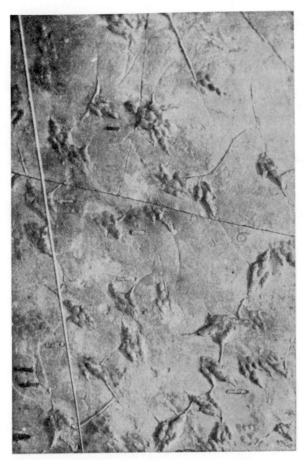

Figure 43. Dinosaur Tracks from the Connecticut Valley.
(Courtesy American Museum of Natural History)

leads evolutionists to believe that the sauropods were semi-aquatic so that their tremendous weight, largely water-borne, did not subject the ends of the limb bones to the mechanical impact that they would be subjected to in an animal that was wholly terrestrial. In fact, it has been suggested that some of them could not have walked on land because of their tremendous bulk and poor legs. Recently, however, footprints have been found which indicate that even these walked on land.[38]

Figure 44. Brontosaurus. One of the larger dinosaurs. He was probably about 66 feet long and weighed 38 tons. (Courtesy Chicago Natural History Museum)

The sauropods are generally believed to represent forms in which evolution went too far and became aberrant. It is difficult to understand how their legs could have supported their huge bulk even though they were somewhat pillarlike.

One of the better-known forms is the *Brontosaurus*, which was about sixty-six feet long and probably weighed about thirty-eight tons. *Gigantosaurus*, to which we referred earlier, also belonged to this group. Another of the better-known sauropods is the *Diplodocus*. Though it attained a length of eighty-seven feet, it was not as heavy as some of the other dinosaurs.

The Ornithischia

All of the Ornithischia were herbivorous. They are also known as the beaked dinosaurs, since they had a sort of horny beak used for grasping food. They gave rise to peculiar forms just as the Saurischia gave rise to the sauropods, but the Ornithischia developed bizarre armor rather than bulk. The first of the Ornithischia are known from fossil tracks in the late Triassic rock of the Connecticut Valley.

The Ornithischia are divided into three suborders, of which the Ornithopoda is the first. These were bird-footed forms, unarmored, bipedal when walking or running, though they probably stood on all fours when resting or feeding. In Cretaceous times a group of duck-billed Ornithopoda developed which possessed more teeth than any other creature known up to the present time.

The second suborder of the Ornithischia were the Stegosauria. These were all armored and all quadrupedal, presumably because of the great weight of their armament. This took the form of high-crested plates or spines sometimes welded into a broad cuirass over the hips, which may have been the most vulnerable part of the creature's anatomy. So well developed is the armor thought to have become that in some of the later forms it is believed the animal was practically invulnerable to any form of animal attack.

The best-known of this suborder was the *Stegosaurus*. This is one of the most grotesque of all the dinosaurs, an awkward angular animal whose back was ornamented with two rows of huge upstanding plates and the end of the tail armed with fearful hornlike spines twenty-five or more inches in length. The tail and hind limbs seem to have been very muscular. It is believed that the armored plates were used for passive defense, and the spines for active defense and possibly offense.

Perhaps the most unusual thing about this form was the small brain. The entire cranial cavity had a volume of only fifty-six cubic centimeters. The brain is believed to have weighed about two and one-half ounces, while the total weight of the animal must have been greater than that of any of the living elephants. The neural canal, though, was large — a fact which would indicate the ability to carry out a great many reflexes. *Stegosaurus* is generally believed to have been a senile side branch, which died out without any further evolution.

Figure 45. Stegosaurus. One of the most grotesque of the dinosaurs. Note the upright spines on the back and the hornlike spines on the tail. (Courtesy Chicago Natural History Museum)

The third suborder of the Ornithischia comprised the Ceratopsia, or horned dinosaurs. These were largely North American, though some have been found in Mongolia. One of the best known of these was the *Triceratops*, which looked very much like a rhinoceros and was about 20 or 25 feet in length. The animal apparently had great strength, especially in the forelimbs and shoulders. The mouth was armed with a sharp cutting beak, like that of the turtle. The nose and the portion of the skull above the eyes bore three huge horns. These horns were used for both offense and defense. The animals were themselves herbivorous.

The Mongolian *Protoceratops* was also a ceratopsian. It is most famous for the fact that it produced the dinosaur eggs found by the Andrews Expedition to Mongolia. It was hornless and is believed to have been ancestral to the *Triceratops*.[39]

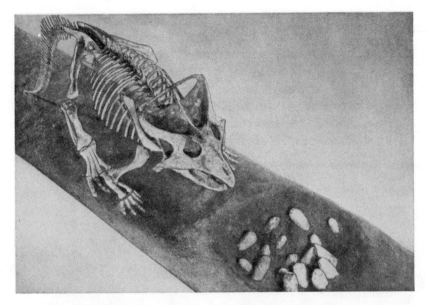

Figure 46. Protoceratops and Eggs. These are the famous dinosaur eggs and a skeleton of the animal that laid them. (Courtesy Chicago Natural History Museum)

The Problem of the Sudden Extinction
of the Dinosaurs

The sudden extinction of the dinosaurs is one of the puzzles with which evolutionists and paleontologists are still struggling. No dinosaur fossils are found in Tertiary rock. In late Cretaceous times, however, the unarmored dinosaurs were still in their prime and in only rare cases showed signs of degeneration. The few heavily armored types found in the late Cretaceous period are among the best-protected of their race, and it is difficult to see any real degeneration in these. Some have suggested that the dinosaurs killed themselves off by a sort of internecine warfare. Others have suggested a slaughter of the young by small, bloodthirsty mammals. In some cases, it has been suggested, these mammals consumed the dinosaur eggs. However, while they were small — many of the Jurassic mammals were smaller than moles and the largest were no larger than kittens —

there is no indication that the early mammals were either bloodthirsty or that they sought eggs. Gregory believes that these early mammals were primarily insectivorous.[40] Nor is there any evidence that the small mammals of the period previous to their disappearance from the fossil record — the Upper Cretaceous — were so bloodthirsty as to wipe out the dinosaurs. Sharp-toothed mammals flourished with the egg-laying dinosaurs in the Middle Cretaceous of Mongolia and

Figure 47. Protoceratops. A restoration of the animal which laid the famous dinosaur eggs. (Courtesy Chicago Natural History Museum)

do not seem to have threatened the dinosaurs in that period.[41]

Others have suggested that their extinction was due to a change in climate or to the mountain building which followed the Cretaceous period. Kraus suggests that temperatures became warmer and these warmer temperatures had a sterilizing effect in large dinosaurs by interfering with spermatogenesis. He believes the huge body size of the

Figure 48. A Mesozoic Scene. In the left foreground is the smallest of the dinosaurs, *Compsognathus.* It was about two and one-half feet long. *Archaeopteryx,* the earliest of the birds, is in the center of the picture. Flying through the air are the pterodactyls, flying reptiles which ate fish. They were pterosaurs. (Courtesy Chicago Natural History Museum)

dinosaurs would mean that these reptiles would cool off very slowly compared to the small reptiles.[42]

The problem remains, for other reptiles, the turtles, the lizards, snakes, *Sphenodon,* and many crocodiles survived in spite of climatic changes, sharp-toothed mammals, internecine warfare, and the like.

The Pterosaurs

The dinosaurs were but one of the Mesozoic reptile groups. Another of these that is supposed to have flourished in geological times but is now extinct is the group of flying lizards, known as the pterosaurs. Some were believed to have had a wingspread of as much as twenty-seven feet. Some of them had slender teeth, but they are believed to have lost these in the course of their evolutionary development, and the later pterosaurs were toothless. They are thought to have lived largely on fish. In spite of the fact that they had wings, they are not believed to have been ancestral to the birds. Actually they glided or soared, rather than flew.[43]

The Ichthyosaurs

The ichthyosaurs constituted another of the Mesozoic reptile groups. These and the plesiosaurs dominated the seas together from Triassic to Upper Cretaceous times. They were superficially fishlike in body form, with a streamlined

Figure 49. *Ichthyosaurs.* These reptiles are supposed to have lived in Mesozoic times. They were fishlike and lived in the water. They had large heads and bill-like jaws. (Courtesy American Museum of Natural History)

back surmounted by a dorsal fin of skin. The head was very large and the jaws bill-like. The eyes, too, were very large. They varied in size from about three to thirty feet. They were equipped with paddle-shaped limbs and had a large number of teeth. Like the whales and dolphins today, they were air breathers. Their eggs are believed to have hatched within the mother's body, so that the young were born alive.[44]

The Plesiosaurs

The head of the plesiosaurs, on the other hand, was small, the neck long, and the tail moderately long. These animals swallowed stones, which they used in a sort of gizzard to grind their food, much as does the modern chicken. They, too, were air-breathing animals. Like the ichthyosaurs they had flexible paddles, but in the plesiosaurs these were not so specialized. They were able to turn very quickly in the water, and this ability, together with the long neck, enabled them to swoop down on their prey. Some, known as pliosaurs, had short necks. They were turtlelike rather than fishlike.

The Turtles

The turtles, another reptilian group, are still represented among living animals today. They are believed to have existed already in the Permian times. The tortoises, land-dwelling turtles, are known as fossils only since Eocene times. The modern sea turtles are supposed to date from Cretaceous times, though there are other marine turtles known from the Upper Jurassic period.

All of these are supposed to have been developed from the stem reptiles, the cotylosaurs. A modified cotylosaur, *Eunotosaurus,* is sometimes postulated as the ancestor of all the turtles in that it comes from the proper time and it appears to be on the verge of developing a shell. But it has one serious drawback as a hypothetical turtle ancestor: the carapace of modern turtles does not develop just from wide ribs but from independent plates of dermal bone which expand markedly and fuse with one another and with the underlying ribs and any bottom shell or plastron. This unique armor and the contortions the skeleton had to undergo to fit into it, combined with the toothless beak, have suggested to some that the turtles are entirely different from any living reptile. Some would even put them along with the platypus, the *Echidna,* and a few other misfits into a new class of vertebrates.[45] This suggestion, however, has not met with a great deal of acceptance.

Turtle evolution is usually regarded as an example of a much-branched evolution.

The Lizards

The lizards, too, are still represented among living animals today. At the present time there are about 3,000 recognized species of lizards. They are believed to have been derived from forms found in the Triassic rocks of South Africa. Today they occupy a wide variety of habitats, and it is suggested that if the mammals were wiped out, they would be able to occupy as wide a variety of habitats as the mammals do today.

The Snakes

Closely related to the lizards are the snakes or serpents. They make up about 2,600 species today. Most of them are tropical, but they are still rather common in temperate zones. They are divided into two groups, the constrictors and the poisonous snakes. The constrictors are believed to be less specialized than the latter group. The poisonous snakes are believed to have been derived from the constrictors, and the two groups are said to be linked through a nonpoisonous primitive group of snakes which have teeth with solid crowns. The common garter snake is an example of this group. They are classed together with some of the poisonous snakes as colubrines and form the first family of that group.

In the second group of colubrine snakes we find snakes with one or more pairs of back maxillary upper teeth which have grooves and are thus capable of acting as poison glands. These include the moon snake of South America, the Indian whip snake, and the Oriental fresh-water snakes.

Later grooves are believed to have developed in the front pair of upper teeth. Today snakes of this type include the coral snakes, the craits, and the cobras. The sea snakes also belong to this group.

Sphenodon: A Living Fossil

One living reptile that is supposed to be almost extinct is the tuatara, or *Sphenodon*, of New Zealand. It is found on several rocky islands off the northeastern coast of New Zealand. It is thought to be related both to the lizards and to the crocodiles and dinosaurs. While it superficially resembles the lizard, its skeletal structure is quite different, and for that reason it is placed in a separate group and is believed to have had a separate evolutionary history.

Sphenodon is most famous for the fact that it has a sort of third eye. It is not visible, but there is a skull opening which accommodates it. The eye itself is covered with skin. This third eye is assumed to have developed into the pineal body in mammals, which in man is very deep in the cerebrum. *Sphenodon* is almost identical in structure with a Jurassic fossil *Homoeosaurus*, of which it is believed to be a direct descendant. Its continued existence presents a problem for the evolutionists, since presumably this living fossil has undergone very little development.

Crocodiles and Alligators

The crocodiles and alligators together make up an order Loricata, or Crocodilia. They differ largely in the fact that the alligators have a relatively short broad snout, whereas that of the crocodiles is longer and narrower. In addition, in the alligators the fourth tooth on each side of the lower jaw enters into pits in the upper jaw, whereas in the crocodiles these teeth slide to the outside of the jaw and are visible. Often the first and second teeth are also visible in crocodiles.[46]

The Crocodilia are generally regarded as an unprogressive, conservative type. The most ancient crocodilians came from the Triassic period and are more or less intermediate between the crocodiles and dinosaurs. Their conservatism presents the same problems as does that of *Sphenodon* and the water monitors.

The Birds

The first of the homothermal or warm-blooded groups of animals is the class Aves, or birds. These are said to have been derived from the same stock that gave rise to the dinosaurs. They are believed to be that branch of the group which exploited the air; and the dinosaurs, various terrestrial habitats. The birds are not supposed to be descended from the dinosaurs, but rather the two are supposed to have had a common origin.[47]

The Origin of Feathers

In order to fly the birds had their forelimbs transformed into wings. The typical reptilian scales, it is believed, were altered into feathers for warmth and to increase the supporting surface. Most evolutionists believe that feathers have originated from a fraying out of reptilian scales.[48] Whether they originated as an insulating device or as a device to make possible flight is a question. Tucker believes that they were originated as an insulating device and that the first birds did not fly. He believes that feathers are strikingly different from scales in their structure. In short, the first step in bird evolution was not the development of the ability to exploit the air, but rather the development of a thermostat to maintain a constant temperature.[49]

In any case, the origin of feathers is still a real problem. The feather cannot correspond to a whole scale but only to the outer half of the scale. The inner half or vascular core is believed to have atrophied. Any theory of the origin of feathers is hypothetical and can only be characterized as judicious speculation.[50]

The Origin of Flight

Another problem is the origin of flight. As we pointed out earlier, the birds are not believed to have originated from the pterosaurs. These latter are believed to represent a side branch of the tree of reptile evolution. Some evolutionists believe that birds originated from tree-dwelling lizards. Others believe that the ancestors of the birds ran along the ground. Still others believe that flying birds had an arboreal ancestry and cursorial birds a terrestrial ancestry.

A cursorial origin of flight suggests that the birds arose from two-footed, long-tailed cursorial reptiles who, while running, oared along in the air by flapping their front feet, which were, of course, not in contact with the ground. This oaring movement could become more effective if the breadth of these anterior extremities were increased to give a greater bearing surface. This is believed to have been accomplished by increasing the size of the scales along the arm margin, and these gradually developed into feathers. Similar scales are thought to have developed along the margins of the tail for the same reason, and these, too, gradually developed into feathers.

Those who believe that the birds originated from an arboreal, or tree-dwelling, ancestor believe that in purely cursorial animals the grasping hind toe tends to vanish and the front limbs tend to be reduced in size rather than to elongate. For that reason they believe the ancestors of the birds to have been tree-dwelling lizards who early divided into two groups. The first of these returned to the ground and became the dinosaurs. The second group developed into birds. Some of these after a long period of evolution returned to the ground and became the modern flightless birds.

Still others postulate separate origins for the two modern groups of birds. They derive the flying birds from arboreal ancestors and the cursorial birds from a terrestrial stock.[51]

Bird Fossils

The earliest birds are known from two well-preserved specimens. One of these is headless and is known as *Archaeopteryx*. The other bears a head and is known as *Arcnaeornis*. Both come from the slate quarry at Solenhofen, Bavaria, and were contemporaries of *Compsognathus*, the smallest known dinosaur. A contemporary of *Archaeopteryx* and *Archaeornis* was the primitive pterosaur *Rhamphorhyncus*. Its wings, however, were only lateral extensions of a skimming membrane, fastened to the rear border of the greatly enlarged fourth finger of each hand.

Archaeornis was about the size of a crow, had feathers, and fair powers of flight. However, he also had some supposedly reptilian characteristics. Teeth were present in both jaws. The fingers of the hand were not yet fused to form a modern wing. Moreover, these fingers still contained claws. The sternum, or breastbone, was poorly developed. There was a long tail on either side of which the steering feathers were arranged. In modern birds the tail is very short, and the feathers are arranged in a fanlike structure.

In Cretaceous times we find two fossils, *Hesperornis* and *Ichthyornis*. Both of these still had teeth. *Hesperornis* measured about four and one-half feet in length with powerful hind limbs, which were probably useful in swimming but were rather awkward on land. Apparently this bird had lost its ability to fly. It is believed to have been similar to the modern loons in its habits except that it was flightless. *Ichthyornis* was a small, ternlike bird and was a good flyer. It is believed to have been quite modern except for the fact that it still had teeth.

Tertiary birds were very similar to the birds that we

know today. It is believed that loss of flight occurred several times during the Tertiary period, since large fossil cursorial birds are rather numerous from that period. The birds as a class are considered by evolutionists to be a very compact group which do not show nearly the range of size and adaptation that the reptiles show. The most highly developed birds are believed to be the small perching birds of the order Passeres.[52]

The Problem of the Constant Temperature Mechanism

One problem in connection with both birds and mammals is the problem of the origin of the constant temperature mechanism, or what is popularly known as the warm-blooded condition. Both birds and mammals have a thermostat which maintains their temperature within rather narrow limits. No such structure is known in any of the other animals. And it is difficult to believe that this difference could have arisen so perfectly in a very short time.

At the same time the very nature of the mechanism makes it almost impossible to trace its evolutionary history. The control center is located deep within the brain, in the thalamus. Since the brain is a soft tissue, fossils give little clue as to the brain structure of organisms.

It is also strange that this mechanism should have developed in both the birds and the mammals. It is not believed that their common ancestor possessed this mechanism, since other groups which do not have it developed from either the protobird or protomammalian stocks after the two separated.

Another difficulty is raised by the suggestion that this mechanism made possible a wide range of adaptations. For while the mammals are a very varied group, the birds are said to constitute a very compact group.

The Origin of Mammals

Turning to the evolutionary history of the mammals, they are believed to have branched off from the reptile stock at a relatively early stage. It is believed that they are descended from the therapsid order of reptiles, which appeared in the Permian period. The therapsids were rather abundant in the Middle and Upper Permian of South Africa.

These later gave rise to the cynodonts, so named for their doglike teeth, and they became the ancestors of the mammals. The teeth of these animals were not all alike but were of different kinds, so that they clearly can be divided into incisors, canines, and molars. The cynodonts are relatively low in the scale of reptilian evolution, so that it is believed that the common ancestor of the modern reptiles, birds, and mammals is to be found in rather remote geological history and that the groups separated very early. It has also been suggested that the ancestor of the mammals may have been similar to the ictidosaurs, another therapsid group found in the Triassic of South Africa.[53] An earlier theory derived the mammals from the Amphibia, but it is now believed that between the Amphibia and the mammals there was an air-breathing stage represented by the cynodonts or ictidosaurs.

The therapsid reptiles were "single arched." The birds, on the other hand, are derived from the "two-arched" archosaurian reptiles. The "one-arched" and the "two-arched" conditions refer to one or two temporal arches on each side of the skull. The archosaurians also gave rise to the crocodiles, dinosaurs, *Sphenodon*, lizards, and snakes. The mammals are the only descendants of the therapsid or "one-arched" reptiles.[54]

The two class characteristics of the mammals are the possession of hair and mammary glands. Both are difficult to account for on the basis of evolution. It has been suggested that hair is the counterpart of feathers in birds and that it, too, has developed from the scales of reptiles. But while feathers develop from connective tissue, hair develops from epithelial tissue. Feathers also have a blood supply, which hair lacks.[55] The two are not homologous. Nor has a satisfactory suggestion been made for the origin of mammary glands and lactation.

Early Mammalian Evolution

The first mammals are found in the upper Triassic strata in Germany, England, South Africa, and China. They are found later in the Jurassic of eastern Wyoming and in the Late Cretaceous in that same general region. The oldest-known mammal is *Tritylodon* found in the Upper Triassic in South Africa and China. This is placed in a separate group of mammals and is not believed to have given rise to any of the higher mammals. There is even some question as to whether it should be classified as a mammal, because the *os articulare* is still fastened to the lower jaw in a typically reptilian manner.

At one time two small jaws found in a coal mine at Egypt, N. C., belonging to the Upper Triassic period, were thought to be mammalian and were placed in the order Protodonta. However, they are now believed to be cynodont reptiles rather than mammals. *Tritylodon* has more perfectly formed teeth. The North Carolina fossils had a single pair of rodentlike incisors above and below. The molars had two or three longitudinal rows of tubercules, or bumps.

Another of these early mammalian orders was the order Pantotheria, which is found in the various Jurassic strata. The dentition is very similar to that of the insectivores, and there are some who believe they were the ancestors of the insectivores. They are thought to have been placental mammals.[56]

All of these ancestral mammals are believed to have been of small size and to have had five digits on the hands and on the feet. In addition, it is believed that all of them were able to oppose the first digit to the others.[57] Many of them were smaller than moles, and none of them were larger than kittens. All of them are believed to have been primarily active seekers after insect food.[58]

In general, they are believed to have been a very conservative group so far as evolution is concerned. Their conservatism is one of the problems for the evolutionist, since rapid evolution of the mammals might be expected. Usually it is explained on the basis of the intensive competition that they experienced from the reptiles. It is believed that mammals could develop only after climatic change or some other condition had brought about the extinction of most of the reptiles.

Archaic Mammals

Mammals are believed to have begun their most intensive evolution in the early Tertiary times. These Tertiary mammals, were, in turn, replaced after a relatively short period of time by the so-called modernized mammals. The archaic Tertiary mammals were deficient in their ability to protect themselves and also deficient in their ability to get food. It is believed that these deficiencies brought about their extinction. For one thing, their feet were relatively conservative, so that they were not able to flee rapidly from an enemy or to chase after an animal which was to serve for food. Their teeth, too, were not well adapted for grinding their food. The brain in general was small and relatively undeveloped in comparison with the brains of modernized mammals of equal bulk.

The archaic mammals included marsupials and five groups of placental mammals. It is possible that the monotremes — simple egg-laying mammals — were also present at this time, or they may have developed later from the marsupials.

One of the Tertiary placental mammalian groups was a flesh-eating carnivorous group known as the Creodonta. Some of them were bearlike, others doglike, or otterlike; some were minklike; others catlike or hyenalike. Six families

Figure 50. Archaic Mammals. A. *Hyaenodon,* a creodont. B. *Dromocyon,* also a creodont. C. *Patriofelis,* another creodont. D. *Phenacodus,* a condylarth. E. *Uintotherium,* an amblypod. (Redrawn from Osborn's *The Age of Mammals,* Scribner's, by permission)

of creodonts are distinguished, one of which is believed to have given rise to modern carnivores.

The Condylarthra were a group of primitive ungulates with a long, heavy tail and rather stocky legs. The teeth were low crowned and suited for feeding on rather succulent herbage. The group is believed to have given rise to the modern ungulates, though none of the genera known as fossils are believed to have been ancestral to the modern ungulates.

The Amblypoda were a group of short-footed ungulates.

Some of them attained a rather large size. Many of them were heavy, unwieldy animals, and a number of them probably lived in swamps, if not in the water itself.

All of these are believed to have become extinct because of an intense competition with better-developed mammalian stocks. Only a few developed into the higher types. Some evolutionists, however, believe that these primitive animals migrated to the Southern Hemisphere and that, together with the other stocks found there, they gave rise to the peculiar fauna which we know today.[59]

The Origin of Modern Mammals

The so-called modern mammals are characterized by the fact that they showed considerable advance in brain, feet, and teeth. In some cases only one was well developed; in other cases two; and in still other cases three of these characteristics were well developed.

Evolutionists are not agreed on whether the modern monotremes and marsupials arose as contemporaries with the modern placental mammals or whether they arose from the same primitive stock as did the archaic mammals.

The monotremes, as we have indicated before, lay eggs, and the young before hatching live on the yolk contained in the egg. The animals lack nipples. The milk is poured on the hair of the abdomen from which the young either suck or lick it up. The monotremes are found only in Australia, New Guinea, and Tasmania.

The marsupials bear their young alive, but in a very immature state. After birth they live in a pouch in the abdomen where they are fed by means of teats. They are found chiefly in Australia and the neighboring islands, but a few of them are natives of America. Even though the monotremes and the marsupials are regarded as fairly simple organisms, the monotremes have a relatively large forebrain, and the kangaroos show a fair learning capacity.[60]

Placental mammals have a specialized structure, made

up of both maternal and fetal elements, for the nourishment of the young before birth. In this way they are born in a fairly mature state, so that fewer young need be produced to preserve the species. Since the monotremes and marsupials are generally believed to be simpler organisms, most evolutionists incline to the theory that these arose relatively early in evolutionary history and that they have continued relatively unchanged for a long period of time.

The Monotremes

The monotremes include the platypus, or duckbill, and the *Echidna*. At one time it was thought that the platypus might be a link between the birds and the mammals, but this theory was rejected many years ago, and few, if any, evolutionists hold it today. It is true that the duckbill has three birdlike features: the duck bill, from which it gets its name; the webbed feet; and the tarsal spurs. However, the bill resembles only superficially the bill of a duck. It is not at all horny like the bill of a duck, but rather is soft, made up of a sort of kidskin leather. The webbed feet are found in a number of organisms, and the webbing in the platypus is believed to be fundamentally similar to the connections

Figure 51. Platypus. This mammal lays eggs. Note the ducklike bill and the webbed feet. (Courtesy Chicago Natural History Museum)

between the bases of the human fingers. The spur is hollow, unlike the spur of a rooster, which is solid. It is connected to a gland which gives off a poisonous secretion. The animal, as indicated above, lays eggs. While this is not exclusively a bird characteristic, it might also suggest a relationship to the bird. However, this egg-laying characteristic is believed to be a heritage from the ancestral reptiles. All of these characteristics are believed to have developed in the birds and monotremes by convergent evolution rather than as a result of the organism's being a link between the birds and the mammals.

The Marsupials and Their Relationships to Monotremes and Placental Mammals

The marsupials are believed to have originated toward the close of the Cretaceous period. They are believed to have originated somewhat earlier than the placental mammals. They are divided into three suborders: the Polyprotodontia, the Diprotodontia, and the Caenolestoidea.

The first of these suborders includes both insectivorous and carnivorous types. They are believed to be the more primitive type. Except for the American opossum they are confined to Australasia.

The Diprotodontia are mainly herbivorous. Their dentition is similar to that of the rodents. This group contains the largest and most highly specialized of the marsupials.

The third suborder is represented today by a few so-called marsupial shrews found in South America. They are believed to be somewhat intermediate between the Polyprotodontia and the Diprotodontia. It has been suggested that their ancestral forms lived in North America. Subsequently, some of them made their way over to Asia and then to Australia, where they gave rise to the Diprotodontia stock. The others came down to South America, where they are found today.[61]

The question as to which came first, the monotremes,

marsupials, or placentals, has still not been decided by evolutionists. It is generally believed that the placental mammals have been derived ultimately from animals that laid a sizable egg. However, the only reason for this statement is the assumption that they are descended from the reptiles. The excessively small size of the egg of the higher placental mammals is believed to represent the end product of a very long course of evolutionary development. The forced feeding of the young found in the marsupials, it is believed, may have been a prerequisite for the development of the sucking mechanism in the young placental mammals. Thus it is generally agreed that the marsupials do represent an earlier stage than the placental mammals and that some of their characteristics had already developed by the time that the first placental mammals branched off from the marsupials. The monotremes are believed to have retained very ancient mammalian characteristics in their reproductive systems and to a considerable extent also in their brains. It is generally believed, though, that a form similar to the Virginia opossum was the ancestor not only of the marsupials but also of all the mammals, that the monotremes separated rather early from this primitive stock, and that somewhat later the placental mammals branched off from this marsupial stock.[62]

Ride suggests a polyphyletic origin for the mammals. He believes the monotreme line was probably separated from the marsupials and placentals even before the mammals evolved.[63]

The Origin of the Placenta

The development of the placenta is one of the problems of evolution. This particular structure, as we pointed out, makes possible the birth of a fairly well-developed organism. It has been suggested that the development of a pouch similar to that found in the modern marsupials was the first step in the development of a placenta, but no real method of the development of this organ has been suggested. It is interesting to note that a placenta is found in one of the species of the Australian skinks (a reptile) and also in the marsupials. This is believed to be an example of convergent evolution, where the same type of structure develops in two separate forms which are not closely related by descent.[64]

Modern Mammals

The various mammalian groups are supposed to have undergone a great deal of evolution and adaptive radiation. At the present time they are recognized as the dominant group of animals, and they occupy almost all conceivable habitats. Not only are there a great number of terrestrial forms, but some of them have exploited the air (bats), and others have gone back to the sea (whales, seals, and dolphins).

The most primitive of the modern mammals are supposed to be the insectivores. On the other end of the scale of development, some evolutionists believe that the carnivores are the most highly developed of the modern mammals. Still others give this honor to the perissodactyls, represented by the modern horse. It is interesting to note that the primates are not regarded as being particularly well-developed mammals. They have advanced by developing their brains, whereas other animals have developed locomotor organs and teeth as well as the brain.

It is believed that when a stock becomes dominant, there is a tremendous outburst of adaptive radiation. This is supposed to have occurred during the periods when the insects and reptiles dominated the world of living things, and it is supposed to be occurring today among the mammals. It is this principle which is supposed to explain the wide variety of mammals found today. However, it should be pointed out that this adaptive radiation has not happened in the case of the most highly developed of all mammalian stocks — man himself. Instead of developing a large number of species, man has developed but one species. This is interesting also because of the fact that man is a fairly numerous species, which would be all the more reason for expecting adaptive radiation.

It is also believed that organisms in general have increased in size as they have developed by evolution.

This large size is believed to be accompanied by the development of a type of organization that is very much dependent upon a stable environment. As a consequence large-sized animals are very susceptible to environmental changes. Many evolutionists believe that the large mammals, such as the elephant, are doomed to extinction. Romer calls them the last futile survivors of Tertiary lines which for the most part did not outlive the Pleistocene epoch.[65] Thus in evolving and becoming large the animal brings about its own extinction.

The Future of Evolution

What about the future? Is evolution still going on? To the latter question the answer is an almost universal "yes." All sorts of suggestions have been made as to the future of evolution. It has been suggested that evolution in man, for instance, will probably come by crossing and recombination. Most, if not all, human evolution will be on the psychic and psychosocial level; very little physical change is expected.[66] But it is generally agreed that evolution is going on and that it will continue into the indefinite future. Not even the highly developed organisms of today, including man, are believed to be the final end products of complete evolutionary progress.

NOTES

1. Willmer, E. N. *Cytology and Evolution* (New York: Academic, 1960), p. 397.
2. Stebbins, G. Ledyard. "The Place of Botany in a Unified Science Curriculum," *BioScience*, XVII, 2 (February 1967), 85.

3. Gregory, William King. *Evolution Emerging* (New York: Macmillan, 1951), I, 501.

4. Coulter, Merle C. "Evolution of the Plant Kingdom," *The Nature of the World and of Man,* ed. H. H. Newman (Chicago: University of Chicago Press, 1926), pp. 217 f.

5. Stebbins, p. 84.

6. Dodson, Edward O. *A Textbook of Evolution* (Philadelphia: Saunders, 1952), p. 136.
   Merrell, David J. *Evolution and Genetics* (New York: Holt, Rinehart and Winston, 1962), p. 151.

7. Dodson, pp. 137–146.
   Merrell, p. 151.

8. Sprague, T. A. "Taxonomic Botany with Special Reference to the Angiosperms," *The New Systematics,* ed. Julian Huxley (Oxford: Oxford University Press, 1940), p. 443.

9. Scott, Dukinfield Henry. *Extinct Plants and Problems of Evolution* (London: Macmillan, 1924), p. 42.

10. *Evolution: Its Science and Doctrine,* Thomas W. M. Cameron ed. (Toronto: University of Toronto Press, 1960), p. 4.

11. Gregory, pp. 20–22.

12. Ibid., pp. 22–24.

13. Willmer, p. 135.

14. Gregory, p. 25.

15. Ibid., pp. 27 f.

16. Ibid., p. 28.

17. Buchsbaum, Ralph. *Animals Without Backbones* (Chicago: University of Chicago Press, 1948), p. 108.

18. Gregory, p. 29.

19. Ibid., pp. 31, 64.
    Dunbar, Carl O. *Historical Geology* (New York: Wiley, 1949), pp. 147 f.

20. Gregory, p. 64.

21. De Beer, G. R. "Embryology and Taxonomy," *The New Systematics,* ed. Julian Huxley (Oxford: Oxford University Press, 1940), p. 376.

22. Gregory, p. 512.

23. Ibid., pp. 90–100.

24. De Beer, p. 376.

25. Gregory, p. 88.

26. Hooton, Earnest Albert. *Up from the Ape* (New York: Macmillan, 1946), p. 57.

27. Gregory, p. 86.

28. Ibid., p. 105.
29. Ibid., p. 103.
30. Jepsen, Glenn L. "Selection, 'Orthogenesis,' and the Fossil Record," *Proceedings of the American Philosophical Society*, XCIII (1949), 491.
31. Romer, Alfred Sherwood. *Vertebrate Paleontology* (Chicago: University of Chicago Press, 1945), pp. 84 f.
32. Huxley, Julian. *Evolution, the Modern Synthesis* (New York: Harpers, 1943), p. 454.
33. Carroll, Robert L. "Lungfish Burrows from the Michigan Coal Basin," *Science*, CXLVIII (1965), 963.
34. Lull, Richard Swann. *Organic Evolution* (New York: Macmillan, 1949), p. 449.
35. Hooton, p. 57.
36. Gregory, p. 301.
37. Lull, p. 464.
38. Gregory, pp. 305 f.
39. Colbert, Edwin H. *The Dinosaur Book* (New York: McGraw-Hill, 1951), pp. 80–82.
40. Gregory, p. 356.
41. Ibid., p. 310.
42. Kraus, Bertram S. *The Basis of Human Evolution* (New York: Harper and Row, 1964), p. 79.
43. Colbert, pp. 97–101.
44. Ibid., pp. 105–108.
45. Carr, Archie. *Handbook of Turtles* (Ithaca: Comstock Publishing Associates, 1952), p. 2.
46. Ditmars, Raymond L. *Reptiles of the World* (New York: Macmillan, 1933, pp. 5, 12.
47. Tucker, B. W. "Functional Evolutionary Morphology: The Evolution of Birds," *Evolution*, ed. G. R. De Beer (Oxford: Clarendon Press, 1938), p. 322.
48. Pycraft, W. P. *A History of Birds* (London: Methuen and Co., 1910), p. 39.
49. Tucker, pp. 330 f.
50. Ibid., p. 332.
51. Lull, pp. 492–494.
52. Ibid., pp. 495 f.
53. Gregory, p. 343.
54. Ibid., p. 326.
55. Hooton, p. 192.

56. Lull, p. 503.
57. Hooton, p. 66.
58. Gregory, p. 356.
59. Lull, pp. 508–515.
60. Rensch, Bernard. "Trends Towards Progress of Brains and Sense Organs," *Cold Spring Harbor Symposia on Quantitative Biology*, XXIV (1959), 294.
61. Newman, H. H. *The Phylum Chordata* (New York: Macmillan, 1939), p. 406.
62. Gregory, pp. 372–374.
63. Ride, W. D. L. "Evolution of Australian Marsupials," *The Evolution of Living Organisms*, ed. G. W. Leeper (Victoria: Melbourne University Press, 1962), p. 289.
64. Flynn, T. Thomson. "On the Occurrence of a True Allantoplacenta of the Conjoint Type in an Australian Lizard," *Records of the Australian Museum*, XIV (1923), 72–77.
    Hill, Jas. P. "The Placentation of Perameles," *Quarterly Journal of Microscopical Science*, XL (1897), 385–439.
    Hill, J. P. "Contributions to the Embryology of the Marsupialia. II. On a Further Stage in the Placentation of Perameles," *Quarterly Journal of Microscopical Science*, XLIII (1900), 1–13.
65. Romer, Alfred Sherwood. "Time Series and Trends in Animal Evolution," *Genetics, Paleontology, and Evolution*, ed. Glenn L. Jepsen, Ernst Mayr, and George Gaylord Simpson (Princeton: Princeton University Press, 1949), p. 109.
66. Huxley, Julian. *Essays of a Humanist* (New York: Harper and Row, 1964), pp. 62 f.

12. Problems for the Evolutionist

Evolution is by no means a complete and perfect theory. We have pointed again and again to problems that arise for the evolutionist, facts which are difficult to explain on the basis of evolutionary theories. The evolutionist, of course, believes that these problems exist because of his inability to know all the facts. His theories and explanations, like the world itself, are in a constant state of flux. Not only are new facts being added, but these new facts require also the constant revision of theories and hypotheses. It is, of course, to be expected that there will be problems for the evolutionist. And yet it is important to realize that these problems do exist lest the impression be created that evolution gives a perfect answer to the organic world as we know it and that only the Biblical doctrine of special creation presents problems.

The Origin of Life

One of the biggest problems for the evolutionist is the origin of life. Various approaches to this problem have been made. At one time it was suggested that this was a philosophical rather than a biological problem, and the problem was evaded by scientists, who refused to discuss it. Others took refuge in a specialized theory of theistic evolution. According to this theory God was supposed to have created the first life, and evolution was supposed to have taken over from that first creation. However, at the present time it is recognized that some explanation of the origin of life must be forthcoming, and a number of theories have been suggested.

a. Life from Another Planet

One of the first theories advanced was that life came from another planet. Arrhenius, for instance, suggested that life came by spores carried through space as a result of radiation pressure.

Blum, however, points out that life could not have come to the earth in this way. Ultraviolet radiation alone, he says, would have killed spores carried in this way during their travels through space. In addition, these spores would have been heated to such high temperatures by radiation absorbed during their travels through space that they could not have survived. Then, too, as Blum points out, this merely pushes the problem back another step and makes necessary an explanation of the origin of life wherever it is supposed to have first developed.[1]

Another theory suggests that life came to this earth in the form of simple organisms carried by meteors or meteorites. If these simple organisms were buried within the meteorite, they would have been protected from some of the ultraviolet radiation. Moreover, if they moved rapidly enough, they might have reached the earth before ultraviolet bombardment destroyed them.

However, it is difficult to believe that these organisms could have survived the intense cold of outer space or that they could have survived the intense heat generated when meteorites strike the earth's atmosphere. Once more, like the suggestion of Arrhenius, this theory merely pushes the problem back a few steps and does not really solve the problem of the origin of life.

One meteorite, the Orgueil meteorite, which contains an assortment of biogenic materials — coal fragments, seed capsules of a reed, other plant fragments, and an optically active, water-soluble protein material — is believed to have been accidentally or deliberately contaminated shortly after it fell in 1864, so that the materials suggestive of life from outer space are actually now believed to have been of terrestrial origin.[2] At present the general opinion is that of Simpson, who says a conservative conclusion would be that it is extremely improbable, almost to the point of impossibility, that any form of life has ever traveled by natural means from one planetary system to another. Travel between the earth and Mars within the same planetary system is still improbable, but the possibility is not absolutely ruled out.[3]

b. Early Theories of the Origin of Life Here on the Earth Itself

Most biologists have rejected the idea that life originated on some other planet, and they look for the origin of life on this earth itself. Almost all of the earlier theories which sought to account for the origin of life on this earth did so by explaining the development of one of the main features of protoplasm. A great many of these theories centered in the origin of proteins. Some of these trace the development of protein through the combinations of nitrogen, hydrogen, and oxygen; and of nitrogen and carbon at the high temperatures which are believed to have existed at the time when the earth began. Others think that protein originated through the formation of the various compounds of nitrogen and oxygen and of ammonia by the action of lightning in the atmosphere. These are supposed to have been washed into the soil where they combined with carbon dioxide to form proteins. It should be realized that the naturally occurring proteins are extremely complex. They do not occur naturally apart from living things.[4]

Another set of theories sought to explain the development of colloidal structure as the starting point for protoplasm. Colloids were believed to have developed as a result of a tendency toward increased complexity. It was believed that under the proper conditions as an end product of this tendency toward complexity colloids similar to those found in protoplasm would develop.

A third theory emphasized the role of the enzymes.

Little attempt was made to explain how these originated, but rather the emphasis was on the ways in which these enzymes got into protoplasm. It was usually suggested that the enzymes built up protoplasm and that protoplasm gradually incorporated the enzymes which produced it.

Most of these older theories have been rejected because they usually assumed that life originated suddenly as a consequence of a fortunate combination of circumstances in a very short period of time. The idea of a sudden origin of life has been almost completely discarded today. Moreover, most of these older theories utilized some materials which it is now believed did not exist at the early periods of the earth's history. Most of them, for instance, assumed that carbon dioxide was the primary carbon compound. But it is now believed that carbon dioxide is the end of the carbon cycle of evolution and that most of the carbon dioxide now present has been produced by living organisms.[5]

c. Modern Theories of the Origin of Life

At the present time it is believed that the origin of life was a gradual process and that life did not come into existence suddenly as a consequence of a combination of a whole series of chance occurrences. The atmosphere of the earth is believed to have contained originally no oxygen at all. Nor is it believed to have contained free nitrogen, though there was nitrogen present in the earth's crust. Superheated water vapor is supposed to have been present in the earth's atmosphere. It is believed that the meeting of superheated steam and of carbides from the earth's crust gave rise to the first hydrocarbons. Shull thinks that these hydrocarbons were the primary organic compounds.[6]

The first nitrogen is believed to have existed in the form of metallic nitrides, which, in combination with the superheated water vapor, produced ammonia, or, in combination with the carbides, produced cyanamides. These latter combined with the superheated water vapor to give ammonia.

Thus ammonia became a part of the earth's atmosphere, just as it is believed to be a part of the atmosphere of some of the other planets at present.

It is generally agreed today that the atmosphere of the primitive earth was a reducing one; that is, it contained no oxygen whatsoever. Some years ago Urey suggested that the original atmosphere was a mixture of methane, hydrogen, ammonia, and water vapor. Combining these into amino acids, the building blocks of the proteins, would require a substantial amount of energy; he believed this came from cosmic rays, only a few of which penetrate the earth at present because of the presence of ozone in the upper atmosphere. At Urey's suggestion S. L. Miller exposed a mixture of these gases to a continuous electric discharge in 1953 and found that some amino acids were produced. Amino acids must combine into linear chains in a process of polymerization which requires the loss of water. Ordinarily this can be accomplished only at relatively high temperatures: however, the chemist S. W. Fox discovered that in the presence of phosphoric acid this reaction would occur at temperatures as low as 70° Centigrade. Fox also reported that when he mixed together 18 amino acids common in living systems these were not distributed in haphazard fashion but exhibited a considerable number of nonrandom combinations. Using energy from the sun and from cosmic rays, organic molecules are believed to have accumulated in the seas. These formed primitive living things which began to metabolize in a fermentation process which released carbon dioxide into the primitive atmosphere. Other anaerobic processes followed.

Photophosphorylation processes came into use. These use the energy of light to provide high-energy organic phosphates. This was followed by photosynthesis which released oxygen as a by-product. Some of the oxygen was changed to ozone, which still serves to screen out most of the cosmic rays. The absence of oxygen prior to this time prevented the oxidation of the relatively simple compounds which could exist in a reducing atmosphere but which would have been destroyed in the present oxidizing atmosphere.

All of these newer theories differ from the older theories in that they assume that life originated gradually and in that they do not draw a sharp line of demarcation between the living and the nonliving. They suggest essentially that life originated in a reducing atmosphere which no longer exists and that life by its very presence modified the atmosphere in such a way that life can no longer originate spontaneously.

The Problem of Free Energy Mobilization

But these theories, too, have their problems. One of these is the problem of some mechanism of free energy mobilization. This involves some mechanism for utilizing various sources of energy. At the present time there are only three types of energy mobilization. There are the heterotrophic organisms, which get their energy from other living things. These are energy spenders, which must be supplied with energy-rich carbon compounds. They include almost all the animals and most of the nongreen plants. A second type of energy mobilization is represented by the chemosynthetic organisms. These are organisms which get their energy from various inorganic reactions. The best-known of these are the iron and sulphur bacteria. The third method of energy mobilization is that represented by photosynthetic organisms such as the green plants.

Blum thinks that the first step in the origin of life must have been some means of energy mobilization. This, he believes, involved the adenylic acid system. He holds that the first proteins were nucleoproteins similar to those found in the nucleus of cells today.

He says that it is hard to imagine the origin of protein molecules without a mechanism for free energy mobilization or the utilization of energy. And yet he believes that it is difficult to explain how this mechanism for the utilization of energy could have developed at a very early stage in terms of the living systems that we now know.[7] Urey's suggestion, which we have outlined above, solves this problem because he believes that life originated during the period when highly reduced compounds were evolving into the highly oxidized ones of today. He points out that the highly oxidized condition that exists on the earth is rare in the cosmos. He believes that the source of free energy for the first living things was the absorption of ultraviolet light in the high atmosphere by methane, water, and other compounds produced from them by photochemical action. This process not only served as a source of energy but also protected primitive organisms from ultraviolet light. He thinks that the red bacteria and some of the species of algae which use hydrogen and carbon dioxide in photosynthesis are living fossils from an early stage in the earth's history.[8]

There is still a serious problem in that cosmic rays are very damaging to protoplasm today; yet their energy is needed in order to synthesize the complex chemicals characterizing life from the relatively simple compounds which are believed to have existed. This would require the origin of life within very narrow limits in the water. The materials being synthesized would have to be close enough to the surface to absorb this energy, yet protected by the water so that when the complex compounds were formed, they were not immediately destroyed once more.

Blum states that neither heterotrophic or chemosynthetic organisms could have lasted very long on the earth without the presence of photosynthetic organisms. Thus he holds that photosynthesis appeared very early in the evolution of life. He believes that the first organisms were very similar to the blue-green algae and that other organisms developed later. Complex chromosome and gene mechanisms, he believes, were a still later development.

Osborn and Kligler have suggested that the first living

organisms were primitive feeder bacteria such as *Nitro-
somonas*, the nitrite bacterium which changes ammonia to
nitrites. These flourished on a lifeless earth and prepared
the earth and its waters chemically for the lower forms of
plant life. But these forms are adapted to living on various
decomposition products, including those which have come
from pre-existing plants and animals. Gregory agrees with
Blum that photosynthetic organisms must have arisen early.
He, too, believes that organisms similar to the blue-green
algae were the most primitive forms.[9]

The Problem of the Origin of Protein

The problem of the origin of the first protein is still a
very serious problem, and one to which there has been no
real answer. Proteins are the most complex compounds
known; they are fundamental to living protoplasm and
characteristic of it. Haldane has suggested that the primal
oceans contained reaction systems having the consistency
of diluted hot soup, and Oparin suggests that they contained
colloidal systems called coacervates. Both of these are
thought to have brought about the development of proteins.

But Blum does not believe that even this explanation
helps to solve the problem of the origin of protein. For one
thing, this problem of the origin of proteins involves the
same problem of the origin of an energy mobilization system
that the origin of life itself involves. Blum points out both
heterotrophic and autotrophic metabolism (energy processes
which depend upon the release of energy from energy-rich
carbohydrates and on the independent capture of energy)
are in modern organisms strictly dependent upon the
existence of proteins in the form of catalysts. This creates
a real problem, for at a time when life did not exist how
did substances come into existence which today are absolutely essential to living systems and yet can only be formed
by those systems?[10]

Keosian points out that there is a wide gap between

coacervates and the most primitive "living" thing and that this is the critical part of the story. Much, he believes, rests on a convincing explanation of the transition based on physical laws. Experimental evidence, he says, is lacking here, and hence the explanations are based on premises that are all mechanistically sound, to be sure, but the inexorability of the argument is gone. He believes that one can make other premises based on other models.[11]

Another difficulty is the mathematical chance of the formation of a compound so complex as a protein. Blum points out that the chance of forming a polypeptid of only ten amino acid units would be something like 10^{-20} (.00000000000000000001). Such a polypeptid is still very small. After the polypeptid stage the proteose stage must be reached, and only after the proteose stage can the protein stage be reached. Blum says that the formation of a polypeptid of the size of the smallest known protein seems beyond all probability.[12] Later he says that he does not see how proteins could have leaped suddenly into being.

It has been suggested that the first protein molecules were formed by some primitive, nonprotein living system. But this suggestion merely evades the question, for such a theory simply pushes the problem back another step, and we are faced with the problem of accounting for the origin of that nonprotein organism.[13]

Ehrlich and Holm point out that the problems of utilizing energy for protein synthesis and the conditions under which it may occur are particularly vexing ones. In present-day biological systems, they note, the enzymes responsible for the mobilization of energy and for the synthesis itself are proteins. Thus if one is to postulate the functioning of such a system in the formation of the first proteins, he becomes embroiled in a "chicken or egg" dilemma. It has been suggested that in the absence of proteins other substances such as clays may have served as catalysts, since many of the known enzymatic phenomena are fundamentally molecule-surface reactions, but this raises the question of how proteins subsequently came to assume this function.[14]

Enzymes, all known examples of which are protein, are vital to living processes. They enable life processes to go on rapidly and at low temperatures. About 100 enzymes have now been isolated, each one catalyzing a particular type of action, and the number of specific reactions in the cell which require an enzyme is believed to be in the thousands.

Horowitz has suggested that there were present to begin with complex organic compounds which were presumably formed in the process of chemical evolution. He believes that the first living organisms utilized some of these complex compounds which they were not able to synthesize. When the initial supply of these essential substances was exhausted, these original organisms perished. But in the meantime mutations had occurred in these early organisms which resulted in living forms that could carry out the synthesis of essential complex compounds from the simpler ones remaining in the environment.

Further mutations provided additional steps in the synthesis until eventually there were organisms which could synthesize all of the essential complex compounds. The intermediate forms which were unable to synthesize all of the necessary compounds tended to be eliminated by natural selection as the intermediate substances on which they were dependent were exhausted from the environment.[15] Blum, however, thinks that natural selection is possible only in systems having a complexity at least as great as that of proteins. He believes that Horowitz utilizes natural selection at too early a stage. It is his judgment that in invoking it Horowitz is postulating the prior existence of that for which an origin is sought.[16]

Another question is just how simple and primitive the organisms we regard as simple and primitive today actually are. Becking discusses the iron bacteria and the sulphur bacteria which some believe to be well fitted to play the role of the original living being. He regards this as a grave mistake. He says that while their outer environment is extremely simple, they need highly complicated internal machinery to translate the simple components into "themselves" and that as far as enzyme systems are concerned, the simple autotroph represents the highest biochemical complexity. He therefore believes that it is most unlikely that similar organisms should have been most primitive.[17]

Steward discusses the complexity of photosynthesis. He says every high school student now professes to know how protein is made because he has learned this in high school and in popular magazines, but Steward asks whether a company set up to make protein in a protein-poor world, on whose board of directors all the recent Nobel Prize winners served, would succeed. He answers, "Perhaps in another century, but not in this decade." He also says, "Despite the most glowing scientific brochures I would not buy shares in a company floated to do this." Living cells, he says, even plant cells, have intrinsic properties by virtue of their organization, the subtle way in which they are put together that enables them to do these things. Cells take the biochemically and biophysically feasible events which can be demonstrated *in vitro* to an often infinitesimal degree, and by a subtle sort of biological engineering they render the merely feasible to be practical.[18] Others say much the same thing and point to the fact that many explanations for the origin of life deal with specific parts of the cell or specific aspects of life processes without attempting to explain all of them. Becking says that until advanced chemistry has made the position of biologists untenable, he will believe that the living cell is more than a pot full of enzymes.[19] Earlier he says that after a lifetime of studying living things he has emerged a vitalist, because he is convinced that while living streams obey physical-chemical laws, they apply these prin-

ciples on an essentially new plane. He refers to the Moscow
Symposium of 1957, in which there was general agreement
as to the possibility of creating living systems out of inan-
imate matter, and goes on to say, "Maybe this confidence
is only given to the biochemist. As a biologist I cannot
share this optimism (or pessimism)." [20] P. T. Mora is quoted
as saying that an understanding of the transition from chemical to life is impossible through modern physics and chemistry.[21]

The Origin of New Life Today

Is life originating today? Almost all evolutionists say
"No." It is generally believed that there is no chance of
living substances originating independently of living things
today. This is in keeping with our modern approach to the
idea of spontaneous generation. At one time it was taken
for granted that the nonliving gave rise to the living.
Decaying meat was supposed to turn into maggots, pond
mud in spring was supposed to spawn frogs, toads, salamanders, etc. This idea, known as spontaneous generation,
has been rejected after careful experimentation by such men
as Redi, Spallanzani, and Pasteur. It is believed that if life
started out to develop today, the substances would be
utilized by living things before they could evolve to that
stage which we recognize as living today. In short, they
would be incorporated into living protoplasm before they
themselves could become alive.[22] Oparin says that there
are no longer any nooks or crannies where such incipient
life could gain a foothold and where it would not be destroyed by the predatory activities of already existing life.
Blum also suggests that it is unlikely for the various chance
happenings which brought about the development of life to
recur today. He also believes that the nonliving world has
evolved and that the critical conditions essential to the
origin of life probably do not exist any longer.[23]

Early Evolution After the Origin of Life

The first protein is believed to have further developed into a viruslike autotrophic organism. These organisms were similar to the blue-green algae but much smaller. Their size was of the magnitude of a virus, and they corresponded more or less to free genes. These, then, later organized themselves as chromosomes, and the chromosomes gradually developed into nuclei and cells. Thus the complex hereditary mechanism involving the nucleus, chromosomes, and genes is believed to have been a very special one arrived at only after a considerable period of evolution.

Yet it must be pointed out that complex nuclear mechanisms are found also in the lower forms — in fungi and some of the algae. Structures that might be called nuclei are also found in the bacteria. Today it is believed that even sexual processes take place in the bacteria. For that reason it is probable that some of the lower organisms are not as simple as was once believed. Indeed, their simplicity seems to have been due to our inability to demonstrate and observe the various complex processes and not to the absence of these processes. Blum believes that even the simplest organism today has come a long way from the earliest organisms.[24]

The Fitness of the Environment

Another point that deserves to be considered in any discussion of evolution is the fitness of the environment itself. Disciples of Darwin and other evolutionists have made much of the fitness of the individual for survival in his environment. But another point that deserves consideration and that is often overlooked and ignored is the fitness of the environment itself for life as we know it.

a. The Fitness of the Earth

From time to time we hear or read discussions on the possibility of life on other planets. As these lines are written, "flying saucers" are much in the news, and there is a great

deal of speculation on the possibility of living things invad-
ing our planet from outer space. Most scientists are convinced, though, that there is no life similar to human life
anywhere in the solar system, and many believe that life
as we know it exists only here on earth.

The planet most frequently mentioned as possibly being
inhabited or at least possessing life is the planet Mars. The
planet has markings which some have suggested are canals
dug and maintained by intelligent beings. In addition,
greenish areas are visible at times which are thought to
indicate plant life. However, Dean B. McLaughlin of the
University of Michigan has suggested that the markings on
Mars are somewhat analogous to the dust bowl areas of the
southwest. The "trade winds" on Mars (where the absence
of oceans and of long mountain ranges permits them to
behave otherwise than they do on earth) pile up the sand,
the dust, and the volcanic ash in drifts and ridges. Some of
this, because of the lack of oxygen in the Martian atmosphere, can have a greenish tone. Thus both the canals and
life on Mars are disposed of as largely illusions produced by
Martian meteorology. Dean McLaughlin's suggestions were
considered one of the astronomical highlights of 1954.[25]

There are many reasons for believing that the earth is the
only inhabited planet. For one thing, the earth is placed just
the proper distance from the sun. Life as we know it can
exist for any length of time only between 0° C. and 100° C.,
the freezing and boiling points of water respectively.
Actually the practical limits are even narrower because of the
susceptibility of proteins and enzymes — so important to
living things and life processes — to even moderately high
temperatures. Most of them break down if they are
subjected to temperatures in excess of 40° C. for any
length of time. It is probably for that reason that most
organisms live between 0° C. and 40° C. If the earth were
closer to the sun, the temperature would be higher, and life
would be impossible. If it were farther from the sun, tem-

peratures would be lower, and once more life would be impossible. Moreover, it is important that the earth should revolve on its axis. If the earth always presented one face to the sun as the moon always presents one face to the earth, then one hemisphere would be relatively hot and the other quite cold.

Three minor constituents of our atmosphere — water vapor, carbon dioxide, and ozone — are largely responsible for the climate of the earth being neither too hot nor too cold. These minor gases screen us from the active ultraviolet rays of the sun. On the daylight side of the earth they shield us from the heat of the infrared solar rays and, in turn, blanket the surface from the cosmic cold of space at night. Without these minor constituents, less than 2 per cent by volume composition of the atmosphere, the earth would be intolerably warm on the daylight side and inhospitably cold on the nighttime side.

b. The Fitness of Water

The chemical compound most intimately associated with living things — water — is also eminently fitted for its role in living things. Water, which makes up eighty to ninety per cent of all living things, has, first of all, a very high heat capacity. This particular physical property is known as its specific heat. Compared with most other substances, a larger quantity of heat is required to bring about a given increase in the temperature of a given quantity of water. The amount of water on the earth's surface, estimated to be enough to form a layer over a mile deep if spread evenly, tends to prevent sudden increases or decreases in temperature, as, for example, between day and night. It is the presence of this large quantity of water that is responsible, too, for the fact that coastal regions are not as warm in summer or as cold in winter as inland areas. For not only the temperature of the ocean itself is kept rather constant by the high specific heat of water but also the atmosphere in its immediate vicinity is affected. This high specific heat of water also prevents the occurrence of catastrophic ocean currents and winds which might result from rapid changes in temperature.

Another important property of water that is extremely significant is its high latent heat of vaporization. In order to change one gram of water from the liquid to the gaseous state as water vapor, it is necessary to add between 500 and 600 calories of heat, the exact number depending on the temperature at which the vaporization occurs. The condensation of the same quantity of water vapor transfers that much heat from the water to its environment.

This particular property is important in cooling plants and animals. The fact that the vaporization of water removes large quantities of heat makes perspiration an effective cooling mechanism in animals. Transpiration, the evaporation of water from the leaves, brings about the same result in plants. This is extremely important because of the fact that proteins and enzymes tend to break down at temperatures above 40° C. Both plants and animals are frequently exposed to situations where the absorption of heat might easily raise their temperatures above this point but for perspiration and transpiration.

Water also possesses a high latent heat of fusion. This means that a relatively large quantity of heat is released when a given quantity of water is changed from the liquid state to the solid state. In freezing, water actually heats the surrounding atmosphere. Our grandparents often took advantage of this property of water in preventing the freezing of vegetables in a root cellar during the winter. When it became extremely cold, they would place large tubs of water in the root cellar. This water would freeze at a temperature higher than the freezing point of the vegetables which they were attempting to protect, and in freezing the water would give off enough heat to maintain the temperature of the root cellar above the temperature at which the vegetables would freeze.

Another point to be considered in connection with the high latent heat of vaporization and the high latent heat of fusion of water is the fact that this makes possible the exchange of a considerable amount of heat between the tropics and the polar regions. As water vaporizes in the tropics, it removes a great deal of heat from these regions; and when it cools and condenses in colder regions, it gives off heat in those regions. Later it changes from a liquid to a solid state and so releases a further quantity of heat. This process is reversed when the ice and snow melt and when the water vaporizes once more. This whole cycle results in a more uniform temperature over the surface of the earth.

Still another property of water, and one which is very unusual, is the fact that it reaches its greatest density at 4° C. (about 39° F.). Most liquids reach their greatest density at their freezing point. This property of water tends to prevent freezing from the bottom up, since water at the freezing point is lighter than water at 4° C. and tends to rise to the top. In this way freezing begins at the surface, and the bottom freezes last, if at all, so that organisms living at the bottom of fresh water ponds and lakes are at least somewhat protected.

This property is also important in the melting of water in the spring. Water is a poor conductor of heat, and if streams froze over from the bottom and melted from the top, they would melt very slowly. Indeed, in many places they would never melt at all. However, as water melts, it becomes heavier and sinks to the bottom, so that the ice is always found at the top where it can absorb the direct rays of the sun.

This property of water is also important in oxygenating the water of ponds and lakes. Water on the surface is relatively well supplied with oxygen; water at the bottom tends to be deficient in oxygen. As the lake or pond cools down in the fall and winter, the oxygen-rich water on the surface tends to sink and replace the oxygen-deficient water on the bottom. As it freezes, the water which is now at the bottom moves to the top once more. In spring, when the ice melts, the water produced moves first to the bottom, and, then, as it becomes warmer, moves to the top once more. Thus this property of water provides for at least two complete turnovers of the water in the pond or lake each year.

Another point to be considered is the "greenhouse" effect brought about by the presence of water vapor in the atmosphere. A greenhouse maintains a higher temperature than the surrounding environment because glass permits sunlight to pass in freely but absorbs and reflects many of the longer heat rays re-emitted by the objects in the greenhouse. Water vapor in the earth's atmosphere does much the same thing. The sunlight is permitted to pass through freely, but many of the longer heat rays re-emitted by the earth are absorbed and reflected back to the earth. This prevents extreme variations in temperature between night and day. At the same time some of the radiation is transmitted; otherwise the surface temperature might go very high during the day.

Still another property of water that is important is that it is the "universal solvent." While not all substances are soluble in water (and it is fortunate that this is the case, since if water were a truly universal solvent, we should find nothing in which to keep it), more substances are soluble in water than in any other solvent. Substances in solution react much more readily than substances that are not. Indeed, it seems probable that all of the chemical reactions of protoplasm take place between substances in solution or in colloidal suspension. A number of the substances which will not dissolve in water form a colloidal suspension with water, and in many ways colloids behave as materials in true solution. Protoplasm itself is a mixture of substances in solution and in colloidal suspension.

The freezing and boiling points of water are unusual. It

is a general rule that elements belonging to the same family in Mendeleev's periodic table behave quite similarly in chemical reactions. Thus both oxygen and sulphur, which are eight elements apart from each other, form a dihydride. The dihydride of oxygen is, of course, water, and the dihydride of sulphur is hydrogen sulfide. It is a general rule that the heavier compound of such a homologous pair invariably has the higher boiling and freezing points, and it is here that we see a unique attribute of water. Hydrogen sulfide has a molecular weight of 34 while water has one of 18; thus the former has almost twice the mass of the latter. Yet the boiling point of water is 161° Centigrade above that of hydrogen sulfide. Had water behaved as could be anticipated from the attributes of the other dihydrides of this family of elements, its boiling point would not be 100° Centigrade but −80° Centigrade.

Still other properties of water which deserve to be considered are its ability to produce ionization of substances in solution, its high surface tension, and the ability of its molecules to associate or react with one another or with other kinds of molecules. All of these have important implications in the chemistry and physics of living protoplasm, and we cannot help marveling at the particular fitness of water for the role which it plays in living things. Nor can we help asking whether such a unique combination of needed properties could be expected by chance.

c. The Fitness of Hydrogen

Another substance that is intimately associated with living protoplasm and which shows a unique fitness is the element hydrogen. It is one of the three most common elements in living protoplasm, and many of the peculiar and unique properties of water may be due to the fact that it contains two atoms of hydrogen to the molecule. In addition to various qualities which contribute to the unique properties of water, the atoms of hydrogen are the lightest and the smallest of all atoms. Their smallness permits them to fit into configurations requiring a volume too small to permit the use of other atoms.

Hydrogen also occupies a central position in the electro-negativity scale, and this makes it possible for it to enter into a very large number of chemical combinations. Indeed, there are more compounds of hydrogen known than of any other element. Its presence on earth is due to the unique position of the earth in relation to the sun. If our planet were smaller, it would not be able to hold hydrogen and its compounds in its crust and atmosphere. Similarly, if it were a little closer to the sun, it would be too hot for hydrogen compounds. Thus the element which is so important to living things might not have been found on the earth had our planet been of a different size or distance from the sun.

d. The Fitness of Carbon

Still another very important element is carbon. Indeed, living protoplasm seems to be built around this element. The number of compounds which it forms is second only to the number of hydrogen compounds. Carbon occupies a central position in the periodic table. Consequently it can achieve a stable configuration by either losing or gaining four electrons. Usually it does this by sharing its electrons. Furthermore, it has the ability to form strong carbon-to-carbon linkages, a rather unique quality which only it and silicon possess. Silicon, moreover, shows this ability only to a limited degree. Because of this ability to form strong carbon-to-carbon linkages, long chains, side chains, and rings are possible. Thus a wide variety of compounds is possible, and these have a great variety of chemical properties.

Another important property of carbon is the fact that its stable oxide, carbon dioxide, is a gas. Silicon has some of the properties of carbon, but its oxide is gaseous only at temperatures of several thousand degrees centigrade. Carbon dioxide is quite soluble in water. Indeed, it forms an unstable compound with water. This is a unique property, since most gases show only a limited solubility in liquids. Carbonic acid, the compound formed by carbon dioxide with water, is a source of the bicarbonate ion. The bicarbonate ion acts as an amphoteric substance, behaving as an acid in the presence of a base and as a base in the presence of an acid. Substances acting in this way are known as "buffers," and they are important in maintaining the hydrogen-ion concentration or pH of a solution. Living organisms are quite sensitive to hydrogen-ion concentration, and most of them are killed if the pH moves very far from neutrality.

The bicarbonate ion is, moreover, a very effective buffer. There are a great many weak acids which will buffer near neutrality, and in some living organisms phosphates and proteins act as buffers. But the buffer system built up by carbon dioxide has a particular advantage in that carbon dioxide is a gas which can be easily gotten rid of and also in that carbon dioxide is a by-product of the organism's metabolism and is, therefore, constantly renewable. Thus, if an acid is introduced, the bicarbonate ion acts as a buffer to keep the hydrogen-ion concentration near neutrality, and at the same time carbon dioxide tends to form more of the bicarbonate ion. If an excess base is introduced, the carbonic acid tends to neutralize it, once more buffering near neutrality.[26]

This solubility of carbon dioxide in water is also important from another angle. At ordinary temperatures a given volume of water dissolves almost an equal volume of carbon dioxide (0.9 volumes at 20° C.). Under the same conditions only about 0.03 volumes of oxygen dissolve. This is significant in the process of photosynthesis, since it makes available to water plants a relatively large quantity of carbon dioxide.

e. The Fitness of Other Elements

Oxygen is the third of the important elements of living things. It is related to sulphur in much the same way that

silicon is related to carbon. However, it forms a compound
with hydrogen more readily than does sulphur. Its fitness is
not quite so apparent as the fitness of water and of carbon
and hydrogen. It might be pointed out, however, that while
hydrogen sulphide could theoretically take the place of
water in photosynthesis, it never does so; and it may be that
there is some peculiar property of oxygen yet unknown
which is responsible for that fact.

Other elements, too, apparently have unique roles in
living protoplasm. Phosphorus is an essential component of
substances concerned with the utilization of energy by the
cells. In this capacity it cannot be replaced by any other
element, though the reason for this is not known at present.
Nitrogen and sulphur are the universal components of proteins. The reason why they should play such an important
part in living protoplasm is not yet known either.

In most of these instances we are struck by the particular fitness of these substances for their role in living
things. Could this fitness be the result of chance?

The Survival of Individual Forms for a Relatively Long Period of Time

In addition, there is the problem of the survival of particular forms for long periods of time. We have referred to
some of these before. The horseshoe crab, *Limulus*, according to the geological time scale, dates back as a genus to
Triassic times. *Protolimulus*, one of its ancestors, goes well
down into Middle Paleozoic times.[27] Presumably *Limulus*
has been unchanged for about 200 million years.

The branchiopods or brine shrimp, simple crustacea, are
already found in what is supposed to be Lower Cambrian
rock, dating from about 500,000,000 years ago. The genus
Apus, which is still extant, is either itself represented in
these early rocks, or is closely related to some of the Cambrian brine shrimp.[28] The ostracods, a rather small group

of the crustacea that still survives, are represented in Ordovician and Silurian rocks.

Among the brachiopods — the lamp shells — one superfamily dates back to the beginning of Devonian times, two to the beginning of Ordovician times, and two to Upper Cambrian times. All of these are still alive today.[29] *Lingula,* a brachiopod, is believed to be the oldest known animal genus.[30]

A fossil *Peripatus,* very similar to the animal we know today, has been found in the Burgess shale of British Columbia. This stratum is believed to date from Middle Cambrian times. The fossil has been named *Aysheaia pedunculata,* but it is almost identical with the *Peripatus* we know today.[31]

Among the insects, ants are believed to have reached the limits of specialization some 30,000,000 years ago and are thought to have survived with very little evolutionary change since that time.[32] Wheeler reports that nearly 69 per cent of the ant genera from the Baltic and Sicilian amber of the Lower Oligocene are still living today. Three species belonging to different genera cannot be separated from living species today.[33]

David G. Hall, Chief, Publications Branch, Agricultural Research Service of the United States Department of Agriculture, reports that some of the insects alive today have shown no major evolutionary changes in the past 250 million years.[34]

An expedition of the American Museum of Natural History reported the discovery in King's Canyon, Calif., of a spider belonging to the family Hypochilidae which is believed to date back to the Carboniferous period.[35]

Among the vertebrates, the lampreys and hagfishes still have the fundamental structure of the Agnatha, the earliest vertebrate group.[36] The shark *Scapanorhynchus owsteni* is already represented by teeth in what is supposed to be Upper Cretaceous rock. It has been found living off the coast of Japan.[37]

The water monitors and sea lizards, one of the groups of the lizards, are believed to be the little-changed survivors from a Lower Cretaceous stock which evolved into the higher lizards. The monitors alive today have retained, at least in all of their essential features, the characteristics already present in the monitors of the Cretaceous times. Gregory believes that they were able to remain unchanged because they escaped genetically predetermined changes in their limbs and other parts that enabled other lizards to shift from the originally mixed environment to a way of life more and more marine. It is not clear, however, what he means by "genetically predetermined changes." [38]

Still other forms that are supposed to have survived for a relatively long time are the hairy-tailed hedgehogs of East India. They are represented by two genera today, *Hylomys* and *Echinosorex*. These are considered to be relatively primitive placental mammals, and it is believed that they survived because they had a very prickly coat and because they were able to roll themselves into a ball which dogs hesitate very much to bite. [39]

Barrett-Hamilton and Hinton report that a number of species of mammals found in Britain are known as fossils from the Late Pleistocene period. These include the brown rat (*Epimys rattus* or *Mus decumanus*), the shrew (*Sorex araneus*), the pigmy shrew (*S. minutus*), the rabbit (*Oryctolagus* or *Lepus cuniculus*), the Irish hare (*Lepus hibernicus*), the vole (*Evotomys* sp.), and *Apodemus flavicollis*. Some of these are made up of several races today; others, like the pigmy shrew and the Irish hare, appear to be remarkably uniform. [40] Apparently these latter have not broken up into separate geographic races in spite of their having existed for such a long time.

Among the plants the well-known ginkgo tree is supposed to have survived since early Jurassic times. It has undergone practically no change and is frequently referred to as a living fossil. Most evolutionists believe that it would be extinct were it not for the protecting hand of man. At the present time it is not believed to exist in the wild state. It is believed to have been preserved by the Orientals and is known only as a cultivated form.

The dawn redwood, *Metasequoia glyptostroboides,* has existed unchanged for over 20 million years. It still exists in the wild state in China.

Similarly *Neopilina* is still alive and seems to have existed unchanged for hundreds of millions of years.

The Cycadales, another of the primitive gymnosperms, are still represented by living forms today. They are found as fossils already at the beginning of the Mesozoic period. They are also known in Jurassic and Cretaceous rock and in early Tertiary rock.[41]

The flora of the Middle and Later Tertiary periods contains only modern genera, and many of these cannot be distinguished from living forms. The species found as fossils in what are supposed to be Miocene strata in southern California are very similar to, if not identical with, modern forms.[42] By the middle of the Pliocene period nearly all of the woody species of California were similar to those which we know today.[43]

It is difficult to explain the survival of these organisms, since the general rule of evolution is change or become extinct. These unchanged organisms should have been in competition with other organisms which did respond to selection pressures. Even if it is postulated that they have lived in the same general area and presumably under the same ecological conditions for millions of years, it would seem that most if not all ranges encompass some average ecological variation and have local and periodic ecological oscillations. In such a situation at least some selection factors would differ on each segment of the periphery of the range.[44]

Length of Life and Degree of Specialization

In this connection it might be pointed out that plants in general are longer lived than animals. Some evolutionists believe that this is the reason why the plants are relatively unchanged. Hitchcock and Chase, for instance, think that many individual plants of buffalo grass on the Western plains are probably the same ones that colonized the plains after the retreat of the glaciers.[45] Some clones of crocus are believed to be 2,500 to 3,000 years old. A clone of *Vaccinium* is believed by Darrow and Camp to be 1,000 years old.[46]

Yet in the animal world the most highly developed and most advanced organisms are the longest lived. In general the mammals are longer lived than other vertebrates and invertebrates.

Problems of Evolutionary Development in Various Forms

a. The Cause of Speciation in Birds

The birds present a number of problems to the evolutionist. Their reproductive environment is least subject to ecological and topographical isolation, since they are able to fly over many land and water barriers. And yet there is supposed to have occurred the development of a large number of species in the birds, even though the number of species of birds is smaller than the number of species in some other groups. How was isolation effected in these groups? It has been suggested that sexual dimorphism and sexual discrimination are responsible for isolation, and this has made possible the development of a number of species.[47] These are subtle psychological differences which are difficult to measure. It is assumed that individual birds were attracted to some members of the species in preference to others. There is no evidence, though, that any such choice is exercised or that such preferences exist.

It has also been suggested that isolation has been effected

by the habit of birds of nesting year after year in the same very restricted area. It is well known that male birds mark off mating territories, from which they jealously exclude all other males. Sometimes the male returns to the same place year after year, and in many cases the female, too, returns to the same place year after year. Thus a single pair or a male and several females occupy a given bit of territory exclusively and continue to occupy this territory during the breeding season year after year. This might account for some isolation. But Lack believes that this instinctive habitat selection, which isolates birds ecologically, plays little part in primary speciation.[48]

b. Instinct vs. Learning in Birds

Another problem in connection with birds is the determination of how much is acquired by instinct and how much is acquired by learning. In general, it has been assumed that most bird behavior is instinctive. Much has been made of the wonderful instincts of the birds which enable them to build complex nests apparently without any education. We have referred earlier to instances in which it appears that under some conditions birds are actually taught to fly and to feed and that these are at least not entirely instinctive procedures. Scott reports observations which indicate that the song of birds may not be entirely instinctive. Baltimore orioles (*Icterus galbula*) reared in isolation developed a song which was quite unlike the normal song of the Baltimore oriole, and they retained this song throughout their lifetime. When other Baltimore orioles were reared with them, they learned this unusual song and sang it exclusively even after the death of their foster parents.[49] Thus it would seem hazardous to generalize and to ascribe so many things to instinct without better evidence.

c. Bird Migration

Another problem in connection with the birds is the explanation for their migratory habits. Why is it that birds migrate often for thousands of miles, that they follow the same general route year after year, and that they spend the winter and summer seasons in almost the identical locations year after year? At one time it was suggested that this was due to the fact that originally all of the land masses were together in a single continent made up of two parts: Gondwana and Laurasia. Gondwana centered around the South Pole, while Laurasia overlapped the equator and extended well into the Northern Hemisphere. This continent drifted apart and together again several times during Paleozoic and Mesozoic times. The birds formed a habit of moving from one part of the continent to another as food became scarcer in one area and more abundant in another. Later this single continental land mass broke up to form eventually the general continental masses that we know today. Gondwana gave rise to Africa, South America, Australia, Antarctica, Arabia, India, and the Pacific Islands. Laurasia gave rise to North America and Eurasia. The birds, however, continued to migrate from one point to another even though these points were now on different continents and separated by large distances.

The continental drift theory is coming to be more widely accepted once more, but according to this theory, the continents were connected much longer than the present distribution of plants and animals would indicate they were. If this theory is true, the various geographical areas should not be as distinct and definite as they are.[50]

Even the distribution of various individual plants and animals does not fit this theory. To mention but one example, Stebbins calls attention to the distribution of the Winteraceae.[51] Their present distribution does not fit the continental drift theory.

Thus the problem of bird migration still remains unexplained.

d. The Arthropod Circulatory System

Another condition that presents difficulties is the circulatory system of the arthropods (crustacea and insects). It is a relatively unsatisfactory system, because it is an open system. The blood does not remain in a system of tubes but passes out of the blood vessels into the various body cavities. It moves quite slowly. The poor circulatory system of the arthropods is supposed to be one reason why they have never become very large. A large arthropod would be impossible; its circulatory or transportation system could not serve a large organism.

The arthropods are supposed to be descended from the segmented worms. These latter have a rather satisfactory circulatory system. It is a closed system similar to that found in vertebrates. The blood remains within a system of tubes. If the evolutionary pattern is correct, then somewhere along the line in the development from segmented worm to arthropod this good quality was lost. It is hard to explain how this happened on the basis of evolution, since the organism which first developed an open circulatory system would have had to compete with a close relative that had a closed circulatory system. Presumably the animal with the open circulatory system would have been at a disadvantage and should have died out. But the very opposite happened, and the form with the poor circulatory system supplanted the form with the better system.

Even more striking is the fact that the insects, which are supposed to be the most highly developed of the arthropods, have the poorest circulatory system. They have only a heart and an aorta. It has been suggested that this is the reason why their circulatory system does not transport oxygen. They have a separate system of tubes, which transports air throughout the body to the individual cells. This, too, is an unsatisfactory arrangement, which limits the size that insects can attain. Transporting oxygen in chemical combination in the blood is generally recognized as a more satisfactory system. The poor circulatory system and tracheal system to transport oxygen serve as limitations on insect evolution. They are believed not to have changed in the last 50 million years and are now barred from all further progress.

e. The Lungfish

The lungfish also create a problem for the evolutionist. It appears that they were among the earliest of the fish. They have a lung — a characteristic which should have been an advantageous one. Presumably they had to compete with fish which had only gills, while they had both gills and lungs. We should expect that the lungfish would have survived and continued to develop while the gill-bearing fish died out. But that is not the case. The lungfish are themselves almost extinct. Indeed, in many respects they are quite primitive — their skeleton is largely cartilaginous — in spite of the fact that they have had a longer period in which to evolve than the other fish.

f. The Absence of Teeth in Birds

Still another difficulty is the fact that birds today lack teeth. We are all familiar with the expression "scarce as hen's teeth." It would appear that a bird having teeth would have some real advantages. He would be able to chew his food before swallowing it. Some of the undigestible material could be more easily expelled than it can be with the bill. As it is, because he lacks teeth, he must have a gizzard, a sac containing sand, grit, and gravel used for grinding the food. But this adds to his weight. Yet anything that adds to the weight of an aerial organism is disadvantageous.

Presumably at one time the birds, or at least their ancestors, did have teeth. As we pointed out, they are supposed to be descended from the lizards — organisms which have teeth. Judging from the fossils, the early birds apparently had teeth. Why should they have lost this advantage? Would it not be reasonable for the organism which first lost its teeth to be eliminated and those organisms which kept their teeth to survive?

g. Bioluminescence

The distribution of bioluminescence, the ability to produce "cold" light, is unusual in the animal kingdom. Harvey says that no clear development of luminosity along evolutionary lines is to be detected but rather a cropping up of luminescence here and there as if a handful of damp sand has been cast over the names of various groups written on a blackboard, with luminous species appearing wherever a mass of sand struck. The Ctenophora have received the most sand, and it is probable that all members of this phylum are luminous. The Cnidaria also contain many luminous species scattered among certain of the orders. At the other extreme are very large groups in which only a few luminous animals are known, as in the gastropod and lamellibranch mollusks. Harvey says that it is extraordinary that one species in a genus may be luminous and another closely allied species may contain no trace of luminosity. Only among animals with more complicated luminous organs does there appear to be a definite series of gradations with increasing complexity that might be regarded as an evolutionary line; elsewhere the ability to emit light is believed to have arisen independently in widely scattered groups.[52]

h. Flight in Insects

According to conventional helicopter flight theory some beetles and even certain bees perform miracles by getting off the ground. In fact, one beetle, *Melolontha vulgaris,* under study at New York University's School of Engineering and Science, should not be able to fly at all. For its average weight of approximately 1.9 grams *M. vulgaris* needs a lift coefficient (a mathematical measure of lifting force) of at least two to three to fly. Yet this insect defies the accepted flight theory and baffles aerodynamicists with an estimated lift coefficient of less than one.[53]

i. Other Complicated Relationships

The adult human botfly catches mosquitoes and attaches eggs to their bodies before releasing them. The eggs hatch when the mosquito lands on the warm skin of a man, and the botfly larva burrow in and start to develop. In the tropical forests the hairs of the three-toed sloth are colored green by the symbiotic algae. There is a moth, the sloth moth, which spends its entire life on the sloth; its larva are presumed to feed on these algae. Ehrlich and Holm say that explaining the evolutionary history of associations such as these and others perhaps even more bizarre is a challenge to the evolutionist interested in the structure of the ecosystem.[54]

Obligate Relationships

a. The Yucca Moth and the Yucca Plant

There are many obligate relationships in nature which can be explained only with difficulty on the basis of evolution. One of the best known of these is the relationship between the yucca moth and the yucca plant, or Spanish bayonet (*Yucca glauca* and others). The yucca flowers hang down, and the pistil, or female part of the flower, is lower than the stamens, or male part. However, it is impossible for the pollen to fall from the anthers or pollen sacs to the stigma, the part of the pistil which receives the pollen, because the stigma is cup-shaped, and the section receptive to the pollen is on the inner surface of the cup. The female of the yucca moth (*Pronuba*) begins work soon after sundown. She collects a quantity of pollen from the anthers of the yucca plant and holds it in her specially constructed mouth parts. She then usually flies to another yucca flower, pierces the ovary with her ovipositor, and after laying one or more eggs, creeps down the style (the stalk of the pistil) and stuffs a ball of pollen into the stigma. The plant produces a large number of seeds. Some of these are eaten by the larvae of the moth, and some mature to perpetuate the species.

It is difficult to imagine what would cause a moth to collect pollen and to stuff it into a stigma. One hesitates to believe that the female knows what the result will be, and it is generally assumed that this is an example of instinctive behavior. Yet this is an obligate relationship, for in the absence of the moth the yucca plant produces no seed, while without the yucca plant the moth cannot complete its life cycle. The moth larvae can feed only on the seeds of the yucca plant. Thus if the moth should fail to pollinate the yucca, the result would be the eventual extinction of both plant and insect.

How can this phenomenon be explained on the basis of evolution? Which came first, the yucca moth or the yucca plant? At the present time the moth cannot live very long without the yucca plant, for it needs the plant to complete its life cycle. The plant cannot live for more than a few years without the moth, for it would not be able to produce seeds and with the death of those plants now alive the species would become extinct. The evolutionist, of course, assumes that this arrangement developed as a result of evolutionary processes, but it is incredible that both the yucca moth and the yucca plant should have reached their present stage of development within a period of just a few years. Yet to assume that at one time both had different methods of completing their life cycles does not solve the problem either, for then the question arises: Why did they give these up? If, for instance, the yucca plant at one time was capable of being fertilized by several species of insects, why should it evolve in such a way as to be dependent on a single species at the present time? And if the yucca moth larvae at one time were able to feed on several kinds of food, why did they evolve in such a way as to restrict their diet to a single food at the present time? Mayr says that it is a considerable strain on one's credulity to assume that finely balanced systems, such as the vertebrate eye or the feathers of birds, could develop by random mutations, and he goes on to say that this is even more true for situations such as the yucca-moth-yucca-plant relationship.[55]

b. The Commercial Fig and Its Pollination

A similar situation is to be found in the relationship existing between the commercial fig and wasps of the genus *Blastophaga*, which pollinate it. The flowers of the fig are produced in structures called syconia. Each of these consists of a hollow, fleshy receptacle with a very small opening at the upper end. There are numerous small flowers which line the inside of this hollow receptacle. Two kinds of syconia are produced. One contains both male and female flowers and is called a carpifig. It is not eaten. The other, which produces edible figs, has only female flowers.

Pollination of both kinds of syconia is accomplished by the female wasps. The openings of the syconia are so nearly closed by overlapping scales that the wasps have great difficulty in getting in and usually tear off their wings in the process. After the female wasp has entered a syconium with both male and female flowers, she lays her eggs and dies. Her eggs hatch, and the young wasps feed on the tissues of the flower. When the male wasps mature, they eat their way out of the flowers in which they have been hatched and into those occupied by females. Here they mate, and shortly thereafter the males die without leaving the syconium. The females become dusted with pollen from the male flowers, make their way to the outside, and fly to another syconium. If this is a syconium with both male and female flowers, the process is repeated. If, however, it is a syconium with female flowers only, the wasp dies without laying her eggs, for the flowers in this case are so long that the female cannot get to the base of them to lay her eggs. In her attempts to do so, however, she dusts these flowers with pollen. These female flowers develop into mature figs, which may then be eaten.

Once more, it is difficult to believe that such an arrangement developed by evolution. For one thing, it is incredible that these two should have reached the present stage of development within such a relatively short time. And if at one time they had several methods of completing their life cycle, it is difficult to see why they should have given up these additional methods. McDougall says that the course of evolution that has brought about such a strange relationship can scarcely be imagined.[56]

c. The Milkweeds

Among the milkweeds (*Asclepias*) the sticky pollen is contained in little sacs or pollinia. These occur in pairs attached by a clip. Pollination is completed by the insertion of the pollinia into slits in the stigma of the flower which match in size and shape the pollinia of the same species. Insertion of the pollinia into the slits of the stigma is a difficult operation, and only a small proportion of the flowers are ever pollinated. Pollination is accomplished by insects. Insertion of pollinia of one species into the stigma of another species is almost impossible.[57] This method of pollination is so complex as to appear to be harmful. What would bring about such a development by evolution? Is this not an example of a type of evolution which has gone too far? It is usually stated that the plant is long-lived and that it produces a great many flowers. Moreover, each milkweed capsule contains a great many seeds. These are all supposed to make up for the difficulty of pollination. But would it not be to the plant's advantage to live long, produce many flowers, and produce many seeds in each flower without being handicapped by this complex method of pollination?

Cause-and-Effect Relationships in Evolution

Another difficulty in the study of evolutionary development is to determine the exact status of cause-and-effect relationships and the sequence of various developments. Is a given characteristic the cause of a second characteristic, or is it the effect of that characteristic? Raymond, for instance, believes that sluggishness and the sessile habit resulted in the formation of a skeleton. He does not believe that the formation of the skeleton brought about the sluggishness and the sessile habit. He believes that because the organism was sluggish more calcareous material precipitated than could be dissolved by the body fluids. He believes that the pre-Cambrian forms had no skeleton and that is why we find no fossils of them. He believes, too, as a further extension of his theory, that among human beings hardening of the arteries develops as a result of a sedentary life and that men who lead an active life rarely suffer from this condition. This would imply that skeletal and armored forms are always derived from naked forms.[58] But Gregory does not believe that this is true. Indeed, he believes that the opposite is frequently true. He believes that in many cases, such as in the fish, armored forms preceded naked ones.[59]

Characteristics Which Seemingly Do Not Meet the Organism's Needs

There are some forms which seem to have characteristics which they do not need, while other closely related forms to which these characteristics would be an advantage lack them. Thus the smaller iguanid lizards are active insect hunters, while the larger iguanid lizards eat leaves, flowers, and berries. We should expect the larger animals to be carnivorous. The big *Conolophus* lizards of the Galapagos Islands have jaws strong enough to chew through shoe leather. But they feed mostly on flowers and fruits, especially on the fruit and spiny pads of the cactus, though they occasionally do eat a grasshopper. The Galapagos sea lizard (*Amblyrhyncus*), another large lizard, feeds only on the tips and sprouts of one of the sea weeds, though it would seem to be fitted to be a carnivore.[60]

The Effect of Specialization

Another problem is the effect of specialization itself. It is generally assumed that the course of evolution is toward more and more specialization. But this very specialization is itself disadvantageous, because as the organism becomes more closely identified with its environment, it is more likely to be adversely affected by changes in that environment. Thus we are told that the probability of survival of any living thing increases with the degree with which it adjusts itself harmoniously to other living things — the organic environment — and to the inorganic environment.[61] Yet in the long run this very adaptation and adjustment may be harmful. Thus among the Caenolestoidea, South American marsupials, the Caenolestinae still survive. These are supposed to be the least specialized of the group and to have been the ancestral form. In the course of time they are believed to have given rise to the Palaeothentinae, which are a little more specialized. These are believed to have become extinct in the Miocene period. They gave rise to the Abderitinae, which were still more specialized. They, too, are believed to have become extinct in the Miocene period. The Abderitinae in turn gave rise to the Polydolopidae, the most specialized of the group, which are believed to have become extinct in the Eocene, earlier than any of the other groups.[62] Thus what is regarded as the least specialized has survived until the present time. The most specialized had the shortest survival period. It evolved latest and became extinct first.

In speaking of the different types of evolutionary development De Beer lists as one type of evolution that which gives rise to large changes and produces evolutionary novelties which exert their main effects at the later stages of the life history. He says that it is characterized by an ever-increasing specialization and consequently by the progressive loss of the potential for future evolution. In other words, those that become highly specialized lose the potential for further evolution. Their very specialization defeats itself so far as progressive evolution is concerned. He believes that these organisms must undergo a change whereby they lose their specialization, become very simple, and effect small changes rather than large changes.[63]

The Effect of High Mutation Rates

A high mutation rate is often regarded as favorable. Yet such is not necessarily the case. Indeed, a high mutation rate may do the very opposite of what it is supposed to do. Wright points out that one effect of mutation seems to be a tendency toward degeneration. This effect is particularly apparent in very small populations, where selection plays almost no role and mutation pressure is the important factor in determining the direction of evolution. He believes that this explains the degeneration of structures of little or no use such as the eyes of the cave fish. But even aside from its effect in small populations it may be harmful. He points out that it has been suggested that at certain times in the earth's history there were tremendous increases in the muta-tion rate, and these are generally believed to have made possible the rapid evolutionary advances which are supposed to have occurred at these times. However, Wright does not believe that this would necessarily be the case. He believes that the real effect of an increase in the mutation rate would depend upon the balance with other factors. A tremendous increase in mutation rate might in itself cause degeneration rather than progressive evolution unless the effect of other factors, particularly selection pressure, were correspondingly speeded up. Thus an increase in mutation rate would have to be accompanied by a tremendous increase in selection pressure, so that selection itself would have to be very intensive at times of high mutation rate. Otherwise deteri-oration might set in.[64]

Closely Related Species Found Side by Side in Nature

Still another problem is the fact that closely related species are often found side by side in nature. This is con-trary to what we should expect, since closely related species are supposed to have diverged as a result of selection for adaptations to particular environments. But if the environment is the same, there is no reason for evolutionary divergence. Hogben mentions a number of examples of this in plant genera such as *Potentilla* (cinquefoil), *Geranium, Veronica* (speedwell), and *Ribes* (currant and gooseberry).[65] We have referred to other examples earlier.

Seed Ferns

Still another difficulty is the fact that at one time seed ferns appeared to have existed. They are not at all uncommon as fossils and must have been very abundant. Today they are usually classified as Pteridosperms and are separated from the ferns; yet they are very fernlike in their appearance and they did bear seeds. The seed is generally regarded as a type of reproductive structure more highly developed than the spore. It is for that reason that spore-bearing plants usually produce far more reproductive cells than do seed-bearing plants. Presumably at one time there were both spore-bearing and seed-bearing "ferns" in existence. It would seem that the seed-bearing "ferns" would be better adapted to survival than the spore-bearers, but in the course of evolution the Pteridosperms have died out and the spore-bearers have survived to this day.

The Complexity of Living Things

The very complexity of living things leads us to wonder whether evolution could take place. No one would seriously entertain the idea that the steel, chromium, glass, rubber, and upholstery that are found in an automobile could have come together by chance in a certain place to form that automobile. The existence of an automobile is evidence of a mind and of planning, not chance. Yet living protoplasm is infinitely more complex than any machine. We have referred to some of these complexities in discussing the physiological evidence for evolution.

Consider the complexity of programming in the cell nucleus through DNA. It has been estimated that the amount

Figure 52. Seed Ferns. These are now extinct, though they appear to have flourished and to have been quite common at one time. Note the prominent seeds in the middle of the illustration. (Courtesy Chicago Natural History Museum)

of zygote DNA needed to specify the characteristics in all of the more than 3 billion people now alive weighs only one-seventeenth as much as a postage stamp.

The human brain itself is a good example of complexity. The cerebral cortex is believed to contain from 12 billion to 15 billion neurons. On the basis of 12 billion neurons the number of possible synaptic pathways in the cerebrum is estimated to be $1 \times 10^{15,000,000}$ — a fantastic figure. Cook says that the nervous system is essentially an intricate electrical system, the degree of complexity of which is hard to imagine. A Pentagon building, he says, would hardly be large enough to house a computing machine with as many synapses as are found in the human brain. All the power developed at Grand Coulee would be needed to operate such a "think factory." All the water of the Columbia River would be needed to dissipate the heat produced and keep its operating temperature down so that it would not burst into flames. And even such a machine would not perform such higher mental functions as imagination and intuition.[66]

Carter, too, comments on this problem of complexities. He believes that they indicate that our theories of evolution are still very incomplete. He calls attention to the complicated organization which we find in an insect or a vertebrate and doubts that our relatively simple theories can completely explain the origin of such complexity.[67]

Stebbins calls attention to the complexity of the adaptive systems in living things and says this is due principally to three factors. The first of these is the highly complex environment including both the physical surroundings of the population and the numerous other kinds of organisms with which the population must be associated. This complexity is increased by the constant change of most environments in a more or less regular fashion through the seasons. Second, Stebbins says that the integration of the body itself is a highly complex affair involving precise adjustments between processes and functions controlled by completely different genes. If a reptile or a mammal is to be adapted to a diet of smaller animals, the limbs must be specialized for seizing and holding its prey; the jaws and teeth for tearing, chewing, and swallowing the prey; and the digestive system for digesting animal proteins. If such an animal is to evolve into a new line of organisms adapted to feeding exclusively on leaves, all its parts must be changed synchronously and in harmony with each other to fit each of them to its new and completely different role. The number of necessary replacements and adjustments of parts, Stebbins says, would be as great as those which would be needed to convert a propeller-driven airplane into one with jet propulsion.

The third basic cause of complexity, Stebbins believes, is

the complexity and indirect nature of the relation between the gene and the character. If the action of a single gene-developed enzyme is altered, many different characteristics of the adult organism are likely to be changed in different ways. Mutation of a gene responsible for one of the enzyme-controlled processes needed to produce cartilage in a higher animal can change bone structure, muscular movements, breathing, and many other activities. Some of these changes could be beneficial, others deleterious. If such a mutation took place as a part of the evolution of a new adaptive system, it would have to be combined with other mutations which would counteract or suppress its harmful effects while leaving unchanged or accentuating its beneficial effects.[68]

Also to be considered is that very often a number of genes interact to bring about even the simplest of structures. Dr. Ake Gustafsson of Sweden has estimated that from 250 to 300 gene loci in barley are concerned with the synthesis of chloroplasts. Chloroplast development consists of a long sequence of gene-controlled processes which must be coordinated so as to follow each other in a precisely integrated fashion. Studies of the development of a flagellum in one of the unicellular microorganisms, *Chlamydomonas*, have shown that its development depends on a similarly complex sequence of gene-controlled processes: one worker found mutations effecting flagellum structure at twelve different loci.[69]

The Second Law of Thermodynamics

Another principle to be considered in this connection is the second law of thermodynamics, a physical principle which states that there is a continual tendency toward greater randomness. Evolution suggests that in the biological world the very opposite is true and that instead of a tendency toward greater randomness there is a tendency toward a higher degree of organization. Evolutionists point out that this second law of thermodynamics applies to the universe as a whole and not to every part of the universe. They point out that a limited tendency in the opposite direction is possible. But the biological world can hardly be regarded as a limited area. Furthermore, these processes which seemingly contradict the second law of thermodynamics cannot go on indefinitely, but in the end the grand total of all phenomena must be in the direction of greater randomness. It would be very unusual for the biological world to follow a principle entirely different from that followed by the inorganic world.

The Problem in Summary

Certainly in view of the many difficulties and problems which exist for the evolutionist and in view of the fact that the problem is of such a nature that no final answer is possible, it would seem that a summary rejection of the Scriptural account is, to say the least, premature even on the part of the scientists. There are many problems in all fields of science to which they must frankly admit they still have no real answers. Some modern cosmologists, for instance, believe that some nebulae acquire a momentum greater than the speed of light and thus recede into unobservability. This is compensated for by the creation of particles relatively near at hand so that the same total quantity of observable matter is maintained at all times. According to this theory, the recession of the nebulae and the creation of new particles must occur at exactly the same rate. Of this theory the president of the Royal Astronomical Society of London says: "Such an extreme example of pre-established harmony . . . is, to my mind at least, harder to credit than a special creation in the past. If I must choose, I choose the latter as the less revolting to common sense, but on the whole I prefer that wise, ingenious, and modest sentence, 'I do not know.' " [70]

As Christians we know that in the Bible we do not have a theory which is subject to all sorts of changes and modifications, a theory which has come about as a result of the restricted reasoning abilities of human beings, but we have the inspired account of the only Being who was present at Creation. True, there are still many things that we do not understand. There are some observations which at present are difficult to reconcile with the Biblical account of creation. It is quite possible that some of these problems will never be solved for us.

But there are great difficulties also with the theory of evolution. No really satisfactory explanation for the origin of life has been suggested. It is difficult to account for the survival of simple forms and for the survival of individual forms for supposedly long periods of time. There are a number of problems of evolutionary development in particular forms. It is difficult to explain the origin of obligate relationships. Some of the characteristics which organisms possess do not seem to meet their needs. The very complexity of living things makes it difficult to believe that these have originated by chance. In the inorganic world we have a tendency to greater randomness: it would be unusual to have the very opposite trend in the organic world. Ehrlich and Holm plead for a "non-Euclidean" theory of evolution; they themselves accept evolution but do not want to be placed in a position of having to affirm a "belief" in evolution.[71] Certainly evolution is by no means proved, and it is not the only possible explanation for the organic diversity that we find. It is not unreasonable, then, to assume that the changes which have occurred have been finite and limited and that they have occurred within closed systems, the "kinds" of creation.

NOTES

1. Blum, Harold F. *Time's Arrow and Evolution* (Princeton: Princeton University Press, 1951). p. 174.
2. Anders, Edward, Du Fresne, Eugene R., Hayatsu, Ryoichi, Cavaille, Albert, Du Fresne, Ann, and Fitch, Frank W. "Contaminated Meteorite," *Science*, CXLVI (1964), 1157.

3. Simpson, George Gaylord. "The Nonprevalence of Humanoids," *Science*, CXLIII (1964), 772.

4. Blum, p. 129.

5. Shull, A. Franklin. *Evolution* (New York: McGraw-Hill, 1951), pp. 286–288.

6. Ibid., p. 290.

7. Blum, p. 176.

8. Urey, Harold C. "On the Early Chemical History of the Earth and the Origin of Life," *Proceedings of the National Academy of Sciences*, XXXVIII (1952), 351–363.

9. Gregory, William King. *Evolution Emerging* (New York: Macmillan, 1951), I, 19.

10. Blum, p. 170.

11. Keosian, John. "Review of Dean Wooldridge's 'The Machinery of Life,'" *Science*, CLII (1966), 1496.

12. Blum, p. 163.

13. Ibid., p. 170.

14. Ehrlich, Paul R., and Holm, Richard W. *The Process of Evolution* (New York: McGraw-Hill, 1963), p. 9.

15. Horowitz, N. H. "On the Evolution of Biochemical Syntheses," *Proceedings of the National Academy of Sciences*, XXXI (1945), 153–157.

16. Blum, p. 171.

17. Becking, L. G. M. Baas. "On the Origin of Life," *The Evolution of Living Organisms*, ed. G. W. Leeper (Victoria: Melbourne University Press, 1962), p. 34.

18. Steward, F. C. "Botany in the Biology Curriculum," *BioScience*, XVII, 2 (February 1967), 88.

19. Becking, p. 39.

20. Ibid., p. 38.

21. Young, Richard S., and Ponnamperuma, Cyril. "Life: Origin and Evolution," *Science*, CXLIII (1964), 384.

22. Shull, p. 296.

23. Blum, pp. 173 f.

24. Ibid., p. 142.

25. *Science*, CXX (1954), 964.

26. Blum, p. 82.

27. Gregory, p. 61.

28. Ibid., p. 59.

29. Ibid., p. 76.

30. Buchsbaum, Ralph. *Animals Without Backbones* (Chicago: University of Chicago Press, 1948), p. 178.

31. Dunbar, Carl O. *Historical Geology* (New York: Wiley, 1949), p. 147.

32. Huxley, Julian. *Evolution, the Modern Synthesis* (New York: Harpers, 1943), p. 495.

33. Wheeler, William Morton. *Ants, Their Structure, Development and Behavior* (New York: Columbia University Press, 1913), pp. 166, 174.

34. Hall, David G. "Recent Developments in Entomology and Their Implications," *The Science Teacher*, XXI (1954), 224.

35. *Science*, CXVIII (1953), 685.

36. Carter, G. S. *Animal Evolution* (London: Sidgwick and Jackson, 1951), p. 329.

37. Norman, J. R. *A History of Fishes* (New York: Wyn, 1949), p. 124.

38. Gregory, p. 280.

39. Ibid., p. 382.

40. Barrett-Hamilton, Gerald E. H., and Hinton, M. A. C. *A History of British Mammals* (London: Gurney and Jackson, 1910–21), pp. 86, 112, 193, 329, 393, 404, 407.

41. Stebbins, G. Ledyard. *Variation and Evolution in Plants* (New York: Columbia University Press, 1950), p. 518.

42. Axelrod, Daniel I. "A Miocene Flora from the Western Border of the Mojave Desert," *Carnegie Institute of Washington Publication* No. 516 (1939), pp. 7–33.

43. Stebbins, p. 521.

44. Ross, Herbert H. *A Synthesis of Evolutionary Theory* (Englewood Cliffs: Prentice-Hall, 1962), p. 140.

45. Hitchcock, A. S., and Chase, Agnes. "Grass," *Old and New Plant Lore*, Smithsonian Scientific Series, XI (1931), 244.

46. Darrow, George M., and Camp, W. H. "Vaccinium Hybrids and the Development of New Horticultural Material," *Bulletin of the Torrey Botanical Club*, LXXII (1945), 10.

47. Hogben, Lancelot. "Problems of the Origins of Species," *The New Systematics*, ed. Julian Huxley (Oxford: Oxford University Press, 1940), p. 280.

48. Lack, David. "Habitat Selection and Speciation in Birds," *British Birds*, XXXIV (1940), 80–84.

49. Scott, William E. D. "Data on Song in Birds, Observations on the Song of Baltimore Orioles in Captivity," *Science*, XIV (1901), 522–526.

50. Dodson, Edward O. *A Textbook of Evolution* (Philadelphia: Saunders, 1952), p. 382.

51. Stebbins, p. 9.

52. Harvey, E. Newton. *Bioluminescence* (New York: Academic, 1952), p. x.
53. *American Biology Teacher,* XXVII, 5 (May 1965), 362.
54. Ehrlich and Holm, p. 84.
55. Mayr, Ernst. *Systematics and the Origin of Species* (New York: Columbia University Press, 1942), p. 296.
56. McDougall, W. B. *Plant Ecology* (Philadelpiha: Lea and Febiger, 1941), p. 87.
57. Stebbins, p. 210.
58. Raymond, P. E. "Pre-Cambrian Life," *Bulletin of the Geological Society of America,* XLVI (1935), 389 f.
59. Gregory, pp. 25 f.
60. Beebe, W. *Galapagos, World's End* (New York: Putnams, 1924), pp. 116 f., 246, 250 f.
61. Leake, Chauncey D. "Ethicogenesis," *Scientific Monthly,* LX (1945), 251 f.
62. Simpson, George Gaylord. *Tempo and Mode in Evolution* (New York: Columbia University Press, 1944), pp. 142 f.
63. De Beer, G. R. "Embryology and Taxonomy," *The New Systematics,* ed. Julian Huxley (Oxford: Oxford University Press, 1940), pp. 376 f.
64. Wright, Sewall. "The Statistical Consequences of Mendelian Heredity in Relation to Speciation," *The New Systematics,* ed. Julian Huxley (Oxford: Oxford University Press, 1940), p. 174.
65. Hogben, p. 273.
66. Cook, Robert C. *Human Fertility: The Modern Dilemma* (New York: Sloane, 1951), pp. 194 f.
67. Carter, pp. 350 f.
68. Stebbins, G. Ledyard. *Processes of Organic Evolution* (Englewood Cliffs: Prentice-Hall, 1966), pp. 31–33.
69. Ibid., loc. cit.
70. Dingle, Herbert. "Science and Modern Cosmology," *Science,* CXX (1954), 519.
71. Ehrlich, Paul, and Holm, Richard W. "Population Biology," *Science,* CXXXIX (1963), 242.

Index

(Numerals in italics indicate illustrations)

INDEX TO SCRIPTURE PASSAGES